Rebuilding Shattered Lives

Rebuilding Shattered Lives

Treating Complex PTSD and Dissociative Disorders

Second Edition

James A. Chu, MD

JOHN WILEY & SONS, INC.

Copyright © 2011 by John Wiley & Sons, Inc. All rights reserved.

Published by John Wiley & Sons, Inc., Hoboken, New Jersey.

Published simultaneously in Canada.

Limit of Liability/Disclaimer of Warranty: While the publisher and author have used their best efforts in
preparing this book, they make no representations or warranties with respect to the accuracy or completeness
of the contents of this book and specifically disclaim any implied warranties of merchantability or fitness for a
particular purpose. No warranty may be created or extended by sales representatives or written sales materials.
The advice and strategies contained herein may not be suitable for your situation. You should consult with a
professional where appropriate. Neither the publisher nor author shall be liable for any loss of profit or any other
commercial damages, including but not limited to special, incidental, consequential, or other damages.

This publication is designed to provide accurate and authoritative information in regard to the subject matter
covered. It is sold with the understanding that the publisher is not engaged in rendering professional services. If
legal, accounting, medical, psychological or any other expert assistance is required, the services of a competent
professional person should be sought.

Designations used by companies to distinguish their products are often claimed as trademarks. In all instances
where John Wiley & Sons, Inc. is aware of a claim, the product names appear in initial capital or all capital
letters. Readers, however, should contact the appropriate companies for more complete information regarding
trademarks and registration.

For general information on our other products and services please contact our Customer Care Department within
the U.S. at (800) 762-2974, outside the United States at (317) 572-3993 or fax (317) 572-4002.

Wiley also publishes its books in a variety of electronic formats. Some content that appears in print may not be
available in electronic books. For more information about Wiley products, visit our website at www.wiley.com.

Library of Congress Cataloging-in-Publication Data:

Chu, James A.
  Rebuilding shattered lives : treating complex PTSD and dissociative disorders / James A. Chu.—2nd ed.
    p. ; cm.
  Includes bibliographical references and index.
  ISBN 978-0-470-76874-7 (pbk)
  ISBN 978-1-118-01505-6 (ebk)
  ISBN 978-1-118-01506-3 (ebk)
  ISBN 978-1-118-01504-9 (ebk)
  1. Adult child abuse victims—Rehabilitation.   2. Post-traumatic stress disorder—Treatment.   3. Dissociative
disorders—Treatment.   I. Title.
  [DNLM: 1. Stress Disorders, Post-Traumatic—therapy.   2. Adult Survivors of Child Abuse—psychology.
3. Dissociative Disorders—therapy. WM 172]
  RC569.5.C55C48 2011
  616.85'8223906—dc22

                                                                                        2010037951

10 9 8 7 6 5 4 3 2

This book is dedicated to the generations of staff and patients of the Trauma and Dissociative Disorders Program at McLean Hospital who have taught and inspired me, and to my family, friends, and colleagues who have provided me the support and love that have allowed me to grow, learn, and achieve at least a modicum of wisdom over the years.

Contents

Foreword

When I was asked to update the foreword I wrote in 1998 for *Rebuilding Shattered Lives*, I accepted with enthusiasm, eager to learn what Dr. James Chu had revised in his now-classic book on the treatment of complex PTSD and dissociative disorders. This revision does not disappoint and, in fact, builds on the first edition and adds to it the insights gained and information published since the original came out. As before, this revision provides clinical wisdom and clarity of discussion regarding the treatment of this challenging population of patients. It also provides support and sustenance to the clinician reader (whether novice or seasoned) facing the challenges these cases present and the dilemmas they often spawn. Dr. Chu's approach is grounded in theory and extensive experience and is thoughtful and thought-provoking but anxiety-diminishing. The guidance provided makes the process more transparent and hence more understandable to the treating clinician.

As in the first edition, Dr. Chu calls upon his considerable inpatient and outpatient experience with these patients and his familiarity with the pertinent literature to elucidate the treatment model and guidelines presented in this book. The model helps the clinician steer a reasonable course in providing treatment to traumatized and dissociative patients, a treatment that does not overwhelm the patient or the therapist and that manages the various risks associated with the treatment. It is a research and training-based model, calling for caution and reason regarding all strategies and techniques, those having to do with memory recovery in particular. It is also a stage-oriented treatment that, using the mnemonic SAFER for the work of the first stage, underscores self-care and symptom control, acknowledgment, functioning, expression, and relationship issues as essential preliminary tasks to be undertaken long before any directed focus is placed on abuse issues per se. Dr. Chu discusses the rationale behind the reworking and abreaction of traumatic material and emphasizes the importance of addressing and resolving the core abuse-related issues and beliefs that so often plague adult survivors. He shows how for the truly traumatized this treatment is far from a search for the missing memories; instead, it is a process of life reconstruction and enhancement.

Dr. Chu is very effective in conveying the challenges posed by these patients (especially early in the treatment process) and cogently discusses ways to manage them. I find especially insightful and useful his discussions on the shift of therapeutic responsibility and chronic disempowerment, empathic confrontation, and relational issues and the therapeutic dance, as well as his sound advice regarding the treatment of dissociative identity disorder. Clinical examples provide realistic, graphic, and compelling illustration of the points under discussion and help familiarize and desensitize the reader to their appearance and management.

The book's additions are all in keeping with the major developments in the field of traumatic stress (in general and as pertains to complex developmental and dissociative posttraumatic stress disorders) and in the treatment advances that have occurred in the field since the book's original publication. Included are discussions of the quality of the child's earliest attachment relationships and its impact on overall development but especially the child's sense of self and self-esteem; the impact of insecure or disorganized attachment on the child's vulnerability to various forms of victimization, within and outside of the family; the relationship between disorganized attachment and dissociation, and the development of dissociative disorders; differences between normal event memory and memory for trauma including attention to their general accessibility and accuracy, whether they were ongoing or returned in delayed fashion as recovered memories; the application of evidence-based treatment strategies where feasible; clinical consensus about a progression of stages of treatment within which the therapist applies techniques hierarchically; a continued specialized focus on dissociation and dissociative process in many of these patients; and an update of information regarding the management of special issues such as patient self-care and self-injury/suicidality, strategies for the containment of posttraumatic and dissociative symptoms, chronic disempowerment and the "impossible" patient, boundary management, acute care requiring the use of hospitalization, and psychopharmacology. As before, Dr. Chu discusses a treatment that is at once relational, relying on the therapist's ability and willingness to be accessible to and active in interaction with the patient, and rational, requiring the establishment of boundaries and limitations and ongoing attention to their maintenance and to the patient's improvement. The therapist is encouraged to be mindful of self and of the client and to use the interaction as both a source of information about the client and his or her history and grist for the mill.

Dr. Chu is especially thoughtful and eloquent in his discussion of controversies and future directions in the field of trauma and dissociation and reasons that clinicians do this work. Complex trauma patients (with and without significant dissociation) make up a substantial percentage of outpatient and inpatient mental health populations, so it is thus important that therapists learn to treat this population. Additionally, much more information is now available about the intergenerational transmission of violence within families and communities; treatment of the sort described here, although time and energy intensive, is very important work in disrupting the cycle of violence in our society. Nevertheless, not all therapists seek out or enjoy this treatment population, and it can generate burnout or lead to therapeutic transgressions and misadventures more quickly than many others. Dr. Chu's emphasis on the therapist's attention to self-knowledge and mindfulness, countertransference, and vicarious trauma in this treatment is invaluable in assisting those of us in the trenches to successfully continue in the work. The need for this work is immense, as is the reward. Thank you, Dr. Chu, for continuing to share your sustaining insight and wisdom in this updated edition.

Christine A. Courtois, PhD

Psychologist, Private Practice: Christine A. Courtois, PhD & Associates, PLC, Washington, DC

Author, *Healing the Incest Wound: Adult Survivors in Therapy* and *Recollections of Sexual Abuse*

Co-Editor with Julian Ford, PhD, *Treating Complex Traumatic Stress Disorders: An Evidence-Based Guide*

Associate Editor: *Psychological Trauma: Theory, Research, Practice, & Policy*

Introduction

The past three decades have seen extraordinary changes in views concerning the traumatization of children in our society. Attitudes of both mental health professionals and the public moved from virtual denial of the existence and effects of child abuse in the 1970s to an almost fervid preoccupation with these issues in the 1980s. In the heady excitement of those days, at least three central tenets were held forth: (1) the abuse of children was a hidden social epidemic with untold human consequences; (2) abuse was the source of innumerable societal ills and mental illness and disability for abuse survivors; and (3) recognition and uncovering of abuse memories were the keys to both individual and societal health. New ways of recognizing and treating childhood abuse were invented, and specialized treatment programs emerged across the United States.

However, in the late 1980s and the 1990s, the pendulum began to swing in the opposite direction. Although many adults who had survived various kinds of childhood abuse were successfully treated, the treatment of those with particularly severe childhood traumatization proved to be complex. Aggressive attempts to help some severely traumatized patients explore and abreact their childhood abuse resulted in profound regression and lengthy, intensive, and expensive treatment. It slowly became clear that extraordinary pitfalls were associated with a simplistic focus on the childhood traumatic events. In addition to experiencing the traumatic events, many survivors of abuse grew up in devastatingly chaotic and disrupted home environments that led to massive disabilities. Their lives, their relationships, and often even their identities were shattered. They developed fundamental assumptions about the world as malevolent and about themselves as defective and powerless, leaving them poorly equipped to cope with even basic life functioning. Perhaps most important, they also learned to approach others with deep mistrust, making all relationships—including therapeutic relationships—tenuous and potentially dangerous.

In retrospect, it is easy to see how severely traumatized persons failed to benefit from a type of exploratory therapy that assumes basic trust and the ability to tolerate intense and dependent therapeutic relationships. In addition to sometimes painful and unsuccessful treatment, a premature emphasis on childhood abuse resulted in a fixation on the trauma as the central theme of the lives of some patients, with their identities becoming organized around their traumatization. Thus, rather than seeing the abuse as events to be overcome, these patients essentially began to see themselves as chronically victimized and disabled.

The 1990s brought further difficulties. Compounding the complexities of treating survivors of extensive early trauma, the mental health community gradually came to understand that in a small minority of patients the reports of their childhood abuse were inaccurate. Some of these patients—especially those who became fixated on their abuse—began to unconsciously embellish what they recalled, leading to ever more lurid accounts of childhood events. Others—especially those with impaired reality testing or who were extremely vulnerable to suggestion—began to believe that they had been abused despite all evidence to the contrary. In addition, a few cases were identified where patients and other persons falsely alleged that they had been abused as children as a means of meeting needs such as avoiding legal responsibility, obtaining compensation, or resolving their internal emptiness and their need for attention from others.

A backlash began to develop. A coalition of parents who claimed that they had been falsely accused of having abused their children—resulting in alienation from their children or even lawsuits against them—joined with skeptical academics in the psychiatric and psychological community to form the False Memory Syndrome Foundation (FMSF). The stated aims of the FMSF initially appeared to have some sense of legitimacy. After all, any false claim of child abuse against an innocent parent has enormous implications for creating heartbreaking emotional pain and suffering as well as disrupting familial ties. And, cognitive psychologists involved in the science of memory research were at least somewhat accurate in pointing out that many in the clinical community lacked knowledge concerning the vagaries of memory, leading them to reflexively believe in the literal accuracy of all patients' reports. However, despite paying lip service to the notion that child abuse is a serious societal problem, the FMSF pursued a well-funded and highly publicized agenda that tended to largely discredit many patients who reported childhood abuse and the professionals who treated them. The FMSF contended that there was no scientific evidence for traumatic amnesia and that misguided "recovered memory therapists" were fracturing families and destroying lives by inducing nontraumatized patients to falsely believe that they had been the victims of childhood abuse by their parents. In the public media, the scientific literature, and the courts, false memory proponents carried out systematic attacks on the validity of "repressed memory," on the diagnosis of dissociative identity disorder, on reports of organized abuse by satanic cults, and on the use of hypnosis and guided imagery in therapy.

What will be the result of these changes in how traumatized patients are viewed? Will the legacy of abuse be once again buried in denial and blaming the victim? Fueled by some instances of naïve or questionable therapeutic practices, some professionals and members of the public have seemed to be willing to dismiss the damaging effects of abuse as predominantly "false memory" or as being a part of a "culture of self-pity," all thought to be encouraged by overzealous or misguided therapists. Against this new wave of denial, some attitudes of concern for the traumatized must be preserved, and the awareness of the effects of traumatic experiences on some of the most vulnerable members of our society must not again be lost. There is some room for optimism, despite ongoing acrimony between clinicians who treat abuse survivors and those who view abuse memories as inherently flawed and unreliable.

Evidence suggests that the intensity of the battle has begun to wane. Some scientists and researchers representing conflicting views have begun to dialogue publicly and privately with progressive integration of views. The clinical community has continued to pursue its work with traumatized patients, albeit with more caution. Since the beginning of the past decade, most of the continuing debate concerning recovered memory and false memory has been restricted to academic discussions and courtrooms. In fact, the controversy has engendered greater sophistication in the understanding of the effects of traumatization, and committed clinicians have been tempered by the strife to become even more effective in their work with traumatized patients.

A large and growing body of knowledge and experience has contributed to developing treatment models and standards of care for the treatment of adult patients who have been severely traumatized in childhood and who present with complex posttraumatic and dissociative difficulties. The treatment is usually lengthy and seldom straightforward, often involving periods of crisis, instability, and personal chaos. However, experience has taught us that with skill, patience, and perseverance, even many of the most traumatized and damaged individuals can be helped to lead more productive and fulfilling lives. Because of the tenuous nature of their ability to sustain connection, work with these individuals requires an unusual level of involvement, and because of their multiple layers of symptoms and functional problems, the path toward recovery is often unclear. But the collective clinical experience of the past three decades and emerging treatment outcome research have demonstrated that thoughtful and skillful treatment often results in fruitful and gratifying therapeutic outcomes.

This book traces the advances of the recent past concerning the nature of childhood abuse and the treatment of its aftereffects. The main emphasis is on some of the most severely traumatized patients and the need to develop a sophisticated understanding of their difficulties, and how to implement a responsible, rational, and balanced treatment. The book is divided into three parts. Part One traces the history of recent findings concerning child abuse and its effects on psychological functioning and an overview of the nature of traumatic memory. Part Two contains the basic principles of the treatment of adults who have complex trauma-related difficulties, including detailed discussions of self-care, symptom control, and relational issues. Part Three discusses various special topics in traumatized patients, including the treatment of dissociative identity disorder, acute care interventions, psychopharmacology, and controversies and future directions in the field of trauma and dissociation.

This book is meant to be a hands-on resource for clinicians. In contrast to the early years in the trauma field, many texts and much literature about the effects and treatment of childhood maltreatment are now available. I have chosen to focus on the actual treatment process of working with complex trauma patients, with an emphasis on how to understand difficult clinical presentations and dilemmas and fruitfully resolve them; to wit, what should clinicians know, what should they do, and how should they go about doing that. Throughout this volume, I have also included many clinical vignettes of problems and impasses that face mental health professionals and many examples of psychotherapeutic interventions and approaches. These clinical situations are better illustrations of clinical wisdom than even the most erudite academic discussions. To protect the identities of the persons discussed, I have altered their descriptions and features and have combined many actual patient accounts to create composite case illustrations.

The field of trauma and dissociation has undergone more growth, change, and debate over the past years than has any other area in mental health studies, except perhaps the study of the neurobiology of mental illnesses. In many ways, the experiences, errors, and growth of the past years have laid a solid foundation for future clinical work, teaching, and research. As a whole, the trauma field has emerged from pervasive denial, progressed through overinvolvement, and led to a more sophisticated and balanced position grounded in clinical wisdom and scientific research. Although we have a much greater understanding of traumatized patients and an enhanced armamentarium of treatment interventions, much can still be learned. We must continue to wrestle with understanding and treating the difficult and complex problems that result from severe and chronic childhood trauma. We must recognize that not all of the extreme beliefs concerning childhood abuse may be factually accurate, but still acknowledge the tragedy and suffering of those who grow up in malevolent environments. We must develop and value new treatments, but continue to rely on the traditional foundations of psychotherapy. As clinicians, we must combine our best knowledge, skill, and expertise to be of maximal help to relieve the distress of those we hope to help.

James A. Chu, MD

Concord, Massachusetts

July 2010

PART I
The Nature and Effects of Childhood Abuse

1

Trauma and Dissociation

30 Years of Study and Lessons Learned Along the Way[1]

Psychological trauma is an affliction of the powerless. At the moment of trauma, the victim is rendered helpless by overwhelming force. When the force is that of nature, we speak of disasters. When the force is that of other human beings, we speak of atrocities. Traumatic events overwhelm the ordinary systems of care that give people a sense of control, connection, and meaning.... Traumatic events are extraordinary, not because they occur rarely, but rather because they overwhelm the ordinary human adaptations to life.... They confront human beings with the extremities of helplessness and terror, and evoke the responses of catastrophe.

— Judith Lewis Herman, MD, *Trauma and Recovery* (1992b, p. 33)

Our current understanding of trauma and dissociation is relatively recent, beginning to emerge only about 30 years ago. Posttraumatic stress disorder and the dissociative disorders—as we currently understand them—were first codified in the American Psychiatric Association's *Diagnostic and Statistical Manual of Mental Disorders, Third Edition* (DSM-III) in 1980. Given what we now know about the effects of severe and chronic trauma, it is extraordinary that so little about it was acknowledged or understood just a few decades ago. What contributed to this pervasive blindness to critical issues that affect the many traumatized persons in North American society? The answer to this question is complex and has historical precedents.

Since the late 19th century the pendulum has swung between recognition and denial of the abuse of children, particularly sexual abuse. Pierre Janet (1907) wrote extensively about the relationship between trauma (including childhood abuse) and dissociation. In his 1896 publication, *The Aetiology of Hysteria*, Sigmund Freud (1896) postulated a link between childhood sexual abuse and psychiatric illness, a theory that he subsequently disavowed (Simon, 1992). Clearly, the Victorian values of Freud's time may have

---

[1] Portions of this chapter were adapted from "Trauma and Dissociation: 20 Years of Study and Lessons Learned Along the Way" (Chu & Bowman, 2000).

contributed to his disavowal of his "seduction hypothesis," which implied that incest was commonly the underlying cause of a wide variety of symptoms that were ascribed to female "hysteria," including fainting, nervousness, insomnia, weakness, muscle spasms, shortness of breath, irritability, loss of appetite, and diminished libido. However, the result of Freud's disavowal was the subsequent denial of the reality of abuse by generations of psychiatrists, psychologists, and other mental health professionals. The noted psychoanalysts Elizabeth Zetzel and William Meissner (1973) captured this stance beautifully in one of their texts on psychoanalytic theory and practice:

> The abandonment of the seduction hypothesis and the realization that the patient's reports of infantile seduction were not based on real memories but fantasies marked the beginning of psychoanalysis as such. The importance of reality as a determining factor in the patient's behavior faded into the background.... The focus of analytic interest turned to the mechanisms by which fantasies were created. (pp. 72–73)

Thus was the foundation laid for professionals to dismiss the realities of their patients' reports for generations. As recently as the 1980s, respected psychiatrists might have interpreted a patient's report of early sexual molestation by her father as "fantasies derived from Oedipal wishes" (meaning that the patient as a child had fantasized the incest because of her wish for a kind of sexual involvement with the parent of the opposite sex). This view implied that adult women were often unable to distinguish between fantasy and reality, and essentially blamed the patient for her own victimization. At that time, psychodynamic psychiatry was still dominated by classic psychoanalytic thinking, where conflicts about sexual drives, instincts, and fantasies were considered more important than the possible reality of occurrence of actual abuse. In fact, even when professionals believed that sexual abuse had occurred, the major emphasis was the resulting intrapsychic conflicts and not on the actual experience and aftereffects of the molestation.

Even among enlightened and sensitive professionals, the harsh facts concerning abuse are easily forgotten. For example, in spring 1992, a national organization released the results of a large-scale study, *Rape in America: A Report to the Nation* (National Victim Center, 1992). The grim statistics reported that one in eight women in this country were likely to be the victims of forcible rape during their lifetimes. Even more striking was the finding that nearly 30% of rape victims were less than 11 years old, and that more than 60% of rape victims were under the age of 17. These statistics actually *underestimated* the prevalence of rape, because although each victim was counted only once, some victims reported having been raped on multiple occasions (as is often the case in incestuous abuse). The results of the study were widely covered in the national press and on network and cable television news. Somewhat surprisingly, in the subsequent weeks, fewer and fewer professionals had any recollection of the essential results of this study—including clinicians who were interested in issues of childhood abuse. Only three months later, I informally polled an audience of more than 200 attendees at a national conference on sexual abuse and found that not one person recalled hearing about the study or the results. While this might be partially ascribed to the process of normal forgetting (in which even important events are progressively unavailable to conscious memory), the all-too-human need to deny these findings is likely to have played a major role in the lack of recall.

When it comes to interpersonal trauma, psychiatrist Judith Lewis Herman, MD (1992b), has pointed to a universal desire to look the other way—a natural human desire not to have to share the burden of the immense human suffering that derives from trauma and to accept some responsibility to ameliorate it. The societal denial of pandemic childhood trauma can perhaps be best understood through Herman's theory that disturbing ideas, such as the etiologic link between child abuse and common adult psychiatric difficulties, can only be sustained in the context of societal support. It is indeed challenging for any society to have the maturity to be able to acknowledge that it has permitted some of its most vulnerable members to be severely abused and as a result to become profoundly impaired. The cultural implications of recognizing the extent of child abuse have strongly influenced the way that the field of trauma and dissociation is viewed and whether its findings can be acknowledged and accepted or denied and reviled. Herman has argued that any single individual does not have the ability to challenge entrenched cultural beliefs and norms, and that the support of a political movement is necessary to allow it to be truly seen and studied. The modern recognition and study of complex posttraumatic and dissociative disorders stemmed from two major political and sociologic phenomena: the Vietnam War and the Women's Movement.

Historically, wars have forced societal attention to focus on the widespread and profound impact of overwhelming violence and trauma in postwar eras. In the United States, after the Civil War, a syndrome labeled "soldier's heart" was described (Da Costa, 1871), which included rapid heartbeat and overall autonomic activation with startle responses and hypervigilance. Following World War I, many American and European soldiers were described as suffering from "shell shock," a condition described as "emotional shock, either acute in men with a neuropathic predisposition, or developing as a result of prolonged strain and terrifying experience" or "nervous and mental exhaustion, the result of prolonged strain and hardship" (Southborough, 1922, p. 92). During and following World War II, clear posttraumatic syndromes were defined. Kardiner (1941) described a "physioneurosis" that included flashbacks, amnesia, irritability, nightmares, and other sleep disturbances. Saul (1945) used the term "combat fatigue" that resulted from overwhelming stress combined with the inability to act, and was manifested by emotional distress along with irritability, nightmares, and increase in heartbeat, respirations, and blood pressure. The original *Diagnostic and Statistical Manual of Mental Disorders* (DSM) was published by the American Psychiatric Association (APA) in 1952 during the Korean War, and the second edition (DSM-II) was published in 1968 during the Vietnam War. Both volumes recognized behavioral and emotional reactions to overwhelming fear or stress.

In the wake of the Vietnam War, an interesting paradox occurred. The war had become extremely unpopular, and by the fall of Saigon in 1975, most Americans were either politically opposed to the conflict or at least relieved to see an end to it. Most clearly did not want reminders of the failed war, and unlike more recent attitudes toward the military, many civilians regarded veterans as somehow tainted by their association with the recent conflict. Public opinion was so negative that veterans were reluctant to talk about their experiences or wear their uniforms in public. However, even in this climate of disavowal, health care professionals and eventually the American public had to acknowledge that a large cohort of young men and women returned from the war profoundly changed and damaged. This phenomenon facilitated the subsequent adoption of PTSD in the DSM-III in 1980. The increasing public and professional acknowledgement of the aftereffects of trauma allowed Vietnam veterans to be treated with a level of compassion and sophistication not seen in other postwar eras.

In 1983, Congress mandated the National Vietnam Veterans Readjustment Study (NVVRS; Kulka et al., 1990). Although the survey found that the majority of combat veterans made a successful adjustment to peacetime life, the NVVRS found that a substantial minority of Vietnam theater veterans continued to suffer from a variety of psychological and life-adjustment problems. Approximately 30% had experienced some form of posttraumatic problems. Even more alarming was the finding that for many veterans (approximately 12%), their PTSD had become a chronic condition. In a more recent study of 1,377 American Legionnaires 14 years after the NVVRS, 11% continued to suffer with more psychological and social problems, including marital problems with higher divorce rates, parenting difficulties, general unhappiness and difficulties functioning, and more physical problems, including pain, fatigue, and infections (Koenen, Stellman, Sommer, & Stellman, 2008).

Just as the Vietnam War focused attention on the effects of combat-related trauma, the Women's Movement and the rise of modern feminism profoundly changed attitudes concerning trauma toward women and the welfare of children. The Women's Movement provided the political will and social support to draw attention to long-neglected issues such as domestic violence, rape, and child abuse. Not surprisingly, many of the pioneers in the burgeoning trauma field in the 1970s and 1980s were women, many of whom embraced feminist values. Ann Wolbert Burgess, RN, DNSc, co-founded a crisis intervention program for rape victims at Boston City Hospital in 1972 (see Burgess & Holmstrom, 1974) and subsequently went on to become a pioneer in the study of the sexual assault on children and their exploitation in child pornography (Burgess, Groth, Holmstrom, & Sgroi, 1978). Similarly, Christine Courtois, PhD, co-founded a campus rape crisis center at the University of Maryland in 1972 and discovered that some clients of the center reported past sexual assault, including long histories of incest. Courtois went on to study and treat the effects of childhood abuse, helping other clinicians who were struggling to find guidance and support when there was a profound dearth of information on the subject of abuse and publishing the first major text on treating victims of incest, *Healing the Incest Wound* (1988). Our current understanding is that early sexual abuse can have devastating posttraumatic effects, but Courtois noted, "the most accurate diagnosis for incest response was posttraumatic stress disorder, an idea that seemed heretical at the time (1981) because PTSD was highly associated in the minds of clinicians with the Vietnam veterans" (p. xv).

In the 1970s, Herman began hearing many stories concerning incest in her adult women patients who had been diagnosed with borderline personality disorder. Despite the skepticism of the psychiatric establishment, she found the incest stories convincing and began a career of studying and treating sexual violence in our society. The result was the stunning book, *Father-Daughter Incest* (Herman, 1981), a scientifically credible work that documented the nature and undeniable harmful effects of sexual violation, which she saw as much more common than had been previously believed. Herman was one of the feminist pioneers who first understood the logical link between the trauma and betrayal of incest and the profound difficulties in functioning experienced by patients with borderline personality disorder.

CHILDHOOD ABUSE: THE HIDDEN EPIDEMIC

The pioneers of the study of childhood abuse and its effects did much to fuel subsequent investigation of the effects of trauma, including understanding the development of posttraumatic and dissociative symptoms and disorders. Little was known in the 1970s and early 1980s about the prevalence or effects of childhood sexual abuse. Earlier estimates of prevalence had reported a very low incidence of incest (e.g., Weinberg's 1955 estimate of an average yearly rate of incest of 1.9 cases per million children). Similarly, no real data existed concerning the effects of child sexual abuse. Kinsey and his colleagues downplayed any negative effects of incest: "It is difficult to understand why a child, except for its cultural conditioning, should be disturbed at having its genitalia touched" (Kinsey, Pomeroy, & Martin, 1948, p. 121). In fact, one of Kinsey's co-authors, Walter Pomeroy, was later infamously quoted as saying, "Incest between adults and younger children can … be a satisfying and enriching experience…." (Pomeroy, 1976, p. 10). Interestingly, Kinsey and his colleagues were surprised by their finding of a high rate of attempted sexual contact in childhood from their interviews with adult women. They found that 24% of the women recalled sexual advances by adult males when they were children, but the researchers downplayed the importance of this finding because most approaches did not result in actual sexual acts (Kinsey, Pomeroy, Martin, & Gebhard, 1953).

Modern research on the prevalence of childhood sexual abuse has yielded disturbingly congruent information concerning the rates of abuse. In 1986, psychologist Diana Russell, PhD, published *The Secret Trauma: Incest in the Lives of Girls and Women*, which reported the results of a landmark survey of the prevalence of sexual abuse in women in the general population. In interviews of 930 women in the San Francisco Bay area, more than one-third reported some kind of unwanted sexual contact in childhood. About half of the reported sexual abuse was incestuous abuse—sexual abuse perpetrated by a family member. These findings were considered surprisingly high when they were first reported but have stood up well in subsequent studies of general population samples in North

America (Briere & Elliott, 2003; Vogeltanz et al., 1999). Russell's work and subsequent studies have made it clear that the sexual abuse of girls is widespread and that it occurs among all ethnic groups and throughout all socioeconomic levels of our society.

Studies of the prevalence of the sexual abuse of boys have shown lower rates as compared to girls, but the rates are still high; when using a broad definition of sexual abuse (e.g., unwanted sexual contact in childhood), studies have found that one in six or seven adult men in the general population report some kind of childhood sexual abuse (Briere & Elliott, 2003; Elliott & Briere, 1995; Finkelhor, Hotaling, Lewis, & Smith, 1990).

Much of the research concerning the rates of childhood abuse has focused on sexual abuse, not only because of the extreme violation of boundaries and roles, but also because it is easier to quantify and study. There are far fewer ambiguities in defining sexual abuse as compared to physical abuse, emotional abuse, and neglect. However, the focus on this one type of childhood maltreatment does not imply that the potential aftereffects for other types of abuse are less serious. The few prevalence studies of physical abuse in childhood have suggested rates of 20% to 30% for both girls and boys (Briere & Elliott, 2003; MacMillan et al., 1997). These studies, combined with other research, lead to the unfortunate conclusion that both childhood physical and sexual abuse is widespread in our society and internationally (Finkelhor, 1994) and is perpetrated on both girls and boys. Although both physical and sexual abuse occurs among all children, girls are more likely than boys to be sexually abused, and, as shown in at least one study, boys were more likely than girls to be physically abused (MacMillan et al., 1997).

BEHIND CLOSED DOORS: SHAME AND SECRECY

In addition to societal denial and disavowal, there are other powerful reasons why the abuse of children is frequently hidden. The nature of child maltreatment—particularly child sexual abuse—and the circumstances in which it occurs also lead to the tendency not to acknowledge its occurrence or its aftereffects. Almost invariably, children feel shamed and responsible for their own victimization. In two remarkable papers, psychoanalyst Leonard Shengold, MD ("Child Abuse and Deprivation: Soul Murder"; 1979), and psychiatrist Roland Summit, MD ("The Child Sexual Abuse Accommodation Syndrome"; 1983), elucidated the way those who are injured by childhood abuse come to blame themselves for having been victimized:

> If the very parent who abuses and is experienced as bad must be turned to for relief of the distress that the parent has caused, then the child must, out of desperate need, register the parent—*delusionally*[2]—as good. Only the mental image

[2] "Shengold's use of the word *delusionally* does not assume a psychotic process or a defect in perception, but rather the practiced ability to reconcile contradictory realities" (Summit, 1983, p. 184).

of a good parent can help the child deal with the terrifying intensity of fear and rage which is the effect of the tormenting experiences. The alternative—the maintenance of the overwhelming stimulation and the bad parental imago—means annihilation of identity, of the feeling of the self. So the bad has to be registered as good. (Shengold, 1979, p. 539)

The child faced with continuing helpless victimization must learn to some-how achieve a sense of power and control. The child cannot safely conceptualize that a parent might be ruthless and self-serving; such a conclusion is tantamount to abandonment and annihilation. The only acceptable alternative for the child is to believe that she has provoked the painful encounters and to hope that by learning to be good she can earn love and acceptance. The desperate assumption of responsibility and the inevitable failure to earn relief set the foundation for self-hate…. (Summit, 1983, p. 184)

Psychologist Jennifer Freyd, PhD (1994), has offered another recent interpretation concerning the children's denial of their own victimization—even to the extent of forgetting it—as a syndrome of "betrayal trauma":

Betrayal trauma theory suggests that psychogenic amnesia is an adaptive re-sponse to childhood abuse. When a parent or other powerful figure violates a fundamental ethic of human relationship, victims may need to remain unaware of the trauma not to reduce suffering but rather to promote survival. Amnesia enables the child to maintain an attachment with a figure vital to survival, devel-opment, and thriving. (p. 304)

Children often fail to disclose abuse, even when they remember it. In addition to feel-ing shame and complicity, they may fear that the family unit would be disrupted, they may feel guilty for possible consequences to the perpetrator, and they may fear retalia-tion, which is often heightened by perpetrators' injunctions "not to tell" with threats of further harm to the victim or other family members (Swanson & Biaggo, 1985). Such patterns of intrapsychic and familial dynamics result in secrecy and shame. The abuse remains hidden behind closed doors and, in many cases of sexual abuse, concealed from other family members. It is not surprising that children not only often fail to disclose abuse, but when they do, they often recant their statements (Sorensen & Snow, 1991). Unspoken and unseen, damage done to victims of child maltreatment continues to grow and fester, often only emerging many years afterward as multiple and varied psychiatric symptoms and disorders and major impediments to healthy functioning.

Patterns of intrafamilial abuse are facilitated by many societies' emphasis on parental rights—to raise children as they see fit—as a cherished principle that supports famil-ial and cultural values (Miller, 1983). Although it can be legitimately argued that this cultural tradition has many positive aspects, its inherently optimistic views of parental child-rearing capacities may be misguided. Through our clinical experience, we know that the capacity to care for and raise children is substantially learned through having been adequately nurtured in childhood; that is, those who have had positive parenting are more likely to become good parents. In cases where parents have been the victims of childhood abuse or neglect, their parenting abilities may be massively flawed. The tragic result can be intergenerational cycles of human misery.

The potential harm to children who are raised by poorly equipped parents is compounded by the lack of any systematic training about parenting. This unfortunate tradition is long standing, existing more than a century ago, as evidenced by a quote by an English author, philosopher, and sociologist, Herbert Spencer, from an 1869 book on the home and families (Beecher & Stowe, 1869):

> Is it not an astonishing fact that, though on the treatment of offspring depend their lives or deaths and their moral welfare or ruin, yet not one word of instruction on the treatment of offspring is ever given to those who will hereafter be parents? Is it not monstrous that the fate of a new generation should be left to the chances of unreasoning custom, or impulse or fancy? ... To tens of thousands that are killed add hundreds of thousands that survive with feeble constitutions, and millions not so strong as they should be; and you will have some idea of the curse inflicted on their offspring, by parents ignorant of the laws of life. (pp. 263–264)

It appears that little has changed from the time of this 19th-century observation, leaving some unfortunate children in potentially abusive families with parents who receive little help in their struggle to raise their children.

NATIONAL STATISTICS AND REPORTING OF CHILD MALTREATMENT

In 1974, Congress enacted the first Child Abuse Prevention and Treatment Act (CAPTA; Public Law 93-247), requiring the states to enact mandatory reporting, investigation, and intervention concerning child maltreatment. Among those required to report suspected maltreatment are educators, law enforcement and criminal justice personnel, social services staff, medical personnel, mental health professionals, child daycare workers, and foster care providers. The number of annual reports rose rapidly, eventually leveling off at around 3.3 million reports each year (Figure 1.1).

CAPTA was amended in 1988 (Public Law 100-294), directing the Secretary of the Department of Health and Human Services (HHS) to establish a national data collection and analysis program that would make available detailed state-by-state child abuse and neglect information. HHS established the National Child Abuse and Neglect Data System (NCANDS) as a voluntary national reporting system, which produces annual reports concerning child maltreatment. As documented in *Child Maltreatment*

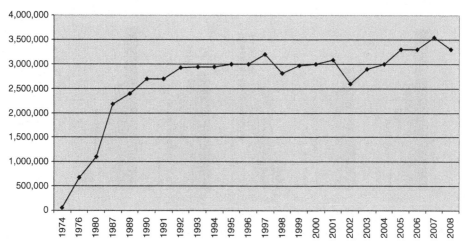

Figure 1.1   Annual Reports of Child Maltreatment Reported to Child Protective Service Agencies

2008 (U.S. Department of Health & Human Services, 2010), there were approximately 3.3 million referrals involving the alleged maltreatment of approximately 6.0 million children received by child protective services agencies. Nearly 63% of the referrals were screened in for investigation by child protective service agencies, and of those, approximately 24% of the investigations determined at least one child to be a victim of abuse or neglect—approximately 772,000 children. Most were victims of neglect (549,000), but there were also substantial numbers of victims of physical abuse (124,000), sexual abuse (70,000), and psychological maltreatment (56,000). Many children suffered multiple types of maltreatment. In 2008, there were 1,740 deaths of children known to be related to abuse or neglect.

As alarming as these statistics may be, they represent only the tip of the iceberg. For example, using a very conservative lifetime prevalence of 5% for serious or damaging sexual abuse, I calculate that there would be more than 200,000 cases per year.[3] In the clinical arena, adult patients rarely report that they disclosed their childhood sexual abuse or that it was discovered around the time that it occurred. This observation is supported by a study analyzed by Finkelhor and his colleagues (1990) of 2,626 American men and women, in which many of those who were victims of sexual abuse never previously disclosed their experiences.

Despite the underestimating of actual prevalence, the NCANDS data elucidate the nature of child maltreatment and expose some commonly held fallacies concerning child abuse and maltreatment (Figure 1.2). For example, it's assumed that victims of abuse and

[3] There are approximately 67 million children in the United States under the age of 16. If unwanted sexual contact occurs in 1 in 20 children, 3.35 million would be victims during the course of their childhood. Assuming that all cases of sexual abuse occur only in one year during a child's lifetime, there would be 209,000 cases per year.

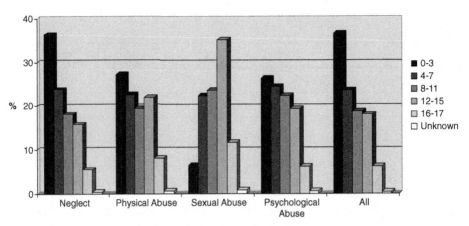

Figure 1.2 Percent of Victims by Age and Type of Abuse

neglect—particularly sexual abuse—are older rather than younger children. In fact, the highest rates of maltreatment in 2008 were in the youngest age group (ages 0–3) and decreased with age. Even with sexual abuse, nearly 30% of victims were under age 8, and 53% were under age 12.

Most child maltreatment occurs within the home. Approximately 80% of perpetrators were parents; 6.5% were other relatives, and another 4.4% were unmarried partners of parents. Of the parents who were perpetrators, more than 90% were biological parents; the others were stepparents or adoptive parents. Mothers and fathers were roughly equally likely to be perpetrators of child maltreatment, although male parents or relatives were more likely to be perpetrators of sexual abuse as compared to female family members. All racial and ethic groups were represented as both victims and perpetrators, with approximately half being white and one-fifth African-American and another one-fifth Hispanic.

Amid all the distressing statistics concerning child maltreatment in America, there may be some reasons to feel optimistic about the future. Despite the high numbers of traumatized children, the actual annual incidence of child maltreatment appears to be decreasing. In the 12 years up to 2008, NCANDS data show that the rate of child victimization may have fallen by nearly one-third (Figure 1.3).

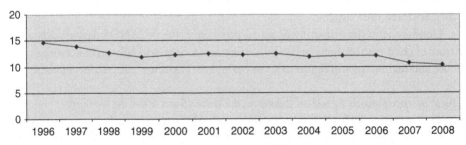

Figure 1.3 Annual Victimization Rate (cases/1,000 children)

Have the public health efforts of government, professionals, and advocacy groups substantially changed the willingness of American society to acknowledge and intervene to prevent the maltreatment of children? If so, it is a remarkable achievement.

CHILDHOOD TRAUMA IN PSYCHIATRIC PATIENTS

Histories of childhood abuse and the symptoms of complex PTSD are extremely common among psychiatric patients. For example, our 1990 study examined nearly 100 women consecutively admitted to McLean Hospital concerning psychiatric symptoms and childhood experiences (Chu & Dill, 1990). The responses were analyzed for reports of childhood abuse and any correlations with adult symptomatology. Using a questionnaire originally developed in another study (Bryer, Nelson, Miller, & Krol, 1987), physical abuse was defined as being "hit really hard, burned, stabbed, or knocked down," and sexual abuse was defined as "pressured against your will into forced contact with the sexual parts of your body or his/her body." A full two-thirds of the group reported significant physical or sexual abuse in childhood. Half of the entire group reported physical abuse, and more than one-third of the group reported sexual abuse. Although these rates are high, the prevalence of sexual abuse does not differ markedly from general population statistics. What differentiates the traumatic experiences of our patients from those of nonpatients? There are many factors, including psychiatric patients being much more frequently the victims of multiple kinds of abuse, long-standing abuse, and intrafamilial abuse. The rates of abuse in our studies have been validated by almost identical results in similar studies of both inpatients (Bryer et al., 1987; Chu, Frey, Ganzel, & Matthews, 1999; Saxe et al., 1993) and outpatients (Surrey, Michaels, Levin, & Swett, 1990).

In psychiatric patients who report physical and sexual abuse, long-standing abuse beginning early in childhood is common. In one of our studies, approximately 80% of such patients reported their physical and sexual abuse as very frequent, e.g., "continuous," "every week," "more times than I can count" (Kirby, Chu, & Dill, 1993). Patients with chronic abuse had strikingly higher dissociative symptoms in adulthood. These patients also had disturbingly early ages of onset of their physical and sexual abuse. Nearly 60% reported that the abuse first occurred prior to age 5, and over 70% reported it occurred prior to age 11. Early age of onset was also correlated with high levels of adult symptomatology. Other studies have demonstrated that both early age of onset and chronic sexual abuse are associated with greater dissociative amnesia (Briere & Conte, 1993; Herman & Schatzhow, 1987).

To a greater extent than in general population samples, psychiatric patients are more likely to be abused within the family. Although the psychological damage inflicted by persons outside the home should not be minimized, intrafamilial abuse may be particularly damaging. In Russell's study (1986) of women in the general population, approximately half of all sexual abuse victims were molested within the family. In contrast, in our studies of psychiatric patients (Chu & Dill, 1990; Kirby et al., 1993), the rate of intrafamilial sexual abuse in patients was much higher, with the vast majority (77%) naming family members as perpetrators. This difference in the rate of intrafamilial abuse between the general population and psychiatric populations strongly suggests that many of the psychiatric patients experienced psychological harm because their abuse was incestuous. In fact, when using dissociative symptoms as indications of psychological harm, we found that in psychiatric patients, intrafamilial abuse was correlated with more adult dissociation, whereas extrafamilial abuse was not as clearly harmful (Chu & Dill, 1990).

The damaging effect of intrafamilial abuse does not imply that abuse that occurs outside of the home is benign. Severe extrafamilial abuse may have profound deleterious effects on a child's development. Even more alarming, the signs of abuse in a child may be far from obvious. In several instances of patients admitted to the hospital for psychiatric care, we have found evidence of serious childhood abuse that was never suspected by caring families. In fact, in a prospective study of young children, psychiatrist Frank W. Putnam, MD, found a significant number of children who had suffered abuse but who were completely asymptomatic (personal communication). Severe abuse is sometimes accompanied by numbing and dissociation, which makes it difficult for children to report abuse. Furthermore, sexual abuse in particular is often accompanied by such a sense of shame that children may be reluctant to reveal what happened. We have seen several families who have guiltily berated themselves for having missed ongoing abuse outside of the home, when the only effects at the time were the child being quieter and preoccupied, or more labile and oppositional, which are hardly unusual behaviors in children. However, our sense is that even when abuse is not known to families, a warm, caring, and nurturing family environment is enormously reparative. The innate resiliency of most children may lead to substantial spontaneous healing from brief traumatic experiences if given the necessary supportive environment.

PROGRESS IN TREATING TRAUMA

Extraordinary advances have been made recently in the study of trauma, particularly including the traumatization of children. Enormous progress has been made in understanding the prevalence of child maltreatment and its aftereffects, including posttraumatic and dissociative responses. Clinical programs, research, and teaching efforts about posttraumatic and dissociative disorders have grown and flourished since the 1980s, as both professionals and the public began to understand the psychological and physiological effects of trauma. The International Society for Traumatic Stress Studies (ISTSS) and the International Society for the Study of Trauma and Dissociation (ISSTD) were founded in the mid-1980s and helped organize efforts to study trauma and treatment of traumatic sequelae. These organizations and the clinicians involved in the treatment and study of survivors of trauma now constitute a large and vibrant worldwide community of professionals who share a commitment to helping victims of trauma.

The trauma field has progressed remarkably in integrating diverse theories and techniques into the treatment of posttraumatic and dissociative disorders. Clinicians treating early trauma now consider its disruptive effect on attachment styles and personality development as they conduct therapy. The perspectives of self-psychology on the narcissistic damage imposed by early abuse have helped clinicians to understand the overlap of trauma-based disorders with borderline, narcissistic, and avoidant personality disorders. The trauma field has made substantial progress in addressing issues of comorbidity with other psychiatric disorders, iatrogenesis, factitious and malingered presentations, somatoform symptoms, and alexithymia that affect the clinical presentations of trauma survivors. The trauma field has also responded to critics with a flood of research on traumatic and recovered memories.

Overall, treatments for posttraumatic and dissociative disorders have become more integrated with traditional therapies. The understanding of the usefulness of hypnosis in trauma has been refined, and modifications of cognitive techniques for use in treating trauma have been developed. Treatment techniques for PTSD and dissociation have proliferated, with the application of new techniques such as eye movement desensitization and reprocessing (EMDR; F. Shapiro, 2001), dialectical behavioral therapy (DBT; Linehan, 1993), and sensorimotor therapy (Ogden, Minton, & Pain, 2006). Improved pharmacologic treatments for PTSD are available, and the trauma field has benefited from revolutionary advances in understanding the neurobiology and neurophysiology of PTSD and traumatic memories.

The Evolution of a Treatment Model

The First Generation: The Early Years—Up to the Mid-1980s

In the early 1980s, a growing number of clinicians began to understand that a significant number of their patients were suffering the aftereffects of childhood trauma. Bewildering and treatment-resistant symptoms were recognized as posttraumatic and dissociative responses to overwhelming and shattering childhood experiences. Although the shift in understanding patients' difficulties offered additional hope for successful treatment, many patients presented difficult treatment challenges, and there were few resources concerning how to treat these patients. Recognizing the role of past trauma in patients with posttraumatic or dissociative disorders, the early treatment models emphasized the importance of abreaction of the traumatic experiences as critical in the early treatment phases. This model was consistent with the reported successful treatment of adults with combat-related PTSD with acute PTSD (Kubie, 1943; Zabriskie & Brush, 1941; reported in Horowitz, 1986).[4] In addition, this model was an extension of the psychoanalytic principles of venting powerful unconscious affects as a way of providing symptomatic

---

[4] Even in the post–World War II era, it was questioned as to whether abreaction alone was effective for combat-related trauma. See Horowitz's *Stress Response Syndromes* (1986, pp. 118–120).

relief. It was believed that aggressive abreaction would lead to the working through of traumatic experiences and, in the case of dissociative disorders, the reintegration of split-off parts of the self. In many cases, patients did benefit from such treatment, but others did less well.

The Second Generation: Growth—The Late 1980s to the Early 1990s

During the period of growth in the recognition of trauma and dissociation, an increasing number of clinicians became knowledgeable and skilled in the treatment of patients with trauma-related disorders. Specialty programs were opened throughout the United States and Canada, many of which became centers for the study of trauma and dissociation as well as the treatment of traumatized patients. Local, state, provincial, national, and international component groups of the ISTSS and ISSTD were formed, and teaching and information about trauma treatment became widespread and increasingly available to clinicians.

Although many traumatized patients with PTSD and dissociative disorders benefited from treatment that emphasized abreaction, others either failed to improve or even became more symptomatic. It became clear that some persons who had suffered extended traumatization in childhood not only developed posttraumatic and dissociative disorders but also had major deficits in ego functioning. The chaos and abuse of their early years interfered with learning vital skills, such as the development of basic trust and relational capacity, affect tolerance, impulse control, the ability to tolerate aloneness and to self-soothe, and a positive self-image and sense of self-efficacy. Thus, when faced with the overwhelming dysphoria involved in remembering and reexperiencing childhood trauma, many patients fled into dysfunctional isolation and sometimes compulsive behaviors, such as self-mutilation, risk-taking, substance abuse, eating disorders, and somatization. Moreover, once the dissociative barriers to traumatic memories were breached, patients became yet more overwhelmed as they were flooded by their past experiences.

The second generation of treatment models focused on the development of a phase-oriented approach, in which there was an initial phase of ego-supportive therapy to improve basic coping skills, stabilize symptoms, maintain safety, and develop affect tolerance, impulse control, stable functioning, and improved relational ability *before* embarking on abreaction of trauma. These tasks often proved difficult and lengthy, and they were sometimes frustrating to both patients and clinicians who wished for a more rapid and definitive resolution of trauma-related symptomatology. Abreaction remained an important component of treatment, but only when patients had achieved an adequate level of stability and were able to tolerate and contain the memories and reexperiencing of traumatic events.

The promulgation of phase-oriented treatment models for the effects of childhood abuse began in the late 1980s at some national, regional, and local conferences. However, little appeared in the scientific literature until the early 1990s (e.g., Chu, 1992c; Herman,

1992b), and acceptance of phase-oriented treatment as a standard of treatment for complex posttraumatic and dissociative disorders was gradual. Given the considerable task of reorienting, reeducating, and retraining a large number of professionals in the clinical community, phase-oriented treatment began to become part of the standard of care for traumatized patients only by the late 1990s.

The Third Generation: Conflict and Maturation— The Mid-1990s to the Present

The False Memory Syndrome Foundation (FMSF) was founded in 1992 and began to promulgate highly publicized challenges concerning amnesia for childhood abuse, the validity of dissociative disorders, clinical research findings concerning childhood trauma, and the practices of clinicians treating victims of abuse. Acrimony and polarization ensued in the wake of FMSF attacks, with the proponents of various points of view taking extreme positions, for example, that traumatic memories (especially "recovered" memories) were either all true or all false. In fact, there was a kernel of truth to all of the points of view. In using new techniques to treat trauma and dissociation, some suggestive techniques may have been used by some therapists that allowed inaccurate reports of trauma memories. However, there was no evidence that the vast majority of trauma therapists had agendas to persuade unsuspecting patients that they were abused by their parents, and actual proof of outright implantation of memories in therapy remained extremely elusive. In fact, studies were able to lend support to the validity of recovered memories in a substantial number of patients, including those with dissociative disorders (Chu et al., 1999; Coons, 1994; Dalenberg, 1996; Kluft, 1987c). Social contagion and contamination concerning abuse memories may well have played a role in the production of poorly corroborated memories, particularly concerning memories of so-called satanic ritual abuse. However, there was no evidence that could obviate the clearly damaging effects of childhood abuse, including some experiences recalled following a period of amnesia for the events. FMSF proponents criticized the scientific methodology of studies that supported the existence of dissociation and amnesia, using arguments that clearly distorted the preponderance of evidence. In fact, dozens of studies demonstrated the correlation of dissociation with trauma and that amnesia for childhood abuse was found in virtually every study of amnesia in traumatized patients (Brown, Scheflin, & Whitfield, 1999).

In what Courtois (1999) has called the third generation of trauma treatment, clinicians have begun to acknowledge the vagaries of memory and the importance of restraint in clinical practices (e.g., recognizing that patients who have high innate dissociative capacities and who develop trauma-related disorders may also be highly hypnotizable and possibly prone to suggestion). Clinicians need to inquire directly about histories of trauma, and posttraumatic and dissociative, including possible amnesia for past events; without direct inquiry, patients who have been victimized routinely fail to volunteer such information because of ongoing shame and secrecy and the need to distance themselves from and disavow such experiences. Yet, such inquiries must be made in a way that is neutral and balanced and minimizes the possibility of suggestion. The third-generation models include more sophisticated evaluations of reports of abuse, better differential diagnosis, and treatment focused on patients' complex and multifaceted symptoms and disabilities.

THE THERAPEUTIC CHALLENGE

The extent of childhood abuse in our society is not simply a health issue. It is also a moral and political issue. Denial and lack of awareness tacitly sanctions the abuse of a substantial number of children in our society. From prevalence study research, mandated child abuse reporting, and our clinical observations, it is clear that *millions* of individuals are suffering (or have suffered) such experiences. This kind of abuse, captivity, and torture is not tolerated in any other group in our society, with the exception of some situations of domestic violence. It is ironic that in our country there are more strictures on operating a motor vehicle than on becoming a parent. In order to drive, one must obtain a license to do so. Driver education programs are universal in our schools, yet little or no training is formally available or seen as necessary to rear children. We assume that the ability to parent is somehow innate or at least learned from being adequately cared for as a child. In many instances, this assumption is correct, but in many other instances, it is tragically wrong. As a society, we give all adults the right to have children without providing them with the education to know how to do so, and we are complacent in allowing parents, many of whom are young and troubled, to struggle with the critical job of caring for children. The legacy of our complacency is a tide of human suffering and even death, which has resulted in untold human, financial, and moral costs to our society. We will require moral courage as a society to be willing to look openly where we previously have refused to see.

This volume is about the treatment of adults who have grown up bearing the scars of severe and chronic childhood abuse. These persons cannot just simply go on with their lives; this kind of abuse cannot be forgotten, disregarded, or left behind, and it continues to have profound effects in almost every domain of their existence. Severe and long-standing trauma introduces a profound destabilization in the day-to-day existence of many victims. They feel unpredictably assaulted by unwanted thoughts, feelings, and reminders of abuse. They are tormented by chronic anxiety, disturbed sleep, and irritability. They have symptoms that alter their perceptions of their environment, disrupt their cognitive functioning, and interfere with a sense of continuity in their lives. They are subject to powerful impulses, many of which are destructive to themselves or others. They have explosive emotions that they cannot always control. They experience self-hate and self-loathing and feel little kinship with other human beings. They long for a sense of human connection but are profoundly alone, regarding other people with great mistrust and suspicion. They want to feel understood but cannot even begin to find the words to communicate with others about their most formative experiences. They wish for comfort and security but find themselves caught up in a world of struggle, hostility, disappointment, and abandonment that recapitulates their early lives.

The therapists and other mental health professionals that treat these patients become a part of this world. Together with their patients, clinicians struggle to provide support, comfort, understanding, and change. Using themselves and the treatment as catalysts for change, clinicians attempt to provide the structure through which victims of childhood trauma may begin to undo the devastation of their early lives and go on to grow and flourish in the world. Given patience, understanding, skill, good judgment, determination, and sometimes just plain luck, survivors of profound child abuse and their therapists who ride this therapeutic roller coaster may survive to end up on solid ground, with a newfound stability and hope for future growth and fulfillment.

2

Complex PTSD

The Effects of Chronic Trauma and Victimization

In the 1980s and early 1990s, as the mental health community became aware of the high prevalence of childhood maltreatment in adult psychiatric patients, attention turned toward identifying the symptoms and problems related to childhood abuse. This focus of inquiry had two purposes: (1) if specific psychiatric syndromes were related to childhood abuse, then treatment would benefit from being trauma-informed, and (2) the presence of such syndromes might alert clinicians to a previously unknown history of trauma. However, the identification of specific sequelae to early trauma proved to be a difficult task. The nature and circumstances of past trauma differ considerably from person to person, and the problems related to childhood abuse are similarly diverse. Hundreds of studies published since the 1970s have shown that childhood traumatization—particularly sexual abuse—is correlated with a wide variety of psychiatric problems, including depression, anxiety, emotional lability, impaired self-esteem, relational difficulties, self-destructive behavior, alcohol and drug abuse, eating disorders, and various physiologic changes, among others (see, for example, Beitchman et al., 1992; Briere & Runtz, 1990; Browne & Finkelhor, 1986; Bryer et al., 1987; Fergusson, Horwood, & Lynskey, 1996; Gelinas, 1983; Greenwald, Leitenberg, Cado, & Tarran, 1990; Hall, Tice, Beresford, Wooley, & Hall, 1986; Herman, Russell, & Trocki, 1986; Mullen, Martin, Anderson, Romans, & Herbison, 1996; Pribor & Dinwiddie, 1992; Silverman, Reinherz, & Giaconia, 1996; Swett & Halpert, 1994). How does one sort through these myriad correlates of early abuse? Which are truly causally related? Many of these problems can derive from multiple etiologies, such as situational stress, genetic loading, or changes in brain chemistry in addition to early life experiences. So, what contribution does childhood traumatization play?

One way of understanding the hierarchy of responses to early trauma is to categorize psychiatric symptoms and syndromes as primary or secondary. Primary responses are direct effects of traumatization, and secondary responses are difficulties that develop as persons attempt to cope with the dysphoria of the primary effects. These latter kinds of responses are considered secondary (but not necessarily less important) because they are not directly caused by early abuse, but rather are the ways in which traumatized persons try to manage their distress.

Research findings and clinical observations strongly suggest that at least three major areas of psychological disturbance result directly from severe childhood trauma or the environment in which it occurs: posttraumatic stress disorder (PTSD), dissociative disorders (including dissociative identity disorder [DID] as the most severe form), and disruption of personality development and maturation such as is seen in borderline personality disorder. Posttraumatic symptoms or outright PTSD are logical consequences of childhood abuse. Adults with traumatic backgrounds often experience many different kinds of intrusive recollections of the abuse, as well as emotional numbing and attempts to avoid reminders of the abuse. Dissociation appears to be an available psychological defense for abused children whose limited coping capacities are overwhelmed by extremely traumatic events. Dissociation enables such events to be "forgotten," or at least emotionally distanced. Many such traumatized individuals have ongoing dissociative symptoms or develop dissociative disorders persisting into adulthood. Finally, symptoms of borderline personality disorder—including ongoing relational disturbances, difficulty tolerating intense affects, impulsivity, and self-hate and emptiness—are consequences of the failures of attachment and the inadequate care and protection that are common in dysfunctional and abusive families.

This chapter discusses the manifestations of PTSD—including the syndrome of complex PTSD that results from severe and prolonged traumatization—and the various secondary responses to trauma. Dissociation and dysfunctional personality adaptations are each discussed in separate chapters that follow.

Many patients who have been severely abused in childhood suffer from the disabling triad of PTSD, dissociation, and borderline personality disorder. They commonly also have secondary symptomatology and diagnoses, as shown in Table 2.1. These persons are particularly vulnerable to various forms of substance abuse, using intoxication as a way to diminish or blunt the intensely dysphoric feelings that they experience—sometimes called the self-medication hypothesis for substance use disorders (Khantzian, 1997). Epidemiologic data in the general population has shown high lifetime prevalences for alcohol and drug use disorders among those who experience PTSD: for alcohol abuse, 52% of men and 28% of women; for drug abuse, 35% of men and 27% of women (Kessler, Sonnega, Bromet, Hughes, & Nelson, 1995). In clinical populations undergoing substance abuse treatment, the rate of co-occurring PTSD and substance use disorders has been estimated at 11% to 34%; in all female substance abuse populations, the rates are even higher, 30% to 59% (Najavits, Weiss, & Shaw, 1997). These data are mirrored by clinical experience; it is very common for survivors of childhood abuse to have a period—either current or past—when they used and ultimately abused alcohol and/ or drugs. In some instances, the substance abuse was so effective in masking the trauma symptoms that evidence of PTSD only emerged after sobriety was attained.

Survivors of childhood trauma frequently become involved in a variety of behaviors that have an addictive quality, including repetitive self-harm as a way of self-soothing, risk-taking behaviors, compulsive spending, and eating-disordered behaviors. In fact, in a significant minority of patients with eating disorders, childhood trauma seems to be a powerful contributor to their compulsive eating, fasting, exercising, and purging. As

Table 2.1   Adult Diagnoses Associated with Childhood Traumatization

Primary Responses

Posttraumatic Stress Disorder (PTSD)	Brewin, Andrews, & Valentine, 2000; Browne & Finkelhor, 1986; Coons, Cole, Pellow, & Milstein, 1990; Donaldson & Gardner, 1985; Schaaf & McCanne, 1998; Widom, 1999
Dissociative Disorders	Boon & Draijer, 1993b; Pearson, 1997; Putnam, Guroff, Silberman, Barban, & Post, 1986; Ross et al., 1990[1]
Borderline Personality Disorder	G. R. Brown & Anderson, 1991; Herman, Perry, & van der Kolk, 1989; Ludolph et al., 1990; Ogata et al., 1990; Westen, Ludolph, Misle, Ruffins, & Block, 1990; Zanarini, Gunderson, & Marino, 1987

Secondary Responses

Substance Abuse Disorders	Fleming, Mullen, Sibthorpe, Attewell, & Bammer, 1998; Kendler et al., 2000; Langeland & Hartgers, 1998; Najavits, Weiss, & Shaw, 1997; Widom & Hiller-Sturmhöfel, 2001; Widom, Weiler, & Cottler, 1999; Wilsnack, Vogeltanz, Klassen, & Harris, 1997
Eating Disorders	Connors & Morse, 1993; Everill & Waller, 1995; Folsom et al., 1993; Hastings & Kern, 1994; Herzog, Staley, Carmody, Robbins, & van der Kolk, 1993; Welch & Fairburn, 1996; Wonderlich et al., 1996; Zlotnick et al., 1996
Somatoform Disorders[2]	Barsky, Wool, Barnett, & Cleary, 1994; R. J. Brown, Schrag, & Trimble, 2005; Loewenstein, 1990; Pribor, Yutzy, Dean, & Wetzel, 1993; Roelofs, Keijsers, Hoogduin, Näring, & Moene, 2002; Spitzer, Barnow, Gau, Freyberger, & Grabe, 2008; Waldinger, Schulz, Barsky, & Ahern, 2006
Obsessive Compulsive Disorder	Huppert et al., 2005; Lochner et al., 2002; Mathews, Kaur, & Stein, 2008

with many other psychiatric difficulties, eating disorders are a final common pathway deriving from numerous etiologies, including self-imposed perfectionism, overt or covert family conflict, or untreated affective disorders—in addition to trauma. However, when childhood trauma plays a critical role in the development of an eating disorder, the resultant difficulties may be more severe, complex, and difficult to treat. Treatment of patients with comorbid PTSD and eating disorders should optimally acknowledge both and incorporate elements of approaches for both problems.

Anorexia and bulimia nervosa are the types of disordered eating that commonly complicate and interfere with trauma treatment, and compulsive overeating—sometimes

---

[1] These studies provide correlations between childhood trauma and dissociative identity disorder. Discussion concerning correlations between trauma and dissociative symptoms can be found in Chapter 3, and a detailed discussion of dissociative amnesia is contained in Chapter 5.

[2] Some somatoform symptoms such as somatoform dissociation and somatic memory may be primary responses, whereas others such as somatization and hypochondriasis are secondary responses.

called binge eating disorder[3]—is also a frequent correlate for adults with a history of childhood trauma, particularly sexual abuse (Fairburn et al., 1998; Grilo & Masheb, 2001; Striegel-Moore, Dohm, Pike, Wilfley, & Fairburn, 2002). In clinical settings, compulsive overeating is described by patients as self-soothing or mood-regulating activity, and the resulting obesity can be a form of secondary gain in making the bodies of sexual abuse victims less attractive, hence alleviating their posttraumatic fears of sexual molestation. Although this type of disordered eating is less troubling in terms of trauma treatment, it is problematic in establishing healthy self-concepts and appropriate relationships, and in the deleterious long-term effects of morbid obesity.

As with eating disorders, there is a significant minority of patients with obsessive-compulsive disorder (OCD) where childhood trauma appears to play a major role in the etiology of their difficulties. There is an emerging consensus that most cases of OCD derive from changes in the neurobiology of brain functioning, with abnormalities in the functioning of central neurotransmitter systems involving serotonin and/or dopamine (for a review, see Pauls, Mundo, & Kennedy, 2002). However, there are some patients—primarily adolescents—whose OCD stems from early abuse, and the obsessional thinking and compulsive behavior have an addictive quality that appears to distract them from feelings and thoughts related to painful past traumatic experiences. There is little research data to document the incidence or significance of childhood trauma in OCD patients, but anecdotal clinical estimates are in the range of 10% to 20%.

Because some traumatized individuals develop and sustain dissociative symptoms to cope with their painful experiences, standard treatment for OCD may be less effective. For example, the cognitive-behavioral intervention of exposure therapy involves repetitively presenting patients with anxiety-producing material (e.g., contamination or forbidden thoughts) to decrease the intensity of their emotional reactions. Over time, the feared situations, substances, or ideas no longer result in anxiety, which reduces the need for obsessional thinking and compulsive behavior. However, if the OCD sufferer reflexively uses dissociation to avoid experiencing the feared exposures, the therapy is less effective. Hence, when OCD is linked to early abuse, treatment must be trauma-informed with particular care regarding the efficacy of specific protocols and interventions.

It has been interesting to observe how the addictive and avoidant behaviors of some childhood trauma survivors ebb and flow. For example, as some more serious behaviors abate with treatment, others are adopted in their place. Repetitive self-harming or risk-taking practices may give way to episodes of substance abuse, which in turn may abate only to be replaced by compulsive eating or spending. At McLean Hospital,[4] my home institution, there are separate, specialized programs for trauma and dissociation, alcohol

---

[3] Binge eating disorder—compulsive binge eating without purging—is categorized under "eating disorders, not otherwise specified" in the DSM-IV.

[4] McLean Hospital is a private, nonprofit psychiatric hospital in Belmont, Massachusetts. It is an affiliate of the Massachusetts General Hospital and the largest psychiatric teaching affiliate of Harvard Medical School.

and drug abuse, eating disorders, and OCD. It is not unusual for some trauma patients, particularly adolescents, to cycle through these various programs as their treatments progress and their symptoms change. However, the primary underlying issue has to do with the traumatic antecedents of their difficulties.

Patients with histories of trauma exhibit a variety of somatoform disorders, or somatic expressions of psychological distress. Some manifestations are primary, direct results of the trauma such as conversion disorders, somatic reexperiencing, and stress-related physical symptoms (e.g., migraine headaches). Other symptoms are secondary effects, such as somatization disorder and hypochondriasis, through which trauma patients attempt to channel their distress by the experience of physical symptoms or becoming preoccupied with the possibility of physical disease. Conversion disorder was recategorized with the somatoform disorders in the DSM-III (APA, 1980) but has a long tradition of being understood as related to the dissociative disorders under the outdated rubric of "hysterical" disorders. In fact, the classic psychoanalytic understanding of hysteria involved physical symptoms such as local paralysis, pain, and anesthesia for which no organic cause could be found, which was termed *conversion*. The definition of hysteria was later extended to include psychological symptoms that resulted from underlying intrapsychic conflict, which was called dissociation.

Conversion disorder is still seen in traumatized persons (Roelofs et al., 2002), but it is relatively uncommon in most clinical settings. This may be an indication of the malleability of the so-called hysterical disorders to conform with socially acceptable norms. In the Victorian age, where mental illness was poorly understood and not widely accepted, it may have been more acceptable for traumatized persons to have physical symptoms rather than psychological difficulties. Such patients literally could not see, speak, or feel, mirroring their inability to acknowledge or communicate about their traumatic experiences.

Although conversion disorders are relatively rare in current psychiatric practice, bodily symptoms related to dissociation are common and frequently co-occur with symptoms of psychological dissociation (Nijenhuis, 2000; Waller et al., 2000). Dutch psychologist Ellert Nijenhuis, PhD (1999) has termed these physical symptoms "somatoform dissociation," which includes many classic conversion symptoms. Somatoform dissociation includes symptoms of bodily dysfunction that have no organic basis, such as the inability to see or speak, alteration of sensory experience, pain, anesthesia, motor dysfunction and nonepileptic seizures. It is strongly associated with reported trauma among psychiatric patients. Somatoform dissociation presumably plays a defensive role—similar to psychological dissociation—in keeping traumatic experiences fragmented so that they are not perceived as overwhelming. In addition, some motor inhibitions and anesthesia/analgesia are somatoform dissociative symptoms that are similar to animal defensive reactions (e.g., freezing) to major threat and injury.

Somatic reexperiencing of traumatic experiences is commonly observed in clinical practice. The psychophysiologic responses to trauma—physical sensations, injury, and autonomic and neurohormonal adaptations—are held in an enduring way in the body

(Rothschild, 2000; van der Kolk, 1994; van der Kolk & Van der Hart, 1991). The often used but somewhat controversial term *body memories* describes somatic reexperiencing of traumatic events, which can include physical sensations (e.g., focused pain) or actual physical manifestations (e.g., involuntary spasms). Although the term body memory is sometimes considered pseudo-scientific, these kinds of somatic memories are well-recognized and well-studied components of the implicit memory system, which includes all of the physical and emotional components of past experience. How else does one explain the physical sensations that are common when persons remember trauma that seem to mirror the actual events? For example, sexual abuse survivors can experience genital, anal, or throat pain, gagging, shortness of breath, and a sense of being crushed. Much less common are well-documented instances where stigmata of past injury appear, such as bruises during the recollection of a traumatic event, which then fade more quickly than would be possible for actual current injury.

In addition to the direct somatic effects of trauma, somatization disorder, pain disorder, and hypochondriasis (all as defined in the DSM-IV) are mechanisms through which traumatized patients experience their psychological distress as bodily symptoms or preoccupation with physical illness. Somatization disorder (also known as Briquet's syndrome)—characterized by multiple physical complaints classically including pain, gastrointestinal, sexual, and neurologic symptoms that have no organic basis—has been linked to histories of early trauma and abuse (R. J. Brown et al., 2005; Pribor et al., 1993; Spitzer et al., 2008; Waldinger et al., 2006). Pain disorder—in which there is no underlying organic reason or the pain is vastly out of proportion to a medical condition—is often also related to childhood trauma (Sansone, Pole, Dakroub, & Butler, 2006), which is not surprising given that complaints of chronic pain are a common sequelae of early abuse (Teegen, 1999). Hypochondriasis—characterized by the persistent preoccupation that one has a serious disease despite the lack of evidence of such—has also been observed in populations of adults who have been traumatized in childhood (Barsky et al., 1994; Pribor & Dinwiddie, 1992).

The ongoing and pervasive effects of early trauma and abuse on the somatic experiences of survivors are quite clear. How to provide effective treatment to such individuals is less apparent. In the clinical arena, somatic dissociation and somatic memories may respond to standard treatments for PTSD and dissociative disorders and to specialized treatment focused on body-mind connections such as sensorimotor therapy (Ogden et al., 2006). However, patients with somatization disorder, pain disorder, or hypochondriasis are notoriously treatment-resistant, often having difficulty accepting the psychological roots of their distress. Perhaps this resistance is so marked because transforming emotional distress as physical illness allows patients to worry about something physical and concrete and spares them psychic pain. Most models of treatment for these disorders have focused primarily on patients in medical settings who have medical complaints unrelated to physical or biologic dysfunction (e.g., the "cardiac cripple" who is incapacitated by worry over insignificant sensations following recovery from a heart attack). There are few models of treatment for trauma patients in psychiatric settings. However, given the frequent presence of somatic aftereffects for patients with early abuse, this area of study should be of great interest and clinical importance in the future.

POSTTRAUMATIC STRESS DISORDER

Traumatization is part of the human experience. Whether by acts of nature or by acts of humans, catastrophic events can overwhelm human beings' ability to cope and result in a variety of posttraumatic responses. If the traumatization is severe, prolonged, or occurs early in life, posttraumatic stress disorder (PTSD) and dissociative disorders are likely to develop. Exposure to traumatic events is extremely common in our society. The National Comorbidity Survey (NCS) was conducted in the early 1990s (Kessler et al., 1995) and sampled 5,877 adults in the general U.S. population for PTSD (Figure 2.1). Lifetime exposure to severe traumatic events was estimated at approximately 61% in men and 51% in women. The traumatic events included experiencing wartime combat, life-threatening accidents, natural disasters, physical assault, rape, sexual molestation, child abuse and neglect, being threatened with a weapon, being held captive, and other kinds of exposure to shocking or terrorizing events, or suffering great shock because one of these events happened to someone close to the person.

Other studies have demonstrated similarly high levels of traumatic exposure in the general population (Breslau, Davis, Andreski, & Peterson, 1991; Resnick, Kilpatrick,

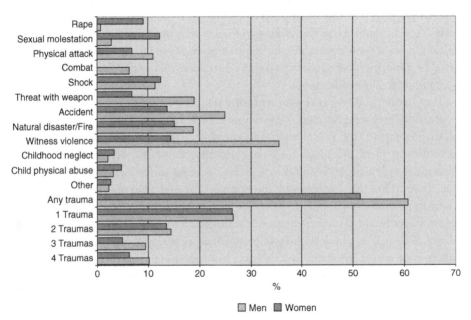

Figure 2.1 Lifetime Exposure to Traumatic Events by Type and Gender

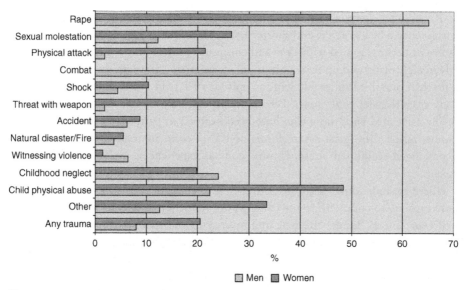

Figure 2.2 Likelihood of Developing PTSD After Trauma Exposure by Type and Gender

Dansky, Saunders, & Best, 1993). However, not all shocking experiences—and perhaps not even most traumatic events—result in PTSD. The NCS determined a lifetime prevalence of PTSD at 7.8% (Kessler et al., 1995), much higher than previous estimates of around 1% (Davidson, Hughes, Blazer, & George, 1991; Helzer, Robins, & McEvoy, 1987), probably because of differences in diagnostic criteria and assessment procedures. The National Comorbidity Survey Replication (NCS-R; Kessler et al., 2005), conducted between 2001 and 2003, sampled 5,692 participants, using DSM-IV criteria. The NCS-R estimated the lifetime prevalence of PTSD among adult Americans to be 6.8%, a very similar figure to the first NCS.

The nature and severity of the traumatic events may influence whether prolonged psychological effects will occur. There were significant gender differences concerning the likelihood of developing PTSD for many different types of trauma (Figure 2.2). In the NCS, the types of trauma in men that were more likely to lead to PTSD included rape, combat exposure, childhood neglect, or childhood physical abuse; women were more likely to become symptomatic following sexual molestation, physical attack, being threatened with a weapon, or childhood physical abuse (Kessler et al., 1995).

The probabilities for developing PTSD were generally higher for life-threatening events than for those that were of lower impact. Of particular note was the finding that although men were more likely than women to be exposed to traumatic conditions, women were twice as likely as men to develop PTSD. This result might point to women's increased vulnerability to develop PTSD, or more likely to the more severe sequelae of certain forms of traumatization, because women were overwhelmingly more likely than men to be the victims of rape or sexual molestation (odds ratio of 13 to 1).

Posttraumatic responses to brief or single overwhelming events in an otherwise intact person tend to be less severe and shorter-lasting. Many such experiences spontaneously resolve or become muted with time and encapsulated deep in the psyche, reappearing only in nightmares and under conditions of severe stress. However, the NCS found that more than one-third of people with an episode of PTSD failed to recover even after many years (Kessler et al., 1995). Persistent and disabling trauma-related responses are usually associated with those who have been exposed to particularly severe or chronic traumatization. The most severe forms of PTSD seem to result from certain types of prolonged childhood abuse, chronic combat experiences, or long-term domestic violence.

There are individual variations in response to stressful events. Some persons have more capacity to cope with trauma and greater resiliency to tolerate and recover from such experiences. Besides the type and severity of the traumatic experience, the reported risk factors for developing PTSD are preexisting psychiatric disorders, adverse childhood experiences, lack of social support, low socioeconomic status, lower intelligence, and family history of mental illness and/or substance abuse (Brewin et al., 2000; Davidson & Fairbank, 1993; Green, 1994; Ozer, Best, Lipsey, & Weiss, 2003). Trauma research has not yet sufficiently explored populations that have been exposed to trauma and do *not* develop posttraumatic difficulties. An emerging area of study in psychology has looked at resilience to loss and trauma and has begun to identify the characteristics of individuals who seem to fare better under adverse circumstances (Bonanno, 2004). A personality trait that has been called "hardiness"—which includes the beliefs that life is meaningful, that one can have control over the outcome of events, and that one can learn and grow from life experiences (Kobasa, Maddi, & Kahn, 1982)—has been linked to resiliency to trauma. However, many patients with severe and disabling posttraumatic responses have histories of extreme trauma such as malignant childhood abuse. Such experiences interfere with the development of healthy resilience, such as the characteristics of hardiness, and it is difficult to imagine that experiences of this sort would be well tolerated by any individual regardless of coping capacity.

The DSM-IV has the following criteria for PTSD (APA, 1994, pp. 427–428):

Criterion A: Stressor

    The person has been exposed to a traumatic event in which both of the following have been present:

1. The person has experienced, witnessed, or been confronted with an event or events that involve actual or threatened death or serious injury, or a threat to the physical integrity of oneself or others.
2. The person's response involved intense fear, helplessness, or horror. Note: In children, it may be expressed instead by disorganized or agitated behavior.

Criterion B: Intrusive Symptoms

The traumatic event is persistently reexperienced in at least one of the following ways:

1. Recurrent and intrusive distressing recollections of the event, including images, thoughts, or perceptions. Note: In young children, repetitive play may occur in which themes or aspects of the trauma are expressed.
2. Recurrent distressing dreams of the event. Note: In children, there may be frightening dreams without recognizable content.
3. Acting or feeling as if the traumatic event were recurring (includes a sense of reliving the experience, illusions, hallucinations, and dissociative flashback episodes, including those that occur upon awakening or when intoxicated). Note: In children, trauma-specific reenactment may occur.
4. Intense psychological distress at exposure to internal or external cues that symbolize or resemble an aspect of the traumatic event.
5. Physiologic reactivity upon exposure to internal or external cues that symbolize or resemble an aspect of the traumatic event.

Criterion C: Avoidant/Numbing Symptoms

Persistent avoidance of stimuli associated with the trauma and numbing of general responsiveness (not present before the trauma), as indicated by at least three of the following:

1. Efforts to avoid thoughts, feelings, or conversations associated with the trauma
2. Efforts to avoid activities, places, or people that arouse recollections of the trauma
3. Inability to recall an important aspect of the trauma
4. Markedly diminished interest or participation in significant activities
5. Feeling of detachment or estrangement from others
6. Restricted range of affect (e.g., unable to have loving feelings)
7. Sense of foreshortened future (e.g., does not expect to have a career, marriage, children, or a normal life span)

Criterion D: Autonomic Hyperarousal

Persistent symptoms of increasing arousal (not present before the trauma), indicated by at least two of the following:

1. Difficulty falling or staying asleep
2. Irritability or outbursts of anger
3. Difficulty concentrating
4. Hypervigilance
5. Exaggerated startle response

In addition, the DSM-IV requires that the PTSD symptoms be present for more than one month (similar symptoms for less than a month are diagnosed as acute stress disorder). PTSD is considered to be chronic if the symptoms are present for more than three months. The DSM-IV describes the occurrence of delayed onset, in which symptoms emerge more than six months after the event. One variant of delayed onset occurs in conjunction with complete or partial amnesia for traumatic events. When the memory is recovered—often years later—acute PTSD symptoms erupt, often with vivid, detailed intrusive memories and flashbacks along with severe autonomic hyperarousal, as though a defensive barrier has been breached. In retrospect, some of these persons with delayed recall realize that they had been in a somewhat chronic, numbed state before the return of the memories.

DIFFERENTIAL DIAGNOSIS

From a treatment perspective, it is important to correctly diagnose patients' difficulties and to understand the etiology of their symptoms. For example, although many traumatized persons meet the DSM-IV criteria for a major depressive disorder, it is more helpful to recognize the symptoms as being trauma related: depressed and anxious mood (related to PTSD and borderline personality), emotional constriction and numbing (related to PTSD and dissociation), social withdrawal (related to PTSD and borderline personality), hopelessness and a sense of foreshortened future (related to PTSD), helplessness (related to PTSD and borderline personality), and self-destructive thoughts and behaviors (related to PTSD and borderline personality). If the symptomatology is truly trauma-related, patients will not optimally respond to treatments for major depression such as antidepressant medication. In our study comparing patients with childhood trauma to nontraumatized patients with major depression (Chu, Dill, & Murphy, 2000), both groups met DSM-III criteria for major depressive disorder and had many classic neurovegetative signs and symptoms of depression, including loss of energy, interest, and motivation, sleep and appetite disturbance, guilt, and suicidal thoughts. The only symptoms that seemed to differentiate the two groups had to do with the characteristics of the sleep disturbance. The depressed group endorsed difficulties in falling asleep despite feeling tired, and midsleep awakening with the inability to fall back to sleep. The patients with trauma had difficulty falling asleep because they were too anxious or fearful to sleep, and they subsequently woke up multiple times during the night with anxiety that was sometimes caused by traumatic nightmares.

Given the distressingly high prevalence of trauma, it is not unusual for some patients to have true comorbidity in addition to trauma-related syndromes. That is, traumatized patients may have major mood and anxiety disorders, schizophrenia and other psychotic illnesses, dementia, delirium, or organic states. In these situations, it is usually imperative to treat the *non-trauma-related* difficulties as the first priority. Serious psychiatric illness is a major internal stress on the body and mind, and because posttraumatic and dissociative symptoms are stress-responsive, these trauma-related symptoms may be heightened by untreated comorbid disorders, as in the following example:

> Esther, a 63-year-old, single woman was admitted to a psychiatric hospital with florid PTSD symptoms. She had intrusive thoughts almost continuously about known physical and sexual abuse that had occurred after she was abandoned as a child and raised in a series of foster homes and institutions. She was particularly fearful at night, having flashbacks and seeing images of menacing men outside her window. A closer examination of her symptoms suggested that Esther was suffering from major depression with psychotic features. She showed extreme psychomotor retardation, barely moving from her bed or chair, had sustained a recent 20-pound weight loss, and spoke of feeling that her "insides" were decaying. A brief course of electroconvulsive treatment followed by medication brought about a remarkable change. She recompensated with improvement in both her mood and PTSD symptoms. Although she still thought about her early abuse, the thoughts did not overly disturb her, and she was able to return to her previous level of functioning.

It is also not unusual for certain psychotic disorders to mimic trauma-related syndromes, as in this clinical illustration:

> A 24-year-old man was referred for evaluation for PTSD. He had recently had several episodes where he had the abrupt onset of episodes of intense anger, agitation, and anxiety, which he attributed to possible sexual abuse by an older family member such as his father, uncle, cousin, or older brothers. When asked if he had memories of the abuse, he admitted that he had no such recollections and had never previously suspected abuse, but he felt that this was the only explanation for these episodes. He was preoccupied with fantasies of avenging himself for having been molested, but he was unclear which family members might have abused him.
>
> It became clear that he also had vague but intense worries about other issues, such as the idea that he might have been sexually abused by a priest in his church (without any memory or indication of such) and that he might be homosexual (despite all evidence pointing to heterosexual orientation). He reported a sense of emptiness and a sense of detachment from others (including parents who he described as caring and supportive) and difficulties functioning; these problems had been increasing since his midteen years. In addition to his apparent paranoia, he admitted that his thinking was often extremely scattered, disorganized, and confused. In consultation with his treating psychiatrist, it was clear that the diagnosis of PTSD was unlikely and that schizophrenia or another psychotic illness was more probable.

COMPLEX PTSD

In several ways, it is not entirely helpful to accept the criteria for PTSD as defined in the DSM-IV as fully describing the aftereffects of trauma. First, PTSD rarely exists in isolation. More often, particularly in cases that become chronic (i.e., symptoms persist for more than three months), extensive comorbid conditions complicate treatment and recovery. Second, the DSM-IV diagnostic criteria are very limited and do not include some important changes that occur universally in PTSD, such as fundamental shifts in the way that trauma survivors see themselves and the world. In order for the concept of PTSD to be most useful, one must consider how it customarily presents in real-world situations and how to optimally understand and treat the multiple difficulties that PTSD sufferers experience. It is also important to understand the limitations of treatment outcome research. In order to have clean participant samples that will elimi-nate unnecessary variables, researchers generally exclude those patients with extensive comorbidities. Hence, some research findings concerning efficacy of treatment have only limited applicability and may not be relevant to many PTSD patients seen in clinical practice.

It is striking to note how commonly PTSD patients have multiple comorbidities (Figure 2.3). In the NCS, the vast majority of participants who had PTSD at any point in their lifetime qualified for at least one other diagnosis during their lifetime; approxi-mately half qualified for more than three diagnoses (Kessler et al., 1995).

Part of the comorbidity found with PTSD results from the overlap in symptom cri-teria with other disorders, which is why many have referred to the umbrella of PTSD. As noted previously, some of the avoidant/numbing symptoms of PTSD may resemble symptoms of depression, and some of the autonomic hyperactivity, such as irritability, hypervigilance, and startle response, may overlap with anxiety disorder symptoms. Even so, it is clear that many, if not most, PTSD sufferers have many areas of psychiatric dif-ficulties in terms of diverse symptoms and disabilities.

Much of the comorbidity of some PTSD derives from the effects of chronic trauma, which have only been recently understood. Psychiatrist Lenore Terr, MD, began studying the effects of trauma on children in the 1970s and published groundbreak-ing accounts that have helped to elucidate the differential effects of acute and chronic traumatization. Terr's best-known work concerns her investigation of the aftereffects of the kidnapping of 26 children in the small California town of Chowchilla in the sum-mer of 1976 (Terr, 1979, 1980, 1983, 1990). The children were abducted from a school bus, packed into two vans and driven around for 11 hours, and then held captive in a buried moving van. They managed to escape from their underground prison late on the following day. In the flurry of police activity and media attention, little thought was given to the children's psychological experience or mental health concerns. The effects of psychic trauma on children were virtually unknown at the time; a local child psy-chiatrist predicted that perhaps only one child would develop psychiatric problems. In fact, all of the children showed striking evidence of residual terror, rage, helplessness,

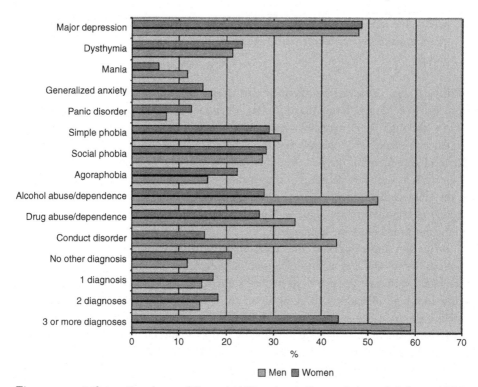

Figure 2.3   Lifetime Prevalence of Comorbid Disorders in Respondents with Lifetime PTSD

and a sense of vulnerability in psychological symptoms (nightmares, premonitions, magical thinking), behavioral reenactments (trauma-related play), and medical symptoms for years after the event. Terr went on to study many other individual children and cohorts of traumatized children, and she began to recognize the varying aftereffects of trauma that depended on the nature of the stressor, the individual characteristics of the children involved, and whether the trauma was a "single blow" or more chronic in nature.

There are differential effects of acute and chronic trauma. In a remarkable summary paper in the *American Journal of Psychiatry*, Terr (1991) observed the following about the effects of acute traumatization:

> The findings special to single, shocking, intense terrors are 1) full, detailed, etched-in memories, 2) "omens" (retrospective reworkings, cognitive reappraisals, reasons and turning points), and 3) misperceptions and mistimings.... Verbal recollections of single shocks in an otherwise trauma-free childhood are delivered in an amazingly clear and detailed fashion. A few details from a traumatic event of childhood may be factually wrong because the child initially misperceived or mistimed the sequence of what happened. But children... seem to remember the event and to give impressively clear, detailed accounts of their experiences. This

remarkable retrieval of full, precise, verbal memories of almost all single blow traumas makes one conclude that these memories stay alive in a very special way. (p. 14)

In this passage, Terr describes the increased clarity of recall (hypermnesia) that results from brief or limited traumatization. The details of the experience are remembered clearly, although there may be some errors caused by misperception and about the sequence of events. The "omens" that Terr referred to are probably more commonly understood as the kind of magical thinking that children often employ to make sense out of events that are overwhelming or out of their control. For example, in the aftermath of the Chowchilla kidnapping, one girl decided to never again wear a blue dress, and another girl resolved to not argue with her mother, both circumstances having occurred on the morning before the kidnapping.

While Terr's investigations concerned children, her conclusions have proved to have applicability to adults as well. Single traumatic events at all ages are generally well remembered, although peripheral details are sometimes misremembered. Adults are also prone to a kind of magical thinking in an effort to gain a sense of control over overwhelming events. For example, in the aftermath of the terrorist attacks of September 11, 2001, many Americans foreswore traveling by airplanes, and Homeland Security officials advised citizens to stock up on plastic sheeting and duct tape to protect themselves against possible chemical or biological attack, even though such measures would be unlikely to ensure their safety.

In contrast to the aftereffects of acute, "single blow" traumas, there are markedly different sequelae in children who are subjected to long-standing trauma. In her 1991 paper, Terr wrote:

> The defenses and coping operations used in the [disorders resulting from chronic traumatization in] childhood [include] massive denial, repression, dissociation, self-anesthesia, self-hypnosis, identification with the aggressor, and aggression turned towards the self, [and] ... profound character changes. ... Children who experience [chronic] traumas often forget. They may forget whole segments of childhood—from birth to age 9 for instance ..." Where one sees the difference between these "forgetful" children and ordinary youngsters is in the multiply traumatized child's relative indifference to pain, lack of empathy, failure to define or acknowledge feelings and absolute avoidance of psychological intimacy. Repeatedly brutalized, benumbed children employ massive denial. (pp. 15–16)

In this brief passage, Terr described some of the multiple domains of dysfunction that eventually have become acknowledged as integral parts of complex PTSD. The elements of "denial, repression, dissociation, self-anesthesia, self-hypnosis" are all automatic psychological defenses to distance oneself from the overwhelming emotions and sensations of traumatic experiences. The massive forgetting serves the need to disavow and block recall of trauma. The extent of the global amnesia—for *all* memories, not just the traumatic ones—suggests that other mechanisms are involved rather than just blocking out distressing events. Finally, Terr notes that chronic childhood trauma alters normal personality development, resulting in profound character changes with "identification with the aggressor, and aggression turned towards the self," "indifference to pain, lack of empathy, failure to define or acknowledge feelings and absolute avoidance of psychological intimacy"—all of which are the building blocks for the development of the characterologic pathology found in borderline personality disorder.

The concept of complex PTSD was originally described by Herman (1992a, 1992b) and includes many features that are commonly seen in individuals who have been subjected to severe and persistent traumatization. In Herman's conceptualization of complex PTSD, the individual is harmed by being held in a state of captivity, under the control of a perpetrator of abuse, and unable to escape. Such conditions are found in situations where human rights are sometimes grossly violated, such as concentration camps, prisoner of war camps, and prisons, but captivity and long-term traumatization can also occur in ongoing domestic violence and in the form of severe and chronic childhood abuse.

The concept of complex PTSD has also been termed "disorders of extreme stress, not otherwise specified" (DESNOS) and was further elaborated by van der Kolk and his colleagues (van der Kolk et al., 1996; van der Kolk, Roth, Pelcovitz, Sunday, & Spinazzola, 2005). It has been assessed using both standard and newly developed instruments (Briere & Spinazzola, 2005; Luxenberg, Spinazzola, & van der Kolk, 2001; Pelcovitz et al., 1997), and validated in DSM-IV field trials (Roth, Newman, Pelcovitz, van der Kolk, & Mandel, 1997; van der Kolk, 2002). In complex PTSD and DESNOS, changes and harm occurs in fundamental alterations in multiple domains of psychological functioning:

- Alterations in emotional regulation and impulse control, such as persistent sadness, explosive or inhibited anger, self-destructive thoughts and behavior, suicidal preoccupation, and risk-taking behaviors
- Alterations in consciousness, such as forgetting or reliving traumatic events, or having episodes in which one feels detached from one's mental processes or body
- Alterations in self-perceptions, such as helplessness, defectiveness, shame, guilt, stigma, or a sense of being different than others
- Alterations in perceptions of the perpetrator, such as attributing total power to the perpetrator or becoming preoccupied with the relationship to the perpetrator including revenge fantasies
- Alterations in relations with others, such as isolation, distrust, being revictimized, victimizing others, or searching for a rescuer
- Alterations in somatic experience, such as chronic pain, conversion, or cardiac, gastrointestinal, neurologic, or sexual symptoms
- Alterations in one's system of meanings, such as a loss of sustaining faith, or a sense of hopelessness and despair

Translated into DSM concepts and language, the syndrome of complex PTSD acknowledges that long-term traumatization has profound effects in many areas resulting in PTSD symptoms, dissociation, and abuse-related personality disturbances—the primary triad of the direct responses to trauma that is so often seen in clinical settings—plus somatic symptoms and psychological responses. Persons with complex PTSD have the classic posttraumatic intrusive symptoms of recurring thoughts, dreams and flashbacks, numbing symptoms of emotional constriction and social isolation, and autonomic over-activation manifested by chronic anxiety, irritability, and startle responses. In addition, the alteration in the way that they view themselves and the world profoundly affects the way that they function and interact with the others. Seeing themselves as defective and vulnerable, but also feeling empty and alone, they approach others with profound mistrust but also sometimes seek a caretaker or rescuer. Sufferers from complex PTSD are frequently overwhelmed with intense feelings, such as deep sadness, suicidal thoughts, explosive or bottled-up anger, aloneness, shame, guilt, hopelessness, and despair. Unable to tolerate such intense affects, they may resort to a variety of dysfunctional behaviors, such as self-destructive acts, repetitive self-injury as a form of tension release, risk taking, and substance abuse.

Severely traumatized patients commonly present with a bewildering range of psychiatric symptomatology and represent diagnostic and treatment challenges. It is understandably difficult to know how to approach patients who manifest such a complex array of symptoms. Perhaps it is because of this complexity of symptoms that these patients are often difficult to treat, and the treatment process is often long, confusing, and complex. Clinical examples best demonstrate how various trauma-related difficulties can present in clinical settings and how clinicians can come to understand them and provide helpful and focused treatment. The following extended clinical vignette of a patient, "Donna," illustrates the mixture of posttraumatic, dissociative, and characterologic features along with extensive comorbidities that can be perplexing to most clinicians. I met Donna on my first day at McLean Hospital and eventually became her psychiatrist and therapist and worked with her for many years. She had already been a patient at McLean for some time when I met her and was well-known—in fact, somewhat notorious—to most of the staff of various inpatient units.

DONNA'S STORY

Donna was first hospitalized when she was 26 years old. She was a college graduate who was working as a teacher's aide. She was unmarried with few friends and had few social interactions other than intermittent contact with a younger brother. She was admitted following a very serious suicide attempt, and she remained hospitalized for more than four months because of unremitting, driven suicidality. Despite the attempts of hospital staff to keep her from harming herself, she ingested overdoses of saved-up medication, mutilated her arms and throat with a stolen metal fork, and attempted to strangle herself with a latex glove. Given her repeated attempts to harm herself and her difficulties engaging productively with hospital staff, she was regarded with anxiety, frustration, and suspicion.

When calm, Donna was a pleasant-looking, somewhat overweight young woman who could be disarmingly direct, humorous, and quite engaging. However, she could also be angry and demanding. Donna felt very demeaned by the necessary safety precautions and the restrictiveness of her treatment that allowed her very little privacy and limited personal freedom. She felt very abused by the hospital staff and did not hesitate to tell them so. She berated them for being cruel, insensitive, and incompetent. Repeatedly, she demanded more privileges and accused the staff of intentionally punishing and hurting her. Donna's treatment team tried to be reasonable, and on one occasion when she seemed to be a bit calmer and less overtly destructive, she was allowed the privilege of going out on grounds with a group of patients and a staff member. She proved unable to maintain the responsibility for this very limited privilege. She eloped from the group, ran off the hospital grounds, bought razor blades, and cut her arms severely in the bathroom of a local bus depot. After being discovered, she was brought back to the hospital, and the cycle of misery and mutual mistrust continued. After an extended period of hospitalization, Donna's self-destructiveness seemed to abate, and she was eventually discharged to a halfway house for psychiatric rehabilitation. However, conflicts over her safety soon erupted, and she was asked to leave the halfway house for violating rules around the use of alcohol. She went to another residence and made arrangements to return to work.

Donna did have some difficulties at work with serious control struggles with her supervisors, as well as problems with absenteeism. When she didn't feel well, which could occur one or two days every two weeks or so, she would not go to work, and that created a serious problem in terms of her reliability. She was also the victim (as she predicted) of prejudice when it became known that she had psychiatric problems. At times she was treated as though she really didn't have any problems and was only trying to get out of working when she called in sick. At other times she was labeled as unstable and incompetent even in situations that would have been stressful to anyone. Donna's behavior varied wildly. She was sometimes able to work competently but at other times seemed so distraught, helpless, and childlike that she was unable even to care for herself. This variability of behavior was very confusing to those who were attempting to treat her. Some believed that she was "just regressed" and was capable of pulling herself together and that she just wasn't trying, whereas others felt that she had little or no control over herself.

Donna's treatment remained problematic. Very few approaches seemed helpful in any kind of sustained way. She was treated with every therapeutic modality in common use. She received intensive individual psychotherapy with me. I prescribed numerous medications, including powerful antidepressants and antipsychotics. She participated in group treatment. Nothing appeared to help. Not only was she despondent and suicidal, but she often became panicked and agitated. She complained of hearing voices inside her head that told her to kill herself and of seeing frightening images of threatening figures at night. She would often try to harm herself when she was distressed, cutting or scratching deep wounds on her forearms or other parts of her body. Periodically, new symptoms appeared, including episodes of seizure-like spasms where she would appear to lose consciousness and convulse on the ground.

Donna remained seriously suicidal. She would frequently present to me looking quite withdrawn, depressed, and distressed. When I asked what was troubling her, she would only respond somewhat incoherently, "I don't feel like myself ..." Attempts to draw her out further were largely futile. She would sometimes mutter or become mute, looking around the room apparently quite frightened, mouthing inaudible words. This behavior would usually escalate into her becoming more upset and agitated, even to the extent of running from the room or trying to hurt herself in some way.

Hospitalization was frequently required, and these admissions continued to be chaotic. Donna would often be agitated and self-destructive, banging on walls with her hands and head and attempting to elope from the unit whenever the door was opened. Some of these agitated episodes could only be contained by putting her into physical restraints, and her cries for help and her piteous sobbing during restraint periods were heartbreaking. Staff members were deeply frustrated by their inability to help Donna. Some continued to feel sympathetic toward her. Others, particularly those who bore the brunt of her articulate verbal (and occasionally physical) attacks, were clearly hostile to her, interpreting her behavior as solely manipulative and attention-seeking. Of particular note was Donna's response after being restrained. She would gradually quiet down and then, often two or three hours later, she would appear to wake up and, in a child-like way, ask the nurse observing her, "What happened?" This response would generally outrage many of the staff who were often convinced that Donna was perfectly aware of what she was doing and should be more honest and cooperative.

For the first several *years* of her treatment, Donna continued to do poorly. Repeated crises of various sorts occurred, many of which resulted in hospitalizations. Even during better periods of outpatient treatment, the unexpected often occurred. On some occasions, Donna would seem to be well grounded and able to discuss her current life situations with increasing insight and more of a sense of trust in her treatment team. At other times, Donna was much less coherent and engaged. She was frequently suicidal, and sometimes her treatment was only focused on attempts to contain her self-destructive impulses and to have her agree to not kill herself—at least until the next appointment. Despite continued therapy and changes in medication, she was sometimes mute, seeming to respond to frightening internal experiences.

Emergency situations were frequent. On several occasions, medical treatment for drug overdoses was necessary. Sometimes Donna would call me for help in a crisis. At other times, she would hurt herself without calling. Her forearms were the sites of multiple self-inflicted lacerations, which sometimes led to serious cellulitis (infection of the skin and subcutaneous tissues with fever, swelling, inflammation, and pain). She claimed to experience no pain when cutting herself, only relief, and she stubbornly resisted any suggestions that she stop this self-mutilation. On several occasions, Donna was at risk for death by drug overdose or for serious medical complications such as the amputation of an arm because of cellulitis.

Donna's treatment finally changed during a particular hospitalization. A perceptive nurse approached me to tell me about certain very striking behaviors she had observed when Donna was placed in restraints, which made the nurse question a history of childhood abuse. Specifically, she would often cower in a corner and put her hands over her head as if fending off attack and then seemingly react as if she were being beaten. This was a light-bulb moment for me, and the observation shifted my understanding of Donna's difficulties as perhaps being trauma-related. For example, her sense of detached spaciness was consistent with depersonalization and derealization (distortions of her perceptions in which the world around her and her body seemed unreal or detached). Her waking up after being in restraints or following a pseudo-seizure could be flashbacks with subsequent amnesia and some kind of somatization. And her ability to abruptly switch from suicidal patient to competent teacher's aide could be interpreted as some kind of switching between self-states. Even more clearly, perhaps some of her hallucinations and intense psychological distress, as well as her stereotyped behavior while being restrained, could be understood as manifestations of reexperiencing of past traumatic events.

Donna had previously been able to report only very general information about her childhood, saying that her father was intimidating and her mother was difficult. Further inquiry revealed that Donna had only fragments of memory for events before the age of 12. She had recall of a few specific incidents, but she remembered almost nothing about such things as routine home life, the house she grew up in, friends, teachers, school, or other early childhood experiences. All she remembered clearly were her adolescent and adult years: details about high school and college, her struggle to leave home against her mother's wishes, her parents' divorce, and then the numbing depression and desperate wishes to kill herself that led her to seek psychiatric treatment. Donna had no memory of overt physical or sexual childhood abuse. She was able to describe a chaotic family with a father who was alcoholic and threatening at times. Her mother appeared to have been chronically overwhelmed and sometimes suicidal, often relying on Donna for comfort and support.

During this period, Donna continued to have terrible symptoms. She began to have nightmares, often waking her roommates with screams of terror. She began to have vivid memories of both being the victim and witness of abuse. She recalled details of how her parents were constantly battling, describing physical assaults between her parents, some of which appeared to be attempts to injure or kill each other. During the course of a hospitalization, she began to have acute reexperiences of a series of physical assaults that had occurred between the ages of 5 and 12. She believed that on multiple occasions when she was left alone with her father that he would become drunk and violent, repeatedly assaulting her.

Therapy became acutely painful for Donna as she felt tortured in her body and mind by her memories and flashbacks of her childhood abuse. The psychological toll was devastating as she spent several months coming to terms with her past. The breakthrough of traumatic memories overcame her brittle defenses of denial and dissociation. She could no longer block out past events; they invaded day and night in intrusive thoughts and nightmares. She could no longer switch into a functional teacher's aide and had to take a leave of absence from her job. In retrospect, the exploration of Donna's childhood abuse was far too rapid and intense, resulting in serious impairment of her functioning. Even so, the previous years of her treatment had resulted in the slow abatement of her mistrust of others and her learning to control destructive impulses and to tolerate intense feelings, and this progress made it possible for the regression to last only a few months.

The ultimate validation of usefulness of understanding the role of trauma in Donna's life was that she actually got better. Several months after the first memory, she was actually asymptomatic for the first time in her life. She was not particularly depressed nor anxious, and she was modestly hopeful about her future. The pseudo-seizures vanished and the nightmares abated. Even more remarkably, she was no longer hated. A new person—warm, compassionate, and funny—began to emerge from behind the mask of fear, defensiveness, and self-hate. Her relationships with others dramatically improved. She continued to have some intermittent crises, but hospitalizations became much less frequent. Her relationship with staff members during these hospitalizations was dramatically different, with virtually all staff members being able to sympathize with her struggles to improve and feeling pleased to be able to help her to do so.

Donna eventually returned to work and tried to create a semblance of a normal life. More than ever before, she was successful. She was able to maintain her own apartment and live by herself. She was increasingly able to make and keep friends and enlarged her network of friends and acquaintances. At age 35 she had a boyfriend for more than a year. However, her life was not trouble-free. There were periods where she was devastated by additional unexpected recollections, and she continued to struggle with episodes of depression. Far from being the end of treatment, the recovery of her past was only the beginning of the rebuilding of her life and her reengaging with the world. She faced the need to examine her fundamental assumptions about the world and herself, and to confront the sense of helplessness and hopelessness that still interfered with her ability to function. Nonetheless, she was able to proceed with the journey from feelings of self-hatred to self-worth, from helplessness to self-empowerment, from despondency to hope. Donna emerged from the nightmare of her struggles with true dignity and the depth of character that only true adversity can forge.

3

Falling Apart

Dissociation and the Dissociative Disorders

It is important to understand the experience of dissociation—the disruption of the normal integration of experience—as a response to trauma or stressful experiences. This feeling of internal fragmentation under stress has become a part of our common lexicon: "I felt as though I was falling apart," "I was shattered," "I was beside myself." This dissociative sense of fracturing results in psychic distress and a paralysis of functioning in which *associative capacity*—access to thoughts, feelings, normal abilities, and judgment—is lost or becomes limited. I can recall a vivid personal example. Many years ago, when I was the director of an inpatient unit, there was a tragic series of suicides of patients in the program—three patients over eight months.[1] On the evening of the third suicide, I was called at home by the charge nurse on duty. After being informed of the circumstances of the suicide, I hung up the phone and was frozen in shock (as suicide is probably the most dreaded event that can occur on an inpatient unit). I had no idea of what I should do, *despite having responded to a similar event on two previous occasions.* I had lost the capacity to access my feelings or even the basic knowledge of how to respond. It was only after I called the hospital director that I remembered the procedures I should follow: go to the hospital, get help from other program psychiatrists and the on-call psychiatrist, assess all of the other patients concerning their safety, investigate what happened to the patient who suicided, designate someone to contact the family, and provide support for the staff.

The DSM-IV defines *dissociation* as the "disruption of the usually integrated functions of consciousness, memory, identity, or perception of the environment" (APA,

---

[1] The dynamics of this kind of suicide cluster are complex. None of the patients knew each other, and to the best of the staff's knowledge, none knew of the previous suicides. Hence, the dynamics behind the suicides were likely held by the staff. My hypothesis is that the staff became overly vigilant in terms of guarding against the risk of patient suicide and essentially held all of the responsibility for keeping patients safe (an impossible task), rather than insisting that patients share in that responsibility. I later observed similar dynamics at another hospital where I was called to consult after a series of episodes of serious patient self-injuries and suicides.

1994, p. 477). Dell and O'Neil's (2009) definition elaborated on the DSM-IV central concept of the disruption of experience:

> The essential manifestation of pathological dissociation is a partial or complete disruption of the normal integration of a person's psychological functioning.... Specifically, dissociation can unexpectedly disrupt, alter, or intrude upon a person's consciousness and experience of body, world, self, mind, agency, intentionality, thinking, believing, knowing, recognizing, remembering, feeling, wanting, speaking, acting, seeing, hearing, smelling, tasting, touching, and so on.... [T]hese disruptions ... are typically experienced by the person as startling, autonomous intrusions into his or her usual ways of responding or functioning. The most common dissociative intrusions include hearing voices, depersonalization, derealization, 'made' thoughts, 'made' urges, 'made' desires, 'made' emotions, and 'made' actions. (p. xxi)

Under conditions of moderate stress, dissociative responses are usually transient and reversible, as the stressful events are progressively integrated into the rest of normal experience. Truly extreme, overwhelming, and prolonged stress, however, can have long-lasting pathological effects in two different ways. If children are exposed to severe chronic stress during critical developmental periods, they may fail to achieve the normal integration of cognition, memory, emotions, perceptions, abilities, and sense of self that supports optimal functioning. This kind of dissociation in response to childhood trauma is a failure of integration, rather than a process of fragmentation. However, older individuals who are subjected to this kind of traumatization may become shattered in a fundamental way. If the stress is long-standing enough, these changes can be difficult to reverse (e.g., the alterations in mental functioning for some combat veterans that can lead to long-term disability).

MODELS OF THE MIND

The concept of dissociation in response to trauma was well described by the French physician and theorist, Pierre Janet (1907), in the early part of the 20th century (van der Kolk & Van der Hart, 1989). Janet was the most articulate theorist to explain the maladies of his era (e.g., hysteria) as characterized by "a tendency to the dissociation ... of the systems of ideas and functions that constitute personality" (1907, p. 32). Janet's work described the effects of trauma on functional losses such as amnesia (that he called mental stigmata), intrusions of traumatic flashbacks and thoughts (that he called mental accidents), and changes in somatic function (e.g., conversion disorders) or intrusive bodily experiences that we now call somatoform dissociation (Nijenhuis, 2000).

Although much of Janet's work was assimilated into Freudian psychoanalytic theory, the dissociative model of the self was largely supplanted by Freud's (1893–1895/1955) psychoanalytic concepts of repression and the unconscious. Both traditional psycho-analytic and dissociative concepts involve the psychological splitting of experience, but in different ways. The classic psychoanalytic concept, based on Freud's (1900/1935) "topographic theory," assumes that persons have a single or unitary psychological state that is experienced as conscious, preconscious (not conscious, but almost conscious), and unconscious in the familiar model of so-called horizontal splitting:

Conscious

Preconscious

Unconscious

In contrast to the theory of repression, the model of dissociation suggests that experience can be split in more complex ways. For example, rather than seeing persons as always having a unitary experience, the dissociative model suggests that over time, one's experience can vary over several different experiential states (so-called vertical splitting). Each state may differ in terms of what is conscious and unconscious (i.e., what is conscious in one state may be unconscious in another).

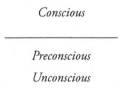

The Freudian notion of the unitary structure of the self remained the predominant theoretical understanding of mental functioning until nearly the end of the previous century, although it was challenged at times. For example, Freud's disciple, Sàndor Ferenczi, diverged from the psychoanalytic community by resurrecting the idea that trauma—particularly childhood sexual abuse—resulted in the splitting of personality states (Ferenczi, 1949). His deviation from the orthodoxy of the day resulted in his being repudiated by Freud and vilified by the psychoanalytic community (Brenner, 2001; Davies & Frawley, 1994; Howell, 2005).

The modern recognition of the importance of dissociation emerged in the mid-1980s through the study of dissociative identity disorder (DID), which was then called multiple personality disorder. In response to newly emerging cases of DID, pioneering efforts were made by many individuals to understand and treat this disorder. Among others, psychiatrists Richard Kluft, MD, PhD; Bennett Braun, MD; and Philip Coons, MD, shared their wealth of clinical experience in treating DID with many clinicians who were just encountering their first cases of DID and struggling in isolation to know how to work with them (Braun, 1986; Braun & Sachs, 1985; Coons, 1984; Kluft, 1984,

1985a, 1985b, 1986). Psychiatrist Frank Putnam, MD, wrote broadly about dissociation in response to traumatic events and the importance of age, gender, and type of trauma in the development of multiple types of dissociative reactions (Putnam, 1985). As the field of trauma and dissociation matured, attention turned to the various manifestations of childhood trauma in adults, broadening the understanding of the complexity of posttraumatic responses. For example, in a 1990 book, *Incest-Related Syndromes of Adult Psychopathology* (Kluft, 1990b), there were discussions of disturbances in the sense of self (Putnam, 1990), somatoform disorders (Loewenstein, 1990), cognitive sequelae (Fine, 1990), posttraumatic stress (Coons et al., 1990), hypnoidal states (Spiegel, 1990), and revictimization (Kluft, 1990a). Thus began the emergence of a new field of study and clinical expertise in psychiatry and psychology, recovering many of the findings of Janet and others that had been buried and lost many decades previously.

Given the rejection of dissociation as a response to trauma by Freud and the early psychoanalytic community, it is particularly interesting that modern psychoanalytic thinking has adopted many of the constructs of dissociation theory to create a more useful model of both normal and pathological mental functioning. Psychologist and psychoanalyst Philip Bromberg, PhD, is one of several in the relational and interpersonal analytic community who have argued that Freud's conceptualizations do not fully explain the adaptations of the mind that patients experience and are reproduced in therapy:

> If one wished to read the contemporary psychoanalytic literature as a serialized Gothic romance, it is not hard to envision the restless ghost of Pierre Janet, banished from the castle by Sigmund Freud a century ago, returning for an overdue haunting of Freud's current descendants.... Freudian theory represented a crucial advance in a certain way over what Janet had to offer.... But Freud's vision was too simple. Though he lent a new coherence to our understand of disparate mental states, he did so at the cost of bequeathing us the therapeutic fiction that for practical purposes, or at least where psychic conflict was involved, the structure of the self could be assumed to be unitary. (Bromberg, 1998, pp. 189, 203)

Bromberg (1998) described pathological dissociated states as arising from interpersonal psychological trauma that results in chaotic affective flooding. He theorized that in order to avoid the sense of annihilation, there must be delinking of self-states so the threatening experiences become "not-me." In many ways, this dissociative model challenges some core beliefs associated with psychoanalysis. For example, the psychoanalytic model of the mind has traditionally focused on intrapsychic conflict producing neurosis and psychiatric disease. Bromberg pointed out that dissociation actually allows conflictual material to coexist in the mind, sometimes in a variety of self-states. He has written that the analyst is able to perceive the patient's shifting self-states by reflections in the analyst's own experience. It is only through this kind of attunement that the analyst is able to understand the interpersonal process of the treatment and how to potentially bring together dissociated experiences. The level of personal involvement implied in this psychotherapeutic stance is in notable contrast to the interpersonal detachment that is stereotypically associated with psychoanalysis.

The theories of interpersonal and relational analyst Donnel Stern, PhD (1997), also involve dissociation as a central mechanism. Unlike Janet, and in the tradition of classic psychoanalytic thinking, Stern has viewed dissociation as an active defense, itself unconscious, that makes an individual unable to reflect on experiences that induce conflict; he describes these unprocessed experiences as being *unformulated*. In contrast to the theory of repression, in which there is pressure for buried conflictual material to emerge into consciousness, Stern has viewed the dissociation of unformulated experiences as being static, with psychic effort required to bring these experiences into awareness. Consistent with traditional psychoanalytic views, Stern has put forth his model as applicable to trauma in the sense of psychological conflict, not necessarily actual terrifying psychological experiences or physical and sexual abuse.

Psychologists Jody Messler Davies, PhD, and Mary Gail Frawley, PhD (1994), were among the first in the psychoanalytic community to explicitly apply dissociation theory to the treatment of adult survivors of childhood sexual abuse. In their model, the sexually abused child consciousness splits vertically as a way of shielding the self from "overwhelming fear of annihilation and, further, to shield oneself from cognitively knowing about the event(s)" (p. 62). They described the emergence of specific types of identities in the analytic therapy of these patients: a depleted adult that has "the semblance of a functioning, adaptive, interpersonally related self ... who struggles to succeed, relate, gain acceptance, and ultimately to forget, and a child who, as treatment progresses, strives to remember and to find a voice with which to scream out her outrage at the world" (p. 67). In this model, the split-off selves are not necessarily the personalities of DID; there may be no amnesia, and the adult and child selves may be mutually aware. However, the identities interact in a way that is very similar to the clinical circumstances found in DID:

> They have entirely different emotional agendas and live in a constant state of warfare over whose needs will take priority at any given time.... The child believes that the adult has "sold out" by progressing with life as a grown-up. After all, grown-ups are bad and do bad things. To become one of them is the ultimate betrayal. The child takes every opportunity, therefore, to subvert the adult's attempt to separate from the past and her identity as a victim to become a part of the outside world.... On her end, the adult persona "hates" the sadistic and disruptive child with bitter intensity. On the most conscious level, the adult views the child as a demanding, entitled, rebellious, and petulant pain in the neck. If she remembers being sexually abused in childhood, she blames her child self for it, thereby refortifying her insistence on the child's thorough and complete badness. (p. 67)

Davies and Frawley noted that the child-self can have several different personas, including the "good-perfect child; the naughty-omnipotent child; and, ultimately, the terrified-abused child" (p. 68). Although these self-states do not reach the dissociative extent of multiple personalities, the therapeutic work resembles that used with DID: promoting mutual acceptance and integration of the parts of the self.

It is ironic that the model of dissociation was once eschewed by the mainstream psychoanalytic community and has now been embraced by this most traditional sector of psychiatry and psychology. Bridging the gap between the clinicians in the trauma field and current analytic thinking, psychologist and psychoanalyst Elizabeth Howell, PhD (2005), has written how the implicit or explicit notion of dissociation has figured in the work of historical and contemporary analysts. To Howell, the complex and sometimes dense abstractions of the analysts have rich applicability to clinical treatment. For example, *enactments* (referred to by Bromberg and Stern) are understood as unconscious ways that traumatized patients use dissociation to avoid productive attachments in therapy, mirroring early relational patterns. Recognition of these enactments presents clinicians with the opportunity to promote integration and relational patterns that are more functional. In addition to noting the ways in which traumatic experiences promote dissociation of intrapsychic experiences, Howell also examined the ways in which trauma and dissociation contribute to characterologic dysfunction, such as pathological narcissism, psychopathy, and even the rarely discussed phenomenon of evil:

> It is not surprising that, collectively, we have become more conscious of evil and dissociation at the same time in current history. In many remarkable ways, the dissociative mind bears witness to a multitude of human contexts and relationships.... [W]hen evil overwhelms us, it may become part of us—until or unless we learn enough about it and our relationships to it. When we face this dilemma, we encounter a completely new realm of moral reality. (p. 10)

From Howell's discussion of dissociation in response to traumatization, it appears likely that dissociation actually permits the evil to exist and flourish. How else to explain the Nazi architects of the Holocaust, many of whom were said to be warm and engaged family men in their private lives? So, too, have been many perpetrators of genocide, of organized crime, of terrorism, and of intolerance and bigotry. In this way, Howell's theory of the "dissociative mind" helps us to understand not only classic posttraumatic responses to trauma but also complex issues of personality functioning.

CLINICAL DISSOCIATION

The dissociative concept of multiple self-states is enormously helpful in understanding both normal experience and pathological conditions. As an illustration, during a typical day, one moves through a variety of experiential states that can be very different from each other (e.g., in different roles such as worker, spouse, parent, member of a social group). Optimally, each state is functionally correlated with specific activities or the particular external environment. In each state, one has different access to certain kinds of mental information specific to that state and less access to information associated with other states. Individuals have considerable control over the nature of their experiential states as well as automatically adjusting to changing situations. There is a continuous sense of the same identity over many different states—all perceived as "me," and there is usually good recall of one's experience in other states.

For the most part, the changes in experiential states occur seamlessly without a person's conscious awareness of them. From the perspective of state theory, in pathological dissociation, the individual loses control of state changes and the ability to adapt to the environment, and can have a discontinuous sense of identity. Thus, a rape victim with PTSD is suddenly triggered into a flashback of the rape during a violent scene on television. Or, for people with certain dissociative disorders such as DID, the changes in states can be less automatic and there can be amnestic barriers between states; they can change abruptly or persist in ways that are inappropriate for the current situation. Furthermore, in DID, other states may not be perceived as "me." The study of so-called state-dependent learning supports this rather rigidly compartmentalized model of the human psyche. Research findings suggest that emotions, learning, memory, and recall are highly state-dependent and that when a person is in certain emotional and physiologic states, it is more difficult to access memories and experience of a different state (see, for example, Eich & Metcalfe, 1989; Tobias, Kihlstrom, & Schacter, 1992; van der Kolk, 1994).

Psychiatrist Bennett Braun, MD (1988), further elaborated the various components of experiential states. In his BASK model of dissociation, he identified four parameters of normal experience: behavior, affect (emotion), somatic sensation, and knowledge. Other parameters might well be added, such as one's sense of identity and the meaning of experiences. Thus, each experiential state has its own unique set of behaviors, feelings, sensations, cognitive awareness, identity, and meaning attached to it. The quality and intensity of the components of states may vary considerably. For example, the parameters connected with someone sitting and listening to a lecture (listening and taking notes as behaviors, a low level of emotional activity, body at rest, alert mental processes, identity as a student, meaning of pursuing educational activity) are quite different from the parameters of the same person performing athletic activity (running and jumping, emotions and senses attuned, the body in motion, identity as an athlete, meaning of engaging in competition or satisfying a need for physical expression).

In Braun's BASK model of dissociation, the different parameters of experience can be split off from each other in a variety of ways. For example, in typical adult-onset PTSD, a person who is experiencing avoidant symptoms can have cognitive awareness of the trauma, but the affect and meaning of the experience can be split off (e.g., "I can remember what happened, but I feel numb and I'm confused about how to think about it."). When the defensive avoidance fails, the person is flooded with full awareness, feelings, body sensations, and meaning in a flashback experience. Conversely, survivors of childhood-onset trauma can often split off the cognitive awareness of the traumatic experience, leaving only the affect. Without the cognitive awareness of the origin of the feelings, both patients and therapists can be confused about their basis, as in this clinical illustration:

> For many years I treated a young woman with complex PTSD and a history of severe neglect and emotional abuse, gradually building trust and a solid working relationship. Yet, every time I informed her of an impending vacation, she automatically froze and became more distant (or in the early years upset, angry, and self-destructive). I might have understood this reaction through the conventional explanation that she was exhibiting typical "borderline" behavior— overpersonalized, narcissistic, and overemotional responses. She might even have agreed with this assessment, as she was puzzled about her own reaction ("I don't know why I react this way; you've gone away many times and you always come back"), thus leading to an unspoken understanding between us that she was essentially inherently defective. Instead, I understood the patient's reaction as an *affective* reexperiencing of known childhood neglect and abandonment that was triggered by my vacation announcement, but without cognitive awareness of the connection to those experiences. Like other humans, she would try to find a reason for her intense emotions, so in the early years of the therapy she would become upset at me as if I was responsible for her distress.

Dissociative experiences range from normal to pathological. Routine adult dissociative experiences include certain kinds of splitting of awareness—for example, what many of us do while driving a familiar route to work. We remember very little about the drive, having been internally preoccupied with personal concerns. Yet, a split-off part of our awareness must be paying attention to the road, as most people suffer very few accidents as a result. The DSM-IV describes several specific forms of dissociation; they are summarized here:

- *Depersonalization* is an alteration in the perception of oneself so that the usual sense of one's own reality is temporarily changed, one's body or feelings are unreal, or one is detached from and can observe one's own body. It is a feature in a variety of psychiatric disorders and can also result from drug-induced states, anxiety, stress, or fatigue.
- *Derealization* is an alteration in the perception of one's environment, feeling that things in one's surroundings are temporarily strange or unreal, or that one is detached from the environment. Derealization frequently occurs with depersonalization.
- *Dissociative amnesia* (previously known as psychogenic amnesia) is characterized by deficits in memory functioning *not* resulting from organic causes such as traumatic brain injury, intoxication, delirium, or dementia. Dissociative amnesia may be partial or complete. It is usually historical and circumscribed—

meaning, loss of memory for discrete periods of time in the past. In rare cases, it is retrograde—meaning, the inability to retrieve stored memories of prior events leading up to the onset of amnesia.

- *Dissociative fugue* is characterized by a temporary and reversible global amnesia for personal identity and past events and is sometimes accompanied by the emergence of a new identity quite different from the person's original identity in terms of personality and other identifying characteristics of individuality.

- *Alteration of identity* is characterized by the manifestation and/or subjective feeling of shifts in identity and a sense of conflicts between internal identities. In some instances, alteration in identity can be characterized as having multiple identities that can emerge in fugue-like states.

Additional dissociative experiences are not fully described in the DSM-IV, most notably various kinds of *trance states* that involve internal focused attention with loss of awareness of immediate surroundings. *Imaginative absorption* or *imaginative involvement* is a normal type of trance-like state involving fantasy (e.g., daydreaming or becoming so involved in a book or movie that one loses track of time and one's surroundings). Meditation and hypnosis also result from dissociative processes where there is a deliberate focus on internal states with loss of awareness of one's environment. Certain religious ecstatic states and possession states are forms of dissociative trance phenomena. Many of these types of dissociative phenomena are nonpathological, including those that are consistent with religious or cultural practices.

A modest scientific literature indicates that the vulnerability to dissociation is highest in early childhood and normally decreases with age (Putnam, 1997; Sanders & Giolas, 1991; Van IJzendoorn & Schuengel, 1996), which is consistent with the observation that a relatively high level of dissociative experiences is commonly observed in young children. Consider many a 5-year-old on Saturday morning in front of the television: part of the child's experience is split off and transported into cartoon-land in a particularly intense way, so that the child is often oblivious to events occurring in the room. The phenomenon of imaginary companionship—a dissociative experience—in young children is also considered normal (Manosevitz, Fling, & Prentice, 1977). The child attempts to disown unwanted impulses and feelings by splitting them off and attributing them to another imagined being (e.g., "I didn't break daddy's CDs. The bad girl did it!"). We intuitively understand this kind of disavowal in children and accept it as a normal part of the developmental process. The disowned feelings, impulses, and behaviors are eventually spontaneously integrated into the child's psyche and sense of self as the child begins to achieve control of them. If seen in adulthood, imaginary companionship would be considered pathological as a kind of dissociative identity disorder.[2]

---

[2] A history of imaginary companions is common in patients with a dissociative disorder, suggesting that at least in some cases the dissociative splitting of identity extends back into childhood (Trujillo, Lewis, Yeager, & Gidlow, 1996).

Researchers in the study of dissociation distinguish between nonpathological trait dissociation and pathological dissociation. There is evidence that nonpathological dissociation has a strong genetic component (Becker-Blease et al., 2004; Jang, Paris, Zweig-Frank, & Livesley, 1998) and has a normal distribution in the population. That is, the trait of dissociation is inborn, and individuals have either a greater or lesser degree of dissociative experiences along a continuum of such experiences. Thus, there is likely to be a population of children who have a higher inborn dissociative capacity. Under normal circumstances, even children who are "high dissociators" would be expected to have a progressive decrease in their dissociative capacity as they grow older. But, if they are exposed to chronic traumatization with ongoing activation of dissociative processes, high levels of dissociative capacity can persist into adulthood, sometimes manifesting as dissociative disorders (Kluft, 1985d, 1990b; Spiegel & Cardeña, 1991). This kind of pathological dissociation, such as chronic depersonalization, amnesia, and fugue states, does not have a continuous distribution in the normal population (Waller, Putnam, & Carlson, 1996; Waller & Ross, 1997). Instead, the distribution is bipolar, with most adults having few dissociative experiences, but a smaller group having a high level of dissociation that is based on environmental rather than genetic influences (Becker-Blease et al., 2004; Grabe, Spitzer, & Freyberger, 1999; Putnam et al., 1996). This distribution can be observed in the clinical arena; when asked, most patients have very few dissociative symptoms, and a smaller group of other patients have florid symptomatology.

Normal adults with lower levels of dissociative capacity (i.e., who do not have antecedent childhood trauma) do have some capacity to activate dissociative processes, such as in adult-onset PTSD in which knowledge of events is often separated from feelings and meanings associated with the trauma. However, they do not develop florid dissociative symptoms or disorders even in response to very overwhelming experiences. For example, in our study of dissociation in psychiatric patients (Chu & Dill, 1990), we found relatively high levels of amnesia for childhood events in samples of psychiatric patients who were exposed to early trauma. However, little amnesia for traumatic events was seen in those patients who were first traumatized in late adolescence or adulthood. Similarly, the vast majority of persons who develop the most severe dissociative disorders—DID and similar disorders—have histories of severe and chronic childhood trauma, usually beginning in early childhood (Coons, 1994; Kluft, 1985d; Putnam et al., 1986; Spiegel, 1984). Conversely, adults who are exposed to even pervasive and harsh trauma (e.g., torture victims or concentration camp survivors) do not develop this disorder.

From a dynamic perspective, the use of dissociation serves as an important psychological defense function in helping the individual to manage overwhelming, conflicting, and intolerable experiences. When a person is overwhelmed, the experience may remain fragmented and separated into compartmentalized components. Different parts of the experience are dissociated (i.e., separated and disconnected). In the face of severe stress, it is common for persons to feel numb (separating feelings from awareness of current events), with a sense of detachment from one's surroundings (derealization) or from one's own body (depersonalization), so-called peritraumatic dissociation. In the face of extreme stress, susceptible individuals actually forget, dissociating cognitive knowledge of events from ordinary awareness (amnesia), or they can feel as though the events are occurring to someone else (depersonalization); these latter responses are far more common in traumatized children than in adults.

Many other kinds of defensive dissociative experiences are less commonly described. For example, the ability to feel removed from external reality and to remain internally preoccupied for minutes to hours (depersonalization, derealization, and imaginative absorption) is extremely common in persons who have been extensively traumatized in childhood. The ability to ignore pain (analgesia) is also frequently observed. In more severe dissociative disorders, one's own thoughts, feelings, or actions may be perceived as alien or *made* (as though placed in one's mind and perceived as thought insertion or auditory hallucinations or acted out through one's body). Finally, in response to the most severe childhood traumatization, we see the dissociative ability to function as a series of different self-states or personalities as the person attempts to adapt as best possible to intolerable events and irreconcilable feelings.

The term *dissociation* is ordinarily used to describe the phenomenon of compartmentalization or fragmentation of mental contents. It does not ascribe any particular mechanism by which the dissociative process occurs. Does dissociation occur as a result of automatic, nonconscious processes, or are there other specific mechanisms by which it occurs? Especially in the context of describing amnesia, the term *repression* is widely used in connection with several different mechanisms. As it is commonly used, it often implies how individuals may block out memories of uncomfortable or conflictual experiences. If done consciously, the mechanism is more accurately called *suppression*, which results from actively trying not to think about negative experiences. This mechanism seems to have played a role in some of the recent cases involving victims of clergy sexual abuse, as in this example:

> In 2005, the defrocked Catholic priest Paul Shanley was found guilty of indecent assault and the rape of a former altar boy and was sentenced to 12 to 15 years in prison. During the 1980s, Shanley served in the parish of St. John the Evangelist in Newton, Massachusetts, where he was a popular hip young priest, known for his progressive and unorthodox views. Unbeknownst to members of the parish (and not presented as evidence at the trial), Shanley had been the subject of many complaints of sexual abuse involving children since the 1960s and had taken public positions defending the practice of pedophilia, including a speech at the founding meeting of the North American Man-Boy Love Association (NAMBLA) in 1969. The key witness at the 2005 trial was man in his 20s, whose family had been part of the Newton parish in the 1980s. He testified that Shanley had taken him out of CCD classes (religious education concerning Catholic Christian doctrine) beginning at age 6 or 7 and had sexually abused him in the church bathrooms, the rectory (priest's residence), and even in the confessional. The man had long blocked out the memories of the events and only recalled

them many years later when he was serving in the Air Force. His girlfriend had called to tell him that articles about sexual abuse accusations against Shanley were appearing in the Boston newspapers.

At first, he denied any recall of being abused, but within days, he had the breakthrough of vivid memories, including numerous instances of fondling and oral sex, and detailed mental images of the church bathrooms and the rectory, including the layout of the rooms and shape and placement of doors and windows. In my role as the Commonwealth of Massachusetts' expert witness concerning the nature of recovered memories, I reviewed numerous documents about the case and was able to interview the witness several months after the trial. He recalled that the sexual abuse had gone on for several years; after it stopped, he consciously tried very hard to not think about what had happened. This strategy worked so well that when he was a young teenager, he attended a farewell party for Shanley's departure from the parish, but he couldn't remember why he felt so uncomfortable around him.

This example concerns conscious efforts to not think about the abuse. If the blocking out of trauma occurs without conscious intent, it might be more accurately called *selective inattention*, a term from cognitive psychology. Or, there is also the classic psychoanalytic concept of repression, which invokes an active process—itself unconscious—that makes memories of overwhelming and conflictual experiences unavailable to ordinary recall. From a dynamic perspective, this mechanism makes a great deal of sense. It is only through forgetting or compartmentalization that a child might be able to deal with the dilemma posed by abuse perpetrated by an authority figure (such as a parent) on whom the child is dependent (consistent with Freyd's betrayal trauma theory). Which of these mechanisms underlie the phenomenon of dissociation? Or, is it even necessary to invoke a psychological mechanism? Does the psyche simply fail to integrate traumatic experiences, making them difficult to access when an individual is overwhelmed? While there is no clear consensus, the answer is that depending on the circumstances and the characteristics of the individual involved, probably *all* of these explanations have an important role.

DISSOCIATION AND THE DSM-IV

Dissociative symptoms are the central elements of the dissociative disorders and also the essential part of certain other psychiatric disorders. As defined by the DSM-IV, the dissociative disorders include dissociative amnesia, dissociative fugue, dissociative identity disorder, dissociative disorder, not otherwise specified, and depersonalization disorder. Dissociative amnesia—the disorder as opposed to the symptom—is defined as "one or more episodes of inability to recall important personal information, usually of a traumatic or stressful nature, that is too extensive to be explained by ordinary forgetfulness" (APA, 1994, p. 481) *not* attributable to organic etiologies such as intoxication or neurologic dysfunction. If it is seen in adult-onset traumatic events, it is usually confined to the trauma itself. Pervasive dissociative amnesia, including major gaps in memory and ongoing periods of lost time, is much more consistent with adults who have histories of severe childhood trauma and is sometimes seen together with other dissociative symptoms as part of a more severe dissociative disorder. Dissociative fugue—again, the disorder versus the symptom—is characterized by global amnesia and identity confusion, sometimes with the assumption of new identity and unexpected travel away from home (APA, 1994). Despite its popularity in the entertainment media (e.g., Jason Bourne in Ludlum's *The Bourne Identity*; Liman, Crowley, & Gladstein, 2002), dissociative fugue is a rare disorder, with new cases being almost always newsworthy. Although dissociative fugue is seen infrequently as a single-symptom syndrome, it is commonly a part of more severe and complex dissociative disorders.

Dissociative identity disorder (DID) is defined in the DSM-IV as

> the presence of two or more distinct identities or personality states (each with its own relatively enduring pattern of perceiving, relating to, and thinking about the environment and self) ... [and that] at least two of these identities or personality states recurrently take control of the person's behavior. (APA, 1994, p. 487)

Although the idea of multiple personalities has captured media attention, the diagnosis of DID sometimes seems dramatic and bizarre to professionals who have not been exposed to actual clinical cases of it. It is perhaps better intuitively understood as a multiple fugue disorder involving the recurrent emergence of different identities with various degrees and types of amnesia between identities. The typical manifestation of DID usually consists of many different identities rather than simple dual identities. It appears that if this type of dissociation is available to a child to defend against intolerable experience and if it is potentiated by chronic trauma, florid dissociation occurs, resulting in complex fragmentation. Extreme versions of DID occasionally develop in response to particularly horrific ongoing trauma (e.g., children exploited through involvement in years of forced prostitution), with so-called poly-fragmentation, encompassing dozens or even hundreds of personality states. In general, the complexity of dissociative symptoms appears to be consistent with the severity of early traumatization. That is, less severe abuse will result in fewer dissociative symptoms, and more severe abuse will result in more complex dissociative disorders.

Dissociative identity disorder, not otherwise specified (DDNOS) is a catch-all category for dissociative disorders that do not fall into other groups. However, included in the DDNOS category is a commonly seen group of patients who do not have the extreme identity separation of DID, but who have a range of dissociative experiences and significant identity confusion and alteration. Patients with this kind of *almost DID* do not see themselves as having multiple identities, but frequently feel so different at the time that they see themselves as a series of different "me's" (e.g., "I know it was me, but I felt as though I was observing myself. I couldn't believe what I was saying and how I was behaving."). Also included in the DDNOS category are *atypical DID* cases in which there are classic DID symptoms but no amnesia between identities, because the DSM-IV diagnosis of DID includes the requirement for the presence of amnesia.

All of the DSM-IV dissociative disorders are nearly universally associated with trauma, internal conflict, or stress, with one exception: depersonalization disorder. In this disorder, the predominant symptoms are intense feelings of detachment from oneself or one's feelings as well as derealization—detachment from one's environment and/or other people. Although traumatic events may play a role in depersonaliza-tion disorder, the clinical manifestations of this diagnosis suggest a different etiol-ogy. Depersonalization disorder has been characterized as typically beginning in late adolescence or early adulthood with a chronic course (Simeon et al., 1997; Simeon, Knutelska, Nelson, & Guralnik, 2003). The onset during a particular age range and a somewhat predictable course suggest an inborn vulnerability to the disorder. The leading American expert in depersonalization disorder, Daphne Simeon, MD, has con-jectured that certain individuals may have genetic loading for ongoing high dissocia-tive capacity (personal communication). In such individuals, dissociative experiences increase rather than decrease throughout childhood, blossoming in late adolescence. The sense of feeling unreal may be episodic or continuous, and there is significant distress and impairment in functioning. Simeon has also observed that in some cases of depersonalization disorder, there is not only depersonalization and derealization but also more amnesia for past events and a greater level of compartmentalization of experience. Some authors have noted a similarity between depersonalization disorder and the anxiety disorders, involving a cycle of increasing anxiety over the deperson-alization/derealization symptoms leading to more such symptoms (Hunter, Phillips, Chalder, Sierra, & David, 2003).

Depersonalization disorder is uncommon though not rare, and because most clini-cians are unfamiliar with the way it commonly presents, it is routinely misdiagnosed as an anxiety or mood disorder. Alternatively, clinicians familiar with the trauma model of dissociation may misdiagnose it as a different dissociative disorder. Correct diagnosis is critically important with this disorder, because it does not respond readily to routine treatments for anxiety, mood, or trauma-based disorders. There are no clearly established treatments, although work on the secondary anxiety produced by the depersonalization symptoms, and cognitive behavioral interventions have been used successfully in some patients. In some cases, medications such as serotonin reuptake inhibitors or other agents have been helpful.

Posttraumatic stress disorder (PTSD) also has dissociative symptoms as an essential feature. PTSD has been classically seen as a biphasic disorder, with persons alternately experiencing phases of intrusion and numbing. As described in the previous chapter, the intrusive phase is associated with recurrent and distressing recollections in thoughts or dreams and reliving the events in flashbacks. The avoidant/numbing phase is associ-ated with efforts to avoid thoughts or feelings associated with the trauma, emotional constriction, and social withdrawal. This biphasic pattern is the result of dissociation; traumatic events are distanced and dissociated from usual conscious awareness in the numbing phase, only to return in the intrusive phase. The proposed diagnostic criteria for the DSM-5 acknowledge dissociation as an essential element of PTSD, describing "dissociative reactions (e.g., flashbacks) in which the individual feels or acts as if the traumatic event(s) were recurring" (APA, 2010a). In addition, patients with PTSD have long-standing heightened autonomic activation that results in chronic anxiety, disturbed sleep, hypervigilance, startle responses, and irritability. This last set of symptoms has led PTSD to be classified with the anxiety disorders rather than with the dissociative disorders. Most of the dissociative disorders and PTSD involve some kind of environmental or psychological stress as a primary etiology, because dissociation seems to play a major role in the psyche's efforts to deal with the stress.

Dissociative symptoms—primarily depersonalization and derealization—are elements in other DSM-IV disorders, including schizophrenia and borderline personality disorder, and in the neurologic syndrome of temporal lobe epilepsy, also called complex partial seizures. In this latter disorder, there are often florid symptoms of depersonalization and realization, but most amnesia symptoms derive from difficulties with focused attention rather than forgetting previously learned information.

THE RETURN OF THE REPRESSED: RELIVING DISSOCIATED EXPERIENCES[3]

The reexperiencing of previously dissociated traumatic events presents in a variety of complex ways. The central principle is that dissociated experiences often do not remain dormant. Freud's concept of the "repetition compulsion" is enormously helpful in understanding how dissociated events are later reexperienced. In his paper, "Beyond the Pleasure Principle," Freud (1920/1955) described how repressed (and dissociated) trauma and instinctual conflicts can become superimposed on current reality. He wrote:

> The patient cannot remember the whole of what is repressed in him, and what he cannot remember may be precisely the essential part of it. ... He is obliged to *repeat* the repressed material as a contemporary experience instead of *remembering* it as something in the past. (p. 18)

If one understands repression as the process in which overwhelming experiences are forgotten, distanced, and dissociated, Freud posited that these experiences are likely to recur in the mind and to be reexperienced. He theorized that this "compulsion to repeat" served a need to rework and achieve mastery over the experience and that it

---

[3] Portions of this section were adapted from the article "The Repetition Compulsion Revisited: Reliving Dissociated Trauma" (Chu, 1991b).

perhaps had an underlying biologic basis as well. The most perceptive tenet of Freud's theory is that previously dissociated events are actually *reexperienced as current reality* rather than remembered as occurring in the past. Although Freud was discussing the trauma produced by intense intrapsychic conflict, clinical experience has shown that actual traumatic events that have been dissociated are often repeated and reexperienced. Past events, affects, behaviors, or even somatic experiences are superimposed on current experience in the form of intrusive thoughts, emotions, bodily sensations, dreams, or full flashbacks. Thus, as in Freud's description of the repetition compulsion, persons are obliged to repeat these experiences rather than simply remembering them. These repetitions range from the need to repetitively talk about relatively minor traumatic experiences (e.g., a minor car accident) to full-blown PTSD symptoms, including recurring dreams and nightmares, intrusive thoughts, and vivid recollections of the event.

As discussed previously, some of the interpersonal and relational analysts (e.g., Stern) believe that the natural state of dissociated experiences is to remain separate, thus contradicting Freud's theory of the repetition compulsion. From my clinical experience, I have observed both dynamics at work, motivated by the defensive need to keep conflictual experiences dissociated and out of awareness, as well as the pressure for them to emerge into consciousness. Differing by the characteristics of individuals, by environmental circumstances, and by experiences at various points in the life cycle, these opposite forces exist in a delicate balance that can change over time. For example, external factors such as survival needs can make persisting dissociation necessary in order to preserve functioning, even with the downside of emotional numbing. At other times, a triggering event or even just the absence of stress may permit dissociated experiences to emerge.

The most striking examples of the emergence of previously dissociated experiences are the flashbacks seen in patients with PTSD. These patients are thrust back into the traumatic events both in their dreams and while awake. Any therapist who has experienced a patient's full-blown flashback has felt the powerful pull into the actual experience of the events along with the patient. The reliving of the trauma is indeed experienced as a real and contemporary event. That is, the patients do not talk about feeling *as if* they remember the experience; rather they feel the experience *in the present*. For example, a combat veteran with PTSD, walking down the street of his hometown, may be triggered into reliving his combat experiences by the sound of a car backfiring. This sound, which is similar to the sound of gunfire, may thrust the veteran into reliving a firefight with enemy forces. He may actually have vivid sensory experiences, visualizing, hearing, and even smelling the combat scenario. He may feel as young as he was at the time of the battle, and he may experience the intense fear, horror, helplessness, and even the bodily sensations of those past events. The power of such an experience is phenomenal and points to the extraordinary ability of the psyche to distance and dissociate experiences, as well as to bring them back into consciousness with full force.

Full and vivid reexperiences of traumatic events are seen in PTSD as sequelae of both acute and chronic traumatic experiences. The overwhelming feelings associated with the events and the meaning of the experiences are dissociated from day-to-day consciousness. When the awareness, affect, and meaning of the trauma are reexperienced all together, they may be relived in very powerful ways. Therapists who work with PTSD patients are familiar with the pull into the traumatic experiences such that patients can lose awareness of their current reality and surroundings. Therapists are also all too familiar with the difficult task of attempting to help patients keep one foot in current reality at the same time as they are consumed by the past. Even this may have some untoward results, as the patients then superimpose their experience onto the current situation, as in the following example:

> Beth, a pleasant but shy woman in her late 20s, entered treatment about three months after being brutally raped by multiple men in a park near her home. I met her during her hospitalization in the early 1980s shortly after finishing my psychiatric residency program. Understanding that Beth's current panic attacks, nightmares, and depression were probably related to the recent rape, I encouraged her to tell me about it. After some resistance to discussing the circumstances of the rape, Beth began to have a vivid flashback of the actual events right in my office. She began screaming and fell to the floor, fighting off unseen attackers as if she was being currently molested. Though trained to appear calm in my role as a therapist, I lost my usual composure when my patient began screaming, and I was forced to abandon my own chair in an attempt to restrain her from banging into the office furniture and injuring herself. At first, I was unable to make any contact with her, as she continued to scream and struggle with her eyes clenched tightly shut. She seemed to be in dire physical and emotional pain. Eventually, I was able to engage her attention enough to let her know that I was there. With great effort, Beth was able to describe the rapists to me and the events she was experiencing, and I tried to remind her that she was in my office and that there was no one else present. To this she demanded, "Then why are *you* hurting me?"

Despite the pitfalls of being confused with the perpetrators of abuse, this contact between the PTSD patient and another person begins a process that is therapeutic and potentially reparative. Traumatic events are often experienced with an intense sense of *aloneness*. With the support and sense of connection to another person, the patient can tolerate, retain, and integrate the events and all attendant feelings into memory as past experience, rather than remaining a dissociated psychological time bomb that is waiting to explode into consciousness. The sense of interpersonal connection is crucial, because reliving trauma without appropriate interpersonal support is simply setting the patient up to be overwhelmed again by the experience and to be retraumatized. Reliving traumatic events in the context of a supportive interpersonal relationship makes true abreaction and catharsis possible and begins the reparative process.

Adult-onset PTSD commonly occurs in the aftermath of such events as combat, assaults, rape, accidents, and natural disasters. However, the prototypical model of adult-onset PTSD can be quite misleading. The person who is disconnected from the

emotional experience of the trauma is prone to report the experience in a rather constricted or matter-of-fact manner. Such persons often deny the importance of these traumatic events in an understandable attempt to keep the overwhelmingly dysphoric feelings from their consciousness. Such a presentation can lead mental health professionals
to collude with the denial and to ignore the importance of trauma in the production of
emotional disturbance and psychiatric illness. Patients may present with a wide variety
of distressing symptoms such as depression or anxiety, or with dysfunctional behaviors
such as addictions or self-destructive behaviors, but they may deny the importance of
known traumatic events. Interestingly, if questioned about whether it *feels* as though the
events happened to them, they often report that they *know* about the events but *feel* as
though they happened to somebody else. Clinicians ignore this kind of history at their
patients' peril. Too much time and effort is sometimes expended on fruitless treatment
efforts to control symptoms, including endless trials of medications, or psychotherapy
directed at issues unrelated to the trauma, as in the following example:

> Susan, a woman in her early 40s, was admitted for suicidal depression to the hos-
> pital unit that I directed. She had been treated for several years for what appeared
> to be classic major depression. She was tearful and angry as she talked about the
> hopelessness of her life. She was convinced that there was no hope of ever feel-
> ing better, and she looked at death as a source of potential relief. Under the care
> of her attending psychiatrist, Susan went through a sophisticated work-up and
> was begun on a series of medication trials that failed to improve the depression.
> Finally, she was given a course of electroconvulsive treatments that seemed to
> result in modest improvement. She bought a bouquet of flowers for the staff and
> was discharged from the hospital, only to make a near-lethal suicide attempt on
> the afternoon of the day of her discharge. The hospital staff and her attending
> psychiatrist were frustrated about her lack of improvement and angry that she
> withheld her suicidal plans from them. One staff member even commented that
> the bouquet looked "funereal" and was furious about how the patient had "set us
> up." However, after regaining some professional composure, the psychiatrist and
> staff agreed to her readmission for further evaluation and treatment.
>
> Susan's current difficulties and past history were reexamined. Interestingly,
> the treatment team had been well aware throughout the course of treatment that
> the patient had undergone a horribly traumatic incident some years previously.
> After giving her infant a prescribed antibiotic medication for an ear infection,
> the child had gone into anaphylactic (allergic) shock and died in her arms. Be-
> cause Susan was able to report the events, and even denied any persistent feelings
> about the death, the staff had assumed that it was no longer a major issue. As
> Susan once again began to talk about the tragic death of her child, it became
> clear that there were (of course) major unresolved issues of grief, loss, anger, and
> guilt. As she relived and shared some of the old feelings with her therapist and
> the staff, she began to appear less depressed. She appeared warmer and more

engaged with others and was eventually discharged uneventfully. One year later, Susan again became severely depressed and required hospitalization. At the time she complained of chest pains that her attending psychiatrist thought may have been side effects of her new antidepressant medication. However, after an observant staff member noted that she was admitted on Mother's Day, we better understood her somatic pain as heartache.

As discussed in the previous chapter, bodily sensations or somatic symptoms that have to do with past traumatic events can also be dissociated from usual awareness. Somatic memory is much more complicated than we currently understand and can have powerful effects on bodily functioning. A medical evaluation of any persisting somatic difficulties is always warranted to rule out true physical etiologies, but posttraumatic causes should also be considered. Medical interventions are generally fruitless for somatic symptoms (including pain) related to trauma and may only further harm the patient. Of course, the presence of other posttraumatic difficulties makes a diagnosis of PTSD-related somatic symptoms more likely. The following example illustrates a case of adult-onset PTSD with prominent physical symptoms:

Harry, a 37-year-old man, was seen by me in psychiatric consultation after a full medical evaluation failed to disclose any cause for his excruciating abdominal pain and intractable nausea and vomiting. He couldn't keep down any food or fluids and was in danger of becoming dehydrated. After a period of medical and psychiatric hospitalization, he was slightly improved and was discharged on a regimen of powerful painkillers and tranquilizers. Harry's treatment with me over the next two years was chaotic. He went through bouts of severe depression and was briefly readmitted to the hospital on two occasions when he became suicidal. In therapy, he continued to have terrible abdominal pains, and he would frequently double over when discussing painful feelings. Even narcotic pain medication was ineffective in relieving the severe abdominal cramping. In therapy sessions, Harry was somewhat self-preoccupied but very likable. He enjoyed telling stories about his past romantic encounters and all the scrapes he had gotten himself into. Over time, he also explored a rather painful childhood and more recent losses and disappointments. Harry gradually improved with less depression and was able to reengage with old friends in a better, more mutually supportive manner. However, he was unable to return to work because of his disabling abdominal pain, nausea, and vomiting.

Finally, in the third year of treatment, Harry came to a therapy session looking very somber. He told me that he had something to talk about that he had never discussed with anyone else. Hesitantly, he began to relate an episode that had occurred in his early 20s. As a way of fleeing a difficult home environment, he had joined a paramilitary organization and had been part of a brief, but disastrous mercenary guerrilla operation in Latin America. He described the combat experience in painful detail, while being doubled over with intense abdominal spasms. He had, at one point, shot a comrade in the head after the comrade had been mortally wounded in the abdomen and was in excruciating pain. It was at this point that he experienced the full horror, pain, nausea, and disgust connected with his combat experiences. These revelations were a major turning point. The physical symptoms abated, and after some additional months of treatment, Harry was free of physical symptoms for the first time in years and was able to function without the use of medications. He received a job offer from an old employer, returned to work, and was able to finish up his course of therapy.

In both of these clinical examples, the patients remembered that the traumatic events had occurred, but they did not connect the trauma to their corresponding feelings and bodily symptoms. It is important to understand that the link between knowledge and feelings could not be easily made in either case because of the enormous psychological benefit of *not knowing*, and therefore not experiencing, the full impact of the traumatic events. This seeming inability to put simple events and feelings together is a defensive function that protects the psyche from being truly overwhelmed by traumatic circumstances and events.

DISSOCIATIVE RESPONSES TO CHILDHOOD-ONSET ABUSE

When children—particularly young children—are faced with terribly abusive experience, they naturally employ a host of dissociative defenses (Dalenberg & Palesh, 2004; Putnam, 1997; Silberg, 1996). Our own research suggests that factors such as early age of onset, severity, chronicity, and intrafamilial involvement are all implicated in the development of severe dissociative symptoms (Chu & Dill, 1990; Chu et al., 1999; Kirby et al., 1993). Unfortunately, these factors are all too common in the histories of many adult patients who report childhood abuse. In fact, among the hundreds of patients who were admitted to the Trauma and Dissociative Disorders program at McLean Hospital over more than 20 years, early, severe, and persistent childhood abuse seem to be more the rule than the exception.

In one of our early studies (Chu & Dill, 1990), nearly one-quarter of our entire participant group (women consecutively admitted to the hospital) showed levels of dissociative symptoms consistent with a diagnosis of PTSD, and 6% showed levels similar to patients with dissociative identity disorder (DID). Similar or higher levels of dissociative symptoms and/or diagnosable dissociative disorders have been documented in other clinical populations of inpatients (Ross, Anderson, Fleisher, & Norton, 1991; Saxe et al., 1993) and outpatients (Foote, Smolin, Kaplan, Legatt, & Lipschitz, 2006; Surrey et al., 1990). In many of these studies, both physical and sexual abuse were independently correlated with a higher level of dissociative symptoms, and multiple kinds of abuse were related to even higher levels of dissociation. Other parameters of traumatic experiences that have been associated with higher levels of dissociation are severity (e.g., penetration versus sexual fondling), chronicity, early age of onset, and intrafamilial abuse. Additional factors such as violence, physical injury, multiple perpetrators, and fear of dying have been associated with amnesia for abuse (Briere & Conte, 1993; Herman & Schatzhow, 1987). Unfortunately, more severe abuse appears to be the norm among hospitalized patients being treated for trauma-based disorders. For example, in one of our studies, more than 90% of patients reporting sexual abuse described childhood experiences of attempted or completed intercourse rather than only fondling or touching (Kirby et al., 1993). This is not to suggest that less severe abuse is benign, but that severe abuse leads to more symptoms and disability and a greater need for intensive forms of psychiatric care.

There are particular differences in dissociative symptomatology between persons who have been first traumatized as adults and those who have been traumatized as children. Chronically abused children develop more dissociative symptoms, including more dissociative amnesia, because some children have a greater innate dissociative capacity as well as less capacity to tolerate stress. In fact, dozens of studies have demonstrated that children who are extensively abused prior to adolescence frequently exhibit either partial or complete amnesia for the abusive events (Brown, Scheflin, et al., 1999). It is common for patients with severe traumatic histories to have extensive loss of memory for childhood events, as discussed in the previous chapter. Typical reports include statements such as, "I don't remember anything before the age of 12," or "I remember some fragments about school, but I couldn't tell you anything much about my childhood." Of note is the amnesia for virtually *all* events, not just the abusive events, suggesting that overwhelming trauma may lead children to actually process their experiences in a way so that they are held separate from ordinary conscious awareness. In the absence of organic reasons for such amnesia, these kinds of statements are highly significant and suggest that there may be reasons why a person might *not* remember substantial portions of their lives. (See Chapter 5 for a more detailed discussion concerning memory and amnesia.)

Even patients who can recall that they were abused will often not acknowledge the impact of the abuse, or they do not connect the abuse with current difficulties. Again, the psychological gain is in *not knowing*, because the reality of the abuse and the implications of the abuse are too overwhelming to be appreciated as a whole. However, not acknowledging abuse does not free persons from reexperiencing aspects of the abuse. Instead, such persons are frequently tormented by intensely dysphoric feelings such as helplessness, depression, anger, and isolation that are connected to the unacknowledged or forgotten abuse. Moreover, because such patients are unable to report the core reasons for their distress, neither they nor clinicians are able to make sense of their painful lives. Because most survivors of childhood abuse carry an internal sense of defectiveness, they assume (as do some of their treaters) that they are simply inherently "crazy and bad." It is striking to realize that it is often easier for many persons to accept that they are inherently defective rather than to acknowledge the enormity and the ongoing impact of their childhood abuse.

ISSUES CONCERNING CLINICAL PRACTICE

Mental health professionals are not routinely trained in adequate interviewing and diagnostic skills to detect either trauma histories or dissociation. A great deal of confusion and misinformation exists about how to ask about childhood abuse, partly because of the concerns raised by some critics that direct inquiries about childhood abuse may be inherently suggestive and may produce false reports of abuse. These concerns must be balanced against the clinical reality that childhood abuse is associated with so much shame and denial that patients routinely do not volunteer such information. Furthermore, there is scant evidence suggests that direct questions delivered in a neutral manner will encourage false reports. My practice is to ask, "Have you had any particularly painful experiences in your life, either as an adult or a child?" Not only does this question avoid any possibility of influencing the patient's response by suggesting abuse, but it also captures traumatic experiences that patients do not acknowledge to themselves as abuse (e.g., because they feel responsible for and deserving of their maltreatment).

Many clinicians are also hesitant to ask about the basic facts concerning abuse experiences for fear of overwhelming and destabilizing patients. In fact, it is often important to know some specifics about any abuse experiences: "What happened?" "How much do you remember?" "How often did it occur?" "How old were you?" "Who hurt you?" and "How did it affect you?" The answers to these questions can yield important information in assessing the nature and impact of any trauma, helping to focus therapeutic interventions. There are differential effects of various types of abuse, and some details about the experiences can help clinicians understand how patients' symptoms and difficulties in functioning have evolved. In the interview setting, I have found that patients' ability to dissociate knowledge from feelings can allow them to divulge sensitive information in a way that is less emotionally charged. Taking a cue from the 1950s police television drama *Dragnet*, where Jack Webb's Sgt. Joe Friday character asks for "Just the facts, ma'am," I ask patients to just tell me as much as they can about what happened and *not* to let themselves get into the feelings about their experiences (i.e., instructing them to dissociate the affective experience of the trauma). I give them explicit permission beforehand to let me know if they are feeling too uncomfortable to answer and that they can stop the line of inquiry at any time.

Despite the increasing awareness of early trauma in the histories of psychiatric patients, specific questions about dissociative symptoms are generally still not taught to mental health trainees as part of a formal mental status examination. Routine examinations may reveal much about mental processes, but clinicians often do not investigate abnormal experiential state changes, gaps in memory, or distortions in perceptions that result from traumatic experiences. The questions needed to elicit evidence of dissociative symptoms are simple. For depersonalization and derealization, one might ask: "Do you ever have the experience of feeling as if your body or emotions are unreal? … feeling detached from your body or that you are outside your body observing yourself? … feeling as though your surroundings are foggy or unreal?" Questions about imaginative involvement include: "Do you ever have the experience of becoming so involved in a book or movie that you actually become a part of the story? … being preoccupied with thoughts or daydreams inside your head for hours at time?" To elicit any evidence about amnesia, one might ask: "Do you have any memory problems? … any gaps in your memory, any lost time? … any problems in remembering events from your childhood? … a sense of general continuity of your memory?" Finally, to ask about evidence of alternate identities or self-states: "Do you have the experience of feeling so different at different times that you almost feel like a different person? … observing yourself do or say things that don't seem like things you'd usually do or say? … hearing voices inside your head talking with each other or to you? … being told that you did or said something you didn't recall doing or saying? … finding belongings that you didn't recall buying/obtaining?"… finding evidence that you must have done something you didn't remember doing?"

It is often impractical and unnecessary to do a full screening for dissociative symptoms in all patients. The bipolar distribution of pathological dissociation in clinical populations results in patients having either few or numerous dissociative symptoms. I usually ask about a history of trauma and follow up with a few screening questions about depersonalization/ derealization and memory. If responses to these questions are negative, it is quite unlikely that other dissociative symptoms or a dissociative disorder exists. If patients endorse the screening questions, more inquiries should be made to determine if they have other dissociative symptoms or meet DSM criteria for the diagnosis of a specific dissociative disorder.

Many of the questions routinely used to assess dissociative symptoms come from the Dissociative Experiences Scale (DES; Bernstein & Putnam, 1986, 1993; see Appendix 1). The DES is a 28-item self-report instrument that was designed as a research tool to screen for dissociation. It contains questions that are extremely useful for clinicians who are not accustomed to asking about different types of dissociative symptoms. An even shorter version, the DES-Taxon (DES-T), utilizes eight questions from the DES that are most closely identified with a taxon (class) of individuals who demonstrate "pathological dissociation" (Waller et al., 1996).

Although not widely used in clinical practice, several other instruments are used to assess dissociative symptoms and dissociative disorders. The *Dissociation Questionnaire* (DIS-Q; Vanderlinden, Van Dyck, Vandereycken, Vertommen, & Verkes, 1993) is a 63-item self-report instrument that measures identity confusion and fragmentation, loss of control, amnesia, and absorption. Developed in Belgium and the Netherlands, the DIS-Q is more commonly used by European clinicians and researchers. The *Somatoform Dissociation Questionnaire-20* (SDQ-20; Nijenhuis, Spinhoven, Van Dyck, Van der Hart, & Vanderlinden, 1996; see Appendix 2) is a 20-item self-report instrument that measures somatoform dissociation such as tunnel vision, auditory distancing, unintended muscle contractions, psychogenic blindness, difficulty urinating, insensitivity to pain, psychogenic paralysis, nonepileptic seizures, and so on. A shorter version, the SDQ-5, consists of five items from the SDQ-20 (Nijenhuis, 1999).

A more comprehensive self-report instrument was developed by psychologist Paul Dell, PhD. The *Multidimensional Inventory of Dissociation* (MID; Dell, 2006a) is a multiscale diagnostic instrument with 218 items that measures dissociative symptoms, generating both scores for classes of symptoms (e.g., derealization, depersonalization, dissociative disorientation and confusion, amnesia, experience of alternate identities, intrusions, trance, flashbacks, body symptoms) and diagnoses (i.e., DID, DDNOS, PTSD and severe borderline personality disorder). The MID and its Excel®-based scoring program are freely available to mental health professionals (see Appendix 3).

There are two structured interview diagnostic instruments for dissociative disorders. The *Structured Clinical Interview for DSM-IV Dissociative Disorders-Revised* (SCID-D-R; Steinberg, 1994a, 1994b, 1995) is a 277-item interview that assesses five dissociative symptoms: amnesia, depersonalization, derealization, identity confusion, and identity alteration. Most items have follow-up questions that ask for a description of the experience, specific examples, and its frequency and impact on social functioning and work performance, which can yield important clinical information. The SCID-D-R diagnoses the five DSM-IV dissociative disorders, yielding a score for each of the five dissociative symptoms and a total score that is based their frequency and intensity. The *Dissociative Disorder Interview Schedule* (DDIS; Ross, Heber et al., 1989; Ross et al., 1990) is a 132-item structured interview that assesses the symptoms of the five DSM-IV dissociative disorders, as well as somatization disorder, borderline personality disorder, and major depressive disorder. In addition, the DDIS also assesses substance abuse, Schneiderian first-rank symptoms, trance, childhood abuse, secondary features of DID, and supernatural/paranormal experiences.

Pathological dissociation—both in terms of its clinical significance and its relationship to traumatic experience—remains a critically important but poorly understood and underdiagnosed condition in clinical practice. Unrecognized dissociative symptoms and disorders result in poor clinical outcomes, frustrating clinicians and leaving patients with unrelieved suffering. This is particularly unfortunate because there are accepted and effective treatments and a body of evidence that shows good clinical outcomes for treating dissociation. Mental health providers continue to need education to understand and use the theory and clinical practices concerning trauma and dissociation. Clinicians who are astute in their observations and practice and who strive to understand their patients in light of both current symptoms and past histories may be the best hope for helping traumatized patients alleviate their painful symptoms and eventually achieve some sense of coherence about their pasts and fulfillment in their future lives.

4

Derailed

Childhood Trauma, Attachment, and the Development of the Self

---

In these cases [of child abuse by close family members], the traumatic experience is apt to become fully incorporated into the child's inner world; the basic building blocks of this world are still in the developmental stage, and the victimization is likely to define the world and self-assumptions of the child. These children are apt to have negative assumptions in all domains, for core beliefs are less likely to be disentangled at an early age. ... The trust and optimism, the sense of safety and security, the feeling of relative invulnerability that are afforded the person with positively based assumptions are absent in the psychological world of these children. Instead, their world is largely one of anxiety, threat, and distrust.

— Ronnie Janoff-Bulman, PhD, *Shattered Assumptions* (1992, p. 86)

The relational disturbances seen in adult survivors of childhood trauma have complex etiologies. The traumatization has profoundly disruptive effects on critical interpersonal attachments when it occurs in childhood, and the negative effects are exponentially increased for the victims of intrafamilial child abuse. When neglect and abuse occur within the family structure, parents' relational deficiencies become mirrored in the way that the children grow up and relate to others. In other words, children suffer not only from the trauma but also from the chaotic and disturbed relational environment in which it occurs. Experts in the trauma field and clinicians have sometimes overly focused on posttraumatic and dissociative symptomatology at the cost of neglecting the profound relational difficulties that cause so much distress and despair in the lives of traumatized patients.

CHILDHOOD TRAUMA AND ATTACHMENT THEORY

The investigation into the harmful effects of childhood trauma has led to reexamination of attachment theory—the contributions of Bowlby (1969, 1973, 1980) and others—to understand the effects of early disruptions of parent-child bonding. Attachment theory examines the nature of the way children relate to parents or caregivers based on how the adults respond to them. Specific relational patterns begin at birth and are established through the infant and toddler years depending on the interactions between the child and parent (or other caregiver). Bowlby described various attachment styles that were subsequently classified into three categories using Ainsworth's Strange Situation Procedure that assesses a child's emotions and behavior in reaction to a strange room, a stranger, and the comings and goings of a parent or caregiver (Ainsworth, Blehar, Waters, & Wall, 1978). These patterns are established early in life and endure through adolescence and into adulthood. Certain adult relational patterns may derive from the different attachment styles in children; these adult patterns can be assessed and categorized by Main and Hesse's Adult Attachment Interview (AAI; Hesse, 1999).

When parents (or other appropriate caregivers) are attentive to the infant's feelings and behaviors and respond appropriately, the child develops *secure attachment*. As toddlers, children with secure attachment freely explore their environment and seek out new experiences but return to the parent as necessary. Such children may be upset at the departure of the parent, but they are able to tolerate the absence, knowing that the parent will return. Children with secure attachments tend to mature into adults with positive views of themselves and their relationships and feel comfortable with both intimacy and autonomy—the *autonomous style* in the AAI classification.

Bowlby described two styles of *insecure attachment* that occur when parents are inconsistent in responding and children come to expect that their parents may not be there when needed. In general, a child with an insecure attachment style does not explore freely and is anxious and withdrawn with strangers. When the parent is absent, the child is highly distressed and inconsolable, and when the parent returns, the child may want contact but avoids it (*avoidant insecure attachment*) or is not easily consoled (*resistant insecure attachment*). As adults, persons with this style of attachment are mistrustful about the intentions of others and ambivalent about intimacy. On the AAI, the adult *dismissing style* (linked to avoidant insecure attachment in children) is characterized by idealization of childhood caretakers and minimizing the need for attachment and relationships. The *preoccupied style* (related to early resistant insecure attachment) is characterized by anxiety in relationships with a heightened level of approval-seeking. Persons with this style can become overly dependent, needy, and sometimes overly emotional. They have doubts about themselves and others and tend to feel responsible for any relational problems.

A fourth category of early attachment—*disorganized attachment*—was introduced by psychologists Mary Main, PhD, and Judith Solomon, PhD (1990), and is characterized by a child's lack of a coherent organized behavioral strategy for dealing with stressful situations (i.e., the strange room, the stranger, and the comings and goings of the caregiver in the Strange Situation Procedure). Disorganized attachment derives from relationships with caretakers that the child finds frightening or alarming, most commonly in situations of emotional, physical, or sexual abuse. The child is placed in an irresolvable situation where the caretaker is "at once the source and the solution"

(Main & Solomon, 1990, p. 163), namely that the child depends on the abusive caretaker for comfort from the abuse itself.[1] The caregivers are experienced as erratic, and children cannot internalize a coherent, organized sense of themselves.

Children with disorganized attachment can show a range of approach-avoidance, "freezing" or confusing behaviors, such as entering trance-like states, moving toward but also avoiding the parent (e.g., approaching with averted gaze) when distressed, or showing odd combinations of nondirected behaviors. Disorganized attachment in children is strongly associated with caretakers who have their own issues of unresolved experiences of trauma and loss—in the *unresolved* category in the AAI classification (Main & Hesse, 1990; Main & Solomon, 1990). Children's disorganized style is a risk factor for a variety of subsequent psychological disturbances, including the development of some of the same relational pathology as their caretakers, suggesting an intergenerational transmission of pathology (Lyons-Ruth & Jacobvitz, 1999; Lyons-Ruth, Yellin, Helnick, & Atwood, 2005).

In 1991, psychologist Peter Barach, PhD, proposed the theory that attachment was a precursor to the development of dissociation—a controversial notion during an era where the actual physical trauma was considered to be the etiology of dissociative disorders:

> In addition to the sadistic, invasive, ritualistic, and humiliating traumatic experiences reported by [multiple personality disorder] patients, clinical material suggests that another kind of childhood trauma may be ubiquitous.... [A]nother type of trauma, which I am calling "the parents' failure to respond," profoundly influences the development of dissociative psychopathology. Under this rubric I am including (1) the parents' failure to protect the child from abuse, and (2) the parents' tendency to dissociate or otherwise detach from emotional involvement with the child.... [T]he mother's chronic failure to respond to indications of distress or emotional need in the child is by itself traumatic, eventually causing a corresponding detachment in the child. The child's reactive detachment sets the stage for reliance on dissociation as a response to "active abuse." (p. 117)

Barach characterized the parents' detachment from the child as a form of dissociation, leading to pathological attachment patterns in which the "abused child has learned to expect no help from mother because she already had emotionally abandoned the child on a regular basis" (p. 118). Thus, in the face of actual abuse, the child does not have the option of seeking external support and instead relies on dissociation—fragmentation into identities that separates the images of good parent and abusive or neglectful parent, and amnesia that shields the child from the memories of the abuse. Freyd's (1996)

---

[1] This is exactly the same dilemma that the abused child faces in the models of Shengold's "soul murder," Summit's "child sexual abuse accommodation syndrome," and Freyd's "betrayal trauma" as discussed in Chapter 1.

betrayal trauma model later echoed this theory, in which she posited that it is the impossible conflicts in attachment that induce dissociation and amnesia in the abused child.

Italian psychiatrist Giovanni Liotti, MD, has expanded the discussion concerning problems with attachment leading to dissociation by emphasizing the interaction between children with disorganized/disoriented attachment styles and their parents who have unresolved loss or trauma.

> Parents of D [disorganized/disoriented attachment style] babies seem, much more often than parents of babies with other types of attachment, to be worried by traumatic memories that divert their attention from the requirements of any efficient style of parental caregiving. These unresolved traumas are related to past abuse, or to loss through death of significant others. (Liotti, 1992, p. 197)
>
> ... [T]he disorganized child has reasons for construing, simultaneously or in quick sequence, both the attachment figure and the self according to the three basic positions of the drama triangle: persecutor, rescuer, and victim. The attachment figure is represented negatively, as the cause of the ever-growing fear experienced by the self (self as victim of a persecutor), but also positively, as a rescuer: The parent, although frightened by unresolved traumatic memories, is nevertheless usually willing to offer comfort to the child, and the child may feel such comforting availability in conjunction with the fear.... Since the frightened attachment figure may be comforted by the tender feelings evoked by contact with the child, the implicit memories of disorganized attachment may also convey the possibility of construing the self as the powerful rescuer of a fragile attachment figure (i.e., the little child perceives the self as able to comfort a frightened adult).... The sequence, in the child's mind, of multiple representations in which both the self and the other person shift among the three incompatible roles of persecutor, rescuer, and victim should be understood as a metaphorical rendition of the construction of contradictory emotional (i.e., preverbal) schemata that arose during the interactions that led to disorganized attachment. These emotional-relational mental structures, encoded in implicit memory, are too complex and intrinsically contradictory to be later synthesized in a unitary, cohesive structure of explicit, semantic memory. In this sense, the [internal working model] of early disorganized attachment is intrinsically dissociative. (Liotti, 2004, p. 479)

In addition to promoting the use of dissociation, dysfunctional and pathological childhood attachment patterns also lead to long-standing relational patterns that persist into adult life. I have routinely observed an intense approach-avoidance dynamic in my interactions with patients who have early trauma histories—what has often been termed the "feel" of abused individuals in the clinical interview. Often one senses strong (or suppressed) object hunger but also intense fear of hurt and intrusion. These patients project a powerful nonverbal expression of "I am the loneliest person you've ever met" along with "Stay the hell away from me!" This is a recapitulation of early patterns of disorganized attachment that are reenacted in adult relationships. These reenactments of the early relational dilemmas lead to disabling difficulties in adult relational patterns in all domains—personal, social, and vocational relationships. However, these dynamics become most evident and powerful in the therapeutic relationship, as the therapist becomes the transferential parent figure, capable of providing care but also the potential source of emotional harm. In terms of adult DSM-IV diagnostic categorization, these relational difficulties are part of dysfunctional personality functioning found in the Cluster B personality disorders in the borderline range.

BORDERLINE PERSONALITY DISORDER

There have been two distinct views of borderline personality disorder in psychiatry. On the one hand, theoretical observations and scientific inquiry have contributed to valuable insights into understanding the etiology and treatment of borderline patients. Early concepts of borderline personality disorder placed it on the border between psychosis and neurosis (Knight, 1958) and emphasized the "psychotic core" that lay beneath a thin layer of normal neurotic functioning (Hoch & Cattel, 1959). Subsequent investigators (Grinker, Werble, & Drye, 1968; Gunderson & Singer, 1975; Kernberg, 1967; and others) described this diagnosis more in specific models of intrapsychic functioning and patterns of behavior in relation to the external world. Based on these observations, the DSM-III (APA, 1980), and more recently the DSM-IV (APA, 1994), defined borderline personality disorder in terms of a specific series of criteria that are necessary to make the diagnosis.

The other view of borderline personality disorder has had to do with the negative associations and connotations connected with this diagnosis. As Boston-area psychiatrist Paul L. Russell, MD, succinctly wrote in his paper, "The Theory of the Crunch": "Diagnosis borderline; prognosis pain" (Russell, 2006, p. 9).[2] In his sympathetic description of the vicissitudes of borderline patients and their treatment, Russell emphasized how their core difficulties with interpersonal connections compel them to repeat and reenact painful conflicts in the therapeutic relationship, which he viewed as not simply a complication in the treatment process but an opportunity to understand patients' dilemmas. Russell suggested that therapists could help advance patients' ability to feel increasingly secure and to tolerate dysphoric affects by providing containment—Winnicott's (1965) concept of "the holding environment." Notwithstanding such sympathetic discussions, the borderline diagnosis has been associated in the minds of many mental health professionals with difficult patients, mostly women, who are thought to be angry, affectively

[2] Russell's paper was originally presented at the Massachusetts Mental Health Center, c. 1970. It was unpublished but widely circulated in the mental health community for many years. Along with several other papers that memorialize Russell's wisdom, it was recently published by the Smith College School of Social Work.

labile, potentially dependent, intrusive, anxiety-provoking, unlikeable, and ungratifying. Trauma psychologist John Briere, PhD, has quipped that, "Borderline is what you call patients you don't like … and staff that you don't like." To counteract this prejudice, noted psychiatrist George Vaillant, MD (1992), in a paper titled "The Beginning of Wisdom is Never to Call a Patient Borderline," advocated the use of other diagnoses that might be applicable to borderline patients but are less emotionally laden.

Through my experience as a supervisor for residents in psychiatry, I grew to understand the origins of the antipathy toward borderline patients. For many years, I did rounds with junior residents in the morning after they had admitted patients to the hospital overnight. On occasion, I inferred that they rather disliked a patient they had evaluated, despite their efforts to present the case with appropriate professional neutrality and decorum. Almost invariably, the patient was an individual who met the diagnostic criteria for borderline personality disorder. Even in the relatively limited clinical encounter, these patients had managed to convey their mistrust of the resident and sometimes expressed hostility and anger based on their assumption that they would be treated badly—through verbal and nonverbal communications that conveyed the message "I know you could care less about me, so let's get this over with"—or worse. Despite their best efforts to feel otherwise, these conscientious young residents resented being regarded as insensitive and uncaring, and they responded with automatic distance and dislike, thus completing the relational reenactment of emotional abuse and neglect. It was only after I asked the residents to consider what may have made the patients relate in this dysfunctional way that they realized that the patients' fundamental assumptions differed from their own. As high achievers, most residents grow up with secure attachments that led them to believe that the world is a benign place and that other people are basically decent (which may not actually be true, but which is a functional and adaptive outlook on life). Borderline patients, on the other hand, grow up with the kind of disorganized attachments that result in negative views of the world and fear and suspicion of other people.

In her book, *Trauma and Recovery*, Herman (1992b) made the persuasive argument that the term "chronic posttraumatic syndrome" be used to describe the characterologic adaptation to abuse, in place of the diagnostic label of borderline personality disorder because of the negative connotations associated with this diagnosis. Although this idea has considerable merit, it blurs the distinction between symptoms of Axis I and Axis II disorders. In the DSM classification, Axis I disorders are seen as syndromes that are superimposed on an existing Axis II personality substrate. In other words, Axis I disorders are seen as symptoms that overlay any Axis II pathology, which consists of long-standing personality characteristics. As one chronically traumatized patient once stated succinctly to me, "It's not 'problems' or 'beliefs' or 'patterns of thinking,' that I can simply reason through. It's *me*, it's who I am." While an understanding of the role of trauma in the development of borderline personality disorder may help both patients and clinicians struggle through difficulties, it does not diminish the intensely painful and often slow process of changing the sense of self, the adaptations made to the world, and the meanings attached to formative experiences.

Elucidating the role of childhood trauma in the development of borderline personality disorder has done much in terms of both understanding borderline symptomatology and helping clinicians to be more sympathetic to the dilemmas of many traumatized patients. Prior to understanding how a traumatic environment affects personality development, classic psychoanalytic theories emphasized the failures of the developing child to build certain kinds of mature intrapsychic structures. For example, psychiatrist Otto Kernberg (1967, 1968, 1970) emphasized the "lower level" defenses of borderline patients and their vulnerability to transient psychosis. He hypothesized that there was a failure of normal psychological development early in life, particularly around the necessary integration of conflictual feelings about primary caretakers. Psychoanalyst Margaret Mahler's (1971, 1972) and psychiatrist James Masterson's (1972) contributions pointed specifically to the rapprochement subphase of the separation-individuation process around the age of 18 months as a time of difficulty. They hypothesized that disruptions of attachment can occur in the mother-child relationship if a proper balance of holding and letting go does not occur.

In recent years, much more attention has been given to actual occurrence of traumatic childhood experiences in borderline patients. Several studies have demonstrated very high rates of traumatic childhood experiences in adolescent and adult borderline patients, generally in the range of 60% to 75% (Herman et al., 1989; Herman & van der Kolk, 1987; Ludolph et al., 1990; Ogata et al., 1990; Westen et al., 1990; Zanarini et al., 1987). These traumatic experiences include reports of physical and sexual abuse and witnessing violence. This growing body of evidence suggests that childhood abuse is often a critical factor in the development of borderline psychopathology. This kind of understanding shifts the conceptual paradigm of borderline personality disorder. Rather than simply focusing on traditional concepts concerning impairments of intrapsychic structure (and a not-so-subtle implication that the borderline patient is somehow defective), one must also consider the developmental adaptations of young children who have been subjected to cataclysmic events. In this context, the intrapsychic structures and behaviors of borderline patients can be understood in a model that emphasizes adaptation rather than pathology (Saunders & Arnold, 1993).

Clinical experience in treating borderline patients mirrors the research findings. Many borderline patients report extensive histories of childhood emotional, physical, and sexual abuse, profound neglect, and the witnessing of violence. However, it is my contention that it is not the trauma per se that results in borderline personality disorder; after all, a significant minority of borderline patients do not have evidence of obvious childhood trauma. Rather, it is the gross disruptions of normal familial attachments and the massive failure of adequate care and protection of the child that result in distortions of normal characterologic development. Experiences of intrafamilial abuse and neglect are extreme manifestations of the failure of normal parental attachment and nurturance. In most of the cases, these disruptions of attachment have been neither subtle nor limited to the rapprochement subphase; the disruptions have been gross lapses in care and attention that occur over multiple critical periods of the child's development.

What about the significant minority of borderline patients who do *not* have traumatic backgrounds? From anecdotal evidence, it appears that there may be major attachment difficulties even when families are well-meaning and nonabusive. In some instances, the child and the parents may have such different temperaments and personality character-istics—either inborn or developed—that the child is figuratively unseen by the parents. For example, a psychologically sensitive child who is born into an action-oriented family that does not understand or dwell on feelings may be very overwhelmed by not feeling held and validated. The importance of emotional coherence in the parent-child relation-ship (even in the absence of inborn similarities) was illustrated for me when I treated a mother for a complicated grief reaction following the accidental death of her teenaged daughter. It was clear that mother and daughter had a very powerful bond, which made the loss even more difficult. When I asked the mother if her daughter was temperamen-tally like herself or her husband, she surprised me with her answer: "No, Leah wasn't like either Stephen or me. I realized that very early on and decided that if I was going to do my job as a mother, that I needed to pay very close attention to who she really was." I was struck that this was at least one perspective on how to define good parenting, but I also realized that many parents who differ from their children in major ways would not be able to have this level of clarity concerning their children or their role as parents.

REFRAMING THE DIAGNOSIS OF BORDERLINE PERSONALITY DISORDER[3]

The DSM-IV (APA, 1994) provides the following criteria for borderline personality disorder (p. 654):

A pervasive pattern of instability of mood, interpersonal relationships, and self-image ... as indicated by at least five of the following:

1. Frantic efforts to avoid real or imagined abandonment ...
2. A pattern of unstable and intense interpersonal relationships characterized by alternating between extremes of overidealization and devaluation
3. Identity disturbance: markedly and persistently unstable self-image or sense of self
4. Impulsiveness in at least two areas that are potentially self-damaging ...
5. Recurrent suicidal threats, gestures, or behavior, or self-mutilating behavior
6. Affective instability due to marked reactivity of mood ...
7. Chronic emptiness or boredom
8. Inappropriate, intense anger or difficulty controlling anger ...
9. Transient, stress-related paranoid ideation or severe dissociative symptoms

---

[3] Portions of this section and subsequent sections in this chapter were adapted from the article "Treat-ment Implications of Past Trauma in Borderline Personality Disorder" (Gunderson & Chu, 1993).

In teaching residents, I have simplified this rather long list into three "buckets": (1) recurring relational disturbances, (2) lack of affect tolerance and impulse control, and (3) negative and empty views of the self. In light of evidence of a history of significant trauma in many borderline patients, these categories of borderline symptomatology are more understandable. The intensity of the borderline patient's relationships and the wild oscillations between idealization and devaluation may well be better understood as recapitulations and reenactments of early abusive relationships. The set of assumptions concerning interpersonal relationships for persons who have experienced abuse is based on their actual experiences with caretakers' narcissistic preoccupation, control, manipulation, and exploitation. It is hence hardly surprising to find that traumatized patients continue to engage others (including therapists) in repetitions of the most powerful interpersonal dynamics that they have experienced. They reenact the roles of both abuser and victim, because in their families of origin, one had to be either one or the other. For the therapist who becomes part of this world, and who is subject to the interpersonal struggles of the reenactments, the experience can be intense and unpleasant. Yet, the patient's dilemmas can be viewed as deficits in learning and deprivation concerning interpersonal experiences rather than as malicious or deliberate. Although abuse-related interpersonal dynamics and dysfunctional behaviors must be challenged, therapists can have more empathy and patience with the necessary and inevitable struggles.

Borderline patients' behavioral dyscontrol, impulsivity, affective lability, and poor affect tolerance can similarly be traced to early abuse. After all, how do children normally develop behavioral control and affect tolerance? Good parents routinely buffer and shield children from situations that produce overly intense affect and out-of-control impulses. If the child is overwhelmed, parents or caretakers mitigate and ameliorate the situation by soothing the child. Parents assist children throughout their developmental years with the gradual process of learning affect tolerance and behavior control, often intuitively utilizing the principle of "optimal frustration," in which the child is progressively exposed to challenging situations in an incremental and stepwise manner, but never allowing the child to become truly overwhelmed.

For example, most parents can distinguish the fussy crying of an infant or young child (that may not require intervention, allowing the child to learn to cope with low to moderate distress) from the cries that signal marked distress or terror (that require immediate intervention). In abusive family environments, these principles are pervasively ignored or violated, and one or more of the caretakers routinely subjects the child to situations in which the child is overwhelmed by unbearable affects and intense impulses. It is hence not surprising that many of the adult borderline patients who come from such family environments have difficulties with these basic psychological and behavioral tasks.

Borderline patients' fear of abandonment and their intense anger may be understood as deriving from actual abandonment, maltreatment, and deprivation. The continuing expectation of being victimized and the recapitulation of abusive and failed relationships lead to a growing reservoir of bitter disappointment, frustration, self-hate, and rage. The result is episodic expressions of intense and poorly controlled anger that break through a barrier of fragile and brittle control. Given borderline patients' disability in being able to utilize supportive relationships, angry outbursts and impulsive and self-destructive patterns of releasing tension such as suicide gestures and repetitive self-injury may be the only outlet for the intolerable experience of explosive rage.

Most of the major theories regarding the development of a sense of self, including psychoanalytic, object relations, and self-psychology theories, point to the importance of a positive, supportive, and validating relational context during critical developmental years. For the adult who has been subject to chronic childhood abuse, the family culture has fostered only confusion about identity, emptiness, and negative views of the self. There is overwhelming consensus that one of the damaging effects of early abuse is the development of self-hate (see, for example, Carmen & Rieker, 1989; Gelinas, 1983; Herman et al., 1986; Shapiro, 1987; Shengold, 1979; Summit, 1983). More recent ideas, particularly concerning the psychology of women, point not only to the importance of the early relational environment but also to the necessity of ongoing relationships that validate one's sense of self, self-worth, and cultural role (see, for example, Jordan, Kaplan, Miller, Stiver, & Surrey, 1991). The childhood experiences of borderline patients predispose them to ongoing relational dysfunction, isolation, and disenfranchisement that compound the early relational damage.

In a paradigm that takes into account the actual occurrence of major trauma in the early background of borderline patients, one must move away from the traditional view of a subtle kind of defectiveness (i.e., that borderline patients—for unclear reasons—inherently have abnormal or excessive reactions to current untoward life events). Rather, one must see many patients with borderline personality disorder as having adapted to overwhelming life events by internalizing and adopting certain patterns of relating and specific defenses, viewing themselves and reacting to others on the basis of long-standing and unresolved abusive experiences. These patterns of adaptation can be seen as currently dysfunctional but eminently understandable in view of past life experiences. This kind of attitudinal shift may be crucial in ameliorating the pejorative associations common to the borderline diagnosis and in providing effective treatment.

From the mid-1980s into the 1990s, there was considerable debate about traumatized patients—especially those with dissociative disorders—as to whether these patients actually had dissociative disorders or were "just" borderline (Buck, 1983; Clary, Burstein, & Carpenter, 1984; Fink & Golinkoff, 1990; Horovitz & Braun, 1984; Marmer, 1991; Marmer & Fink, 1994). Some clinicians viewed trauma-related treatment as ineffective and overgratifying, and they argued that the primary treatment should be containment of behaviors through strict limit-setting and maintaining clear boundaries. Although this contention was reductionistic and simplistic, many patients who have dissociative and posttraumatic disorders *also* have borderline personality disorder, and *part* of their treatment involves containment, good boundaries, and clear limits. After all, severe and persistent intrafamilial abuse fosters not only the development of posttraumatic and dissociative conditions but also borderline psychopathology that results from the failure of adequate caretaking and relational support.

Over many years at McLean Hospital, we have seen hundreds of patients with severe PTSD and dissociative disorders, and the vast majority had borderline personality disorder characteristics or similar difficulties in personality functioning. Our observations may be somewhat skewed, as only the more disabled subset of the traumatized population is seen in a hospital setting. However, the contention that severely traumatized patients present with posttraumatic and dissociative symptomatology *and* characterologic difficulties is supported by research that has shown a substantial overlap in patients with trauma histories, dissociative disorders, and borderline personality disorder (Ross, 2007; van der Kolk, Hostetler, Herron, & Fisler, 1994; Zanarini, Ruser, Frankenburg, & Hennen, 2000).

TREATMENT IMPLICATIONS OF TRAUMA AND DISORDERED ATTACHMENT

The prominence of disordered attachment in the etiology and expression of trauma-related disorders suggests that relational issues must have a central role in the psychotherapy of these disorders. The resolution of relational issues is at the heart of most phase-oriented models of trauma treatment and is described at length in the subsequent chapters of this book as well as by other authors (see, for example, Courtois, Ford, & Cloitre, 2009; Herman, 1992b; Lebowitz, Harvey, & Herman, 1993; Steele, Van der Hart, & Nijenhuis, 2001). However, several models of psychotherapy for trauma-related disorders explicitly focus on disordered attachment as the essential part of the treatment process. In his 2000 book, *Not Trauma Alone: Therapy for Child Abuse Survivors in Family and Social Context*, psychologist Steven N. Gold, PhD, describes his model of Contextual Therapy. Rather than having a simplistic focus on trauma processing, the model emphasizes building collaboration (especially in the therapeutic alliance), correcting maladaptive negative beliefs about the self (e.g., being unworthy of and incapable of sustaining relationships), and learning skills to reduce symptomatology and enhance interpersonal ties. In a 2001 paper, Gold and colleagues describe three cases of considerable complexity where unexpectedly rapid progress was achieved by leading with a focus on building relational capacities, which then facilitated the resolution of posttraumatic and dissociative symptoms.

In a 2001 paper, psychologist Ruth Blizard, PhD, highlighted the relational issues of disorganized attachment in persons who grew up with abusive primary caretakers, leading to dissociated victim/masochistic and perpetrator/sadistic ego states. Her treatment model is focused on understanding the defensive structure of ego states and ameliorating the relational conflicts between them:

When alternating ego states are understood as evolving from defensive schemas developed to negotiate the dilemmas of attachment to an abuser, the following therapeutic techniques can be derived: 1. identifying adaptive needs and maladaptive defenses, 2. interpreting ego state switches as attempts to resolve relational dilemmas, 3. gradually bridging dissociation between states, 4. using transference and countertransference to understand relational patterns, and 5. cultivating more adaptive interpersonal skills within the therapeutic relationship. (p. 37)

Issues related to attachment and traumatization must be interwoven into the therapy. One of the more important ways of encouraging a positive therapeutic attachment and developing a sense of alliance is for therapists to validate the essential elements of patients' abuse. Whereas an earlier generation of psychoanalytically oriented therapists may have been concerned about the symbolic distortions of such retrospective accounts of abuse, it is now clear that such accounts can often be corroborated (Chu et al., 1999; Feldman-Summers & Pope, 1994; Herman & Harvey, 1997; Herman & Schatzhow, 1987; Kluft, 1995). A reflexively skeptical response is likely to appear hostile and will almost certainly damage the fragile therapeutic alliance. Therapists who focus *only* on the intrapsychic conflicts produced by past abuse or on possible distortions of initial accounts of abuse are guilty of empathic failure. Such stances tend to devalue patients' perceptions of their experiences, resulting in increasing their sense of shame and fearfulness within the therapy or even precipitating flight from therapy. This is not to suggest that therapists should encourage patients to believe in the literal truth of *all* recollections (including those that may be poorly or hazily remembered) or to conjecture about what might have happened. Similarly, therapists should not conclude that all borderline patients, or all patients with certain behaviors or traits, have been subject to gross abuse. Rather, when appropriate, therapists can ally with their patients' sense of having been victimized, which can help these patients to begin to understand their own feelings and behaviors.

Acknowledgment of the reality of past victimization is also helpful when coping with issues concerning therapeutic responsibility. Most patients with histories of abuse are typically burdened by undue feelings of responsibility for their having been victimized or abandoned. The coping strategies and defenses characteristic of traumatized patients make them particularly likely to take flight or to become defensively angry in response to interventions that emphasize their being responsible for creating their own problems. It is necessary to help patients distinguish clearly between the need to take responsibility for caring for themselves in the present and wrongly assuming the responsibility and blame for having been abused in the past.

An approach that emphasizes the importance of empathizing with patients' abuse experiences and their adaptation to such experiences mandates alteration of traditional therapeutic interventions. For example, interpretations concerning the centrality of anger in the patient's life or pointing out the manipulativeness of patients' actions are often counterproductive early in the therapy. These types of interventions may ask patients to "own" their angry feelings and behavior before validating the reasons why they are angry or behave in dysfunctional ways. Such approaches may be especially likely to evoke negative therapeutic reactions in traumatized patients with borderline characteristics (Adler, 1985; Brandchaft & Stolorow, 1987; Kolb & Gunderson, 1990). Indeed, premature confrontations and interpretations have been shown to be a major cause of borderline patients dropping out of therapy (Gundersonet et al., 1989). Interpretations that identify a patient's angry motives and feelings usually need to be accompanied by empathy and validation of past trauma. For example, the therapist could convey that the patient's anger about past abuse is understandable, but that angry feelings must be identified and expressed in a manageable fashion.

Reports of successfully treated patients have documented the importance of support and the significance of patients developing a positive attachment to the therapist (Waldinger & Gunderson, 1987; Wallerstein, 1986). Early interventions are most successful when behaviors (including even those that may be dysfunctional, such as self-destructive behavior or flight) are understood and reframed as being understandable, sometimes even admirable, adaptations to childhood experiences, but the behaviors are misplaced and no longer useful in the present. More generally, whereas virtually all patients must make a personal commitment to their own self-care before they can work as allies in treatment, those with histories of severe abuse require added support during the early phases of treatment, gentleness about interpretations directed at their traumas, and patience about expecting them to engage in stable therapeutic alliances or to do transference-based work.

Establishing and maintaining a positive therapeutic alliance is critical throughout the treatment of traumatized patients and begins the healing process for disordered attachment. Of course, validation of trauma and other supportive interventions are only the first step in the treatment of traumatized patients, as empathy and understanding alone can result in patients becoming mired in a chronically victimized and helpless position. As the therapy continues, ongoing efforts to maintain a sense of engagement must be supplemented by interpretations and confrontation (e.g., around dysfunctional behaviors and dissociated affects such as hate and aggression). However, an ongoing effective alliance and an empathic sense of the traumatic antecedents of patient's feelings and behaviors will make such interventions more acceptable. Establishing empathic resonance before interpretation or confrontation is essential (Chu, 1992a). As Mann (1973) noted,

> [T]he gentle, caring concern of the therapist for the patient may well be the most important element in a proper, effective confrontation.... It communicates to the patient his privilege to choose the direction that he would like to move in rather than communicating a directive to which the patient feels impelled to yield. (p. 44)

5

The Memory Wars

The Nature of Traumatic Memories of Childhood Abuse[1]

Dissociative amnesia is at the core of the controversy concerning traumatic memory of childhood abuse. The idea that overwhelming experiences can be forgotten and then later recalled has a long tradition, originating in major schools of thinking concerning intrapsychic experience. Early in the 20th century, French physician Pierre Janet (1907) described psychogenic amnesia and theorized that traumatic events could be dissociated from conscious awareness, only to be remembered at some later point in time. Sigmund Freud's psychoanalytic theory included the belief that events that were traumatic or that resulted in intense intrapsychic conflict could be repressed and become unconscious, and could later be repeated and reexperienced (Freud, 1893–1895/1955, 1896, 1920/1955). As described in previous chapters, Freud's notion of repression involves an active process—itself unconscious—that holds unacceptable or overwhelming thoughts and impulses outside of conscious awareness. These theoretical constructs laid the groundwork for modern investigators who were interested in the effects of traumatic events on memory.

In the clinical arena, dissociative amnesia has been observed for overwhelming and traumatic experience. For example, psychiatrist Bessel van der Kolk, MD, reported a clinical anecdote of a woman who was repeatedly arrested for pulling fire alarms and shouting for people to get out of buildings that she believed were on fire (van der Kolk & Kadish, 1987). The authors believed that she was completely amnestic for having survived the infamous Coconut Grove nightclub fire in which hundreds had perished more than 30 years previously. In the course of treatment, she recovered the memory of being in the burning building filled with smoke and toxic gases.

Numerous other anecdotal accounts of amnesia for traumatic childhood events have also been reported. For example, in the mid-1990s, the media reported the story of Ross Cheit, PhD, who was at the time an associate professor of political science at Brown University (National Public Radio, 1996). In 1992, Professor Cheit learned that his nephew was joining a boys' chorus. He became quite depressed but could think of

[1]Portions of this chapter were adapted from the article "The Nature of Traumatic Memory" (Chu, Matthews, Frey, & Ganzel, 1996).

no reason for his depression. However, shortly thereafter he had the abrupt recovery of memories of childhood sexual molestation by an administrator of a boys' chorus summer camp. Cheit set out to corroborate his memory. He found other men who as boys had been molested at the same camp, as well as two former employees of the camp who had witnessed some episodes of sexual molestation. He subsequently located and telephoned the perpetrator, who admitted to the acts. He filed civil suit against the organizers of the boys' chorus; the case was settled in 1994. Cheit has gone on to establish the Recovered Memory Project, which has documented more than 100 cases of individuals where there is clear confirmation of the accuracy of recovered memories of traumatic events for which they previously had been amnestic (Cheit, 2010).

Perhaps even more striking are the many adult patients who report extensive amnesia for childhood events. To some patients, much of their childhood is foggy. Others can recount the events of their past but feel as though they happened to someone else. Many patients describe a kind of Swiss cheese memory with gaps in their recall of their early experiences, or even complete amnesia for any events over months or years. In clinical settings, this level of amnesia may be highly significant. Many patients with this kind of amnesia eventually recover memories that they had forgotten completely or in part.

In the current clinical arena, clinicians generally accept that some recovered memories of childhood abuse are essentially valid reports of repressed or dissociated early experiences. Indeed, for some patients, clinical work with recovered memories has been a vehicle to resolution of psychiatric symptomatology and has led to an enhanced understanding of the traumatic etiologies of their difficulties. However, as documented in the introduction and earlier chapters of this book, some academics have questioned the validity of repression and recovered memory and the existence of severe dissociative disorders—see, for example, Holmes (1990), Loftus (1993), McHugh (1992), Ofshe and Singer (1994), Piper (1997), and Pope and colleagues (Pope & Hudson, 1995; Pope, Hudson, Bodkin, & Oliva, 1998). Some of these academic skeptics and others have served on the Scientific Advisory Board of the False Memory Syndrome Foundation (FMSF), joining a coalition of parents who vehemently denied accusations that they had abused their children. Among the concerns expressed by the leadership and members of the FMSF were that: (a) clinicians were largely unaware of the science concerning memory, especially concerning memory distortion and the creation of pseudomemories; (b) there was no evidence to support the validity of repression or the accuracy of recovered memories; (c) certain self-help books, e.g., *The Courage to Heal* (Bass & Davis, 1988), encouraged persons to believe that they had been victims of abuse when they had particular nonspecific symptoms but no actual memory of abuse; (d) so-called recovered memory therapists were influencing patients to believe that they had been abused and, in some cases, to sue their parents or family members for having abused them; and (e) some clinicians were wrongly supporting the validity of extreme and bizarre organized child abuse, such as the existence of widespread organized satanic ritualized abuse.

The viewpoints and concerns expressed through the FMSF have been largely regarded by the mainstream mental health community as extreme and hyperbolic. In fact, although many traumatized patients have always remembered some abusive childhood experiences, most also recover additional previously unrecalled memories of abuse or additional details of partially recalled memories. Such memory recall occurs both within and outside of therapy sessions. Newly recalled trauma memories frequently precede a patient's entry into psychotherapy (Chu et al., 1999; Herman & Harvey, 1997), which may be the reason why they seek treatment. Memories that are recovered—those that were forgotten and subsequently recalled—can often be corroborated and are no more likely to be confabulated than are continuous memories (Dalenberg, 1996; Kluft, 1995; Lewis, Yeager, Swica, Pincus, & Lewis, 1997).

Many of the relevant professional societies have issued statements concerning recovered memories of abuse (American Psychiatric Association, 2000; American Psychological Association, 1994, 1996; Australian Psychological Association, 1994; British Psychological Society, 1995). These reports all present a balanced view: that it is possible for accurate memories of abuse to have been forgotten only to be remembered much later in life, but that it is also possible that some people may construct pseudomemories of having been abused. Some of the statements note that therapists cannot know the extent to which someone's memories are accurate in the absence of external corroboration, which may be difficult or impossible to obtain given the passage of time. And, as is true of all memories, recollections of childhood abuse may mix memory of actual events with fantasy, confabulation, misremembered details, or displacement or conflation of several events.

Amidst the hyperbole and acrimony in the debate about traumatic amnesia and recovered memory, there were legitimate concerns about clinical practices in regards to recollections of abuse. In the 1980s and early 1990s, the clinical community was largely uninformed about the scientific research concerning memory. But, the FMSF mischaracterized the extent and practice of recovered memory therapy, a type of treatment that was unknown to most legitimate clinicians. However, a minority of overzealous therapists did use unorthodox practices (including checklists of nonspecific symptoms thought to indicate past sexual abuse) designed to elicit and explore possible sexual abuse in patients with no memory of such experiences; such practices that place importance on a therapist's idiosyncratic belief system were and are simply substandard.

In the 1990s and into the early years of this past decade, the memory debate was argued in the courts. Numerous lawsuits resulted in large settlements or judgments in civil cases (and some criminal convictions) against practitioners. For a review of legal cases, see Lipton, 1999 (note that the paper is written from the FMSF perspective). In retrospect, many of these lawsuits derived from clinical situations where there was uncritical acceptance of patients' reports (however bizarre) and before there were established models of treatment for complex PTSD and dissociation. As Lipton observed, the number of cases being litigated has declined significantly, and to my knowledge no large settlements or judgments have been made against practitioners since 2004.

Several authoritative reviews have been written on the complex subject of traumatic amnesia (see Appelbaum, Uyehara, & Elin, 1997; Brown, 1995; Brown, Scheflin,

& Hammond, 1998; Brown, Scheflin et al., 1999; Courtois, 1999; Dallam, 2002; Gleaves, Smith, Butler, & Spiegel, 2004; Pope, 1996; Scheflin & Brown, 1996; Williams & Banyard, 1997). Dalenberg (2006) and Brown, Scheflin, and Hammond (1998) have also provided excellent summaries of the legal challenges that are still being adjudicated in various jurisdictions in the United States and elsewhere. The focus in this chapter is to provide an integrated view of trauma and memory by reviewing recent findings concerning progress in cognitive memory research, issues concerning memory distortion, prevalence studies of traumatic amnesia, the psychobiology of traumatic memory, and clinical practice concerning traumatic memory.

THE CONTRIBUTIONS FROM COGNITIVE PSYCHOLOGY MEMORY RESEARCH

The central questions raised in the debate concerning amnesia and recovered memory are (a) Is traumatic memory different from ordinary memory? and (b) Is recovered memory of traumatic experiences essentially valid? Is it subject to distortion, or is it essentially false memory resulting from suggestive psychotherapy? The answers are far from simple. There have been serious problems even in finding a common language in the recovered memory debate. Different disciplines and schools of thought have vastly different viewpoints and terminology to describe observable phenomena. For example, the traditional clinical community tends to use terms such as *the unconscious, suppression,* and *repression,* invoking psychoanalytic mechanisms that involve active and dynamic intrapsychic processes. The cognitive psychology community favors terms such as *normal forgetting, selective inattention,* and *nonconscious processes* to describe similar phenomena. For this discussion, I am using the terms *dissociative amnesia, traumatic amnesia,* and *recovered memory* rather than *repressed memory,* as the latter term invokes a specific mechanism through which it is thought to occur.

The Malleability of Memory

Memories can be remarkably inaccurate at times. Earlier ideas going back to the 1950s erroneously held that precise details of a traumatic scene are permanently etched in memory in a potentially retrievable manner—so-called flashbulb memories (Brown & Kulick, 1977). Despite the difficulties of simulating traumatic experiences in the laboratory, investigators have studied the nature of memory in stressful experiences. Experimental procedures have included testing college students under demanding conditions (Eriksen, 1952, 1953; Tudor & Holmes, 1973) and exposing research participants to shocking photographic material (Christianson & Loftus, 1987; Kramer, Buckhout, Fox, Widman, & Tusche, 1991). Participants in these studies were often remarkably inaccurate in recounting details of their experience (e.g., the sequence of events), although experiences that were central to the individual seemed to be accurately retained. These investigations have suggested that an individual's recall of events is a direct function of the intensity of the affect associated with the experience; the more emotional the experience, the better it is remembered. Thus, because traumatic events are by definition associated with higher emotional valance, they may be better remembered.

However, aspects of actual traumatic experiences can also be misremembered. The central features of traumatic events are generally accurately retained, but many of the peripheral details of the experiences can be inaccurate. For example, studies of memories of the horrifying explosion of the space shuttle *Challenger* in 1986 showed that many individuals—especially children—had incorrect recollections of the events (Neisser & Harsch, 1992; Warren & Swartwood, 1992). Psychologist Elizabeth Loftus, PhD (1993), has described other shocking situations such as war and accidents that were misremembered. This is consistent with my own personal experience. I long had a vivid memory of how I heard about the assassination of President John F. Kennedy. In my recollection, I had been in my sixth-grade classroom when a friend and classmate burst into the room saying that the President had been shot. There is obviously no question about the fact of the assassination, but when I met up with my former classmate at a high school reunion many years later, we were able to determine that we were actually in our seventh-grade homeroom during the incident.

The role of suggestion in shaping actual memory content has also been well established in laboratory studies (Loftus, 1979; Loftus, Korf, & Schooler, 1989; Schooler, Gerhard, & Loftus, 1986; Schumaker, 1991). In some protocols, such as those designed by Loftus and research psychologist James Schooler, PhD, participants were shown pictures, slides, or videotape of an event and were then asked to recall the event. When participants were given cues or suggestions regarding the event, they often made errors concerning what they recalled. For example, in a protocol for one experiment (Schooler et al., 1986), participants were shown slides depicting an automobile accident. For one set of participants, the slides did not contain a stop sign, but its existence was suggested in a question that was asked after they viewed the slides. This post-event suggestion was quite subtle: "Did another car pass the Datsun while it was at the intersection with the stop sign?" or "Was the Datsun the same color red as the stop sign?" When later asked, many participants reported seeing the sign and could provide a verbal description of the sign, particularly when an individual was asked to mentally visualize a memory. It is important to understand that actual memory content is changed—in this case through the retrieval mechanism. In fact, memory content can be influenced at all stages of the memory process: perception, consolidation (organizing and encoding), storage, retrieval, and reconsolidation.

In these studies and many others, a person's conviction concerning the accuracy of memories was *not* related to what actually happened. Individuals typically have a high level of subjective confidence in the accuracy of their memories. It has long been known that study participants have equal confidence in memories that were suggested as in truly accurate memories (e.g., Cole & Loftus, 1979; Greene, Flynn, & Loftus, 1982; Loftus, Miller, & Burns, 1978). Even if they have recollections that are distorted or false, persons are generally are convinced that their memories represent what actually happened (which explains many an argument in which members of a couple vehemently disagree about past experiences that they shared but remember differently). This phenomenon has clear implications for work in psychotherapy. Even when patients have clear memory content and are convinced of their validity, the therapist cannot automatically assume the accuracy of their recall.

Pseudomemories: Memories for Events That Never Occurred

Despite evidence that memory content can be influenced by suggestion, emotional arousal, and personal meaning, the bulk of memory research actually supports the accuracy of remembered events that are known to have occurred. However, there is also evidence that persons can "remember" events that did *not* occur. One personal pseudomemory was described by the Swiss psychologist, Jean Piaget (1962), the well-known theorist of cognitive development in childhood. For many years during his childhood, Piaget had a clear visual memory of someone trying to kidnap him from his stroller when he was two years old. The memory also involved his nanny chasing away the potential kidnapper and then going home and telling the family. Years later, when Piaget was 15, the nanny returned to the Piaget family and confessed that the incident had never occurred. Her motive had been to enhance her position in the household, but she subsequently had suffered guilt about the fabrication and about the watch she had received as a reward.

In a National Public Radio show (Gross & WHYY-FM, 1989), *Fresh Air* host Terry Gross interviewed Julia Child, the French Chef, who described other pseudomemories. She reported being repeatedly approached by fans who insisted they "saw" her throw a chicken on the floor and "saw" her drink wine from a bottle. Mrs. Child denied ever having done these things, although she admitted to once having flipped a potato pancake onto the stove. Television viewers may have seen numerous Julia Child parodies, including a *Saturday Night Live* show in which she was lampooned in a sketch where she tried to bone a chicken and created mayhem in her kitchen (Michaels & Wilson, 1978). It is possible that viewers may have confused such parodies with the actual cooking show, suggesting that memory content may consist of a combination of actual events, displaced events, and fantasy. When I have used this anecdote in lectures, I have intentionally misstated the identity of the actor who portrayed Julia Child as Chevy Chase; in fact, it was actually Dan Aykroyd. I further enhance the suggestion by asking members of the audience to see if they can picture the scene in their minds. I then debrief the audience and point out that if I hadn't disclosed the suggestion, some of them would have fully incorporated the pseudomemory and would have subsequently recalled the wrong actor in the sketch.

An experiment by Loftus and colleagues (1993) further demonstrated that vivid visual memories can be created simply by being told of events by a trusted other person. In the experimental protocol, a family member attempted to instill a memory of an episode of being lost at the age of 5 in another family member. All family members agreed that the episode had never occurred. In one example, a story was told to Chris, age 14, by his older brother:

> It was 1981 or 1982. I remember that Chris was 5. We had gone shopping at the University City shopping mall in Spokane. After some panic, we found Chris being led down the mall by a tall, oldish man (I think he was wearing a flannel shirt). Chris was crying and holding the man's hand. The man explained that he had found Chris walking around crying his eyes out just a few moments before and was trying to help him find his parents. (p. 532)

Over the following days, Chris began to have fragmentary memories of this event. By the end of two weeks, he had a vivid memory of being lost:

> I was with you guys for a second and I think I went over to look at the toy store, the Kay-Bee toy, and uh, we got lost and I was looking around and I thought, "Uh-oh. I'm in trouble now." You know. And then I ... I thought I was never going to see my family again. I was really scared, you know. And then this old man, I think he was wearing a blue flannel, came up to me ... he was kind of old. He was kind of bald on top ... he had like a ring of gray hair ... and he had glasses.

Even after being told about the experiment, Chris still had trouble believing that the incident had not occurred. Although this experiment has been criticized for ethical and methodologic problems (Crook & Dean, 1999), it does illustrate the potential creation of pseudomemories when an individual is urged to believe false events by a trusted other person, which has obvious implications for the process of psychotherapy.

Is there a population of persons who are susceptible to creating pseudomemories? Psychologist Ira Hyman, PhD, and colleagues attempted to implant false memories of childhood events in college students. In serial interviews over a few weeks, participants were asked to describe both real events (from information supplied by parents) and told that they had experienced events that hadn't actually occurred. Over several interviews, approximately 8% of participants developed vivid pseudomemories of false events, as in the following description (Hyman, Troy, & Billings, 1995, p. 191) (I = interviewer, S = subject):

First Interview
  I: The next one is attending a wedding. At age 6 you attended a wedding reception and while you were running around with some other kids you bumped into a table and turned over a punch bowl on a parent of the bride.
  S: I have no clue. I have never heard that one before. Age 6?
  I: Uh-huh.

S: No clue.

I: Can you think of any details?

S: Six years old, we would have been in Spokane, um, not at all.

Second Interview

I: The next one was when you were 6 years old and you were attending a wedding.

S: The wedding was my best friend in Spokane, T___. Her brother, older brother was getting married, and it was over here in P___, Washington, because that's where her family was from and it was in the summer or spring because it was really hot outside and it was right on the water. It was an outdoor wedding and I think we were running around and knocked over like the punch bowl or something and um made a big mess and of course got yelled at for it. But uh.

I: Do you remember anything else?

S: No.

I: OK.

In a similar experiment, researchers found that vivid pseudomemories increased from 9% to 25% if participants were asked to internally visualize the false events in detail (Hyman & Pentland, 1996). These studies support the contention that pseudomemories can be induced, particularly with repeated suggestion, rehearsal, and the use of imagery. It should be noted, however, that only a minority of participants responded to cues to remember false events, suggesting that certain individuals may have more vulnerability than others to creating pseudomemories.

The suggestibility of younger children has been studied by psychologists Stephen Ceci, PhD, and Mary Lyn Huffman, PhD (1997). In their studies, preschool children were interviewed on multiple occasions and were given suggestions about fictitious events. For example, in one protocol (Ceci, Huffman, Smith, & Loftus, 1994), children were asked to "think real hard before answering" a variety of different events, including a presumably false experience of "get[ting] your hand caught in a mousetrap and go[ing] to the hospital to get it off." Over the course of 10 interviews, a majority of 3- and 4-year-old children remembered these false events as true, as did a lesser number of 5- and 6-year-olds. Subsequent to the experiments, neither parents nor researchers were able to convince some of the children that the events had not occurred. Videotapes of some of the interviews of children were shown to experts in the field of children's forensic testimony. These experts were unable to distinguish between true and false accounts. These studies support the intuitive notion that younger children have difficulty distinguishing between reality and fantasy, and they are vulnerable to suggestion. This type of research further complicates the issue of validity of memory, not only in children who report abuse, but in adults as well. Even if adults report that they have always remembered past events, it is possible that the original events could have been related to fantasy or suggestion, or misremembered.

The 1989 criminal prosecution case of Paul Ingram added evidence to the notion of the creation of pseudomemory. As described by social psychologist Richard Ofshe, PhD (1992), and Loftus (1993), Ingram, a devout Catholic and the chair of his county Republican Party committee, was accused of the sexual abuse of his daughter and other children and participation in satanic cult activities including ritual sexual abuse and murder. At first, he denied everything. However, after interrogation and pressure from advisors, Ingram began to have vivid memories of his involvement in the alleged abuse. Ofshe, an expert witness, attempted to test Ingram's suggestibility. He told Ingram that he had been accused of forcing his son and daughter to have sex together, an event that his children agreed had *not* occurred. Ingram initially had no memory of this event, but after being urged to think about the scene, he began to vividly recall it and eventually confessed to the alleged activities. This apparent pseudomemory does not necessarily invalidate Ingram's other recollections. In fact, another psychologist involved with the case reported that Ingram pled guilty to six counts of child molestation after "care was taken to eliminate those allegations that could have been contaminated by the investigator's questioning or by contact with the daughters and Mr. Ingram" (Peterson, 1994, p. 443). However, this case does raise issues concerning the effect on memory of questioning, suggestion, and interrogation in both legal and clinical settings.

From the perspective of the FMSF, pseudomemories of traumatic events that never occurred derive principally from suggestive therapy techniques. In fact, several other mechanisms are much more likely to produce inauthentic reports of childhood abuse. *Contagion* is a powerful mechanism in which individuals unconsciously adopt other persons' personal narratives as their own. One of the liabilities of specialized treatment programs for trauma patients is that patients are exposed to the personal stories of other patients and can possibly come to believe that they too were similarly victimized. Closely related to the mechanism of contagion is what I call *unconscious elaboration*, in which individuals come to erroneously believe that they were (or may have been) traumatized in ways that they do not remember or have only vague hints about, as in the following example:

> Meg, a 52-year-old single financial advisor, had been in various forms of psychotherapy most of her adult life for reasons that were unclear but compelling. She had always felt that something was missing in her life, and that kept her feeling isolated from intimacy with other people. Attractive, accomplished, and articulate, Meg had always wanted marriage and children, but these dreams had eluded her. She often wondered if her difficulties stemmed from secrets buried by her Christian Science family's insistence on dwelling on only the positive and not acknowledging illness and distress, including secrets about sexual abuse. She recalled her father as a sexual man who had confided in her that he had no active sexual life with her mother. In a therapy session, while recalling various times when she had been ill as a child and received no medical care, Meg had the memory of being a young child and feeling her father's body lying on top of

her while he kissed her on the mouth. She immediately concluded that this was evidence of the sexual abuse she had long suspected. However, as she continued to think about the memory, she recalled that as a child she had come down with croup (swelling of the vocal cords resulting in a barking cough and difficulty breathing) and that there were family stories of her father performing mouth-to-mouth resuscitation, forcing air into her lungs to keep her alive. This was not the confirmation she sought, and the question of possible childhood sexual abuse remained unanswered.

There are clinical situations where patients fail to perceive that what they already remember accounts for their current distress and difficulties, and they continue to look for evidence of more obvious and egregious abuse. These kinds of situations need to be managed with particular care. While not ruling out the possibility of unremembered abuse, clinicians should counsel restraint in advising patients on how to approach their search for memories, as in the following clinical illustration:

Sarah, a 47-year-old marketing executive, consulted me for her long-standing depression and current life adaptations, which included a sense that she was unworthy of anyone else's care or attention. Many of her difficulties clearly derived from her childhood experience where she was devalued by her parents for being a girl, unlike her two brothers who were praised and supported. Her parents were either distant or angry and physically abusive. Despite all the chaos that she experienced growing up, Sarah did quite well, marrying a kind and loving (though somewhat distant) man and raising a family in addition to having a successful career. However, she was left with a sense of lingering emptiness and an indefinable sense of being defective. It was a struggle for her to know how to ask anyone else for help despite her sense that others generally liked her.

In the course of the evaluation, Sarah told me that she had always wondered about whether she had been sexually abused by her father. Although she had no memory of such abuse, she wondered if that was the reason she felt defective and somewhat alienated from others. Plus, she added, she was aware of her father's sexuality and that on various occasions he looked at her in an inappropriately sexual way. Sarah had no memories of sexual abuse (despite trying to remember), and her memory for her childhood was generally intact and continuous. After some continued discussion, I remarked that while I couldn't rule out sexual abuse, it didn't seem likely given her efforts to remember it and her years of psychotherapy. I explained that the history that she already knew could fully account for her psychological distress. I suggested that while we couldn't rule out the possibility of sexual abuse, her efforts should be directed at fully understanding how profoundly the early attachment problems and persistent denigration affected the way she came to feel about herself and what she deserved from others. Sarah seemed generally relieved by our discussion.

Under different circumstances, it might have been entirely possible for this patient to falsely believe that she had been sexually abused (and maybe even to develop pseudomemories), because her perception of her childhood difficulties were not enough to justify how bad she sometimes felt. However, developing erroneous beliefs about sexual abuse would have been a red herring at best and a major impediment to progress at worst.

The contributions of memory research raise many thorny questions, some of which challenge clinical observations. For example, cognitive psychology research does not empirically substantiate the existence of the psychoanalytic theory of repression, despite the utility of this concept in clinical practice. Memory research does not provide an explanation of how traumatic memories that were once conscious become nonconscious other than through normal forgetting, selective inattention, or avoidance. However, it is problematic to extrapolate experimental findings to clinical situations. As several investigators have noted, experimental conditions are often quite different from actual clinical situations—so-called ecological factors (Erdelyi, 1985; Holmes, 1974, 1990; Schacter, 1990). Experimental investigations of traumatic memory are limited by the ethical constraints, and thus cannot expose participants to truly overwhelming and prolonged traumatic events. Thus, results from experimental psychology may be limited in understanding the actual impact of traumatic events. Nonetheless, a clear understanding of the mechanisms of memory is critical in evaluating clinical reports of traumatic memory and clinical situations.

STUDIES OF TRAUMATIC AMNESIA

Memory loss as a component of stressful events is a part of our cultural heritage (e.g., stories in literature and film about persons who have been through some kind of trauma and lose their sense of identity and/or memory of the event). As discussed in previous chapters, amnesia for traumatic events first experienced in adulthood is relatively uncommon but does occur. In past decades, amnesia was observed in combat veterans from World War I (W. Brown, 1919; Thom & Fenton, 1920) and World War II (Henderson & Moore, 1944; Sargant & Slater, 1941; Torrie, 1944), and in Holocaust survivors (Jaffe, 1968; Kuch & Cox, 1992; Wagenaar & Groenweg, 1960). However, given the higher dissociative capacity of some children, amnesia is much more common for traumatic events that occur at an early age.

Amnesia for Childhood Sexual Abuse in Clinical Populations

How common is amnesia for childhood events in the aftermath of trauma? There has been an explosion of studies in this area published since 1987. In a review paper on the evidence for dissociative amnesia and recovered memory, Brown, Scheflin, and Whitfield (1999) identified 68 studies, all of which found some degree of dissociative amnesia following sexual abuse. Since that time, more than two dozen additional

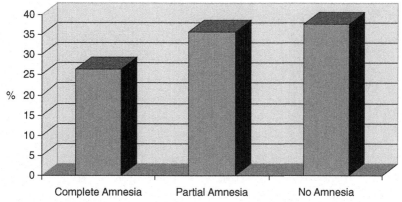

Figure 5.1　Percent of Adult Patients Reporting Amnesia for Sexual Abuse ($N = 53$)

papers have been published in this area. Given the number of papers, I will not attempt to summarize them all, instead presenting only those that are of particular interest from a clinical or historical perspective. The first published study concerning the nature of amnesia for childhood abuse and validity of recovered memories was reported by Herman and her colleague Emily Schatzhow (1987). Their study involved 53 women who had sought treatment in time-limited incest survivors' groups at Cambridge Hospital in Massachusetts. A majority of these women reported that they had experienced some kind of amnesia for their sexual abuse at some time in the past (Figure 5.1). Twenty-six percent (26%) reported that they had severe amnesia (e.g., at some point had no memory for the abuse), 36% reported moderate amnesia (e.g., remembered only some or part of the events), and the remaining 38% always fully remembered the abuse.

More amnesia was correlated with early age of onset of the abuse, chronic abuse, and severity of abuse, such as violent or sadistic abuse. Perhaps even more notable was that the overwhelming majority of these women were able to find some corroborating evidence of the abuse (Figure 5.2). Seventy-four percent (74%) were able to find convincing evidence that the incest had occurred, such as family members who confirmed it, or in one case, papers and other evidence from a deceased brother who had been the abuse perpetrator. Another 9% found family members who indicated that they thought the abuse had likely occurred but who could not confirm it. Eleven percent (11%) made no attempt to corroborate their abuse, leaving only 6% who could find no validating evidence despite efforts to do so.

Rates of amnesia remarkably similar to these were found in several subsequent studies. In one study (Gold, Hughes, & Hohnecker, 1994), patients who reported sexual abuse at an initial intake at an outpatient mental health center were asked detailed questions about their ability to recall the abuse. Thirty percent (30%) reported periods of no memory of the abuse, 40% had some partial memory (i.e., evidence of abuse but no clear memory, memory of some aspects, or memory of some but not all episodes), and

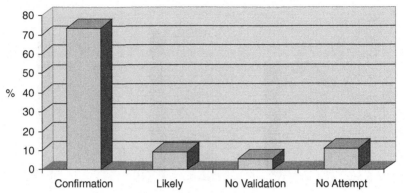

Figure 5.2 Percent of Adult Patients Who Sought Corroboration of Sexual Abuse (*N* = 53)

30% reported complete and continuous memory. Another study investigated the experiences of 60 patients in psychotherapy who recalled being sexually abused (Cameron, 1994). Of the participants in this study, 42% had a period of complete amnesia for the abuse, 23% reported partial amnesia, and 35% had no amnesia.

Psychologists John Briere, PhD, and John Conte, PhD (1993), recruited therapists to administer a questionnaire to their patients who reported sexual abuse memories. The questionnaire consisted of a variety of scales about current symptomatology and past life experiences. Of the 450 subjects who reported childhood sexual abuse, 54% reported having had some amnesia for the abuse between the time of occurrence and age 18. Greater levels of amnesia were correlated with greater current levels of psychiatric symptoms, early age of onset and severity (e.g., multiple perpetrators, physical injury, fear of death if they revealed the abuse). Interestingly, the researchers also asked about factors that were likely to produce a greater level of psychological conflict, such as enjoying aspects of the abuse or accepting bribes. These factors were not correlated with amnesia, suggesting that the physical noxiousness of the experience, rather than intrapsychic conflict, may produce amnesia.

Herman and psychologist Mary Harvey, PhD (1997), reviewed detailed clinical evaluations at the Victims of Violence program at Cambridge Hospital for documentation of amnesia and corroboration of their abuse experiences. For those reporting sexual and physical abuse or witnessing of intrafamilial violence, approximately half (53%) reported continuous memory, 17% described both continuous and delayed recall (for different incidents of abuse), and 16% reported a period of complete amnesia for their abuse followed by delayed recall. Forty-three percent (43%) spontaneously described some corroboration of their abuse experiences, and there were no significant differences in the rates of corroboration between those with and without delayed recall. Most patients cited reminders of the trauma or a recent life crisis or milestone as the precipitant for recovering memory; only 28% described psychotherapy as the reason for memory recovery. In fact, the recall of new, disturbing memories was frequently cited as the reason these patients sought psychotherapy.

A study by Loftus and colleagues (Loftus, Polonsky, & Fullilove, 1994) is particularly interesting given Loftus' advocacy of the false memory hypothesis. More than half (54%) of 105 women in outpatient treatment for substance abuse reported childhood sexual abuse. Most (81%) reported remembering part or all of the abuse (partial amnesia or no amnesia), and 19% reported that they forgot the abuse for a period (complete amnesia).

The rates of amnesia in the studies cited in this chapter and others in the literature are remarkably consistent. As noted in Brown, Scheflin, and Whitfield's (1999) review, "[R]oughly one-third of patients across [the 25 clinical] studies reporting that they had completely forgotten the abuse for some period of time. Substantial forgetting of the childhood sexual abuse was found in *every clinical study*, without exception" (p. 54).

Amnesia for Childhood Sexual Abuse in Nonclinical Populations

Studies in nonclinical populations of individuals with documented histories of sexual abuse—who presumably have fewer distressing symptoms than patient groups—have nonetheless shown high rates of amnesia for childhood abuse. Psychologists Linda Meyer Williams, PhD, and Victoria Banyard, PhD, studied women (Williams, 1994) and men (Williams & Banyard, 1997) who had been treated for documented sexual abuse 17 years earlier in a city hospital, and asked them to participate in a study about hospital services. Thirty-eight percent (38%) of the women and 55% of the men did not recall the abuse or chose not to report it. Although the investigators did not ask specifically about the documented abuse, the participants were asked about sexual abuse experiences; many of the women in Williams' studies who did not report the early abuse did disclose other intimate details about their lives, including subsequent sexual victimization. Hence, there is a strong implication that many were actually amnestic for the experiences. There was a correlation between amnesia and younger age at time of abuse, which would be expected because verbal recall of events is limited for events experienced before age 3. However, this factor alone could not explain the degree of amnesia in the subject population. Few of the women had been under 3 years of age at the time of their abuse, and there was actually more amnesia in the 4- to 6-year-old group versus the under age 3 group. More amnesia was associated with perpetrators being family members. Amnesia was not correlated with any particular kind of abuse or severity of abuse (e.g., fondling versus penetration).

Psychologists Shirley Feldman-Summers, PhD, and Kenneth Pope, PhD (1994), studied another nonclinical population. They surveyed 330 randomly chosen psychologists and found that 24% reported a history of physical abuse and 22% reported a history of sexual abuse. Of the participants with histories of abuse, 40% reported a period when they had no memory for the abuse, and 47% reported that they had obtained some kind of corroboration of the abuse experiences. Fifty-six percent (56%) identified psychotherapy as a factor in recalling the abuse.

Corroboration of Childhood Abuse

Several of the studies cited previously involved asking about participants' attempts to validate their memories of childhood abuse and reported relatively high rates of some kind of corroboration (Feldman-Summers & Pope, 1994; Herman & Harvey, 1997; Herman & Schatzhow, 1987). At least two studies have used relatively stringent standards of corroboration. Psychiatrist Richard Kluft, MD (1995), surveyed the detailed records that he had kept of 34 patients with dissociative identity disorder (DID) that he had flagged for either confirmed or disconfirmed memories. For corroboration of memories, he required a report (either directly or through the patient) that another person, such as a family member, relative, or friend, had actually witnessed the abuse, or a confession by the alleged perpetrator of abuse. Nineteen of the patients (56%) had been able to obtain confirmation of childhood abuse. Three of the patients (9%) had memories that were later disconfirmed. Of the 19 patients who obtained confirmation of particular abusive experiences, 10 (53%) had always remembered the events, and 13 (68%) first recalled specific events in therapy. Two patients were able to ascertain that they had both valid memories and pseudomemories. The use of hypnosis was not a factor in the validity of memory recall; many of the corroborated memories (85%) were accessed through hypnotic techniques.

In the study that our McLean group published in 1999 (Chu et al., 1999), we attempted to replicate findings concerning childhood abuse experiences and resulting amnesia in psychiatric patients, the circumstances concerning memory recovery, and the extent to which patients had been able to corroborate their recovered abuse memories. The participants in our study were 90 patients in the Trauma and Dissociative Disorders Program at McLean. Not surprisingly, they endorsed a high level of childhood maltreatment, often having been the victim of multiple types of chronic abuse beginning at an early age. They also had experiences concerning amnesia and recovered memory consistent with previous studies (Figure 5.3).

Participants endorsed both complete and partial amnesia for all types of abuse— physical and sexual abuse and witnessing violence—generally in the 20% to 30% range.

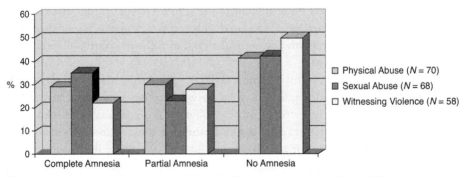

Figure 5.3 Percent of Participants With and Without Amnesia by Type of Abuse

Table 5.1   Corroboration of Recovered Memories of Childhood Abuse

Participants who reported complete amnesia and recovered memory for:	Attempt to corroborate?	
	Yes	No
Physical abuse (*N* = 20)	14	6
Sexual abuse (*N* = 25)	19	6
Witnessing violence (*N* = 12)	6	6

Participants who attempted corroboration of recovered memory of abuse for:	Physical evidence?		Verbal validation?	
	Yes	No	Yes	No
Physical abuse (*N* = 14)	5	9	13	1
Sexual abuse (*N* = 19)	5	14	17	2
Witnessing violence (*N* = 6)	3	3	3	3

Our findings concerning corroboration were quite striking (Table 5.1). We asked patients whether they had ever sought to validate abuse experiences that they had previously forgotten and subsequently recovered, and found that a high percentage of those who reported physical and sexual abuse had made some attempt to do so. We considered the recovered memory of abuse experiences to have been corroborated if there was concrete physical evidence (e.g., scars, medical or police records) or if the participants told us that others (such as a family member or the perpetrator) had confirmed that they knew the abuse had occurred. We did not accept reports that a family member thought that the abuse might likely have occurred or that a sibling had been similarly abused as corroboration of recovered memories.

Approximately three-quarters of participants who had amnesia and recovered memory of physical and sexual abuse had made some attempt to corroborate their memories; fewer participants felt the need to corroborate witnessing violence. There was little physical evidence to validate recovered memories, but for physical and sexual abuse, the overwhelming majority of participants had been able to find others who confirmed that the abuse had occurred: 13 of 14 (93%) for physical abuse and 17 of 19 (89%) for sexual abuse.

Critiques of Studies of Amnesia for Childhood Abuse

One of the criticisms of prevalence studies of childhood trauma and subsequent amnesia is that many of the studies are based on a self-report methodology, and individuals may falsely report early abuse (for reasons including confusion, confabulation, and fantasy, among others). However, self-report methodology is widely used in clinical research, and there is no reason to suspect that traumatized persons are more likely than others to distort or fabricate their histories. In fact, false-negative responses concerning amnesia are more likely than false-positive ones. For example, if an individual develops amnesia for childhood abuse and has not yet recovered those memories, that individual would be categorized as having "no amnesia."

There is another source of possible false-negative responses. When asked about childhood maltreatment, research participants do not always characterize clearly abusive experiences as such. For example, in Widom and Shepard's (1996) prospective study of recall and accuracy of sexual abuse, significant percentages of both men and women with confirmed childhood sexual abuse did not report it when interviewed 20 years later. However, it is unclear whether this was the result of traumatic amnesia, normal forgetting, or—as was the case with more men than women—that they did not acknowledge the childhood sexual encounters as sexual abuse.

There have been other criticisms of the methodology of various studies, including the vagueness in the definition of *forgetting* or *remembering*; not taking into account the phenomena of normal forgetting and normal infantile amnesia for very early experiences; the lack of clear, independent corroboration of abuse experiences; sampling biases; and methods or questions used in inquiries (Loftus, 1993; Ofshe & Singer, 1994; Pope & Hudson, 1995). However, the weight of the evidence is clear, as articulated by Brown, Scheflin, and Whitfield (1999):

> What is the fairest conclusion that can be made based on the totality of the evidence across all 68 studies on forgetting childhood sexual abuse? The reader should note that not one of the 68 studies failed to find complete forgetting/recovery of abuse memories in at least some portion of the sampled respondents.... The consistent finding favoring dissociative or traumatic amnesia across 68 separate studies representing five diverse research designs and using different methods of measurement by more than 100 authors in nearly all independent studies across several countries greatly increases the likelihood that dissociative or traumatic amnesia demonstrated in each of the 68 studies is a real phenomenon, as opposed to being an artifact of methodology (e.g., retrospective or prospective), sample variation, or measurement error that might or might not have occurred in single studies. (pp. 67–68)

MULTIPLE MEMORY SYSTEMS

In terms of personal experience, individuals tend to equate the term *memory* with verbal and visual memory—mental narratives and images associated with past experiences. However, since the late 19th century, the study of memory has produced descriptions of several forms of memory, suggesting that memory is not a unitary entity but more likely a multidimensional function consisting of various domains and representations of recollections (Polster, Nadel, & Schacter, 1991). Separate and distinct memory systems have been described by many investigators (Milner, 1962; Tulving, 1972, 1983). Harvard research psychologist Daniel Schacter, PhD, ultimately coined the currently accepted descriptive distinctions of two primary memory systems: *explicit* and *implicit memory* (Graf & Schacter, 1985; Schacter, 1987).[2] Explicit memory consists of the recollection of prior experiences with intentional or conscious recall and is generally considered to include verbal and visual memory. Implicit memory refers to performance or behavior based on prior experiences of which one has no conscious recall, including conditioned responses, "priming," and procedural memory (nonconscious motor memories, e.g., bicycle riding). Implicit memory is likely also to be the active process in affective and somatic memory—that is, recall or reexperience of emotions and bodily sensations (Crabtree, 1992; Erdelyi, 1990).

Research on "priming," a type of implicit memory, sheds further light on the nature of conscious and nonconscious mental processes (Schacter, 1985, 1992). Priming is generally a laboratory procedure that refers to facilitation of a simple cognitive task (e.g., object recognition or word completion) as a result of a prior encounter with the cue and independent of conscious recollection of that encounter. For example, college student research participants who have previously been shown lists of words are much more likely to recognize those words in other lists even after several weeks when they have no conscious recollection of the original words. Even more remarkably, patients with organic amnesia (who for reasons of brain injury are unable to prospectively retain conscious information) do similarly well on such tasks, indicating that implicit memory is a nonconscious process that operates quite separately from conscious recall. The findings strongly suggest that memory and memory processing are highly complex, with multiple memory systems involved in the acquisition, retention, and recall of information. This theory of separate and independently functioning memory systems supports the clinical observations in PTSD patients that certain kinds of emotions and somatic sensations may be experienced without conscious awareness of their traumatic origins.

Prospective studies by Burgess and her colleagues of 42 children who had been sexually abused in military day care centers highlighted the differences between types of recall (Burgess, Baker, & Hartman, 1996; Burgess & Hartman, 2005). In their studies, the investigators interviewed the children and their parents several times during the 15 years after the documented abuse. The mean age of the children at the time of abuse was 3.6 years. In the investigations following the revelation of their abuse nearly all of the children had verbal memory of the experience (i.e., they were able to verbally describe what had happened). When they were interviewed 5 to 15 years later, only some were able to verbally recall what happened, although many had behavioral reenactments of their

---

[2] These categories replace the older terminology of *declarative memory* and *procedural memory*. Declarative memory is defined as conscious recall of information and experiences ("knowing what") and is further subdivided into semantic memory (general recall independent of context, e.g., facts) and episodic memory (recall that depends on context such as time, place, or personal experience); declarative memory falls within the category of explicit memory. Procedural memory is defined as the nonconscious retrieval of the ability to do things ("knowing how," e.g., motor skills) and is considered part of the current classification of implicit memory.

abuse. Is this evidence of traumatic amnesia? Possibly, but alternative explanations include normal forgetting and immature memory functioning in the very young children. However, this study is particularly interesting; some of the accounts of the aftereffects of the abuse demonstrate the different kinds of recollections of some of the children:

> Tim had initially disclosed to being driven to an off campus house, tied to a tree in the woods and being physically hit. He said that something had been pushed into his bottom. Somatic and behavioral memories were noted in his persistent complaints of anal pain and fear that something was in his rectum. He would clench his legs, defecate and urinate on the floor and rug and avoid using the bathroom. Abdominal pains were frequent as well as the preoccupation that something was in his rectum. He and his parents did not link this to the abuse itself, although he could recollect that he was hurt at the day care center. (Burgess, 2008)

This account demonstrates the presence of both explicit and implicit memory of the abuse, and that the two systems can be dissociated from each other in conscious awareness. The psychological gain of the dissociation of information from the different memory systems is that both the parents and child can avoid being overwhelmed by the full impact of the experience and the aftereffects of the abuse by recalling and experiencing it in a compartmentalized way.

Terr observed the existence of various kinds of memory in response to traumatic events in childhood. In one study of preschool children who had been subjected to known traumatic events (Terr, 1988), verbal recall of the events depended on the child's age when traumatized and on the chronicity of the trauma. Children under 3 years of age tended to have less verbal memory of their experiences, a finding that is consistent with the development of verbal abilities around this period (Miller, 1979; Williams & Banyard, 1997). However, even some of these very young children appeared to have retained some type of nonverbal learning concerning the traumatic events, engaging in behavioral reenactments (e.g., trauma-related play, fears, and dreams) despite having no conscious recall. In her 1988 study of 20 children who were under the age of 5 at the time of the trauma, Terr noted that

> Ages 28 to 36 months, at the time of the trauma serves as an approximate cut-off point separating those children who can fully verbalize their past experiences from those who can do so in part or not at all.... At any age, however, behavioral memories of trauma remain quite accurate and true to the events that stimulated them. (p. 96)

Bruce D. Perry, MD, PhD, a noted expert on the effects of trauma on children, has also observed that implicit recall of trauma can exist even when there is no explicit memory. In a 1999 book chapter titled "Memories of States: How the Brain Stores and

Retrieves Traumatic Experience," Perry provided several fascinating (albeit tragic) examples of unusual expressions of recall in traumatized children:

> D. is a nine-year-old boy. He was victim of chronic and pervasive physical threat and abuse from his biological father. From the age of two until six he was physically and sexually abused by his father. At age six he was removed from the family.... He suffered from serious brain injury such that he was in a coma for eight months following the injury. He continues to be difficult to arouse, is nonverbal, no form of meaningful communication is noted. In the presence of his biological father, he began to scream, moan, his heart rate increased dramatically. Audiotapes of his biological father elicit a similar response. Clearly the sensory information (sounds, smells) which was associated with father was reaching this child's brain in a way that elicited a state memory. This child's brain did not have the capacity to have conscious perception of the presence of his father.... Exposure to his father elicited no cognitive, narrative memory; his agitation and increased heart rate were manifestations of affective and state memories which were the products of many years of traumatic terror which had become associated with his father—and all of his father's attributes. (p. 25)

In another example, Perry described implicit recall in a child who was too young to have narrative explicit memories of an extremely traumatic event:

> K is a three-year-old boy referred to our clinic following the murder of his eighteen-month-old sister.... Approximately two months after the event, a semi-structured interview was conducted. During the non-intrusive part of the interview, K was spontaneous, interactive, smiling and age-appropriate in his play. When the direct questioning [about witnessing the murder] began, his heart rate increased but his behaviors remained constant. Within five seconds of being asked about his sister, his heart rate dramatically increased and his play stopped. He broke eye-contact, physically slowed and became essentially non-responsive. This dissociative response was accompanied by a decrease in his heart rate to the previous baseline level of the free play portion of the interview. Similar alterations in heart rate and induction of a protective dissociative response could be elicited by exposure to cues associated with the murder. In this situation, this child, upon direct questioning, gave no verbal or narrative information about the event. This lack of a narrative memory, however, did not mean that the child had not stored the experience. Clearly, he demonstrated clear and unambiguous evidence of emotional and state memories when verbal or non-verbal cues were used to evoke the event. (pp. 30–31)

As in these examples, multiple memory systems are active in the recall of trauma, and the various parameters of traumatic experience—visual, verbal, affective, somatic, and behavioral—can be later reexperienced in a variety of ways, both conscious and non-conscious. Thus, it is important in the clinical arena to have a broad understanding of the diverse ways that traumatic experience can later manifest, which is necessary to adequately treat patients who suffer from the effects of early abuse. In particular, understanding the implicit memory of behaviors, feelings, and sensations of trauma in the absence of—or dissociated from—conscious explicit memory can help patients (and their treaters) make sense of their current experiences.

THE NEUROBIOLOGY OF TRAUMATIC AMNESIA

What are the underlying causes and mechanisms for traumatic amnesia? In many of the aforementioned examples, neurodevelopmental factors as well as psychodynamic and cognitive mechanisms have profound effects on persons' inability to recall traumatic events. However, there are likely additional neurobiological etiologies for amnesia, particularly in relation to the pervasive amnesia for "whole segments of childhood" (Terr, 1991, p. 16) as a response to chronic traumatization at an early age. The forgetting of all memories—not just the negative ones—implies that the underlying mechanism for this kind of amnesia is not repression of overwhelming experiences or selective inattention to noxious events. Instead, the massive failure to integrate entire periods of childhood strongly suggests that intensely traumatic experiences may result in a different way of processing and storing information, perhaps mediated by chronically elevated levels of stress-induced neurohormones. This model is consistent with the concept of dissociation, in which various mental contents exist in different states held separately from each other, which may derive from numerous different mechanisms.

The psychobiology of learning and memory suggests that traumatic memory is quite different from ordinary memory. Many investigators propose that the symptoms of PTSD result from the multifaceted neurohormonal changes that occur in response to acute and chronic stress (for reviews, see Charney, Deutch, Krystal, Southwick, & Davis, 1993; Krystal, Bennett, Bremner, Southwick, & Charney, 1996; van der Kolk, 1996; Vermetten & Bremner, 2002a, 2002b). These changes may powerfully affect the ways in which memory is encoded, stored, and retrieved.[3] At least three stress-responsive neurohormonal systems have emerged as critical in the development of PTSD: (1) catecholamines, including adrenaline, noradrenaline, and dopamine, which modulate bodily activation and arousal particularly in stressful emergency situations; (2) hormones of the hypothalamic-pituitary-adrenal (HPA) axis, including corticotropin-releasing factor (CRF), adrenocorticotropic hormone (ACTH), and the

---

[3] It should be noted that although many physiologic changes have been observed in PTSD patients, some of the stress-responsive neurohormonal changes (especially in the brain) have been observed only in animal models, and the applications of these models to humans with PTSD remains somewhat speculative.

glucocorticoids, which have an essential role in maintaining physiological and psychological homeostasis; and (3) endogenous opioids, which are opiate-like substances produced by the body in response to stress. Persistent increases in catecholamine activity, alterations in hormonal functions in the HPA axis, and opioid responses have all been documented in patients with PTSD (Bremner, Krystal, Southwick, & Charney, 1996a, 1996b; McFall, Murburg, Roszell, & Veith, 1989; Pitman & Orr, 1990; Pitman, van der Kolk, Orr, & Greenberg, 1990; Southwick et al., 1997; Yehuda, Giller, Southwick, Lowy, & Mason, 1991; Young & Breslau, 2004).

Patients with PTSD exhibit multiple symptoms of heightened autonomic arousal, including exaggerated startle response, increased response to stress-related stimuli, panic attacks, and hypervigilance. Many investigators have suggested that the physiological arousal found in PTSD is caused by chronic elevations in both central and peripheral catecholamine functioning (for reviews, see Pitman & Orr, 1990; Southwick et al., 1997). In the model of "inescapable shock," for example, laboratory animals who are unable to avoid aversive stimuli show dramatic increases in catecholamine activity and persistent elevations of catecholamines that are slow to subside (van der Kolk, Greenberg, Boyd, & Krystal, 1985). Even brief reexposure to the aversive stimuli results in a similar increase in catecholamine activity with a delayed decline. This animal model appears very similar to the physiologic reactivity in humans with PTSD. After being triggered with a reminder of the trauma, the individual's autonomic system is oversimulated (experienced as anxiety, jumpiness, startle responses, difficulty sleeping), and this overactive response is abnormally slow to subside.

In extensive animal studies, neurophysiologist James McGaugh, PhD, and others have shown substantial effects of neurohormones such as catecholamines on retention of newly learned material (McGaugh, 1989; McGaugh, Introini, & Castellano, 1993). Exposure to catecholamines immediately post-learning affects performance in a dose-dependent fashion. Low to moderate levels of epinephrine enhance retention of newly learned material. However, higher doses actually interfere with learning. Thus, an attenuated catecholamine response to a traumatic event might enhance memory, whereas unusually high levels of catecholamines (such as seen in chronic traumatization) might block memory formation. In a study of catecholamine enhancement of memory retention (Cahill, Prins, Weber, & McGaugh, 1994), participants were shown slides of a neutral story and a more emotional story about a boy in a life-threatening situation. One group of participants was given propranolol, a drug that blocks the activity of the beta-adrenergic receptors of the autonomic nervous system, and inhibits the release of catecholamines. Both groups had a similar level of recall for the neutral story, but the group receiving the drug had significantly less recall for the details of the more emotional story as compared to the control group. This study supports the theory that acute catecholamine elevations enhance memory, making traumatic memories more indelible than ordinary memories.

Hormonal activity in the HPA axis is highly responsive to acute stress, producing an immediate increase in CRF, ACTH, and glucocorticoids (Yehuda et al., 1991). Findings concerning glucocorticoid levels in traumatized populations have varied considerably. Although several studies have found elevated glucocorticoid levels as compared to control subjects (Lemieux & Coe, 1993; Maes et al., 1998; Pitman & Orr, 1990; Rasmusson et al., 2001), other studies have found similar levels (Baker et al., 1999; Mason, Wang, Riney, Charney, & Southwick, 2001; Young & Breslau, 2004), and at least one study demonstrated lower levels (Yehuda, Teicher, Trestman, Levengood, & Siever, 1996). A more recent study suggests that some of the variability may have to do with age when an individual was traumatized, if the trauma was recent, or total lifetime trauma experiences (Friedman, Jalowiec, McHugo, Wang, & McDonagh, 2007).

Glucocorticoid receptors are particularly abundant in the hippocampus, a brain structure thought to be central in memory function. Hippocampal neuronal degeneration has been demonstrated in monkeys after either prolonged stress or prolonged administration of glucocorticoids (Sapolsky, 1986; Sapolsky, Krey, & McEwen, 1986; Sapolsky, Uno, Rebert, & Finch, 1990), leading some investigators to suggest that elevated levels of glucocorticoids may be toxic to the hippocampus, resulting in actual neuronal cell death. Reduced hippocampal volume (as measured by magnetic resonance imaging) has been demonstrated in studies of veterans with combat-related PTSD (Bremner et al., 1995; Wignall et al., 2004) and in patients with PTSD associated with childhood physical and sexual abuse (Bremner et al., 1997), but other studies have not observed such changes (Jatzko et al., 2006; Yehuda et al., 2007). However, irrespective of hippocampal volume changes, attentional and short-term memory difficulties are found in PTSD (Bremner et al., 1997; Bremner et al., 1995; Yehuda et al., 2007); if they are associated with changes in brain structures, they may not be reversible, implying that treatment interventions should focus on compensating for these deficits (e.g., using different learning strategies).

Stress-induced analgesia that is attributed to the release of endogenous opioids has been observed in both animal models and humans (Hemingway & Reigle, 1987; McGaugh et al., 1993; Willer, Dehen, & Cambier, 1981). In several studies, the effects of endogenous opioids have been indirectly measured by using the opiate antagonist, naltrexone, to block stress-induced analgesia in PTSD subjects (Ibarra et al., 1994; Pitman et al., 1990; van der Kolk, Greenberg, Orr, & Pitman, 1989). Endogenous opioids are known to have inhibitory action in the amygdala (McGaugh, 1989, 1992), a brain area believed to be central in the emotional evaluation of information (Davis, 1992). McGaugh's studies in animals showed that low doses of opioids suppress learning and diminish the enhancement effects of epinephrine (McGaugh et al., 1993), suggesting that activation of the endogenous opioid system may have a negative effect on establishing memory for traumatic experiences.

Perry (1999) described a traumatized boy who may well have been shown evidence of an endogenous opioid response to reminders of early abuse:

F. is a fifteen-year-old male. From birth to age eight, he was continually exposed to severe physical abuse from his biological father. He witnessed many episodes of his mother being severely beaten by his father. As he grew older, he attempted to intervene and was seriously injured on several occasions. At age eight, his mother left his father.... At age ten he began having syncopal [fainting] episodes of unknown origin. He received multiple evaluations by neurologists and cardiologists who ruled out psychogenic causes of his fainting.... His resting heart rate was 82. When asked about his father, his heart rate fell to 62 and he became very withdrawn. On a walk in the hall, when asked about his abuse, his heart rate fell below 60 and he fainted. He was placed on Trexan, an opioid receptor antagonist, with a marked decrease in his syncope. (pp. 25–26)

A considerable body of research points to state dependence in learning, memory, and recall. That is, when a person is in one emotional and physiologic state, it is more difficult to access memories and experience of a different state (Eich & Metcalfe, 1989; Tobias et al., 1992; van der Kolk, 1994). Because a traumatic experience induces a marked physiological arousal and altered neurohormonal state, it is likely that both the encoding and recall of memory is specific to this state. This may explain trauma-related amnesia and dissociation; especially when PTSD numbing symptoms are predominant and the individual is not physiologically aroused, it may be more difficult to access the traumatic state. Conversely, when presented with cues that are reminiscent of the trauma, access to the traumatic state may be facilitated, leading to flashbacks and other reexperiencing phenomena that may be experienced as disruptive PTSD symptoms, or if modulated, may be useful in certain kinds of exposure therapy.

Finally, based on clinical observation, some investigators (Crabtree, 1992; Kolb, 1987; van der Kolk & Ducey, 1989; van der Kolk & Van der Hart, 1991) have suggested that traumatic memories are stored segregated from ordinary narrative memory and are less subject to ongoing modification in response to new experiences. In contrast to narrative memories that are integrative and malleable, and thus fitted into the individual's personal cognitive schemas, traumatic memories are inflexible, non-narrative, and disconnected from ordinary experience. This lack of integration may be the basis for dissociated remembering through behavioral reenactment, somatic sensation, or intrusive images that are disconnected from conscious verbal memory of events. Because the memories are unprocessed and unassimilated, they retain their original force—"unremembered and therefore unforgettable" (van der Kolk & Ducey, 1989, p. 271). Ordinary narrative memory is dynamic and both changes and degrades over time. In contrast, traumatic memory may be less changeable and has been described as "indelible" (Le Doux, 1992).

EVALUATION OF MEMORY

Given the complexity of memory and memory systems, the risks of distortion of memory content, and the possibility of the creation of pseudomemory through a variety of mechanisms, how does a clinician assess the validity of patients' reports?

Though the primary role for clinicians is not as an investigator, it is critical for patients and their treaters to know what is based on objective reality, what is a screen memory[4] or metaphor, what is conflated or displaced, and what did not actually happen. There is often no possibility of independent corroboration of events that may have taken place long ago, and much of what any individual recalls probably contains distortions. However, the ultimate measure of the accuracy of memory may be the sense of both the patient and the therapist that the patient's history is credible and fits with what is known about the patient's past, with the patient's symptoms, and with who the patient has come to be. Some specific factors may also be helpful in making this determination (Table 5.2).

In clinical practice (and supported by clinical research findings), it is more common for patients to have some—albeit often incomplete—memories of past trauma. They often subsequently recover more details or new memories, although complete amnesia for all abuse experiences does occur in a minority of patients. When patients begin to talk about their abuse histories and/or have new memories of past traumatic events, they do so with difficulty and enormous ambivalence. Not only do they have difficulty finding the words to describe their feelings, but they are reluctant to speak of the events that have been long held in shame and secrecy, which they feel responsible for bringing on themselves. It is thus uncharacteristic for patients with genuine histories of trauma and abuse to embrace their pasts with certainty and easy acceptance.

If clinicians are generally open to the reality of abuse, it is of great importance if they find themselves incredulous when hearing a patient's account of past trauma. For an interested and committed therapist to feel disengaged, or even bored or annoyed, derives from some sensed inauthenticity in the patient's story. Such feelings of the therapist should be carefully heeded and are a sign that the nature and origins of the patient's presentation should be examined. Such reactions may also occur in response to some patients' fixation on the trauma—real or imagined—as if a sole focus on the trauma would fix their entrenched and dysfunctional ways of coping and their sense of disenfranchisement in the outside world. It is perhaps a sign of the lack of their own certainty about their pasts when patients demand that their therapists must validate what they can't possibly know (e.g., "You have to believe me!"). Therapists should maintain appropriate therapeutic neutrality concerning the objective reality of past trauma. If the account of past trauma is credible and fits well into the narrative of a patient's life, there is no contraindication to acknowledging that the memories may likely be accurate. But, in the absence of such clear indications, the therapist must help the patient sit with uncertainty until a reasonable consistency among the patient's sense of identity, personality, symptoms (current and past), and history can ultimately be established.

---

[4] Deriving from psychoanalytic theory, a screen memory is one that is acceptable to the individual and is used unconsciously as a screen against an allied memory that would be distressing if remembered.

Table 5.2 Factors in the Evaluation of the Validity of Traumatic Memories

Patient Factors

More Likely to Be Valid	More Likely to Be Questionable
The patient has always had some memories of traumatic situations or conditions.	The patient has no previous memories of any trauma despite efforts to recall them.
The patient has ambivalence about accepting or believing the memories and initially has great difficulty verbalizing them.	The patient accepts and embraces memories, is willing to discuss them, and has no difficulty verbalizing them.
The patient's trauma memories are believable and credible to the therapist.	The patient's memories are not credible and/or become increasingly bizarre or outlandish.
The patient is willing to explore the meaning of memories and their validity.	The patient is fixated on recollections of trauma and demands that the therapist validate them.
The patient has current and past symptoms of complex PTSD that are consistent with the remembered trauma.	The patient's symptomatology is atypical for complex PTSD (over- or under-endorsed) or has a confounding diagnosis such as psychosis.
The patient is determined to improve and works toward taking control of life and functioning.	The patient is strongly identified with being a patient and is passive and dependent.

Therapist Factors

More Likely to Be Valid	More Likely to Be Questionable
The therapist is well trained in a recognized school of psychotherapy and seeks consultation as needed.	The therapist lacks in-depth training or experience and is reluctant to seek consultation.

More Likely to Be Valid	More Likely to Be Questionable
The therapist maintains professional neutrality in regards to the validity of the trauma memories.	The therapist is focused on the trauma memories as the source of the patient's difficulties.
The therapist has good boundaries and is able to compassionately set limits.	The therapist easily loses therapeutic perspective and is enmeshed with the patient.
The therapist uses good, traditional psychotherapeutic techniques and employs specialized modalities (e.g., hypnosis) if adequately trained and as is appropriate.	The therapist doesn't adhere to traditional psychotherapeutic techniques and uses specialized modalities excessively with or without adequate training.

Factors That Do Not Necessarily Determine If Memories Are Valid or Questionable

The patient or therapist is convinced that the patient was abused without credible memories or corroboration.

The patient has dreams, fantasies, or feelings about abuse.

The patient has symptoms that correspond to those on abuse checklists.

The patient has apparent memories or flashbacks—however vivid—about possible abuse.

Trauma histories are generally more credible if patients are focused primarily on improvement and gaining a sense of control over their lives. Individuals are more prone to develop inaccurate memories when they lack an internal locus of control and become strongly identified in a victimized patient role, maintaining a passive and dependent stance. In this identity, there is strong motivation to develop memories that reify the patient role through fantasy, contagion, confabulation, unconscious embellishment, or even deliberate fabrication.

Effective therapists are usually well trained and experienced in at least one form of traditional psychotherapy and are less likely to either encourage or accept questionable accounts of past trauma. They are willing to seek consultation if therapeutic problems or impasses occur. They maintain a well-boundaried treatment frame and avoid enmeshment with their patients. They primarily use traditional forms of psychotherapy, and, if using specialized modalities such as hypnosis or EMDR, are well trained in these modalities and use them as appropriate to the treatment. Conversely, if therapists are poorly trained, overinvolved, or enmeshed, they can easily lose therapeutic perspective. Ill-advised treatment strategies or inappropriate use of specialized modalities can permit regression and make it more difficult for patients to distinguish between fantasy and reality.

In the course of helping patients shift through the confusing exploration of traumatic experiences—some of which emerge from the haze of amnesia—there is often much ambiguity. Dreams, vague feelings, and even PTSD-like symptoms such as apparent flashbacks and recollections are not necessarily true indicators of past trauma unless they become coherent parts of a credible life story that fits what is known about the person's past and who they have become. However, such experiences should not be reflexively dismissed. I have often had patients who "know that something happened" without clear memories or other evidence of early abuse; many of them subsequently recalled credible childhood trauma. Conversely, even in instances where it appeared that there was no trauma, it was important and necessary to understand how and why patients had such feelings.

IMPLICATIONS CONCERNING TRAUMATIC MEMORY FOR CLINICAL PRACTICE

From experimental investigations, clinical research, and clinical practice, substantial evidence supports the existence of complex memory processes that are affected by traumatic experiences. Dissociative amnesia for traumatic events has repeatedly been shown to be correlated with early age of onset, chronicity, severity, and family involvement. Thus, children who experience abuse at very young ages, who suffer multiple kinds of abuse, whose abuse continues over years, and who are abused by family members are most likely to develop serious dissociative symptoms, including dissociative amnesia and severe dissociative disorders such as DID. Unfortunately, at least in some clinical populations, this kind of abuse is more the rule than the exception.

Important implications from Terr's work (1991) begin to explain that both a heightened clarity of memory (hypermnesia) and impairment of memory (amnesia) can result from traumatization. Hypermnesia—enhanced memory—is seen in situations that involve single-blow or circumscribed trauma, and pervasive amnesia results from chronic traumatization. Some evidence shows that there may be nonconscious behavioral, affective, and somatic memory of traumatic events even when there is no conscious recall. However, it should be emphasized that the accuracy of memory, particularly recovered memory, following chronic traumatization is not well established. Given that chronically traumatized children use massive denial and dissociative defenses, these children may not encode traumatic memories with the hypermnestic clarity that is characteristic of single event traumas. Thus, these chronically traumatized patients are most likely to suffer amnesia for their abuse, and, given the level of denial and dissociative defenses they use, the accuracy of recovered memory in these patients may be vulnerable to distortions and errors in recall. However, the essential features of recovered memories of severe childhood abuse cannot be easily dismissed. In fact, the limited clinical studies of the corroboration of recovered memory strongly support the essential validity of many recovered memories of childhood abuse.

Therapists should understand the findings from memory research that memory content can be highly influenced by the mechanisms of memory retrieval, and caution must be exercised in inquiring about histories of childhood abuse. Research concerning the use of suggestion and certain kinds of coercive interrogation (Gudjonsson, 1992) has shown that memory content can be changed, introducing distortion and even pseudomemories. However, in the general clinical setting, there is little evidence that direct questioning about abuse per se results in false memories of abuse. The laboratory findings from cognitive psychology memory research suggests that only a small minority of individuals are predisposed to develop pseudomemories, and no competent therapist pursues the aggressive kind of suggestion used in false memory research protocols. However, it is possible that patients with high dissociative capacity (e.g., those that develop dissociative amnesia and dissociative disorders) may be particularly prone to confabulating memories. Although experts have pointed out that there are similarities and distinctions between dissociation, hypnotizability, and fantasy proneness, these traits clearly tend to cluster in particular individuals (Lynn & Ruhe, 1986; Merckelbach, à Campo, Hardy, & Giesbrecht, 2005; Pekala, Angelini, & Kumar, 2006; Putnam, Helmers, Horowitz, & Trickett, 1995; Spiegel, Hunt, & Dondershine, 1988). Hence, therapists must be careful not to inquire about possible abuse in a way that even subtly suggests a particular kind of response.

Therapists who treat survivors of abuse must be open to understanding patients' difficulties in a variety of ways and should not impose any particular idiosyncratic model of treatment on patients. Fantasies about abuse, suspicions or partly formed ideas about abuse, and dreams about abuse are not the same as the actuality of abuse. Especially when memories are fragmentary, therapists must support the psychological validity of the memories but avoid making premature conclusions when insufficient evidence supports the actual occurrence of abuse. Similarly, when recovered memory begins to replace amnesia, therapists must remain open to the possibility of real abuse but must also encourage patients to reconstruct their personal history in a way that is thoughtful and rational. Therapists must also scrupulously avoid regressive clinical practices. Current reality, past realities, fantasies, dreams, and fears become inextricably entangled under conditions of profound regression, making it difficult or even impossible to establish a coherent personal history.

So, finally, what is the nature of traumatic memory? In my estimation, ample evidence demonstrates that traumatic memory is quite different from ordinary memory. Events that are truly overwhelming—and especially if chronic may be "unspeakable"—are experienced, processed, and stored in a way that is very different from ordinary memory. As van der Kolk, Hopper, and Osterman (2001) observed:

> For over 100 years clinicians have observed and described the unusual nature of traumatic memories. It has been repeatedly consistently observed that these memories are characterized by fragmentary and intense sensations and affects, often with little or no verbal narrative content.... While the sensory perceptions reported in PTSD may well reflect the actual imprints of sensations that were recorded at the time of the trauma, all narratives that weave sensory imprints into a socially communicable story are subject to condensation, embellishment and contamination. While trauma may leave an indelible imprint, once people start talking about these sensations, and try and make meaning of them, it is transcribed into ordinary memory, and, like all ordinary memory, it is prone to become distorted.... Like all stories that people construct, our autobiographies contain elements of truth, of things we wish did happen, and elements that are meant to please the audience. The stories that people tell about their traumas are as vulnerable to distortion as people's stories about anything else. However, the question about whether the brain is able to take pictures, and whether some smells, images, sounds or physical sensations may be etched into the mind, and remain unaltered by subsequent experience and by the passage of time, still remains to be answered. (pp. 9, 28–29)

Working with patients concerning traumatic memory has not only the potential for enormous benefits but for serious detrimental effects as well. In order to be most helpful, therapists must combine an understanding of trauma, knowledge concerning memory processes, cautious inquiry, validation and support, and sound psychotherapeutic practices. Work of this kind may be maximally helpful to patients who suffer from sequelae of childhood abuse and who struggle to remember and make sense of their painful and chaotic lives.

PART II
Phase-Oriented Treatment for Complex PTSD

6

The Therapeutic Roller Coaster

Phase-Oriented Treatment for Complex PTSD[1]

The recognition of the profound effects of early abusive experiences, and the complexity of adult clinical syndromes related to such experiences, underscores the need for a sophisticated understanding of the treatment process for childhood abuse survivors. Because of patients' many and varied comorbid psychiatric symptoms, clinicians need to understand which problems and symptoms have priority in treatment. Over the past 20 years, a standard of care for complex PTSD has evolved that conceptualizes a sequence of treatment approaches designed to address specific issues in a way that is maximally helpful to patients.[2] Several clinician-investigators have advocated using a phase-oriented or stage-oriented approach (Chu, 1992c; Courtois, 1999; Courtois, Ford, & Cloitre, 2009; Herman, 1992b; Lebowitz et al., 1993; Steele, Van der Hart, & Nijenhuis, 2005). All of these treatment models are based on the clinical experience that many survivors of severe childhood abuse require an initial (sometimes lengthy) period of developing fundamental skills, including maintaining supportive relationships, developing self-care strategies, coping with symptomatology, improving functioning, and establishing some basic positive self-identity as a prerequisite for active work on memories of traumatic events.

Much of the earlier literature on the treatment of PTSD focused primarily on the treatment of adult war veterans and others who were traumatized as adults. Some treatment paradigms for this population place a priority on abreaction (see, for example, Foa, Steketee, & Rothbaum, 1989; Frueh, Turner, & Beidell, 1995; Keane, Fairbank, Caddell, & Zimering, 1989). The positive value of abreaction is thought to involve the reexperiencing of the traumatic event in a context of high social support so that the experience is tolerated, attitudinally reframed, and integrated into conscious experience. For example, in the treatment of adults who have been through wartime experiences

---

[1] Portions of this chapter were adapted from the article "The Therapeutic Roller Coaster: Dilemmas in the Treatment of Childhood Abuse Survivors" (Chu, 1992c).

[2] Although this has been a new approach in the modern study of trauma treatment, as early as the late 19th century, Pierre Janet advocated a phase-oriented treatment for dissociative disorders (see Van der Hart, Brown, & van der Kolk, 1989).

or similar events, abreaction is sometimes brought about by exposure or flooding techniques whereby the patient is deliberately exposed to stimuli designed to trigger reexperiences of the traumatic events in a supportive and controlled environment (e.g., veterans being shown film clips that simulate combat, individualized trauma scripts based on trauma experiences, computerized virtual reality scenarios). For many veterans with combat-related PTSD, such therapeutic strategies have been effective in alleviating acute symptomatology.

There are no similar studies of the use of abreactive techniques in survivors of extensive childhood trauma. Based on clinical experience, however, it is widely believed that the *eventual* reexperiencing and working through of childhood trauma is part of the definitive treatment for the resolution of posttraumatic and dissociative symptomatology. Persons who have been able to successfully confront and work through abusive childhood events often experience dramatic changes, reporting that they are able to proceed with their lives unencumbered by their pasts. This abreactive process promotes improvement, such as fewer and less troubling intrusions of the abusive experiences, a reduction in dissociative symptomatology, a new sense of identity as being psychologically healthy and functionally competent, and a much improved ability to relate to the world and to others.

The clear value of abreaction of childhood trauma in some patients led to an unfortunate belief system that is still remarkably ubiquitous among some patients and their therapists. In this belief system, it is assumed that in any clinical situation where childhood abuse is discovered in the patient's history, all efforts should be made to explore and abreact those abusive experiences. Moreover, some clinicians appear to believe that if current difficulties seem related to past abuse, then abreaction is the treatment of choice. Unfortunately, in the treatment of many patients, such a belief system is conceptually flawed and inappropriate, and can have untoward effects such as increasing acute symptomatology and difficulties with functioning and coping, as illustrated in the following clinical example:

A 22-year-old woman was admitted to our inpatient psychiatric facility after taking an overdose of her antianxiety medication. She had a long history of severe depression, panic, suicidal impulses, poor relationships, and a low level of functioning. She had recently begun treatment with a new outpatient therapist. In the context of therapy, the patient began to reveal evidence of severe early childhood sexual abuse. The patient began divulging more and more information about the abuse, and she became increasingly fearful, isolated, and suicidal. She was referred for hospitalization in order to "work through the abuse issues." Following her admission, the patient was noted to have flashbacks of presumed childhood sexual abuse. Despite cautions from the hospital staff concerning the need for stabilization as a treatment priority, she and her therapist were insistent on the need to "get the bad feelings out" in order to heal from the abuse. The patient was encouraged by her therapist to explore these issues in therapy, and she related horrific details of repeated victimization, which she reported that she was just remembering. On the unit, her behavior became more and more out of control, particularly at night, necessitating intensive suicide precautions and even the intermittent use of restraints for head banging. After six weeks of hospitalization, she was unable to be discharged and was put on a leave of absence at her job.

The key element that appears to be missing in premature attempts at abreactive therapy in patients with complex PTSD is the ability to utilize social and interpersonal support. Unfortunately, the ability to relate to and feel supported by others is a primary area of disability in many patients with a history of severe childhood abuse. The relational difficulties that complex PTSD patients experience also arise within the therapeutic relationship, often in a particularly intense fashion. The therapist is viewed with great suspicion, and many severely abused patients are unable to take the emotional risk to have a normal level of trust in the relationship. Because therapy involves intimacy, vulnerability, and the potential for arousing painful and overwhelming feelings, the therapist and the therapeutic process are experienced as major stressors and may precipitate negative therapeutic reactions. Characteristically, when faced with any major stressor (internal or external), severely abused patients flee into isolation as the perceived safest alternative, but once again are alone with the burden of their symptoms, feelings of emptiness, despair, and self-hate, and their dysfunctional and self-destructive behaviors.

My clinical experience over three decades with severely traumatized patients with complex PTSD has suggested that the best prognosis has been associated with persons who attempt to gain control of their inner experience and their outside lives, who challenge themselves to overcome obstacles, and who persist in their efforts to attain some semblance of a normal life. In the face of an underlying reservoir of powerful feelings of despair related to their early abuse, these persons struggle to achieve some measure of healthy functioning in the world and in their interpersonal relationships. The initial achievements of these efforts may feel fragile and superficial. However, persistent efforts at functioning result in a sound foundation that consists of a more positive sense of self-identity and self-worth, a sense of control over internal feelings and impulses, an ability to interact with the external environment, a daily structure that provides stability in daily living, and a network of social supports. These accomplishments then may provide some solid ground on which the patient may stand when exploring the quagmires of early abuse. The establishment of this kind of stability is often arduous and lengthy, requiring untold efforts from patients, guidance from skilled clinicians, and endless patience and persistence. There are few shortcuts, and even with competent treatment and maximal effort from both patients and therapists, the early treatment process is often punctuated by crisis and anxiety. It is a common experience for therapists and patients to feel as though they are riding some kind of roller coaster with little sense of control or direction, and to have a constant feeling of impending crisis and potential danger.

Most phase-oriented treatment models consist of three phases or stages:

1. Establishing safety, stabilization, control of symptoms, and overall improvement in ego functioning
2. Confronting, working through, and integrating traumatic memories
3. Continued integration, rehabilitation, and personal growth

For example, Herman's model, described in her much acclaimed 1992 book, *Trauma and Recovery*, delineated three such phases, rather poetically named Safety, Remembrance and Mourning (the essential processes of coming to terms with momentous past trauma), and Reconnection (in Herman's conceptualization, the effects of trauma result in disempowerment and disconnection, so healing inherently involves re-empowerment and reconnection). In a somewhat obscure paper published in the same year (Chu, 1992c), I described a treatment model for complex PTSD with three phases that I named (much less poetically) Early, Middle, and Late.

The division of the course of treatment is somewhat arbitrary, because patients generally move back and forth between phases, rather than progressing in a neat linear fashion. However, this delineation is useful in specifying the components and sequence of treatment. The discussion in this volume focuses extensively on the early phase of treatment, as the dilemmas encountered here are the most formidable for patients and clinicians. The middle or abreactive phase of treatment is summarized in this chapter. By the time patients have done the arduous work of the early phase of treatment, they are much more stable, and work on traumatic memories often proceeds in a much more intuitive fashion, largely free from crisis (although it is still very emotionally painful). For more lengthy descriptions of this process, some fine texts discuss in detail the abreactive and integrative process with complex PTSD patients (Courtois, 1999, 2010; Courtois & Ford, 2009; Davies & Frawley, 1994; Gold, 2000; Herman, 1992b) and those with dissociative disorders (Kluft & Fine, 1993; Putnam, 1989; Ross, 1997). The late phase receives the least emphasis here, as it is more familiar to experienced psychotherapists as the work with individuals who are largely functional but who have patterns of thinking, feeling, and behaving that affect the quality of their lives. Three areas that are part of the focus of early treatment—self-care, symptom control, and relational issues—are described in this chapter in brief, as the scope and importance of these areas merit a fuller exploration; they are more extensively discussed in the four subsequent chapters of this volume.

EARLY PHASE TREATMENT

For many childhood abuse survivors with complex PTSD, abreaction and resolution of early traumatic experiences are limited by deficits in being able to tolerate the intense affects and experiences associated with the traumatic events, and their inability to utilize supportive relationships—specifically including the therapeutic relationship. Abreactive work must be deferred pending the development of basic skills concerning relating and coping. In the early phase of treatment, emphasis should be placed on establishing a therapeutic alliance, educating patients about diagnosis and symptoms, and explaining the treatment process. Certain areas of focus can be identified as crucial in the early phases of treatment. These are discussed here as part of the mnemonic SAFER:

Self-care and Symptom control
Acknowledgment of the role of trauma
Functioning
Expression of affect and impulses in a productive manner
Relational work

Self-Care

Survivors of childhood abuse are prone to become involved in a wide variety of self-destructive and self-harming behaviors (see, for example, Briere & Runtz, 1987; de Yong, 1982; van der Kolk, Perry, & Herman, 1991). Chronic reexperiencing of the affects related to early abuse—including intense dysphoria, panic, helplessness, and hopelessness, as well as a chronic sense of aloneness and disconnectedness—often lead to suicidal impulses and behavior. Self-injury of a nonlethal nature is also extremely common, and paradoxically is often used as a soothing and coping mechanism (Himber, 1994; Shapiro, 1987). Patients with histories of extensive childhood abuse often describe their repetitive cutting, burning, or picking at the skin as tension-relieving rather than painful. Interestingly, this may have an underlying biologic mechanism in the release of endogenous opioids (Kirmayer & Carroll, 1987; van der Kolk et al., 1989).

As described in Chapter 2, survivors of childhood abuse often have other self-destructive and dysfunctional behaviors, such as substance abuse and eating disorders, and also addiction to risk-taking behaviors such as addictive traumatic reexposure (van der Kolk & Greenberg, 1987) or unsafe or risky sexual practices (Koenig & Clark, 2004; Purcell, Malow, Dolezal, & Carbello-Diéguez, 2004). Finally, revictimization is remarkably common, including repetitions of emotional, physical, and sexual abuse (Briere & Runtz, 1987; Chu, 1992b; Cloitre, Tardiff, Marzuk, Leon, & Portera, 1996; Coid et al., 2001; Dutton & Painter, 1981; Follette, Polusny, Bechtle, & Naugle, 1996; Russell, 1986), even within the presumed safety of the therapeutic relationship (Kluft, 1990a).

Childhood abuse survivors tend to be ambivalent about self-care. Perhaps one of the most damaging legacies of chronic childhood abuse is the compulsion to continue the patterns of abuse long after the original perpetrators are no longer actively abusive. In addition, a sense of inner worthlessness may make self-care seem internally consistent or unimportant. And perhaps most significantly, when self-harm is used as a mechanism for self-soothing or affect modulation, alternative coping mechanisms that involve reliance on others may seem extremely risky to the abuse survivors who have backgrounds of abandonment and betrayal. Patients' propensities toward inadequate self-care through both self-destructive behavior and vulnerability to revictimization must be controlled before beginning any exploratory therapy. Failure to do so increases the likelihood of serious self-harm when traumatic material is broached.

Analogous to the situation of abused children who must be removed from abusive environments as the first priority of treatment, abuse survivors must create an environment of personal safety before they are able to make progress in treatment. To this end, therapists need to insist that the therapy focus on self-care. In the early phase of treatment, this often takes the form of therapists asking for agreement on a therapeutic agenda (e.g., "I know that hurting yourself has been a long-standing coping mechanism for you, and that you may not feel that self-care is important. However, if we are to get anywhere in this therapy, you will have to make a commitment to work very hard to take care of yourself, even when you may not want to.").

It should be noted that in the early phase of treatment many patients will lack the ego strength to fully achieve self-care. In many situations, lapses will occur, and patients may retreat to self-harming or self-destructive behavior. Such lapses are tolerable if—and only if—patients are able to demonstrate a commitment to the principles of self-care over time and are able to make consistent progress toward reducing dysfunctional behaviors. It is essential to the treatment process that patients ally with their therapists around preventing self-harm, oppose their own self-destructive impulses, and understand the mechanisms of their vulnerability to revictimization. They must also begin to learn how to soothe themselves using alternative and less self-destructive ways of coping with stress.

Symptom Control

Many of the symptoms associated with complex PTSD and dissociative disorders need to be modulated and controlled as part of the stabilization process in the early phase of treatment. Patients are likely to remain in crisis as long as they continue to have frequent reexperiencing symptoms, such as flashbacks, nightmares, intrusive thoughts, feelings, and sensations, along with the accompanying physiologic hyperarousal symptoms of chronic anxiety and disturbed sleep. Hence, limiting the intrusion of traumatic thoughts and feelings during the initial phase of treatment is a crucial part of the therapy of many patients with complex PTSD. In addition, patients with dissociative identity disorder (DID) need to be able to control symptoms such as abrupt state changes (including personality switching) and amnesia; see Chapter 12 for a discussion of interventions more specific to the treatment of DID. Although the goal of early phase treatment is to defer abreaction of traumatic memories to when patients are stable, premature reexperiencing of symptoms frequently and routinely occurs before patients are prepared to process them, contributing to more instability.

In the 1990s, with the shift away from a direct focus on abreacting traumatic events in the early phase of treatment for patients with complex PTSD, the question arose concerning what to do when patients experienced acute posttraumatic and dissociative symptoms. Especially if the symptoms were related to particular experiences (e.g., flashbacks or nightmares of specific events), was it necessary to retrieve memories of the event, or could the focus be just on the symptoms? Over time, on the basis of clinical experience, it became clear that patients could be stabilized without accessing the memories. In fact, any premature exploration of memories often leads to a cascade of more memories, resulting in an unraveling process that is similar to making the mistake of pulling on a loose yarn in a sweater.

The approach can be fairly straightforward. The clinician can certainly listen to what patients have to say about the memories they have recalled; it is almost never appropriate to silence patients or ignore what they are saying. But instead of asking about more details, clinicians can encourage patients to try and manage the symptoms (i.e., stopping further recall and regaining present-day orientation) and provide suggestions on how to do so. On the Trauma and Dissociative Disorders inpatient unit at McLean Hospital, members of the nursing staff have been the most skilled at doing this. Because memories tended to surface in the evening and night (the time of day when many traumas such as sexual abuse occurred), it was not uncommon for a staff member to find a patient huddled in a corner or hiding in a closet having a full-blown flashback. In the early days of the program, staff members rapidly became expert at helping patients focus and reorient to their present circumstances. I and others learned a great deal from their innovative approaches and expertise.

If patients are working in alliance with therapists and other treaters, many behavioral interventions can be effective. Most of these fall into the category of grounding techniques, which help patients to focus on their immediate surroundings in the current reality when they are beginning to be overwhelmed by posttraumatic symptoms. Grounding techniques, if learned and practiced regularly, are effective at increasing voluntary control over such symptoms. Focusing on persons' immediate environment can help pull out of reexperiencing past trauma. (I recall once receiving a panicked telephone call from a patient who was experiencing a terrifying flashback. I asked her to tell me where she was in her house, and then to go look out the window and to tell me what she saw. With this help, she was able to ground herself in only a few minutes.) Contact with other persons, particularly eye contact, is also enormously effective and conveys two critical therapeutic messages: control of posttraumatic symptoms is possible, and other people can be helpful and safe. Focused activities, familiar objects, and soothing or energizing sensations can be helpful in reorienting patients who are having difficulty with reexperiencing symptoms. Preplanned strategies for achieving control should be formulated for use in managing the crises that can often occur outside of the therapy office at inopportune times. More details concerning strategies and interventions for symptom control are presented in Chapter 8.

Control of intrusive symptomatology can be achieved, but only if patients ally with the goal of attempting to control the rate and nature of reexperiencing past abuse. Therapists must have patience and take the time to provide education and support about how this can be done. In this way, patients can be recruited to ally with the therapeutic process of achieving adequate symptom control. Both patients and therapists should recognize that this process may be quite difficult, and early attempts may be only minimally successful. However, the ultimate goal of the therapy has to do with achieving a sense of mastery over past traumatic experiences, and unless patients are allied with this goal, it will not be attained. *Not* to strive for control is acceptance of the notion that reexperiencing symptoms are inherently beyond patients' control and essentially dooms therapeutic efforts.

Acknowledgment

Although intensive exploration of past traumatic experiences may be inadvisable in the early phase of treatment, acknowledgment of the significance of early trauma is crucial. Childhood abuse is perhaps the most important determinant in the lives of trauma survivors, not only in terms of posttraumatic symptomatology, but also in terms of their ability to function in the world and to relate to others. To ignore the role of abusive experiences is to tacitly collude in patients' denial of the impact of the abuse and in their erroneous beliefs of being responsible for their own victimization. The simple acknowledgment of the possible role of early traumatic experiences begins the process of helping survivors to understand many of their current difficulties as normal adaptive responses to extraordinarily overwhelming events.

Therapists must reiterate that although patients must shoulder the responsibility of the recovery process, they are not responsible for the abuse itself. Therapists often need to repeat variations of the normalizing message: "You are not crazy or bad. You have had normal reactions to very abnormal and traumatic experiences. You could not have stopped the abuse, and you are not responsible for having been hurt." Somewhat ironically, this message is often poorly received. Patients who are abuse survivors are often remarkably ambivalent about acknowledging the role of trauma in their lives. Although they may be able to understand intellectually the relationship between their early abuse and their current difficulties, on an emotional level they tend to resist acknowledgment of any such linkage.

Patients' denial concerning the effects of early trauma is both an effort to distance themselves from overwhelming experiences and the very powerful need to maintain a bond with idealized caretakers—even when the caretakers were perpetrators of abuse. Their adaptations to the abusive experiences have formed the core of meaning in their lives ("I was hurt because I was so bad"), and they resist seeing how much their lives have continued to center around flawed assumptions about themselves and others. As a result, it is striking how much many trauma survivors continue to minimize obviously abusive experiences and their effects; for example, one of my patients angrily accused me of being "patronizing" when I used the word "abuse" in describing the pattern of constant denigration and contempt that she experienced as a child. Even bright and perceptive patients—who can acknowledge that no other children could possibly deserve what they experienced—persistently maintain that they were to blame in their personal family situations. Hence, it is not surprising that the corrective messages acknowledging the consequences of early trauma need to be supportively reiterated throughout the early phase of treatment.

Functioning

It is almost impossible to overstate the importance of traumatized patients maintaining an appropriate level of functioning in their lives. Patients who have suffered early abuse are frequently overwhelmed by reexperiencing their trauma. Without persistent efforts on the part of both patients and their therapists to maintain a semblance of normal functioning, these reexperiences can rapidly intrude into every aspect of patients' lives. A syndrome of recurrent flashbacks precipitating crises, desperate efforts to obtain comfort and reassurance, dysphoric dependence on treaters, and massive regression are seen frequently in treatments that are out of control.

Maintaining functioning is far from a trivial matter. Without some kind of anchor in the current reality, patients can become consumed by the emotional reality of their past abuse. That is, the feelings of victimization, hopelessness, powerlessness, and aloneness are experienced not just as related to the past, but can be overlaid on individuals' current lives. Over the years on our inpatient unit, we frequently observed patients who were admitted in crisis—and were sometimes intensely suicidal—based on such feelings. They were not able to perceive that their actual current lives were not abusive and well worth living; in short, they lost perspective of the difference between the present and the past. Too often, we saw scenarios in which patients began to psychologically unravel while pursuing premature work concerning past abuse. Many such patients, who may have been marginally compensated in terms of coping, quickly became incapable of functioning at all, and over time they become bereft of any kind of identity other than as a victimized and dependent patient. This kind of result is not only a poor therapeutic outcome but also a major problem that carries considerable risk in terms of increased symptomatology, permanent loss of functioning, chronic depression, and even suicide.

During a crisis, individuals sometimes benefit from the milieu and tasks associated with work. The work setting provides a focus that can distract one from worries and preoccupations associated with painful personal experiences such as loss or conflict, and it can provide balance and perspective in one's outlook on life. Interaction with others, whether friends or coworkers, is also an antidote to personal distress, providing diversion, support, and a sense of community. Without the demand characteristics of work or other reality-based roles and activities, it is all too easy for traumatized patients to become trapped in the past. Maintaining some appropriate level of functioning is often difficult but is nonetheless essential. Therapists, even those who have been trained to be nondirective in their approach, need to respond with a clear "No" to the often-asked question from patients, "Do you think it might be worthwhile for me to take time off from my usual activities in order to get to the root of my difficulties?" Even if efforts to function seem to patients to be superficial or just going through the motions, they are important in terms of balancing the internal pull toward becoming totally immersed in past trauma.

Another critical therapeutic benefit is derived from functioning. Survivors of childhood abuse routinely have negative self-perceptions, feeling empty, defective, and disenfranchised from others. How does one's negative sense of self change into something positive? During the course of my formal psychiatric training, I don't recall ever being taught the mechanisms for such change. But, based on years of experience observing and assisting patients in their recovery, I am convinced that insights achieved in therapy are only the beginning, and the roots of self-esteem and a positive self-image are in actually *doing* things in life. Summoning up the courage to reach out and connect with others, going to work reliably, following through with an exercise program, and engaging in recreational activities are some examples of types of functioning that begin to instill new positive ways of thinking about oneself to replace the old negative ones (e.g., "friendly," "productive," "fit," "fun-loving"). Over time, healthy functioning in all domains—relational, vocational, educational, and recreational—leads to self-esteem and a positive self-identity.

Therapists must emphasize the importance of maintaining both functioning and supportive relationships, especially in the early phase of treatment. Without this emphasis on functioning outside the therapy, problems such as regression and overly intense transferences are prone to flourish. A sense of mastery in functioning helps reinforce patients' sense of internal control of their own lives, rather than feeling controlled by their past negative experiences. Paid employment, a volunteer job, regular activities in the home, at school, or in training programs are preferable because they not only provide a positive sense of self but also compel patients to function in the current reality. To the extent to which patients' activities are not therapy-related, they can provide a balance for the heavy emotional weight of their treatment. However, if patients are unable to meet the challenges of vocational or educational settings, treatment programs such as therapeutic groups, day programs, or AA/NA-related activities are important as areas of functioning.

Expression

The intense affects associated with posttraumatic symptomatology must be expressed in a nondestructive and therapeutic manner. Although full exploration of the traumatic events may not be advisable in the early phase of treatment, patients do experience some of the overwhelming negative affects associated with the trauma, including such intolerable feelings as intense depression and hopelessness, panic and terror, and rage. Particularly because one of the goals of early therapy is to help patients avoid use of ingrained and destructive coping mechanisms, the therapy must help patients find healthier means of expression.

A more subtle difficulty for persons with early childhood abuse has to do with the way that childhood trauma is experienced and recalled. Prior to adolescence, and especially in early childhood, the primary modality of experiencing the world is not verbal, symbolic, and linguistic as it is in adults, but is largely sensorimotor. Traumatic events that occur early in childhood are encoded in the psyche in a modality that is primarily nonverbal. Neurologic studies of the effects of child abuse on brain function suggest that trauma results in overactivation of right brain (nonverbal) activity as compared with left brain (verbal) activity (Schiffer, Teicher, & Papanicolaou, 1995). Thus, when traumatic events are relived in current reality, they retain a strikingly nonverbal quality. In the clinical arena it is quite striking to encounter patients who are otherwise highly intelligent, verbal, and articulate, but who literally seem to have no words to describe their childhood experiences. For these patients, their experiences of early childhood abuse remain both literally and figuratively unspeakable.

The inability to find words to describe feelings and events concerning early abuse has important implications. Achieving a sense of control over internal mental processes depends on the verbal ability to organize and contain powerful emotional processes. For example, the verbal thought, "I am afraid because I feel as though everyone will hate me like my mother did" is much more manageable than nameless dread. Not only can the feeling be named and described, but it can be consciously countered with other verbal narratives, such as "My mother was a unhappy and tortured person who hated everyone, and other people have no reason to hate me." Thus, the difficulties that traumatized patients have in being able to verbalize their experiences leave them more vulnerable to being repeatedly overwhelmed. This inability to verbalize experience also results in patients being unable to communicate with and to receive support from others. It is a common experience for patients to be flooded by powerful but wordless feelings and memories, but to feel intensely alone even in the presence of a therapist or other supportive persons. Finally, intense nonverbal experiences often leave little alternative to traumatized patients other than acting out. Because the underlying basis of this kind of acting out cannot be communicated and may involve avoidance, flight, or even self-destructive acts, such behavior is often poorly understood and sometimes characterized as deliberate misbehavior. However, true acting out is an expression of intense underlying affects without conscious awareness of them, not just another undesirable and difficult patient behavior. Acting out is also an opportunity for the patient and therapist to begin to search for words to describe the patient's chaotic and inarticulate internal world.

Unspeakable feelings need to find expression in words. However, in the early phases of treatment, verbalization of very intense feelings may be a difficult task. This process may be facilitated through therapeutic nonverbal expression, and the expressive therapies may have a special role in encouraging and working with trauma patients. After all, the expressive therapies are specifically designed to help patients translate nonverbal feelings into words. It is a common experience for abuse survivors, who are unable to speak about their feelings, to be able to find some relief through art, music, or physical activity (movement, dance, exercise, or sports). Even writing is sometimes nonverbal; certain patients describe sitting with a pen and paper and allowing words to flow out onto the paper without conscious awareness of their content. In the early phase of therapy, such efforts should be directed primarily at therapeutic expression (e.g., venting tension) rather than exploration of traumatic events and can be powerful forces in helping patients to find words for their previously unspeakable feelings.

Formal expressive therapy is best left to trained and qualified expressive therapists. However, even verbal psychotherapists can help patients find nonverbal channels for explosive feelings. Therapists can support patients in pursuing expressive activities or can even simply encourage a program of regular physical activity. The latter modality can be a very effective outlet for a variety of dysphoric affects. After all, intense panic or rage is a visceral experience that is normally felt more in the body than in the mind and is not easily verbally expressed even among those who have not been traumatized. Training in relaxation techniques, guided imagery, or autohypnosis (self-induced trance states) can be useful to combat both dysphoric feelings and the bodily overactivation that occurs in posttraumatic conditions. However, early in treatment, it is important that any such efforts be directed at containment of feelings, especially anxiety, and not at exploration of traumatic events.

Relationships

Negotiating relational minefields with survivors of early abuse is undoubtedly the most challenging aspect of the therapeutic work and is usually the rate-limiting aspect of the treatment. Survivors of childhood trauma bring the abuse-related interpersonal assumptions of their childhood environments into all of their adult relationships, including the therapeutic relationship. These relational assumptions often transform the therapeutic relationship into an emotional battlefield in which the patient and therapist take on abuse-related roles. Through complex interactions including projective identification, the patient and therapist end up playing out these various roles, making collaborative work on resolving past traumatic experiences extremely difficult. The most important task of early phase treatment is beginning to replace the model of abuse-related relationships with patterns of interpersonal interactions that are mutual and collaborative.

In the early phase of therapy, the patient and therapist must repeatedly renegotiate the therapeutic alliance. As the patient is repeatedly unconsciously compelled to precipitate abusive reenactments that disrupt the treatment relationship, the therapist must empathically interpret the process and help the patient in developing a sense of collaboration and mutuality. This process of disconnection and reconnection must occur on seemingly endless occasions with endless variations before a minimal sense of basic trust is formed. The following clinical example is a rather dramatic illustration of this process:

I once supervised a doctoral student in her psychotherapy of several patients with histories of early trauma. The student had already had extensive experience as a master's-level therapist, but she was finding one of her patients—Ruth, a 34-year-old woman with a history of severe childhood abuse—particularly difficult to treat. My supervisee was confident enough to bring actual audiotaped recordings of therapy sessions to our meetings, which lent a striking note of reality to my experience of the therapy. There had been some blurring of the therapeutic boundaries as the patient anxiously sought reassurance, and because the frantic calls had become numerous (almost daily) and intrusive, the therapy had been focused on reestablishing the treatment frame. Ruth was quite unhappy (understandably) about limits being placed on the out-of-the-office contacts and complained angrily that she was being treated unfairly and that her therapist was cold and uncaring. In very angry and accusatory tones she said, "I've seen many other therapists, but when I met you I thought you were the first person I could really trust—and now you betray me. I can't believe you're doing this to me. You don't care about me and just want to get rid of me. You're just like everyone else! No, in fact you're *worse* because you *pretend* that you care."

The therapist was initially taken aback by the vehemence of the verbal barrage, and feeling defensive and unfairly attacked, had difficulty even finding words to respond to the patient (a common reaction even for very experienced therapists). However, after a number of fruitless interchanges, she finally was able to say, "I'm sorry you feel so hurt. It is not my intent to abandon you. In fact, I am just trying to work out this relationship so that I can continue to help you over the long haul. I realize that I may have been somewhat unilateral in talking about my limits, and I would be very interested in your ideas about how we might solve the problem of phone calls, as it's very important we find ways to work together." Ruth almost instantly became calmer and replied, "You're really interested *my* ideas? I didn't know you cared about how I felt. You have to remember that in my family you could literally scream all you wanted and nobody heard or cared." In this way, mutuality was reestablished. However, the vicissitudes of the interpersonal process soon continued, as the patient said, "But I still can't believe how you talked to me as though I was just a bother to you."

This is the therapeutic dance, a seemingly endless cycle of disconnection and reconnection that occurs repeatedly, sometimes in the course of even a single therapy session, and certainly over the weeks, months, and sometimes years in the early phase of treatment. This process makes this phase of therapy long and arduous, but this process also provides a new model of relatedness that is in sharp contrast to the abusive style of relatedness the patient has experienced and expects. The therapy helps the patient to actually experience mutuality and collaboration in the relationship, rather than the control, aggression, exploitation, abandonment, and betrayal that formed the core experiences of the patient's early life. Establishing and providing this alternative interpersonal process is the core of the so-called corrective emotional experience. That is, the reparative process is providing patients with a new experience of a relational model with which to obtain support, to resolve conflict, and to feel a powerful sense of connection with others. The corrective emotional experience is *not* about taking care of patients. Although most therapists are compassionate and do a certain amount of caretaking of their patients, this alone does not bring lasting change in the patient's basic relational assumptions.

Therapists who expect patients to respond positively to an approach that consists primarily of caretaking or reassurance will be ill-equipped to weather the vicissitudes of the therapeutic process with abuse survivors. Patients who have been damaged by early interpersonal trauma cannot be "loved into health." Therapists must learn the hard lesson that the process of therapy with severely traumatized patients is rarely straightforward. It is not easy for therapists to understand and accept that they will not be able to consistently relieve patients' suffering, avoid conflict, or be seen as positive and helpful. In fact, to the extent that the therapy sometimes does provide help and relief, it can be all the more frustrating to patients and therapists that such experiences occur only intermittently.

Despite therapists' efforts to be helpful and benign, they will not always be regarded as such. Therapists must recognize that no matter how kind and compassionate, tolerant, or skilled they may be, they will likely find themselves as the objects of "traumatic transferences" (Spiegel & Spiegel, 1978), being regarded as abusers, and the object of patients' anger, suspicion, and even sadism. They must also be prepared to feel themselves being pulled into the position of feeling enmeshed, helpless, and violated, which are repetitions and reenactments of the experience of the abused child. Many, if not all, of these experiences in the therapeutic relationship are an integral part of working with patients who have had horrific life experiences, and they should be viewed as opportunities for work and change. Therapists must be prepared to work with such situations and to deal with their own countertransferential feelings. Using the framework of the "therapeutic dance" to understand the cycles of the therapeutic relationship can assist therapists to help advance the process and to formulate strategies to move the relationship toward a more psychologically healthy and stable collaborative position.

Patients vary widely in ego capacity, motivation, social support, economic resources, and other factors that may make them more or less able to use treatment to make fundamental changes. Accordingly, some patients may need to continue in early phase treatment for years—and sometimes even for the entire course of treatment. Such patients are often able to improve considerably in terms of overall stabilization and functioning, but they may not have the internal resources to engage in an intense (and potentially destabilizing) exploration of their trauma memories. Many factors may contribute to chronic low functioning, including severe attachment problems, ongoing enmeshment with perpetrators, serious and unstable comorbid conditions, ongoing medical problems, and unremitting life stresses, among others.

MIDDLE PHASE TREATMENT

In the middle phase of treatment, the focus turns to working with the patient's memories of traumatic experiences. Effective work in this phase involves remembering, tolerating, processing, and integrating overwhelming past events. This work includes the process of abreaction—the release of strong emotions related to an unresolved past experience.

Herman (1992b) speaks of abreaction as the reconstruction of a comprehensive verbal narrative of such unresolved traumatic events, where "the therapist plays the role of witness and ally, in whose presence the survivor can speak the unspeakable" (p. 175). When traumatized patients have mastered the tasks of the early phase of therapy, they may then cautiously proceed to the exploration and abreactive work of the middle phase of treatment. Patients vary considerably concerning the pace of treatment. Some enter therapy with excellent coping skills and may quickly move toward middle phase treatment. However, as noted in the previous section, many others require months or years of preliminary work.

Abreactive work should always be undertaken from a position of strength rather than vulnerability. Without adequate preparation and support, patients are prone to reexperience traumatic events once again in isolation and to be repetitively overwhelmed by them. In treating hospitalized patients over many years, the precipitating factors for decompensation have sometimes involved unstable patients undertaking a torturous process of going through a long series of out-of-control abreactions, with therapists making sometimes heroic efforts to help contain these explosive events. Although abuse survivors may be able to vent affect and release internal tension through uncontrolled abreactions, these experiences have resulted in very little lasting therapeutic value. Effective abreaction involves emotional processing, cognitive change, and achieving a sense of mastery concerning the trauma in addition to the intense discharge of emotions related to the traumatic experiences. If the only process is emotional discharge, it is simply retraumatizing, and thus is contraindicated.

Abreactive work should not involve crisis. Achieving full understanding and integrating past traumatic experience certainly involves confronting very painful feelings about past realities, but it should not result in patients feeling so overwhelmed that a crisis is precipitated. For the most part, effective abreactive work takes place in an outpatient office setting. Many patients enter into therapy with the expectation of resolution of traumatic issues through a kind of cataclysmic catharsis. Although there may be breakthroughs of understanding and instances of intense emotional release, working through trauma should be a somewhat modulated and progressive process that is accomplished over time. As early abreactive work is successfully completed, patients draw strength from new understandings about their lives and feel progressively freed from conflict, intrusive memories, and self-hate. This new strength is then an asset that allows them to go on to achieve resolution of other conflictual areas, or even to return and rework other aspects of areas already broached. Clinical experience suggests that working through each major issue or important event may entail a prolonged process lasting days, weeks, or months. The process must often be repeated until all major issues or events are resolved. However, it is *not* necessary to process every single traumatic event in the patient's past; this would be almost endless given the chronic victimization in the histories of some patients. Rather, only key traumatic experiences need to be processed in order to give new meaning and perspective to similar experiences.

Significant regression is commonly observed in the face of abreaction of traumatic experiences. That is, under the stress of reexperiencing early abuse, patients may return to former patterns of isolation and dysfunctional or self-destructive behavior. If and when these patterns reemerge, clinical attention should return to early phase issues until these issues are once again mastered. In fact, it is precisely because of the inevitable regressive pull of abreactive work that early phase issues *must* be mastered. Patients need to establish powerful relational bonds and be prepared to withstand extremely dysphoric affects without resorting to dysfunctional behavior in order to tolerate abreactive work. Plus, they need to have begun the work of establishing a more positive sense of themselves and their lives in order to be able to distinguish the present reality from the feelings related to the past.

Clinicians should provide education about the nature of the abreactive process, including the likelihood that symptoms may be exacerbated, as well as the benefits of successful memory processing. Work on traumatic memories can sometimes be planned out and scheduled. The patient and therapist can discuss and reach an agreement upon which memories will be explored, what interventions might be employed, how much of the memories can be accessed in any given session, how to titrate the emotional reactions, and how to contain the memories if the process becomes overly intense. There are many ways to access and work with memories. My preference (based on very traditional training) is to allow the memories to surface naturalistically, and then simply to gently explore their content and the associated feelings and meanings, how to understand them, and what the events have meant in the patient's life. However, some specialized modalities have been used to facilitate the abreaction, such as hypnotic interventions to access and process memories (e.g., Brown & Fromm, 1986; Spiegel, 1988), EMDR (Shapiro, 2001), and specialized techniques to help control and modulate the intensity of the abreactive experience, for example, visualizing the traumatic experience on a screen with controls for the speed and volume (Spiegel, 1988). These specialized modalities should be used only with appropriate training and as needed to facilitate therapeutic processes.

Although patterns of abreaction differ according to the individual characteristics of patients, I have observed several common phases. These are (1) increased symptomatology, particularly more intrusive reexperiencing, resulting in (2) intense internal conflict, followed by (3) acceptance and mourning, which is transformed into (4) mobilization and empowerment. An increase in the reexperiencing of traumatic events is a common early feature of the abreactive process. Again, I should emphasize that this reexperiencing should occur without a major breakdown of functioning. The patient should have the ability to maintain grounding in current reality throughout the abreactive process. Acute reexperiencing may take many forms. Major traumatic events may be reexperienced with symptoms such as nightmares and disturbed sleep, increased anxiety, dissociative experiences, and generalized autonomic hyperarousal. Other kinds of reexperiences may be more subtle. For example, the past experience of being subjected to pervasive hatred and denigration may be reexperienced as intense feelings of shame, self-hate, helplessness, aloneness, and despair.

Paradoxically the initial reexperiencing symptoms are sometimes accompanied by the patient's efforts to deny any link to traumatic events or to even use dysfunctional defenses (e.g., isolation), but the denial and defenses begin to break down as patients are able to utilize the support of the therapist and others in their lives. With the help of this kind of support and utilizing newfound coping skills, patients begin to tolerate the reality of past events, including the associated overwhelming affect and bodily sensations. They find words to describe the memories, translating the experience into a verbal narrative. The function of the therapist is to witness, support, and empathize, to reframe perceptions and meaning, and to help with pacing and containment. The reframing of the traumatic experiences is a crucial step, and being able to remain connected with others is crucial in this process. These connections enable the patient to utilize the perspectives of others—perspectives that often cannot be gained by the patient alone. In fact, it is sometimes useful to encourage patients *not* to try and work out painful issues on their own between sessions, especially when they find themselves going over the issues repetitively without being able to resolve them. With appropriate outside perspectives, the events that were originally experienced from the perspective of a helpless abused child can be seen from a more adult viewpoint, and patients can understand them in a different way (e.g., that they were victimized and exploited because of the failings of their abusers, not because they were deserving of such treatment).

New perspectives about past abuse produce intense internal conflict. For example, patients are often unable to let go of long-held feelings of self-blame at the same time that they begin to understand that they were not responsible for their abuse. Patients may retain a sense of identification with the perpetrators of abuse or may still feel intensely protective of them, even though they realize that they were victimized by them. Abuse survivors may also experience intense shame about not having been strong enough to stop the abuse, or having "given in" to the abuse, even though they understand that they were helpless in the abusive situation. In the face of markedly different ways of thinking about internal beliefs and attitudes about the abuse, it is almost universal for patients to try to reject old ways of thinking (e.g., those related to helplessness, powerlessness, and guilt). However, this rarely works, and patients often end up feeling tormented and conflicted. The resolution of such conflicts involves the patient's new, stronger, and healthier aspects of themselves coming to understand and developing compassion for the old and dysfunctional aspects. That is, patients must understand that some intrinsic aspects of themselves—including unpleasant feelings, thoughts, behaviors, and identities—were molded in very painful ways by extreme events, and that these self-identities need to be accepted and nurtured rather than hated and rejected. Acceptance and integration of past feelings and behaviors, as opposed to rejection and disavowal, leads to the resolution of these internal conflicts.

Persons with dissociated and unresolved abusive experiences frequently underestimate and minimize the extent of their own victimization as a way of protecting themselves from the full impact of the abuse. Despite the intense dysphoria that often accompanies fragmentary memories of the abuse, survivors are often stunned when they fully realize the extent and meaning of past abuse. One severely traumatized patient was finally able to give some eloquence to her experience after years of treatment:

> I have been struggling for years to "get it." I've realized for some time now that I'm smart, but I still couldn't understand it. I went all around in circles rather than just realizing what had really happened. I now know why I couldn't understand it. To accept what happened takes away the whole meaning of my childhood. I had to believe I was hurt and hated because I was so bad, and so all these years I hurt and hated myself. And I was so alone with my self-hate—no wonder I tried to kill myself. It's so unbelievable that they could have done that to me if I didn't deserve it. It makes everything seem so pointless—nobody really benefited. It didn't have to be that way—but it I guess I have to accept that it was that way.

As patients begin to accept the reality of their past abuse, they are often overcome by the extent of their former helplessness and by the abandonment and betrayal of important people in their lives. This part of the abreactive process often leaves patients emotionally drained, analogous to survivors of a natural disaster who are just beginning to take in the extent of the devastation that has destroyed their lives.

Full realization of the extent of their abuse, and the subsequent toll it has taken on their lives, allows patients to begin to mourn the losses that have resulted from the abuse—those things that they missed and those that couldn't happen as a result of their victimization. This slow and painful process may involve patients examining each significant aspect of their pasts and reframing their understanding of the events and their meaning. Patients begin to accept that they were truly not to blame for their victimization and to understand how the early abusive experiences pervasively influenced the course of their lives. Supported by these insights, patients begin the process of surrendering the role of victim and replacing it with a sense of self as a survivor of abuse. Over time, the abreactive process enables abuse survivors to mobilize their strengths and to gain a sense of control over their lives. Another patient once remarked to me:

> I once read a story about a man who had been a political prisoner. For years he was kept in a cell that was five feet wide and nine feet long, separated from anyone else. His routine was the same each day—he got up at 6:00 each morning, ate twice a day, and was allowed to bathe once a week. The rest of the time, he spent walking up and down the nine feet of his cell, back and forth, back and forth. As an old man, after almost 30 years, he was released and went to live with relatives. For the rest of his life, he got up at 6:00 each day, ate twice a day, bathed once a week, and spent his time walking back and forth in his bedroom—up nine feet and back nine feet. I realize that's what I've done most of my life—living in captivity although I'm no longer a captive. I now know I don't have to stay in my cell. My life has been ruled by fear, but I finally feel as though I can escape and be free.

Pervasive distress becomes more focused as nameless feelings become understood and can be verbalized in words. For example, rather than experiencing wordless automatic terror and numbness in close proximity to all men, sexual abuse survivors may be able to recognize that specific men were responsible for the abuse and to verbalize, "These men are not the men that hurt me and are not looking for ways to destroy me." They may then be able to focus their fear, anger, and outrage at the perpetrators as opposed to a more generalized displacement of these feelings.

Abreaction of past trauma frees traumatized patients from fear of their own dissociated memories. Their nightmarish childhood realities lose the power to overwhelm and control them—huge and malevolent abusers are seen as smaller and less powerful, and even horrific events become part of the past rather than repetitively intruding into the present. A remarkable transformation slowly occurs, as the sense of self is enhanced by an understanding that they have been able to tolerate and overcome their past abuse. Having understood and overcome extraordinary past circumstances, abuse survivors can find a new sense of empowerment, including the sense that they can protect themselves from future victimization. Having been able to acknowledge their own victimization and to come to terms with the realities of human failings such as selfishness, aggression, and malevolence, abuse survivors often begin to take on a depth of character in terms of self-understanding and true empathy toward others. After her long and continuing struggles to overcome the effects of abuse, one of my patients reported:

> You asked me months ago if I would like to trade places with someone else—someone that I admire. A few years ago I would have said "Yes!" in a minute, but now I don't think so. This is my life, and even though I wish sometimes it wasn't, it has made me who I am and I don't want to be someone else. I've had to look at myself and examine myself and learn how to accept myself, which has been incredibly painful. I know a lot more about myself and about others than most people—probably as a result of what I have been through. I like myself, and I really think that I'm okay. I've been told that adversity breeds character and I suppose it's true, but I can't help from thinking that I would have settled for a little less adversity and a little less character.

Gaining this kind of perspective through integrating past traumatic memories into normal experiences and existing mental schemas permits the memories to be understood and accessible to ordinary recall. After all, the therapeutic work with traumatized patients is not about trauma per se or abreaction as the goal of treatment—such a focus only leads to an endless parade of traumatic experiences and endless abreactive processes. Abreaction is the *means* through which survivors of trauma begin to build a credible, personal narrative that helps them truly understand how they have become who they are, why they feel what they feel, why they do what they do, and how they can go on with their lives.

LATE PHASE TREATMENT

Much of the process of late phase treatment is similar to that of nontraumatized patients who may have entered therapy functioning well, but experiencing emotional, social, or vocational problems. The abreaction and resolution of past abusive experiences enables trauma survivors to proceed with their lives relatively unencumbered by their pasts. Late phase therapy involves consolidation of gains, achieving a more solid and stable sense of self, and increasing skills in creating healthy interactions with the external world. The resolution of the all-encompassing and overwhelming past events reduces patients' inevitable narcissistic preoccupation with their symptoms and difficulties, and allows them to have more appreciation of others as separate individuals. Moreover, an empowered sense of self leads patients to have increased confidence in their abilities to participate successfully in interpersonal relationships and other activities in ways that previously eluded them. In persons with a fragmented sense of identity, a profound sense of an integrated self arising from new psychic structures often emerges, which facilitates their ability to engage with the external world.

It is common for patients in the late phase of therapy to find areas of unresolved trauma or trauma-related issues as they proceed with their lives and encounter new situations. This process should be construed only as a need to complete further abreactive work and not as a failure of therapy. In fact, it is sometimes necessary for patients to revisit traumatic memories that had previously been processed from a more adult and integrated perspective. The history of successful experiences with abreactive therapy often facilitates and often shortens any additional similar subsequent treatment.

A final quote from another patient illustrates the new perspective of those who have been able to rebuild their shattered lives:

When I look back, it's incredible I ever made it this far. How many times did I feel I couldn't get any further? How many times did I try to kill myself? I think if I knew in the beginning what it would take to get to this point I never would have tried. There were so many years spent just getting through, and then so many years *undoing* what was done to me—so many years just getting to the point that I could have a chance just like anyone else. In a way, it's so unfair that I have had that job of "undoing." I've had to struggle and struggle to do what seems so easy for everyone else. But, I guess I've learned that no one else could do it for me, although God knows I've needed a lot of help. Life isn't always easy for me now, but I don't expect that. I feel lucky and very thankful for having the chance to do all the things I've done and to have a real future. It's scary to admit this, but I'm looking forward to the rest of my life.

7

Staying Safe

The Paradox of Self-Care

The concept of self-care for adult survivors of childhood abuse is an inherent paradox. Learning self-care is an essential early step in the treatment of traumatized patients, but most persons who have been victims of early abuse have a very debased sense of self—as worthless and defective—and have no concept of the need to care for one's self. Not only do traumatized patients often fail to care for their emotional well-being, but they also often fail to take basic care of their physical health. Adults who have been chronically abused, particularly those who have been physically or sexually abused, have little sense of ownership of their own bodies, which derives from the depersonalization that was necessary to tolerate the noxious physical experiences. Patients often describe a kind of discomfort about their bodies: "I know that somehow this body belongs to me, but it doesn't feel like my body." When they look in the mirror, they sometimes feel as though they are seeing someone else. Most of the feelings that traumatized patients have about their own bodies are negative—echoes of what they were told and how they were treated: "ugly," "fat," "disgusting," "cheap." Patients with dissociative identity disorder (DID) have the most extreme distortions of the way they see their bodies; with a bit of mental *leger-de-main*, reflections in the mirror or photographs of themselves are perceived as having the imagined physical appearance and bodies of their alternate identities.

One of the extremely destructive paradigms in abusive families is that the victimized child's mind and body are available for exploitation. Thus, adult impulses such as rage, sadism, or sexual tension are vented on the child. It is not at all surprising that children who have been exploited in this way employ the same paradigm when they become adults: they use themselves and their bodies to relieve tension or to act out impulses that often result in self-harm. This tendency to use the self as a vehicle for tension release is heightened by the relational disturbances that result from the abusive early environment. When distressed, most humans seek connection with others in order to feel understood and to alleviate the distress. This avenue of assistance is unavailable to many abuse survivors, because their cries for help have been met with either further abuse or indifference at best, and they have learned to avoid human connection.

The need for comfort and soothing is evident in all of our relationships and is especially prominent with young children (see Chapter 4). Even the most independent toddler or young child seeks a protective adult when the child is stressed or frightened. A normally nurturing parent establishes physical contact and comfort, by picking up and holding an infant or toddler, or by making connection through eye contact or words with an older child once the child has acquired some ability to use verbal communication. This behavior of seeking support from another human being is innate and is in marked contrast to the reactions of many patients with backgrounds of childhood abuse. In times of stress or difficulty, these patients flee from any kind of contact with others into a dysfunctional isolation, relying only on their own resources. The innate response to seek contact with others when in distress has clearly been replaced by the conviction that opening oneself to another when vulnerable will inevitably result in more harm.

MANAGING COMORBID SUBSTANCE ABUSE, EATING DISORDERS, AND SOMATIZATION

Being unable to effectively utilize others for support, many abuse survivors seek relief in a variety of dysfunctional behaviors that do not rely on anyone else. Some persons attempt to numb themselves through drug or alcohol abuse or excessive reliance on prescription medications. Others change the focus of their distress by engaging in eating disordered behavior or by becoming excessively preoccupied with real or imagined somatic problems. Not surprisingly, histories of childhood abuse are extremely common in patients with substance abuse, eating disorders, hypochondriasis, and somatization (see Chapter 2). Sometimes these problems are relatively minor in terms of impact—patients who occasionally abuse alcohol or drugs, who struggle to be able to eat properly, or who try to avoid becoming preoccupied with somatic concerns. In other instances, these problems are major impediments to effective treatment. To the extent that these problems are a prominent and consuming focus in patients' daily lives, they must be addressed as a priority in treatment. Little, if any, work on learning the skills needed to address trauma-related difficulties can be done with patients who are recurrently intoxicated, endangering their lives through starving, bingeing, or purging, or whose activities center almost entirely around somatic concerns. In that these difficulties offer a kind of relief for patients, there is often considerable ambivalence to addressing them as problems. Patients sometimes regard them as secondary difficulties that will remit if only work is done on trauma-related issues. I have often heard patients minimize their difficulties: "I only lose control of my drinking (or drugging, or eating) when I have flashbacks, and I need to work on my trauma," or the patients with DID who maintain, "*I* don't have a drinking problem—I don't even like to take aspirin; it's my alters who drink." This last statement is probably familiar to those who work in the addictions field as a form of common denial.

Among experts in both the trauma and substance abuse fields, the conventional wisdom has been that any serious substance abuse in trauma patients must be the primary focus of treatment (i.e., that patients must achieve stable sobriety before working on trauma issues). However, psychologist Lisa Najavits, PhD, has proposed an evidence-based model called Seeking Safety that provides integrated substance abuse and PTSD treatment (Najavits, 2004). She has pointed out that common messages such as "Don't work on the PTSD until you've been sober for a year," or "Substance abuse is the only thing you need to focus on" can be experienced as invalidating for traumatized patients (Najavits, 2002).

Furthermore, in clinical practice, it has been particularly difficult for patients with PTSD to maintain abstinence with traditional treatment, especially if they have more intrusive PTSD symptoms when they stop abusing substances (Ruzek, Polusny, & Abueg, 1998; Solomon, Gerrity, & Muff, 1992). The Seeking Safety model has an integrated treatment approach for the concomitant treatment of both disorders. Using structured sessions, cognitive-behavioral approaches, attention to interpersonal processes, and case management, the model emphasizes safety as a priority of treatment, including stopping substance abuse, reducing self-harming and risky behaviors, establishing healthy relationships, and gaining control over the symptoms of both disorders. In many respects, the Seeking Safety model is a dual-diagnosis approach that incorporates many of the elements of the early phase of trauma treatment.

Addressing and modulating out-of-control behaviors should be a prerequisite task that must be undertaken as a part of any trauma-related treatment, and clinicians must be clear in their advice and expectations. Referral to inpatient or outpatient substance abuse treatment programs, Alcoholics Anonymous, Narcotics Anonymous, eating disorders programs, or other resources, or establishing effective protocols for somatization may be an important part of addressing self-care. Somatization may offer particular difficulties in terms of treatment, as most work in this area has been focused on patients in medical and surgical settings, not on psychiatric patients. It may be useful to establish a program of regular and predictable medical appointments with a primary care physician who can both provide support and exercise appropriate limits concerning access to excessive and harmful medical care (Barsky, 1996). In addition, an educationally oriented cognitive-behavioral treatment, particularly in a group format, has been found helpful for some patients to alleviate their somatic concerns (Salkovskis, 1989).

SILENT CRIES: SELF-HARMING IN ABUSE SURVIVORS[1]

Self-cutting is known to be common among a variety of populations including adolescents (Kumar, Pepe, & Steer, 2004; S. Ross & Health, 2002), patients with eating disorders (Favazza, DeRosario, & Conteiro, 1989; Paul, Schroeter, Dahme, & Nutzinger, 2002), patients with dissociative disorders (Putnam et al., 1986), and patients

---

[1] This section draws on the clinical research and practice of Judith Himber, PsyD, and portions were incorporated, as noted, from her article, "Blood Rituals: Self-Cutting in Female Psychiatric Patients" (Himber, 1994).

with borderline personality disorder (Russ, Shearin, Clarkin, Harrison, & Hull, 1993; Shearer, 1994). Repetitive self-cutting has been correlated with histories of childhood sexual abuse (Briere & Runtz, 1987; Himber, 1994; Shapiro, 1987; van der Kolk et al., 1991; Wise, 1989) and is by far the most common kind of bodily self-harm seen in adolescents and adults with abuse backgrounds. Either delicate or substantial cuts to the arms, abdomen, breasts, genitals, legs, throat, or face (in approximate decreasing order of prevalence) are used as repetitive tension-reducing mechanisms. I have seen a variety of similarly destructive behaviors that seem to be variants on this behavior, including picking at, burning, or abrading the skin; repetitive banging of the hands, arms, head, or feet; swallowing objects such as razor blades, glass, or pieces of metal; and inserting objects or foreign bodies into body orifices (most commonly vaginally) or actually into the flesh or veins. While this kind of self-harming behavior may seem somewhat horrifying and perplexing, it is widespread among patients who experience explosive inner tensions and who cannot access support from others. In most cases, these self-harmful activities are considered to be parasuicidal and not truly attempts to kill or endanger the self; one of the more dramatic examples I can recall was a young woman who repetitively swallowed broken razor blades but became quite concerned and immediately sought help about her medical condition immediately after swallowing them.

The primary gain for many self-harming behaviors is often an immediate relief of tension. Patients use self-cutting to manage their dysphoric internal states; there are two opposite patterns—most commonly, to induce a relaxation response, or conversely, to cause pain in order to end unpleasant depersonalized states (Grunebaum & Klerman, 1967; Himber, 1994). Most patients act in a way that is stereotyped and consistent over time; that is, most patients seem to choose specific forms and methods of activities (e.g., cutting in specific places with certain kinds of sharp objects). In the most common variant of repetitive self-harm, there is usually very little pain associated with the behavior. Before patients cut themselves or engage in other parasuicidal behavior, they often describe experiencing an intolerable sense of inner tension that may include anxiety, dysphoric dissociative states, or anger, which is immediately alleviated after the self-harming behavior. If cutting is involved, it is often the visualization of blood that results in the feeling of relief from tension (Himber, 1994). The underlying mechanism is thought to derive from the release of endogenous opioids—perhaps a bodily response to an evolutionarily adaptive reaction to the sight of blood—which in some studies has been blocked by naltrexone, an opioid antagonist (see, for example, Roth, Ostroff, & Hoffman, 1996). Thus, repetitive self-harming acts are remarkably prompt and effective solutions for self-soothing in patients who cannot obtain comfort or support from others.

In addition to tension relief, self-cutting and other similar behaviors are often an acting out of patients' deep-seated sense of defectiveness and self-hate. Some patients describe the need to "get the bad blood" out, or the impulse to cut out something bad from inside of them (Grunebaum & Klerman, 1967; Himber, 1994). Although repetitive self-cutting results in substantial psychological and physiological gains, it almost always is associated with shame and secrecy. Patients are generally quite aware that self-cutting is aberrant in terms of normal human behavior and that others tend to react to this behavior with horror and disgust. Some patients also describe their cutting as compulsive and out of control, requiring more frequent or extensive cutting to achieve the desired outcome. This kind of loss of control also leads to increased feelings of shame.

Nonlethal self-cutting or similar behavior has also been described as a mode of communicating distress. Otto Kernberg, MD (1968, 1984), a psychiatrist who helped establish the current understanding of borderline personality disorder, has interpreted self-harming behavior as acting out—for example, as attempts to discharge transferential anger. Other experts have noted the motivation to manipulate others, to gain attention, or to deal with threatened loss (Grunebaum & Klerman, 1967). Some patients may harm themselves for these reasons, particularly in situations of acute distress and explosive anger. When cutting occurs in the context of intense rage over feeling abandoned, ungratified, or misunderstood, cutting may convey messages such as: "This shows you how angry I am!" "*Now* do you take me seriously?" or "See what you made me do?" However, I infer from my clinical experience that the central intent of self-harmful behavior is not always about attempts to influence the response from others, or at least not the primary motivation. After all, most patients began this kind of activity in isolation and secrecy, long before it came to the attention of anyone else. Much self-cutting begins as an inarticulate cry of pain from patients who have no words to adequately describe their distress and/or who feel repeatedly unheard and unseen. Self-cutting almost always originates as a solitary act that occurs when patients feel intensely alone, overcome by their distress, without a conscious intent to communicate or manipulate.

When revealed in the context of a therapeutic relationship, self-harming behavior may take on the additional role of conveying unspoken messages. Revealing self-injury is a mute cry for help, but it often also appears to be an invitation for a reenactment of abuse-related scenarios. There is a nonverbal communication of, "Do you see how much I hurt?" as well as an almost defiant statement of, "Do you see how different I am from other people, and how I don't need help from anyone else?" The therapist is in a difficult position in terms of knowing how to respond. A response of only concern or sympathy is certainly gratifying for the patient who then feels heard, but little is gained in terms of promoting direct or verbal communication. A response that ignores or minimizes the behavior increases the patient's sense of being alone and unheard. A response of disgust, frustration, or anger (especially when the self-harming behavior is in violation of a therapeutic "safety contract") inevitably provokes shame and a confirmation of the patient's perceived defectiveness, and sets into motion the abuse-related scenario of patients feeling shamed that they have been bad and deserve to be punished.

Perhaps the best response in these situations is one that is modulated in terms of expressed emotion and conveys concern and interest along with a gentle confrontation concerning the dysfunctional aspects of the behavior: "I can see that you have been in a great deal of pain, and I would like to learn more about your cutting and what leads to it. I am sorry that you have not found another way to let me or other people know about your pain, and that you have had to continue to do something that interferes with your ability to grow and heal." Responding in a matter-of-fact, calm, but serious manner with gentle confrontation about the need to change is essential in transforming the self-harming behavior into a more adaptive solution, such as interpersonal communication and developing a sense of mastery. The therapist also needs to assess the dangerousness of the self-cutting, both in terms of suicide potential (unusual) and physical well-being. Even in the absence of suicidal intent, blood loss, serious scarring, and the potential for serious infection may mandate referral to a physician for ongoing monitoring and treatment.

Given the addictive quality of self-cutting, it is not surprising that the most effective treatment uses an addictions model. In this model, self-harmful behavior should not be regarded moralistically, but as a maladaptive effort at coping that has negative consequences. As in other addictions, there is a wide range of severity. At one extreme, there are patients who are so drawn to the behavior that they are at risk for seriously harming themselves. I remember several patients who had cut themselves so badly that they developed life-threatening cellulitis from the nonhealing wounds. Another patient, once she began to cut, felt strong impulses to cut more and more deeply. For such patients, total abstinence from cutting is required. However, for most patients, it is important to make the distinction between establishing safety and extinguishing self-harm. For many patients, the cutting has no serious medical implications, and it may be permissible for them to hold on to a reduced level of self-harming behavior until they have developed or restored basic abilities to engage productively with others. However, establishing an alliance around the progressive goal of stopping self-harm is essential. As in the treatment of other addictive behaviors, slips and relapses are common, and a sustained commitment to the ultimate goal of abstinence is the most important part of successful treatment. Emphasis must be placed on the patient to supply the primary motivation to control the behavior, although it must be acknowledged that the patient will require considerable support. As noted by Himber (1994):

> Establishing an alliance around safety proceeds hand-in-hand with the development of understanding and communication. Although stopping self-cutting is a final goal of treatment, there are useful intermediate steps. If the patient cannot agree to stop cutting, can she identify and agree to goals which will help her recover? Some patients may disavow the seriousness of their behavior or the shame and fear associated with it, insisting that "it's no big deal," not suicidal, and not worth paying attention to. This can set the stage for a struggle between the patient and the therapist. In such struggles, the patient projects her distress and anxiety about self-harmful behavior onto the therapist, and then both attacks and devalues the therapist's interventions. As the patient acts less and less concerned about cutting the therapist may become more and more alarmed and the struggle can escalate. It is important to keep the focus on the patient's responsibility for her own safety and to name her attempts to disavow her own distress. (pp. 629–630)

Clinicians must be extremely careful not to take on one side of this ambivalence (the "good" side), which allows the patient to actually feel less conflicted about the self-harmful behaviors. Clinicians should provide expert advice and empathic support, but must make it clear that patients must carry the primary responsibility for their own behaviors, for ambivalence about the behaviors, and for changing the behaviors. The following case illustrates some of the dilemmas and the negotiations concerning the treatment of repetitive self-harm:

> Barbara, a 35-year-old mother of two young children, was admitted to the hospital for severe depression and suicidal ideation. She reported a 20-year history of repetitive self-cutting, and although she had no major medical problems related to this behavior, both of her forearms were crisscrossed with hundreds of small scars and more recent wounds. Despite several years of therapy, Barbara was making little progress, which she attributed to both a sense of hopelessness about her own condition and to passivity on the part of her outpatient therapist: "She just listens and doesn't actually *do* anything." In regards to her self-cutting, she reported that she cut for a variety of reasons, but mostly when she felt intense feelings such as despair, anger, or aloneness. The cutting replaced these feelings with numbness.
>
> Barbara's outpatient therapist knew about the cutting and had actually tried a number of interventions to make it stop. Several safety contracts had been established, but despite Barbara's superficial compliance, she continued to cut secretly and somewhat defiantly: "I know she wants me to stop, but it's my body and she doesn't understand how much I need it." Barbara's hospital therapist asked about details of the cutting and the circumstances under which it occurred. She also underscored both the adaptive role of the cutting and its impact on Barbara's life: "I know that cutting has been a kind of friend to you over the years in helping you cope with intolerable feelings and circumstances. However, you should realize that if you can't stop the cutting, you will not be able to find more adaptive ways to express your feelings and move on in your treatment. Only *you* can decide when you are ready to stop cutting. Rather than placing the responsibility on your outpatient therapist to 'make' you stop cutting, I think you should remember that the cutting makes you feel ashamed and out-of-control at times, and has interfered with your treatment."
>
> After considerable discussion, Barbara agreed to try and find ways to stop the self-cutting. She used several grounding techniques to try and control dysphoric dissociative states and followed through with a plan to try to talk to others when she had the impulse to cut. She also developed new techniques of controlling her impulses—for example, rubbing her forearms with an ice cube that produced a numbing feeling that was similar to the sensation of cutting and somehow made it less necessary to do so. Finally, Barbara devised a unique solution. Using a craft kit of wooden beads, she painted the name of each of her sons on two large

beads, which she then fashioned into bracelets, one for each arm. Subsequently, when she would find herself looking at her arms for a place to cut, she would see the bracelets and recall that she had made a commitment to herself and her family to try and stabilize her life. This proved very effective and she was able to stop cutting—for the first time in decades. However, two weeks after discharge from the hospital, the outpatient therapist noticed fresh scars on her arms. Barbara shamefully admitted, "I guess I've been forgetting to wear the bracelets." Barbara and her therapist were then able to discuss Barbara's essential role in controlling the self-cutting, and were able to devise a new strategy for addressing this issue in the context of her treatment.

THE MANAGEMENT OF SUICIDE RISK

The risk of suicide is a very real threat with many patients with complex PTSD. A heightened level of suicidal behaviors has been correlated with childhood trauma (Afifi et al., 2008; Nelson et al., 2002; Sarchiapone et al., 2009; Ystgaard, Hestetun, Loeb, & Mehlum, 2004), PTSD (Amir, Kaplan, Efroni, & Kotler, 1999; Ben-Yaacov & Amir, 2004; Kotler, Iancu, Efroni, & Amir, 2001; Sareen et al., 2007; Sareen, Houlahan, Cox, & Asmundson, 2005), and dissociative disorders (Foote, Smolin, Neft, & Lipschitz, 2008; Putnam et al., 1986; Ross & Norton, 1989). The specter of suicide is frequently omnipresent in the early treatment of severely traumatized patients. Many patients who have survived extensive early abuse have made suicide gestures or attempts, and nearly all such patients chronically contemplate suicide as a potential relief from their intolerable daily experiences.

The management of true suicide risk should be relatively straightforward. First, truly suicidal impulses and behavior must be distinguished from the parasuicidal behaviors involved in self-cutting or other self-harming behaviors. Second, clinicians must insist that the threat (or implied threat) of suicide not be used as a form of communication or negotiation. Third, therapists and patients must agree—in advance—that the real possibility of suicide is a crisis situation, and that any and all interventions can and should be used. Fourth, although both therapists and patients together may help determine the risk of suicide, therapists have the ultimate responsibility for acting to preserve patients' lives and well-being. These principles are central to managing chronic suicidal threat and necessary for the sanity of both patients and therapists. They cannot be compromised, and clear limits must be set concerning any violation of these principles.

Interpersonal conflict and struggle are often inherent features of the therapeutic relationship. It is a far safer therapeutic strategy to set clear limits concerning the principles about suicide from the outset, and to permit the inevitable conflict and negotiation to occur in other less lethal areas. I am indebted to my colleague and co-teacher in workshops for treating complex dissociative disorders, Audrey Wagner, PhD, for her clarity concerning the goals of therapy. As she clearly reminds our workshop attendees, therapy should be about improving the quality of life, *not* about deciding whether to live or die—an observation that has helped innumerable clinicians in their work. Agreement concerning this principle must be a prerequisite for starting or continuing therapy. Without such an agreement, treatment may well be unnecessarily prolonged, mired in endless negotiations about the possibility of suicide, or may even become therapeutically untenable with little hope for a positive outcome, with a greater likelihood of stalemate or even death through completed suicide.

The difference between suicidal and parasuicidal behavior is determined best by direct discussions with patients regarding the motivations and goals of their behavior. Patients are often able to be quite clear that there is no suicidal intent in certain self-harming activities. However, there are often areas of ambiguity, such as patients who hurt themselves in ways that might or might not be lethal, or in behavior that is not intended to be suicidal but might well result in serious injury or death (e.g., repeatedly driving while intoxicated). Because of the extreme consequences of this kind of ambivalent behavior, therapists should clearly err on the side of acting to safeguard patients' well-being if there is any substantial question of personal safety.

Patients' hints or threats about suicide can be a form of communication or negotiation. Statements such as "I'm not sure I can keep myself safe" are often a disguised way of asking, "Do you recognize that I am in pain and feel desperate?" or "What will you do for me if I don't hurt myself?" Therapists should confront such implied communications directly and ask if the patient is trying to communicate the intent to commit suicide—or some other message. Because unresolved questions concerning suicide are likely to result in hospitalization or other unwelcome outcomes, the burden is on patients to try to clarify the underlying message in their statements. Frank and direct discussion about suicide is the best deterrent against self-endangering behavior. If patients and therapists are unable to engage in such direct discussion, suicidal behavior may even increase. For example, the patient who says, "I'm been thinking about killing myself" as a way of asking, "Do you care about me?" may actually feel impelled to act if the question is not clarified and the patient feels disappointed or upset by the therapist's response.

Agreements that the patient will not attempt suicide, so-called *safety contracts* or *safety agreements*, can be very effective, particularly because many trauma patients have a rigid personal commitment of having to adhere to their promises ("I always keep my word"). However, from both a clinical and a medicolegal perspective, safety contracts do not substitute for the clinician's judgment about the patient's safety. For example, for a safety contract to be effective, the patient must have intact reality testing and—with all patients—there must be a sense of alliance between the patient and therapist. The presence of delusional beliefs may impel patients to make suicide attempts despite previous agreements not to do so, and in the absence of a basic alliance, patients may not feel bound by their contracts. Safety contracts must be interpreted in the total context of the patient's clinical situation and should be reviewed regularly.

The best safety contracts are made face-to-face with direct eye contact and with therapists sensing a level of sincerity (although often with reluctance on the patient's part) about the agreement. Safety contracts also have limitations. For example, it is almost impossible to devise a formal safety contract without loopholes, and patients may stick to the letter of the agreement but may find ways to violate the substance of the agreement (e.g., "I said I wouldn't overdose, but I didn't agree not to drive my car off the road" or "I agreed to be safe until our next appointment, but you canceled it and rescheduled it."). Furthermore, safety contracts are usually time-limited, because few patients can agree to long-term or indefinite contracts not to attempt suicide. For the convenience of not having to renegotiate the contracts, it is advisable to ask for as long a period of time as possible, for example, a year. However, few patients are able to make such a prolonged commitment, and contracts for a few months or weeks are much more common. It is incumbent on the clinician to keep track of the end date of safety contracts. They must be renewed, and any failure to do so may well be seen by the patient as permission to engage in self-endangering behavior, as in this clinical illustration:

> Ashley, an adolescent with a history of severe childhood abuse, had made several serious suicide attempts in her young life. She began working with a therapist, who helped her decrease her self-destructive behavior through a series of safety contracts that were established on a session-by-session basis. Ashley and her therapist took these contracts very seriously, including very detailed provisions in the contracts concerning not only the time period of the contracts but also various prohibitions against all sorts of self-harming and risk-taking behaviors. Following a therapy session approximately 18 months into the treatment, the therapist suddenly recalled that she had gotten an emergency telephone call near the end of the session and had neglected to renew the safety contract. After some thought, she decided that given the trust that had developed in the relationship and the precedence set by previous agreements, a continued safety contract was clearly implied, and she did not act further. Ashley, on the other hand, was acutely aware of the absence of the safety contract and was convinced that this was a clear message from her therapist that the therapist had finally gotten tired of her and wouldn't mind if she killed herself. She took an overdose of all her medication and was subsequently admitted to a hospital after being found by her roommate.

It is hence crucial that patients be asked to adhere to the spirit rather than the letter of any safety contacts. Although safety contracts may be useful, establishing some kind of ongoing commitment by the patient to continue to struggle to stay alive is much more important. As with safety contracts, this commitment must be repeatedly discussed and reaffirmed.

As is the case with most self-harming behavior, traumatized patients have intense ambivalence about suicide. After all, those who unambivalently wish to die have unfortunately already suicided. Many abuse survivors have intense internal conflict about being alive. When patients are unable to tolerate the pain of their own intense conflicts, therapists may find themselves assuming one side of the ambivalent feelings—once again, usually the good or positive side. Unfortunately, this sometimes permits patients to be unambivalently negative about this complex issue. Therapists and patients may find themselves battling over the issues involving actual survival rather than recognizing them as the projections of the patient's ambivalence and internal conflict:

> In the early years of my psychiatric career, I began treating Deborah, a 36-year-old mother of two, who entered therapy with the goal of wanting to feel "less tortured." She began to describe fragments of memory that suggested truly horrific physical, sexual, and emotional abuse in a highly chaotic family environment. As the therapy progressed, she became more and more aware of the extent of her abuse and more overwhelmed by feelings of depression, despair, and loneliness. Her suicidal ideation and self-destructive impulses increased. In therapy, Deborah claimed that she could no longer be responsible for her own personal safety and that I had to "hold the hope" for her. This resulted in many instances in which she would persuasively argue that her life had become a constant torment, and that I should understand and allow her to kill herself. I would then counter with reasons why she should live, including hopes for the future and the value of her life for herself and for others. Deborah rejected all of these arguments as false assertions. She even rejected the notion that her children would be devastated, arguing that they would be better off without her. I found myself becoming more and more anxious that she might suicide.
>
> Finally, I was able to say: "I understand that you wish to die and that life is a torture for you. However, I think you may be oversimplifying the situation to yourself. I think you have very mixed feelings about living and dying. Although you desperately wish to die, you have a remaining small hope that life might get better. Although you know that *I* want you to live, it is much more important for *you* to know that you both want to live and to die. I cannot convince you to live, but I can help you sit with the very uncomfortable feelings about not knowing what to do." Much to my surprise, Deborah acknowledged the validity of these observations, and the therapy then continued in a more stable manner.

Specifically concerning the issue of suicide, the therapist may need to temporarily assume responsibility for maintaining the patient's safety, such as arranging hospitalization when the patient is unable to commit to safety. However, any such stance should be short-lived, because the therapy is untenable unless patients assume the burden of working through their own conflicts about living.

Making a commitment to stay alive is essential for maintaining a workable alliance and therapeutic relationship. This simple fact is too often overlooked by desperately tortured patients and their well-intentioned therapists. Patients often may be so filled with their own pain that they ignore the fact that they have a basic responsibility in any relationship including the therapeutic relationship: that they must be alive to participate in the relationship, and that this assumption is a prerequisite for expecting that anyone else will make a commitment to them. Therapists may be afraid to bring up this issue of the patient's responsibility to remain alive because of the principle that therapists should not let any of their own feelings contaminate the therapy. However, even the therapeutic relationship depends on the most basic contract—that *both* parties agree to make a commitment to continue working together. Thus, another effective intervention is often the therapist confronting the patient's abandonment of the relationship, for example:

> "I know that you have many reasons to want to die. However, do you remember that you have often asked me to make a commitment to you? I am glad to do so for the foreseeable future, but it is only fair to ask that you do so too—by making some commitment to remaining alive. I have no wish to take away your ultimate control of the decision to live or die, but I do want to ask you to make a decision for now not to destroy our relationship."

Emergency interventions are required in situations where patients' lives are in danger. Too often, therapists feel they are not allowed to pursue critical options. Therapists should never agree to relinquish vital therapeutic interventions, for example, agreeing never to hospitalize the patient ("I'll just be put into restraints and be retraumatized"), to always discuss all options beforehand ("I'll never be able to trust you again"), or to never contact family members ("They'll never let me forget it"). Although it is always clinically desirable to discuss matters with patients and to respect their wishes, a possible imminent suicide is an emergency situation that may require extraordinary measures. Such measures may be necessary to save a life, even at the cost of destroying an ongoing therapeutic relationship.

No matter how well-managed a therapy may be, there is always the possibility of broken contracts and attempted or even completed suicides. The burden of the living with the sequelae of horrific abuse may be more than some victims can tolerate. Fortunately, the number of completed suicides is quite small considering that self-harmful behavior, chronic suicidal impulses, and even suicide attempts are quite common in severely traumatized patients with complex PTSD. In some respects, patients' ambivalence about living or dying is expressed in their use of suicide gestures such as medication overdoses rather than more lethal means such as self-inflicted gunshots or hanging.

In situations where there is a serious breach of the substance or spirit of agreements concerning safety (and the patient survives), the therapist needs to consider several options. First, is the therapist willing to continue the treatment? A chaotic and anxiety-provoking therapy places a considerable burden on the therapist, and therapists need to consider whether they are able and willing to continue. It is very important for therapists to be truly candid with themselves about this issue, as both the patient's and therapist's well-being depends on it. Too often, therapists convince themselves they can continue to treat difficult patients and then subtly act out their frustrations and anger much to the detriment of the treatment. Second, if therapists are willing and able to continue the treatment, they must determine what basic requirements must be met by the patient (e.g., agreements concerning safety, behavior, outside supports, shift in attitudes, etc.), and then ask the patient to meet these requirements in order to continue the therapy. A serious suicide attempt is a major breach of the therapeutic relationship, and it is then incumbent on the patient to demonstrate a willingness and ability to heal the rupture in order to continue the therapy.

REVICTIMIZATION[2]

One common failure of self-care results in the revictimization of childhood abuse survivors. I have observed a variety of behaviors in patients with traumatic backgrounds that range from seeming obliviousness to potential danger to repetitive reenactments of their abuse to chronic risk-taking that sometimes appears almost addictive in nature. These behaviors result from a variety of different and complex psychological processes that are tied to early abuse experiences and place many traumatized patients at considerable risk.

Shortly after developing an interest in understanding and treating patients with histories of childhood abuse, it seemed to me that there was an unusually high incidence of adult physical and sexual assaults in this patient population. In our study that was published in 1990 (Chu & Dill), we found that patients with a history of childhood sexual abuse were more than twice as likely to be victims of adult sexual assault than those with no sexual abuse history. Subsequent focused studies have confirmed that the rate of sexual revictimization is double for women who had been sexually abused in childhood compared to those without such histories (Gidycz, Coble, Latham, & Layman, 1993; Tjaden & Thoennes, 2000), and one large study of men showed a fivefold increase in the rate of adult sexual abuse if they had been sexually victimized in childhood (Desai, Arias, Thompson, & Basile, 2002).

In settings such as emergency rooms and crisis centers, adults with histories of childhood abuse have been shown more likely to be victims of multiple rapes and other kinds of revictimization (Briere & Runtz, 1987; Dutton, Burghardt, Perrin, Chrestman, & Halle, 1994; Follette et al., 1996). Even in psychotherapy, patients with a history of childhood sexual abuse are more likely to be the victims of therapists' sexual misconduct (Kluft, 1989b, 1990a). Therapists who have sexually exploitative impulses or who are repeat sexual offenders pose a serious risk to all patients, but particularly to those who have been previously victimized (Schoener, Milgrom, Gonsiorek, Luepker, & Conroe, 1990). Finally, revictimization is not limited to sexual abuse (which has been more widely studied than other types of abuse). In our 1990 study (Chu & Dill), women who had been physically abused in childhood were dramatically more likely to be physically abused as adults, with an odds ratio of 17:1.

---

[2] Portions of this section were adapted from the article, "The Revictimization of Adult Women with Histories of Childhood Abuse" (Chu, 1992b).

The underlying causes of revictimization are complex. In the case of repetitions of childhood victimization, there is the impetus for reenactment. By this, I do *not* mean to imply that the victim seeks subsequent harm (a version of perpetrators' "explanations" that victims "asked for it"). Rather, early abuse sets into motion powerful underlying psychological forces that can consciously or unconsciously affect subsequent thinking and behavior. The repetition compulsion in relation to childhood trauma may be one of the key factors behind revictimization. In his discussion of the repetition compulsion, Freud (1920/1955) postulated the "need to restore an earlier state of things" and a need for the person to rework the original experience, specifically taking an active versus a previously passive role, as a way of gaining a sense of mastery over the experience. He also noted that repetitions of repressed experience allowed venting of affects associated with the experience, particularly sadism and hostility. These two last dynamic issues—the active mastery of prior passive unpleasant experiences and the expression of affects associated with past experiences—are important in understanding the role of the repetition compulsion in the revictimization of survivors of childhood abuse. The compulsion to repeat may involve persons taking active (although unconscious) measures to reenact prior traumatic events, as in the following case example.

> Many years ago, I met Susie, a 27-year-old, single woman, with a childhood history of extreme physical and sexual abuse, who I began treating for chronic depression, emptiness, and self-destructive behavior. Frequently, when overwhelmed by her feelings (and often while somewhat intoxicated), she felt compelled to park along the side of major highways late at night, waiting to be "rescued." I would often hear about such episodes in the early morning hours when I was called by the state highway patrol; somehow Susie would let them know I was her therapist. I was then in the position of being her rescuer. After one of these episodes, I brought up my concern that she could be hurt by pursuing such behaviors. Susie was unable to understand why I objected to her behavior, saying that she only wanted someone to pay attention to her and that she knew how to take care of herself. After one episode in which she was picked up and sexually assaulted by a law enforcement officer, she withheld this information from me, feeling angry that I would probably say, "I told you so."

Perhaps the clearest examples of attempts at mastery through the repetition of early sexual trauma come from the reports that have linked prostitution with childhood sexual abuse. Studies of prostitutes have shown extremely high levels of childhood sexual abuse, and levels of both incest and rape that are far higher than in control groups of women (James & Meyerding, 1977; Silbert & Pines, 1981; Widom & Kuhns, 1996). Herman (1981) documented both promiscuity and victimization in women who had been sexually abused. It is in clinical situations that the elements of this type of repetition are clearly evident. One patient who frequently prostituted herself remarked, "When I do it, I'm in control. I can control them through sex." Her contempt for the men who used her was evident, and she was only minimally aware of how she may have been exploited. In this situation, it is clear that there was an attempt to have active control of a previously passively experienced victimization, and that a great deal of the affect (contempt and hostility) associated with previous sexual abuse was expressed.

The repetition of past abusive experiences might result in favorable outcomes if persons were actually able to master past aversive experiences through reenactments. Unfortunately, these attempts usually seemed doomed. The inherent interpersonal betrayals of childhood abuse frequently lead adults to avoid supportive alliances. Hence, when they are confronted with overwhelming repetitions of past abuse, they have only their own resources to draw upon and are frequently again overwhelmed, retraumatized, and revictimized. Moreover, the venting of bitterness and anger often results in further disruption of the interpersonal ties, which might otherwise provide protection and support. In this way, the childhood interpersonal arena is recreated and reexperienced, leaving its victims unprotected and exploited, ultimately leading to isolation, helplessness, and despair.

Trauma-related symptomatology is another key factor related to revictimization. When overwhelming life events (or the feelings associated with them) are dissociated, individuals are not only compelled to repeat the events but may also experience additional posttraumatic syndromes that place them at risk (Chu, 1992b; Gold, Sinclair, & Balge, 1999; Sandberg, Lynn, & Green, 1994). As Kluft (1989b) noted:

> They often have dissociative defenses that cloud their perceptions and leave them with a discontinuous experience of themselves and their mental contents. . . . Their defenses leave their sense of self and identity fragmented and experience becomes more compartmentalized than integrated. (p. 487)

Such persons, who are unable to bring their full experience to bear on a potentially dangerous situation, may act with less than their best judgment, leading to revictimization. The symptoms of chronic posttraumatic stress disorder, with the classic biphasic response of periods of intrusion alternating with periods of avoidance and numbing, are evident in many survivors of childhood abuse in their adult lives. During periods of intrusion, individuals have recurrent reexperiences of the traumatic events along with associated affect. Individuals who are actively reexperiencing abuse are unlikely to be revictimized; in fact, they may be hyperreactive even to circumstances that contain no real threat. However, during the numbing phase, when individuals avoid recalling their abuse, they have markedly constricted affect and are detached from others, placing them at higher risk for revictimization. Past traumatic events and the associated affects (including fear and anticipatory anxiety) are quite dissociated from conscious awareness. Thus, individuals may be in a quite threatening situation and be seemingly unaware of potential danger, as in the following example:

> Nancy, a young woman who was in treatment for the sequelae of extensive childhood physical and sexual abuse, was accustomed to taking long walks through

the woods around her home. She found these walks to be quite soothing and particularly helpful in allowing herself to block out painful memories of her childhood. One evening, while walking along a trail, Nancy found her path blocked by a young man riding a motorcycle and dressed in Army fatigues— apparently from a nearby Army base. With no qualms, she stopped and allowed herself to be engaged in conversation and accepted a ride on his motorcycle. She was shocked when he subsequently made sexual advances and raped her.

Dissociative symptoms and unavailability of normal anticipatory anxiety is most marked in patients with severe dissociative disorders. Their rigid compartmentalization of experience and identity places them at substantial risk for revictimization. Not only are traumatic experiences dissociated from consciousness, but many dysphoric affects (including anticipatory anxiety) are split off into separate self-states or alternate personalities, resulting in increased vulnerability of revictimization.

One other posttraumatic phenomenon is of note. The model of "inescapable shock" described by van der Kolk and others (van der Kolk et al., 1985; van der Kolk & Greenberg, 1987) is based on situations where the victim of trauma is helpless to prevent or escape from the aversive events. Inescapable shock leads to an impairment of the ability to learn how to escape from new aversive experiences. Thus, when persons with childhood abuse histories are faced with potentially threatening situations, they may feel extremely constricted in their choices and helpless to escape. Not only do they have difficulties in conceptualizing new ways to deal with traumatic circumstances, but they often feel overwhelmed by the return of feelings of helplessness associated with the original abuse that is triggered by the current trauma. This is often manifested in patients' descriptions of going limp, freezing, or becoming automatically submissive in the presence of a powerful, threatening, and abusive person.

The absence of nurturing interpersonal attachments in childhood is another powerful factor in revictimization. Disturbances of attachment, particularly separation and disruption of early childhood nurturing relationships, leave individuals vulnerable to being overwhelmed both in childhood and later as adults (Bowlby, 1980; Rutter, 1987). Thus, children who are subjected to traumatic experiences within the context of inadequately protective social environments are at greatest risk for ongoing difficulties in relating to others (see Chapter 4). They are hence deprived of any model of healthy relationships and lack the support that is inherent in a social network of relationships. Clinical and research psychologists David Finkelhor, PhD, and Angela Browne, PhD (1985), summarize the relational effects of traumatic childhood abuse, citing betrayal as a major dynamic issue:

Sexual abuse victims suffer from grave disenchantment. In combination with this there may be an intense need to regain trust and security, manifested in the extreme dependency and clinging seen in especially young victims. This same need in adults may show up in impaired judgment about the safety of other people. (pp. 536–537)

For many trauma survivors, the assumptions and schemas associated with early abuse are perhaps the most powerful factors that predispose individuals to revictimization. Having existed in an environment where they were chronically physically or sexually abused, individuals may later accept a level of either actual or threatened physical or sexual assault. Individuals who have not previously been abused would not tolerate such situations, but for those who have been victimized such situations are part of their assumptive world; their adult revictimization is experienced as painfully familiar. Investigation of so-called *traumatic bonding* suggests that prolonged exposure to intermittent abuse predisposes persons to form powerful emotional bonds to abusers and later to others like them (Dutton & Painter, 1981). Thus, victims of early abuse may tolerate abusive adult relationships, caught in a repetitive scenario of abuse and dependency. For such persons, the choice may seem to be either remaining in a battering relationship or being doomed to an endless state of aloneness. For many persons who lack a basic sense of self-efficacy and self-sufficiency, the logical choice may be to opt for the security of a continuing relationship and to accept continuing interpersonal abuse as an unavoidable inherent drawback.

There are also particular difficulties with individuals who have a negative self-image. Individuals who have been subjected to abuse and victimization and those who have not received positive reinforcement and validation in childhood are likely to have extremely negative self-regard and to view themselves as powerless (Bagley & Ramsey, 1986; Carmen, Rieker, & Mills, 1984; Gelinas, 1983; Herman et al., 1986; Shapiro, 1987; Swanson & Biaggo, 1985). Feeling responsible for the abuse or neglect that they suffered and sometimes seeing themselves as loathsome and defective, they cannot conceive of situations in which they would be regarded with esteem and respect. Hence, it is hardly surprising that individuals who hate themselves often allow themselves to become involved in situations in which they are revictimized. The role of victim, although painful, is consistent with their self-image.

In patients with a history of childhood abuse and patterns of revictimization, specific psychotherapeutic stances should be taken. The traumatic antecedents of revictimization should be acknowledged, but if patients are currently at risk for physical or sexual violence, the therapist should be highly sensitive to the danger of dismantling the dissociative and posttraumatic defenses that they need to cope with their current life situation. Because of the powerful unconscious dynamic factors that predispose abuse survivors to revictimization, therapists have the responsibility to educate patients about their vulnerability and to point out potentially risky or dangerous behaviors in relationships. An emphasis on relational issues is particularly important, as a solid therapeutic relationship and an interpersonal support network may be the most effective way of helping patients avoid revictimization. Finally, every effort should be made to identify situations, internal emotional states, and triggers that are connected to revictimization and to be aware of important protective defenses such as anticipatory anxiety.

Although therapists must insist that patients take personal responsibility for their own safety, this is not to imply that patients are to blame for being revictimized. An understanding of how persons with histories of early abuse are intensely vulnerable to subsequent revictimization should only underscore the responsibility of perpetrators who intentionally inflict harm on others. Similarly, the availability of vulnerable individuals does not absolve predators, who often seem to search out those whom they can exploit. Although abuse survivors need to understand the mechanisms through which they may be exploited and to control any behaviors that leave them more vulnerable, they cannot be held responsible for the sadistic and often illegal actions of others. To blame childhood abuse survivors for their own vulnerability and for causing their own subsequent exploitation may be one final form of revictimization.

8

Containment

Controlling Posttraumatic and Dissociative Symptoms[1]

The concept of a phase-oriented treatment approach for survivors of childhood trauma mandates that basic ego-supportive psychotherapy is the first order of business prior to exploration and abreaction of traumatic events. This work is a formidable task given the pervasive symptomatology that many traumatized patients bring to treatment. Florid posttraumatic and dissociative symptoms create chaos in patients' lives. These experiences include reexperiencing of past abuse (e.g., flashbacks) and numbing responses, out-of-control state changes such as identity switches in patients with dissociative identity disorder (DID), and the discontinuity of experience seen in partial or complete amnestic events. All of these symptoms can be severe in their expression and are often intolerable to patients, and all must be modulated or stabilized to reduce the level of crisis in patients' lives. This is the real and important trauma therapy that sets the stage for later abreactive work.

Much of our understanding of the effects of childhood abuse is founded on psychodynamic and psychoanalytic principles. Psychologists Laurie Anne Pearlman, PhD, and Karen Saakvitne, PhD (1995), have observed:

> Much if not most of our fundamental premises about insight-oriented psychotherapy with trauma survivors—what it is, how it works, and why it works—are originally psychoanalytic in origin.... The fact that current relationships are influenced by internalized objects and object relationships is a fundamental psychoanalytic concept essential to understanding transferences and reenactment in trauma therapies.... This relatively simple idea elegantly incorporates a developmental perspective and sets the stage for the recognition of the roles that unconscious processes and early relationships play in adult functioning and identity. (pp. 43–44)

----

[1] I wish to credit my colleague, Audrey Wagner, PhD, for her contributions to this chapter. When you have taught together for years, it sometimes becomes unclear as to who first thought of what. To the extent that I was able to disentangle our work, I have noted her contributions (or it is obvious in the examples). I am grateful to Dr. Wagner for her personal and professional support over the years, which has helped me hone my understanding of the complex issues that we encounter in our work.

Traumatic experiences in childhood disrupt the normal formation of psychic structures that are gradually formed over the course of development. Thus, severe and persistent early abuse strongly affects ego capacities and defenses, self-regulatory mechanisms, and concepts of the self and others.

Although trauma theory derives extensively from psychodynamic and psychoanalytic perspectives, effective treatment interventions draw on an eclectic variety of perspectives, including not only psychodynamics but cognitive-behavioral, object relations, self-psychology, and family/systems theories as well. The overall philosophy of the treatment of trauma survivors is consistent with psychodynamic principles: understanding the role of past experience, transforming conflicted unconscious processes into conscious thoughts and feelings, and integrating repressed and dissociated experiences (Matthews & Chu, 1997). However, early in treatment, when the control of symptomatology is a priority, cognitive-behavior interventions are particularly useful. Although clinicians trained in this modality may have particular expertise, the basic principles involved in a cognitive-behavioral approach can be understood and used by all clinicians treating patients with complex posttraumatic and dissociative disorders.

PSYCHOEDUCATION AS A COGNITIVE-BEHAVIORAL PARADIGM

The basic paradigm for therapeutic interventions used to contain dysphoric or dysfunctional symptomatology has two parts. The *cognitive* component involves setting out a psychoeducational framework and conceptualizing approaches to achieve treatment goals, and enlisting the patient in an alliance to work toward these goals. The *behavioral* component consists of instituting and rehearsing interventions, and then repeating or modifying interventions until the treatment goals are attained. This type of cognitive-behavioral approach is not only pragmatic but also tends to minimize the often overly intense transferential aspects of the therapeutic relationship. It offers a task on which both patient and therapist can focus and alleviates the all-too-common pitfall of struggles as to whether the patient or the therapist is going to control the agenda of the therapy. As I have often said to patients, "It isn't a question of doing it *my* way or *your* way. These are the ways that have been shown to help persons like yourself overcome the difficulties that you experience."

When it comes to the task of controlling posttraumatic and dissociative symptomatology, the cognitive psychoeducational component is more important by far than the behavior techniques. Educating patients about the necessary and possible goal of achieving control of their symptoms is essential to collaboration around this task. Without an alliance concerning symptom control, no interventions or techniques are likely to be effective, and patients are likely to reflexively oppose such efforts: "I've tried that and it doesn't work!" Conversely, with such an alliance, many interventions may work, and patients are then often able to devise individualized techniques that are effective for their particular symptoms. Given that pervasive mistrust is a hallmark of persons with extensive interpersonal abuse, forming and maintaining an alliance around the goal of symptom control with traumatized patients is a major undertaking. Moreover, one of the inherent characteristics of posttraumatic and dissociative experiences is that they feel out of control. That is, patients experience these symptoms as happening *to* them—overwhelming feelings and sensations that emerge from within, often triggered by unanticipated events in their environments. Very few patients easily accept the idea that they can have much control over the flashbacks and state switches that are part of their daily lives, and it is often difficult to engage them in this task.

One way to approach this dilemma is to clarify that perfect control is not the goal and is not immediately expected. Rather, the expectation is only that patients begin to look at these uncontrolled experiences in such a way that they can begin to have even a minimal impact on them: "I know that you feel as though your flashbacks are totally out of control, and that you have no way of knowing when they will hit and how you can get out of them. However, if you are willing to work very hard with me we may be able to find some small ways that you can alter these experiences to some degree. Do you think it might be possible to get even as little as 5% more control over these difficulties?" Presented in this way, patients are more easily able to see the process as incremental advances in control over the symptoms that are inherently experienced as uncontrollable.

Even some of the most uncontrollable posttraumatic and dissociative symptoms *can* be contained through extraordinary efforts of patients if they are motivated to do so. The following case illustrates both the possibility of controlling posttraumatic and dissociative symptoms and the difficulties of such control in traumatized patients. The patient was treated many years ago, and at the time, her symptoms were not recognized as probably being posttraumatic in nature:

Mary, a 38-year-old, married woman and mother of two, was hospitalized in 1978 for problems with depression and difficulty functioning in the inpatient unit of a teaching hospital where I was a psychiatric resident. She was known to have a background of considerable trauma, but her difficulties were characterized as "pseudo-neurotic schizophrenia," which implied a kind of surface functioning over a core of schizophrenic-like psychosis. Her symptomatology included periods of acute decompensation—then described as transient psychosis but now more easily recognized as reexperiencing of the trauma—in which she would become paralyzed with fear and act in a very young and regressed manner. Her clinical course was prolonged (even by the standards of the pre–managed care era) because of the fragility of her condition. Despite sophisticated psychotherapy and use of medications, she had frequent decompensations, making it difficult for her team to see how she could be discharged to home.

Nonetheless, it was eventually decided to begin the transition process to home, and Mary was put on a bus for a home visit and an appointment with her outpatient therapist. The bus headed down a major highway toward her hometown, only to be snowed in by the Northeast blizzard of 1978, and became stranded on the highway, miles from any help. Somewhat surprisingly, Mary did not fall apart. Rather, she rallied both herself and the other passengers on the bus, leading them in camp songs ("100 Bottles of Beer on the Wall," etc.) to help keep up their spirits and melting snow for drinking water. Eventually, after being rescued by the highway police, she abruptly decompensated and was brought back to the hospital in a disorganized and helpless state.

A similar clinical situation occurred a few years ago with a patient with a dissociative disorder whose seemingly out-of-control symptoms were brought under control by external circumstances:

Jill, a thin and athletic young woman with DID, was hospitalized for suicidal impulses and aggressive acting out. Despite her rather frightening history of florid posttraumatic and dissociative symptoms, and self-destructive and violent behavior, she presented as cooperative and articulate for the most part—but only during the day. As the evening progressed, she began to have episodes of apparent identity switching and flashbacks. During these periods she appeared to be reliving physical and sexual assaults (that had originally occurred during the evening). She would become agitated, panicked, and angry, striking out at any-one who approached her. This behavior continued on a daily basis over several weeks, often necessitating the use of restraints.

Restraining the patient was particularly traumatic for all involved, because while in restraints the patient apparently reexperienced her childhood assaults and sexual molestation. Her screams were piteous, and she could not be reas-sured or soothed. The hospital staff was split concerning how to intervene. While some staff members believed that she was manipulatively trying "to get attention," others felt that she had no ability to control the episodes and would continue to need this level of external support. The uncontrollable behaviors escalated to the point that the patient began to throw heavy furniture, and a staff member was injured. After this incident, the staff agreed that better control was necessary, and the patient was told that if the episodes continued for more than three days, arrangements would be made for her transfer to another facility. The patient had made strong attachments to various members of the staff and was panicked at the thought of transfer. The violence never recurred, but it was obvi-ous that the patient had to exercise very intense efforts (with the mental strain clearly visible in her face and tensed and rigid body) to maintain control in the evenings, and she was able to utilize a high level of support through numerous verbal interventions from staff.

Both of these patients were highly symptomatic, decompensated, and regressed. Feel-ing helpless and exhibiting a certain amount of passivity, they seemed to expect oth-ers to assume control of their behavior. The posttraumatic symptoms that they both experienced were quite powerful, and they usually felt unable to control the changes in their experiential states. However, under fairly dire conditions that made it necessary to exercise more control, both patients were able to do so, albeit using an extraordinary amount of personal resources and drawing on the support of others.

A kind of medical analogy may be apt here. Persons with acute viral gastroenteritis almost inevitably suffer from explosive vomiting and diarrhea. These unpleasant events cannot be suppressed beyond a certain point, but given some effort, one can exercise how and when they occur in order to avoid public embarrassment. Similarly, posttraumatic and dissociative symptoms have a kind of powerful urgency, and yet patients can utilize their own resources (and those of others) to help bring them into control. Very frequently, if an alliance is formed between patients and their therapists around this task, patients can consciously work toward the goal of control and make substantial progress over weeks and months. In some circumstances, however, external control may be necessary, and the use of hospitalization and/or sedating medication can be indicated. Persisting, ongoing, uncontrolled symptomatology makes therapeutic gains impossible and eventually destroys the therapeutic process. As a result, such seemingly drastic measures as ending or suspending therapy, hospitalization, or transfer to other caregivers are logical consequences of the failure to *begin* to establish control.

STRATEGIES FOR CONTROLLING POSTTRAUMATIC AND DISSOCIATIVE SYMPTOMS

There are a variety of techniques for controlling posttraumatic and dissociative symptoms that my colleague, Audrey Wagner, PhD, categorizes as management strategies, safe/special places, and overall crisis planning.

Management Strategies

Many of the management strategies for patients who experience posttraumatic and dissociative symptoms fall into the category of *grounding techniques* and utilize a focus on the five senses: sight, hearing, touch, smell, and taste. One of the most basic strategies is to ensure good ambient illumination. A well-lit environment can be very helpful in grounding patients, particularly in the evening or at night. Whether in the office, hospital, or at home, this means providing adequate lighting and encouraging patients not to sit in dark or dimly lit environments when they feel anxious and vulnerable. When frightened or overwhelmed, many patients feel compelled to retreat to darkened rooms, hiding in their beds, closets, or other confined spaces. Seeking safety in such places only increases their propensity to lose their bearings in current reality and become more pulled into the flashback experience.

Maintaining visual contact with cues in the environment is also crucial. In many ways, the syndrome of so-called ICU psychosis has similarities to the loss of control of posttraumatic and dissociative symptoms. In intensive care units, severely ill medical or surgical patients are placed in an unfamiliar environment that is dimly lit with few cues as to date or time of day, and they are in contact with many unfamiliar people. Under such conditions, some ICU patients become quite disorganized and disoriented. The solution is often simple. Adding extra lighting, a clock and calendar, and ensuring contact with familiar people and objects often restores patients' orientation and equilibrium. In a similar way, patients who tend to get lost in dysphoric dissociative states benefit from focusing on their physical environment and on familiar and comforting objects. Psychiatric nurse and expressive therapist, Elizabeth Benham, RN, worked with patients in our program for years and published a description about some of these kinds of interventions in a hospital setting (Benham, 1995):

> It is by example that we first teach patients how to ground themselves. When a patient is experiencing florid dissociative symptoms,... we approach the patient and call her by name and identify ourselves. We tell the patient where she is and what month, day, and year it is. We repeat this information over and over in reassuring tones. If the space... is darkened, we illuminate the area by turning on the lights, or opening the drapes. We ask the patient to open her eyes if they are closed, so that the patient can see where she is and who we are. We also ask the patient to try and move her eyes so as not to be in a daze; as this seems to keep patients locked into a dissociated state of flashback. We encourage the patient to look at our faces so that eye contact can be made.... We tell the patient we know she is frightened, but that she is safe. We ask her to begin naming what she sees in the room such as the color of the rug, or chair, how many chairs are in the room. We might ask her to identify what color her shirt is, the color of our clothes, or even how many shoelace holes are in her sneakers. If we know the patient well enough, we might remind her of significant others such as a child or a spouse. Instructing patients to feel their own weight in the place they are sitting is also useful, as is having them sense where their other body parts are touching. For example, we ask, "Can you feel your elbow on the chair?" "How about the glasses on your nose?" "What about the rings on your fingers?" or "Can you feel your watch on your wrist?"
>
> Once the patient is alert enough to recognize us, it is helpful to have the patient reposition the posture that is held during the dissociative or flashback experience. Having her stand up and walk with us allows the patient to connect with the ground.... As we walk with the patient, the patient continues to identify the surroundings. If she is not alarmed by our suggestion, we encourage her to look in a mirror, so that she can see she is an adult and not a child in a traumatic situation. (p. 33)

This description of interventions for posttraumatic symptoms contains several critical elements. It is particularly important to note that although the patient's emotional state that is induced by reexperiences of early abuse is acknowledged, the etiologic traumatic experience is not explored. That is, patients are asked to find ways to cope with the dysphoric experiences and not to deepen them. In the early phase of treatment, premature exploration most often leads to further loss of control and the emergence of more memories rather than containment. The tone of voice that one uses is also important. It should be reassuring, but it should not be overly soft, soothing, and rhythmic. Some posttraumatic symptoms such as flashbacks can be understood as autohypnotic phenomena, and a tone of voice that is meant to be soothing can have the reverse effect of prolonging the trancelike reexperiencing state. A calm and firm tone of voice with a normal level of pitch and volume that avoids rhythmic cadences will often help orient the patient.

In an interpersonal situation, eye contact is enormously effective. In fact, direct and focused eye contact makes it impossible for patients to remain in dysphoric dissociated states. There are inherent qualities in eye contact that produce a powerful interpersonal connection that is enormously grounding. Many crisis situations have been resolved simply by therapists being quietly and firmly directive, asking patients to look at them and to focus on the therapist's face and make eye contact. Some traumatized patients have difficulty with direct eye contact, perhaps fearing the anger or hatred seen in the eyes of abuse perpetrators. Even when asked to look directly, some patients may be so fearful that they cannot do so, or they have a terrorized, blank, and unfocused gaze. In these situations, the therapist may direct the patient to look around and name other objects in the room or to look at parts of the therapist's body that are less threatening (e.g., legs, hair, shirt). Aside from being effective as a grounding technique, eye contact demonstrates that some kind of interpersonal connection can be helpful and not hurtful as it was in the past.

In addition to using sight, the other senses can be used for grounding as well. Hearing and sounds can be used by listening to music, singing, or reading aloud. Using touch can take the form of feeling familiar and soothing objects or paying attention to one's body and the feelings of one's surroundings (e.g., the support and the feel of the fabric of a chair). Pleasant, strong-smelling substances can counteract the olfactory hallucinations—most commonly the smells of alcohol, sweat, and semen—that are associated with early trauma such as sexual abuse. Patients can carry a vial or small container of fragrant substances such as coffee beans or potpourri for this purpose. Drinking hot or cold, pungent, or fragrant liquids (e.g., hot coffee or tea, ice water, or juice) can be a part of the grounding strategies as well. For some years there was a sign over the door of the Trauma and Dissociative Disorders Unit at McLean Hospital that read "The Land of the Frozen Oranges." This referred to the supply of whole oranges that was kept in the freezer for use in grounding. The cold, hard oranges and the pungent smell of them when patients would dig their fingernails into the skins proved to be very helpful for patients to regain a sense of their current reality.

In recent years, there have been initiatives through state mental health divisions for crisis intervention in inpatient programs specifically designed to reduce the use of restraint and seclusion, particularly for patients with histories of trauma. So-called sensory stimulation rooms are designed to provide soothing and grounding sensory input for patients who are agitated or distressed. These rooms are painted in a pleasant color and have comfortable seating. Music can be played, and weighted blankets, squeezable toys, colored glasses, aromatic substances, and a variety of other visual and tactile objects provide sensory input to help calm and ground patients.

Transitional objects—items that remind patients about the presence and support of their therapists—can also be useful grounding tools. Dr. Wagner keeps a bowl of small, smooth stones in her office for just this purpose. Patients may take and keep a stone to use as a tactile grounding strategy and also as a reminder of her presence in their current lives. She also uses photographs and written notes and audiotaped messages (done in the therapy session) as transitional objects. Her patients also can call her office voicemail and listen to the outgoing message as a reminder of her role in their lives, and they can leave a message to simply establish a sense of connection. (She does instruct them specifically to ask for a callback if that is necessary, but otherwise she just listens to the message.)

Using grounding techniques in an office or hospital setting provides the opportunity to learn more about the internal emotional events that precede loss of control. Flashbacks and state switches are experienced as happening abruptly and unpredictably without any warning. However, careful monitoring of emotional states often shows that dysphoric posttraumatic or dissociative states are often preceded by certain specific kinds of internal emotional states that escape the awareness of most patients. Practicing grounding in a treatment setting offers an opportunity to learn about these internal states, as in the following example:

Jane, a young woman with a history of severe physical and emotional abuse, was prone to flashbacks of being berated, humiliated, and beaten by her father whenever she began to feel too close (and hence vulnerable) to another person. Shortly after beginning therapy, I noticed that she wasn't able to maintain eye contact, and she seemed to drift away into some internal state. She seemed oblivious to my efforts to attract her attention, and then she appeared quite frightened and almost as if she was fending off blows. After considerable efforts on the part of both Jane and me, she was able to maintain visual focus on a small toy rocking horse that was part of the office decor.

After several months of work on grounding, she was even able to look at me briefly for a few seconds at a time. During this process, I asked about her internal emotional experience: "I wonder if you can tell me what you are feeling inside when you begin to have trouble looking at me. Is there some feeling or sensation that you are experiencing during those times?" Eventually, Jane was able to identify levels of increasing anxiety that she experienced as a tightness in the pit of her stomach. She could then recognize that whenever this feeling became worse, she was beginning to lose contact with her current reality. We were then able to devise various relaxation techniques, including simple measures such as taking a series of deep breaths, which tended to reduce the feelings and sensations associated with the anxiety. I also allowed her to borrow the toy rocking horse from my office, which she found helpful when trying to ground herself at home.

Therapists who are familiar with cognitive-behavioral techniques (including some DBT interventions) may also wish to use formal mood monitoring or behavioral chain analysis to help patients track the specific emotions they experience, as well as the intensity of particular emotions that call for therapeutic interventions. This kind of attention to internal emotional states may be extremely helpful for patients to become more aware of their emotional functioning and more able to have control over them.

When patients have intense reexperiencing (e.g., flashbacks and intense emotional states related to the trauma), they can lose the ability to distinguish the past from the present. *Cognitive strategies* are designed to help them tell the difference between *feelings* from the past and *facts* about the present. Dr. Wagner has observed that patients can easily get stuck in the past. She works with patients to put together a list of facts about the present, particularly anything that is true about the present that *contradicts* the emotional experience about the past, as in this example:

The FACTS
My name is Sally Smith.
I am 38 years old.
My children's names are Rose and Joseph.
I live in Natick, Massachusetts.
My father lives in New Jersey; he doesn't even know where I live.
I have two dogs, Bert and Ernie.
I work at the State Bank.
I use computers at my work.
It is July 2010.
Audrey is my therapist.

Patients are able to personalize the list of The Facts as a way of reminding themselves about the reality of their current lives and to realize that many of their intense and dysphoric feelings belong in the past. Using the list proactively—reading it or even reciting it out loud when patients start to feel destabilized—can enhance grounding and prevent dysfunctional reexperiencing.

Specialized techniques such as *putting away* painful experiences or feelings can provide containment between sessions or seal over premature breakthroughs of memory. Dr. Wagner often helps patients visualize mental images such as a container that has an opening that only allows one to put things in but not to take things out, much like the deposit slot at an ATM machine. After patients are well grounded they can deposit memories or intense feelings to be put away in the container. In further elaborating the imagery, the container can only be opened with two imagined keys—like a bank safe deposit box—with one key to be held by the patient and the other to held by the therapist. In this way there can be agreement about only accessing those memories and feelings in the office when both the patient and therapist agree to do so. In imagination, the container can be put away—in a vault or even in a more imaginary place like the bottom of the ocean. In this way, posttraumatic and dissociative symptoms can be symbolically contained, allowing patients to seal over overwhelming memories and feelings, to pace the therapy, and to limit the most difficult work to the therapy sessions.

Putting away is a guided imagery technique—a meditative or hypnotic intervention used without formal trance induction involving internal visualization. In guided imagery, a person is asked to imagine all of the details of a particular scenario or situation. Although this technique has uses for a variety of therapeutic purposes in many types of clinical situations, it has particular utility in treating trauma-related disorders—in this case, to pace the therapy and allow painful memories to be available only when working in therapy.

Safe/Special Places

Guided imagery can also be used to promote relaxation and a feeling of safety. In the early phase of trauma treatment, it can be used to help patients to imagine and visualize a place where they can feel completely safe and secure, hence the name of a *safe place*. Some patients cannot conceive of a place that feels completely safe, so they may wish to refer to a *special place*, which is relatively secure. The goal of this intervention is to produce a relaxation response. Once patients learn to use guided imagery, they are able to go to their safe/special place at will and to induce the relaxation response, which can be especially useful when they are feeling overwhelmed by reexperiences of the past. This, in turn, helps them manage the cycle of anxiety that they will become overwhelmed, knowing that they have a way to counter the waves of panic and fear.

The exact characteristics of safe/special places are determined by the individuals. Some choose a natural setting such as a beautiful woodland clearing, a sunlit garden, or a beach. Others have rooms in imagined structures (which is particularly common for patients with DID who may already have an organized internal architecture). Still others create a safe/special place that could not exist in reality, such as a comforting room made of flannel or full of cotton balls. The crucial element in making effective safe/special places is to fully develop them in imagination and to practice accessing them so that patients can do so at the first sign of posttraumatic and dissociative problems.

Formal relaxation techniques, guided imagery, and even autohypnosis have an important adjunctive role for therapists who are skilled in these modalities. It should be emphasized that early in the treatment process these techniques are used for stabilization, containment, and relaxation, *not* for exploration of traumatic experiences. Hypnotherapeutic techniques such as age regression, affect bridges, and various forms of visualizing traumatic experiences are usually contraindicated until stabilization is achieved. All such techniques need to be used skillfully and cautiously, because some of the altered states or trance states induced by these techniques can have adverse results, as in the following clinical illustration:

> Steve, an adolescent young man, repetitively suffered from extremely painful dysphoric states in which he relived the beatings that he received as a child. After identifying some of the emotional cues that seemed to presage these reexperiences, he and his therapist used some visual imagery to help him relax. Because Steve was fond of swimming and the ocean, his therapist helped him visualize sitting in warm tropical waters and feeling the waves wash over his legs and lower body. This technique worked well, and the therapist encouraged him to try this technique at home; in retrospect, this was premature given that they had not had much chance to practice accessing and to fully develop this safe/special place. That evening, when Steve was starting to feel anxious, he was successfully able to visualize the ocean scene, but he quickly panicked when he lost control of the scenario and experienced being pummeled by crashing waves and being drawn out into the ocean and deeper waters.

Crisis Planning

Therapeutic efforts in the office or hospital setting are crucially important, not only for their immediate impact, but also as rehearsals of the interventions that patients can adapt for use out of the office. Most crisis situations happen at inopportune times. For example, patients with PTSD and dissociative disorders often report that they become most panicked and develop dysphoric symptoms in the evening or nighttime. The timing of these symptoms is caused by the lessening of visual cues in the environment and the loss of control that results from fatigue. In addition, some patients identify evening as the time when sexual abuse occurred, and they become more anxious as the day progresses. Thus, unless therapists and patients subscribe to the view that therapists should be available at any hour of the day or night to provide therapeutic support (a very bad idea for both parties), every patient must develop a crisis plan for use at anytime.

A crisis plan is a simple strategy that involves formulating a list of sequential activities or interventions to be used in situations when patients feel anxious or overwhelmed. It is often helpful to ask patients to go through the concrete process of actually writing down the list, which reinforces the interventions in the crisis plan that are easy to forget when patients are overwhelmed. The preplanned interventions may include grounding techniques, cognitive strategies, various activities and distractions, as well as the timing of when to reach out for more help. Some interventions are applicable to a wide variety of patients. Such interventions include turning on lights or pulling up blinds and opening curtains, turning on the television or radio, and calling friends or other supportive persons. Other interventions are more specific to individuals and may include such activities as relaxation exercises, accessing one's safe/special place, reading or looking through art or picture books, expressive modalities including painting or singing, taking a warm bath (or cold shower), calling a hotline, doing physical exercise such as jogging or simply walking, or playing with pets or comforting objects such as stuffed animals. Here is one example of a crisis plan:

> Read "The Facts" while holding ice.
> Spend time in safe/special place at home.
> Soothing activities—take a warm bath, read, make some tea.
> Distracting activities—listen to a CD, play with Bert and Ernie.
> Stress-releasing activity—go for a walk, clean the stove, tear paper, throw ice into the bathtub.
> Listen to Audrey's tape.
> Call Audrey to leave a message.
> Repeat all steps above.
> Call Audrey and leave a message asking her to call me back.

Calling one's therapist is at the end of the list for two reasons. It is important to ask patients to respect therapists' time and personal life outside of therapy sessions. But more importantly, it is therapeutically beneficial for patients to see if they can use their own resources to regain their baseline stability without having to be dependent on their therapists.

As an overall plan to avoid crisis, patients should maintain a regular structure to promote grounding and self-care, especially during periods of predictable stress. For example, if evenings are consistently difficult, routine activities such as drawing the curtains, turning on lights, and engaging in specific activities are important for ongoing containment and stability. Patients may use safe/special places both in their imagination and in their real-world environment, such as well-lit comfortable areas with soothing objects where they may go when feeling especially frightened or impulsive. (These should *not* be places that are similar to the places where they took refuge from trauma as a child, e.g., in a closet or under a bed, because they evoke feelings from the past.) Patients must be engaged in the process of formulating their personal crisis plans, as they are often able to provide some very individualized or unique solutions. One married woman was able to use her wedding ring as a comforting and grounding object that reminded her that she was an adult and not being abused as she was when she was a child. Another patient, described by Benham (1995), who loved to cook and bake, used these activities to provide relaxation. Because it was too difficult to organize a baking activity when she was panicked, she prepared kits of premeasured ingredients packaged in shoeboxes along with recipe cards. When she began to feel overwhelmed, she simply opened a box and began to cook.

All of the interventions in the crisis plan may need considerable practice and rehearsal. As Benham (1995) aptly points out:

> These interventions have a cumulative effect. The patient will not necessarily feel immediate relief the first time that the intervention is tried. Over time and with

practice, the interventions become progressively more effective. Most patients initially see their only choices for relating to their emotions as either "stuffing it" as they did in their painful past, or losing control, which usually leaves them with a poor self-image. With practice, the patient finds that she can process feelings without being overwhelmed by them or letting them take over her life. (p. 33)

Patients' ability to achieve some measure of control over their posttraumatic and dissociative experiences has enormous benefits. They begin to have a sense of being empowered in areas that formerly left them feeling helpless and traumatized. They can begin to limit the intrusion of symptomatology to times that such experiences are useful and appropriate, such as in the therapy sessions. In treatment sessions, patients can use their newfound abilities to limit regression, putting away overwhelming experiences until the next session. This ability is crucial to maintaining a balance between therapeutic work and functioning, and is essential in order to limit regression while attempting to resolve the effects of traumatization. Well-developed skills in containing and controlling symptomatology are prerequisites for the effective abreaction—working through and integrating experiences of past abuse. The process of learning control may be difficult and time consuming. There are few shortcuts, but patients and therapists who invest the time and energy to achieve these fundamental skills will be able to rely on them to facilitate the process of recovery.

9

The Therapeutic Dance

Relational Dilemmas in Treating Complex PTSD

Many of the survivors of the battlefields of childhood abuse carry with them the scars of family wars. Having been repeatedly victimized and defeated, they remain wary—fearful of attack and prepared to retreat, mistrustful of alliances and expecting betrayal from others, and alienated from the rest of the world. Many investigators and clinicians have described these difficulties that impair the relational capacity of chronically traumatized patients (see Chapter 4). However, the experience of this interpersonal world is most vividly communicated by abuse survivors through their relationships with others, including the relationships with the clinicians that treat them. Their communications—in the form of unarticulated feelings and behaviors based on fear, anger, and despair—speak with mute torment about their past relationships and the harshness of the interpersonal world they continue to inhabit. Only by entering this interpersonal world—and by intermittently sharing the experience of the chronically abused patient—are clinicians able to understand their patients' dilemmas and effectively treat their relational dilemmas.

ASSUMPTIONS CONCERNING BASIC TRUST

Survivors of severe interpersonal abuse experience intense internal conflict about their relationships with others. Despite having been abused, exploited, controlled, betrayed, and abandoned, many still have a persistent wish to engage with others in ways that might alleviate their pain. Yet, even these wishes are influenced by their early experiences and their own sense of disempowerment. They see other persons only through the lens of their victimization. Having little sense of their own self-worth or self-efficacy, they cannot engage in relationships that are partnerships between equals. Rather, others are seen as powerful potential rescuers who may also become powerful abusers. In this sense, relationships provide little gratification and perpetuate only uncertainty, conflict, and fear.

Underestimating the fundamental level of basic trust for survivors of childhood abuse leads to one of the most common forms of empathic failure on the part of therapists and other clinicians. Clinicians often bring their own set of assumptions about the world—usually intact assumptions about the benevolence of others and their own sense of self-empowerment and self-worth—that are often at considerable odds with patients' assumptions about the malevolence of others and their own vulnerability. In fact, in order to maintain a normally optimistic set of assumptions, therapists frequently exercise a kind of self-preserving denial concerning the experiences of abused patients, only to be startled at times by the reactions of their patients, as in the following clinical example:

> Tracy, a 16-year-old girl, had experienced a lifetime of pervasive abuse. In her infant and toddler years, she had been brutalized by her father and neglected by her impaired mother. She was subsequently removed from her home by a social service agency and was brought up in a series of foster homes and group homes that ranged from grossly abusive to distantly caring. Following placement in a residential school setting, Tracy appeared withdrawn and angry, and she had difficulties with both her schoolwork and her social interactions with peers. She was referred for therapy with a well-meaning psychiatric resident.
>
> During an initial period of several weeks, Tracy was rather quiet. Although she responded with only silence or monosyllabic answers, she seemed willing in coming to the therapy sessions. As the resident continued to express interest in Tracy's current and past experiences and pressed her to express her feelings, she became more withdrawn in sessions. Although she continued to show up reliably for her therapy, she appeared more and more uncomfortable. When pressed by the resident about the cause of her anxiety, she finally blurted out, "What do you want from me? Everybody wants something from me." Panicked by her own outburst, she then tried to run out of the room. The resident quickly rose from his chair and went toward Tracey, who was blindly struggling with the door handle. She recoiled and cried out, "Please don't hit me!"

It can be difficult for clinicians who have always trusted in the basic benevolence of the world and other people to understand the vulnerability that abused patients experience in interpersonal relationships. Although they long for a sense of interpersonal connection in the therapeutic relationship, the increased intimacy actually causes heightened anxiety rather than being reassuring. Their basic assumption—based on their early abuse experiences—is that others will exploit their vulnerability to find a way to hurt them. Even if a therapist is able to get through the interpersonal defenses of a patient and to be seen as kind or helpful, the patient is thrown into more internal conflict, trying to juggle the fragile sense of the therapist as benevolent with the certainty that the therapist will use or abandon them. This point was brought home to me when a patient in the early phase of treatment somewhat angrily told me how she felt about me: "You asked if I was able to hold onto a sense of you when I'm not here. Are you crazy? You think I *like* to think about you? You *seem* okay, but that just makes me feel more worried, wondering when you're going to turn on me."

This kind of conflict can be intolerable to patients and may lead to a classic type of negative therapeutic reaction. From the therapist's perspective, the therapeutic process may seem to be going well, with patients making progress with increased interpersonal connection, more sharing of information, or more expression of feelings. But, panicked by the increased sense of intimacy and vulnerability, patients may regress or even sabotage the therapeutic process. It can be confusing and unexpected when patients retreat to dysfunctional isolation and many of the negative and sometimes self-destructive ways they previously used to deal with the world—for no apparent reason. Unless this negative therapeutic process is seen for what it is, this reenactment of early abuse-related relational dilemma can stalemate the therapy as the patient views the therapist with hostility, fear, and suspicion, and the therapist sees the patient as uncooperative, unmotivated, and difficult.

One of the most primary developmental tasks, as described by the developmental psychologist Erik Erickson (1968), is the development of basic trust. Based on experiences from the earliest years of life, children come to expect that fundamental needs for nurturing and care will be met. If such needs are not met, or are subsequently denied through pervasive victimization, children do not acquire a sense of basic self-worth, nor do they develop a sense of basic trust or interpersonal safety, beliefs that they carry into adulthood—described by Janoff-Bulman (1992) as the "fundamental schemas of their assumptive world, their core psychological structures" (p. 87). How can clinicians who have not experienced childhood abuse begin to understand the deficits in basic trust and interpersonal assumptions of their traumatized patients? I use the following imagined scenario when I teach about this subject:

In order to provide you with a new kind of learning experience, I am going to help you to understand something wonderful and dramatic about the power of the human mind. I'm proposing that we go up on the roof of this rather tall building. We will join hands and spend a minute or two concentrating on feeling that we are as light as air, and when I give the signal, we will step off the edge of the building and float lightly to the ground. Now I know that you'll probably think this is a bad idea. But, what if I were able to demonstrate that this unimaginable feat is possible? Let's imagine that you could see me step off the roof of the building and float to the ground, landing softly and completely unhurt. I would then turn and look up at you and say, "Now you try!" If you have any sense, you'd decline the invitation and come back down by conventional means using the stairs.

This is the kind of challenge that we offer traumatized patients when we say, "Trust me." This seemingly innocent suggestion is perceived by patients as an invitation to participate in their own self-destruction. Many traumatized patients have observed that others around them have been able to safely participate in trusting interpersonal relationships. However, such relationships seem to present an impossible risk for them, further reinforcing their beliefs about their own incompetence and defectiveness and their sense of disenfranchisement from others.

In the early 1980s, it was often suggested that the first step in the treatment of traumatized patients involved establishing trust. For survivors of pervasive childhood abuse, this kind of recommendation now appears quite naïve, as a stable sense of basic trust is often not established until well into the later stages of recovery. Nonetheless, this difficult task must be addressed from the outset of the therapy, and it requires much time and patience on the part of both therapists and patients. For example, a patient in her fourth year of therapy once remarked, "Do you remember all the clever things that we were trying to do in the first two years that we worked together? I now realize that what I was really doing was trying my best to sit in the same room with you and to cope with the vulnerability and terror of your actually *seeing* me." There are inevitable disruptions in the therapeutic relationship when patients become frightened, flee from the relationship, or try to undo the work of the therapy. Misunderstandings and miscommunication on the part of the patient or therapist, mistimings, and even errors by the therapist are an inherent part of the substance of the treatment. As the conflicts that result from these events are resolved, the patient gradually builds an interpersonal history with the therapist that becomes the foundation for a more secure attachment that enhances future growth and recovery. This process is almost never easy or predictable. Even attempts to empathize and expressions of caring can be misunderstood as threatening or intrusive by patients who have grown up in environments of pervasive victimization.

THE THERAPEUTIC STANCE

Although a psychodynamic and psychoanalytic understanding concerning early traumatic experiences is valuable in the therapy of abuse survivors, certain aspects of the classic psychoanalytic stance are not. Traditional psychoanalytic distance (i.e., the therapist as a "blank screen") is contraindicated in work with many trauma patients. For patients with backgrounds of healthy attachments and who have benevolent interpersonal assumptions, the therapist's quiet passivity might be interpreted as respectful or perhaps challenging. However, given traumatized patients' backgrounds of abuse and their lack of a sense of basic trust, inactivity or withholding on the part of the therapist allows traumatic transferences to flourish. Patients often find themselves unable to articulate their concerns and feelings, resulting in silence. For patients with backgrounds of interpersonal abuse, the lack of response from therapists is commonly misinterpreted as a sign of disapproval, hostility, or even repugnance. Such traumatic transferences have their origins in a past reality and can rapidly become functionally psychotic. They frequently become the basis for interpersonal reenactments of abusive situations and can be a source of retraumatization in the present relationship.

Traditional psychoanalytic distance is designed to encourage transference distortions, which may be useful in breaking through the armor of well-defended persons in order to examine underlying feelings and attitudes. In contrast, many abuse survivors have only brittle defenses; when they break down, patients can become almost paranoid and disorganized by overwhelming thoughts and feelings. Thus, therapy with abuse survivors should generally attempt to *minimize* transference distortions. Therapists' active involvement in therapy sessions is essential, and therapists must monitor periods of silence in the therapy and determine whether the silence is perceived by patients as helpful or disorganizing.

Maintaining strict neutrality with abuse survivors is at times both difficult and inappropriate. Such patients routinely have fixed and skewed negative beliefs about themselves and others, and such beliefs are likely not to change if unchallenged. For example, survivors of sexual abuse may fail to understand that the sexual involvement of adults with children is wrong. Or, even if they understand the concept, they may feel that it was permissible in their particular circumstances. Abuse survivors—even those who are bright, articulate, and educated—almost universally accept the blame and responsibility for their own abuse; their belief that they somehow caused the abuse allowed them to have a sense of control over their own helplessness and powerlessness. Therapists must be willing to be unequivocal about the idea that the exploitation of children is always wrong and that children do not cause their own abuse even in circumstances where they were provocative or took an active role. While the principle of therapeutic neutrality has merit, it must not be confused with inappropriate *moral* neutrality concerning such basic issues. Failure to state a clear moral position may be damaging to the therapeutic process, as it can be understood by patients as collusion with their own negative beliefs about themselves.

A stance of caring and willingness to engage on an interpersonal level is important in any effective psychotherapy, but it is particularly essential in the therapy of most abuse survivors. Whereas persons with healthy interpersonal assumptions assume that others are interested in their experience and are able to empathize with them, patients who have been interpersonally abused assume that others are disinterested and do not understand their experiences. The stereotyped response of "Um-hmm" will be quickly interpreted as inauthentic (e.g., understood as, "I can't be bothered to try to respond"). Even saying, "I understand" can be misinterpreted. In one instance, a patient of mine erupted in an angry response: "You understand? How could you understand? You've had a privileged life. You haven't been through what I've been through!" As a result, therapists by necessity must sometimes make extra efforts to demonstrate that they comprehend their patients' difficulties, for example, reiterating what they have heard or how they have understood the patient dilemmas ("Do I understand you correctly that you are trying to tell me . . .?" or "I understand how difficult it is for you to tell me this") or to acknowledge that the patient has evoked a personal emotional response ("I can feel how sad this is for you").

Because of the tenuousness of their capacity to remain connected, patients with backgrounds of severe abuse seem to pull for therapists to be actively involved in the therapeutic relationship as *participants* and not just as observers. Thus, it is normative for therapists to feel much more personally involved both in the therapy and with the patients. As a result, therapists' overidentification and overinvolvement—not too much distance—is a major hazard in the therapeutic relationship. Such therapists (particularly those who view their role as taking care of or reparenting their patients) are prone to becoming so involved in empathizing with patients' experience that they lose their sense of therapeutic perspective. Uncritical acceptance of patients' helplessness and their subjective sense of being overwhelmed can lead therapists and patients to a shared sense of immobilization in the treatment. Therapists in this situation also commonly feel that others do not adequately understand their patients' pain and disabilities. They find themselves at odds with their colleagues, particularly in settings such as inpatient units (where team treatment is necessary) and defensively reject consultation. Therapists in this position may take extraordinary measures to alter the external environment for their patients, as in the following example:

> I was called by a community therapist, Dr. Smith, about a possible referral of a patient to our inpatient unit. She asked a number of questions, such as whether the staff had experience working with dissociative identity disorder (DID), whether it would be possible for her patient, Karen, to be given full privileges to freely walk the grounds, whether we could guarantee that restraints would never be used during the admission, etc.—all seeming to indicate that Karen needed special care and considerations in order to be hospitalized. Even though I was unable to agree to numerous preconditions, Karen was eventually admitted to our inpatient unit after a suicide attempt. She remained extremely isolated, refusing to interact with various staff members who she claimed were controlling and demeaning to her. She demanded that all the staff address her by the names of her various personalities as they appeared from time to time. She also superficially cut herself repeatedly when she was anxious or angry.
>
> When confronted with her dysfunctional behavior, Karen angrily referred staff to her therapist so that the therapist could tell them how to manage her: "You better talk to Dr. Smith—*she* knows how to work with me!" The therapist was, in fact, very confused and angry at the situation. She called the unit director and complained that the staff were too impatient with Karen and did not understand the difficulties with dissociation. She also demanded that Karen's self-cutting behavior be accepted since it was clearly not lethal, and she had no other way to express her feelings. When the inpatient team suggested a consultation to the therapy, the therapist responded by questioning the clinical competence of the unit staff. The patient then signed out of the hospital with her therapist's agreement.

The essential problem in this clinical illustration was the therapist's overidentification with the patient. In her empathic understanding of her patient's dilemmas, she overlooked the obvious fact that the patient would need to learn to live within the constraints of reality—in this case, the rules and procedures of the unit, the necessary comfort level of the staff around issues of safety, and the legitimate questioning of whether the ongoing therapy was maximally helpful.

Therapists working with abuse survivors need to maintain a dual role. While they must actively participate in the therapy and empathize with the patient's experience, they must also maintain a sense of therapeutic perspective and direction. They must recognize that although patients feel overwhelmed and helpless, there are ways to achieve mastery over these feelings. Therapists must empathically confront patients' demands that the external world adapt to their disabilities and ask patients to make efforts to change in order to deal with the world—a task that initially may feel impossible. Rather than becoming enmeshed in and enabling their patients' helplessness, therapists must reiterate that patients have the choice and ability to make changes. It is helpful for the therapist to understand patients' despair but to also express the conviction that the therapeutic process can help patients ameliorate or overcome their difficulties. For example, it is not enough for therapists to "get" why patients feel suicidal ("Given your background of betrayal and abuse and the pain you experience every day, I understand why you wish to die"); an alliance around this point alone leads only to mutual hopelessness. In addition, the therapist must also model the expectation that it is necessary for patients to move from that position ("I know it may seem impossible at times, but I think it is possible for you to play an active role in changing the course of your life so that you will not always feel so tormented").

REENACTMENTS OF CHILDHOOD ABUSE

As outlined in the previous chapters, survivors of childhood abuse not only bring their abusive experiences to the therapeutic arena, but they also make them part of the therapeutic relationship. That is, they compel the therapist to actually assume a role in the reenactments of their traumatization. It is crucial to understand that this process is often inevitable. Given their traumatically based interpersonal assumptions, traumatized patients must see all of their adult relationships through the lens of their abuse. These powerful assumptions transform all important relationships into reenactments and recapitulations of their early experiences. However, this process is not simply a pitfall to be avoided or sidestepped; it is an intrinsic part of the treatment of these patients. The *therapeutic dance*, with its endless repetitions of disruptions and reengagements in the early phase of therapy, provides a model of interpersonal connection, conflict resolution, and collaboration. If recognized and skillfully managed, the interpersonal reenactment of the abuse offers an opportunity to be able to provide the experience of a relational world that is positive and growth-producing, enabling patients to learn new relational skills.

Davies and Frawley (1994) have described the four major roles that are recapitulated in the therapy of abuse survivors: abuser, victim of abuse, indifferent or neglectful bystander, and hoped-for rescuer. Patients repeatedly take on and reenact these roles, and because therapists are involved by necessity as active participants in the therapeutic relationship, they assume similar and complementary roles. These abuse-related interpersonal dynamics are extremely powerful, as are patients' projective identifications that compel therapists to experience many confusing and overwhelming countertransferential feelings and impulses. Certain relational positions may be recurrently assumed or even become the predominant relational dynamics during phases of therapy. However, it is also my experience that these relational positions may be quite fluid, changing frequently and abruptly as they mirror and reenact the kaleidoscope of the malignant interpersonal disturbances that characterized the childhood abuse. As has been observed by several experienced clinicians and investigators (see, for example, Chu, 1992c; Dalenberg, 2004; Davies & Frawley, 1994; Pearlman & Saakvitne, 1995), therapists must both allow themselves to be engaged in these reenactments and maintain perspective and clarity concerning the process in order to facilitate a benign resolution. Again, the therapeutic dance—the cycle of abuse-related difficulties in the therapeutic relationship with repeated resolutions involving healthier relational experiences—eventually allows patients to leave behind their trauma-based assumptions and experience a more benevolent world.

In the typical crisis of a reenactment of the relational dynamics of early abuse, patients feel angry, disappointed, and/or betrayed by therapists' responses (or lack of responses). In this situation, patients once again feel abused and may act abusively toward therapists or themselves; therapists feel cast in the role of abuser, may feel abused by their patients, and have certainly failed as the hoped-for rescuer and feel—at best—like the indifferent bystander. Davies and Frawley (1994) described a series of transference-countertransference positions that commonly occur in the therapy of abuse survivors. Transference-countertransference is a remarkably apt description, because these interpersonal dynamics are dependent on both the patient's abusive past and the therapist's own personal experiences.

My assumption in this discussion is that therapists should be reasonably free of any major relational pathology of their own in order to work with abused patients. Even normal personal characteristics of the therapist are heightened and distorted by the powerful interpersonal forces of the therapy (e.g., caring evolving into rescuing, facilitation becoming control, personal restraint transformed into withholding). Serious interpersonal pathology on the part of the therapist (e.g., problems with aggression, major narcissistic or social deficits) will almost certainly result in therapeutic impasses, serious boundary violations, and/or harm to both patient and therapist. One particular scenario deserves special emphasis. Not uncommonly, clinicians are drawn to the mental health professions in response to their own backgrounds of conflict or deprivation. The resulting countertransference need to rescue patients, provide caretaking, or to compensate for past abuse must be strictly examined and limited. The dynamics of the therapy must be largely driven only by patients' past experiences, and hence become a kind of interpersonal Rorschach test that elucidates and expresses the nature of patients' past interpersonal experiences.

As discussed by Davies and Frawley (1994), the interpersonal dynamics in the therapy of traumatized persons are varied—as varied as the individual circumstances of the abuse. Perhaps the most common interpersonal scenario occurs as the patient reenacts the position of being abused. This abused child role can take on many characteristics: helpless and devastated, angry and manipulative, appeasing or caretaking, or demanding and entitled. Each of these roles produces a complementary response in the therapist. The patient who reacts in the therapy by becoming a helpless and devastated victim often induces a rescuing response and even overidentification, but may also elicit anger or distance in response to the patient's passivity and dependence. Patients' hostile and angry stances frequently produce withdrawal or retaliatory rage in the therapist. Idealization or caretaking from patients may induce therapists to become passive recipients who collude with avoiding or seeing the covert agendas in a reenactment of hidden abuse. And patients' entitled demands often produce attempts to placate or rescue, or anger at the patient's narcissism.

The roles of the patient who defensively takes on the position of abuser are similarly varied. Patients may be overtly hostile and demeaning, covertly intrusive and invasive, distant and uninvolved, or seductive and insidiously ingratiating. Such interpersonal positions also elicit specific responses from therapists. Rageful attacks often produce attempts to appease or placate, interpersonal withdrawal, or retaliatory hostility. Covert intrusion concerning personal boundaries induces therapists to feel helplessly violated or angrily defensive. Patients who become uninvolved in their therapy—as if it is the therapist's job to make the treatment occur—can result in therapists redoubling their efforts or angrily withdrawing. And, seductive responses can cause therapists to become troubled and passive (replicating and enacting the confusion of the abused child) or to become angry and rejecting.

All of these interpersonal positions have the potential for either providing invaluable information about the patient's experience or resulting in impasses and failure of the therapeutic process. Resolution of these conflictual transference-countertransference positions depends on an accurate understanding of the dilemma, clarification and interpretation, reality testing, and patience. As in any effective interpersonal psychotherapy, therapists must learn to examine their own responses as a way of understanding their patients' dilemmas. Therapists must not be afraid to acknowledge (to themselves) dysphoric feelings of anxiety, enmeshment, coldness, hostility, sadism, or even sexual arousal that can be evoked in the therapy of severely traumatized patients. Such feelings enable therapists to make clarifications and interpretations that allow patients to understand the confusing interpersonal world that their abuse continues to evoke.

Therapists must also be prepared to maintain personal and therapeutic boundaries and to set appropriate limits. Out-of-control aggression or violation of therapists' personal boundaries are not helpful to the patient or the therapy and should not be tolerated. Therapists must ask patients to examine their relational patterns in the context of their early abusive experiences. This process is often long and difficult—to patients the dysfunctional relational dynamics are real not transferential—and therapists must use all of their patience and skill to help patients move toward mutual and collaborative relationships and healthy interpersonal perspectives. The following clinical example illustrates some of the vicissitudes involved in the shifting interpersonal reenactments of past abuse:

Joan, a 42-year-old, divorced woman, was hospitalized following a difficult series of events in which she was intrusive concerning the personal life of her therapist, Dr. White. She had initially begun to ask questions about the therapist's personal life "in order to feel more equal—like a friend and not just a patient," and made frequent telephone calls to the therapist's office and home in states of crisis. Joan appeared to become increasingly preoccupied with her therapist and made personal comments in ways that made him quite uncomfortable ("You dress so nicely, but you know you really shouldn't wear brown shoes with that suit."). Dr. White felt unable to bring up any of these intrusions in the therapy, as he was quite aware that Joan would feel upset about her perceived sense of his rejecting her. Instead, he became quite distant in sessions, even to the extent of falling asleep on one occasion.

Joan then accused her therapist of not wanting to be involved with her, and she redoubled her efforts to find out more about him—even following him home and covertly watching him, his wife, children, and visitors to the house. When she finally confessed to this last activity, Dr. White became quite angry and threatened to terminate the therapy if such behavior ever recurred. Joan became intensely ashamed and begged him not to abandon her. Later that night, she called Dr. White and confessed to having taken an overdose of a tranquilizer that he had prescribed, and she was hospitalized. When the inpatient case manager introduced herself, Joan seemed angry and withholding. After being asked about her life and daily activities, Joan blurted out, "I know you think I'm pathetic because of my involvement with Tom—I mean, Dr. White—but I am somebody, too! You therapists all think you're something special." The case manager, aware of how angry Joan was becoming, controlled her wish to say something quite demeaning, and instead commented on Joan's anger, "You seem quite upset with me as if I have insulted you. I want to make it clear that I have no preconceived notions about you, and I am just trying to understand how you have come to be involved in this very uncomfortable situation."

After some further discussion, Joan was able to become less defensive and to discuss her distress about her relationship with Dr. White. Although she was aware that her behavior was pushing him away, she felt so exposed in the therapy and felt compelled to find out more about him both to "feel closer" and to "get something on him." Dr. White also admitted to the case manager that he was feeling trapped in the relationship, and although he genuinely liked the patient and was committed to helping her, he felt very uncomfortable about the relationship. After some discussion, it became clear that the patient was reenacting the dynamics of the relationship with her father, who was generally demeaning and neglectful, and only becoming attentive and seductive during times leading up to his sexual abuse of her. When Dr. White broached this subject with Joan, she responded angrily, "So you're saying that my feelings for you aren't real and that I can't tell the difference between you and my father! I thought you were nice—my father's a bastard!" However, after some discussion and explanation concerning abuse-related relationships, the patient was able to calm down as she at least felt less blamed for the problems. Although she remained unconvinced about the basis of her relational difficulties, Joan and Dr. White were able to renegotiate some basic agreements concerning their relationship and the treatment. She was discharged from the hospital to continue the long process working with her therapist to try to understand and cope with her assumptions and the effects of her incestuous past.

MANAGING COUNTERTRANSFERENCE RESPONSES

Countertransference responses in the treatment of abuse survivors are quite complex and can cause considerable difficulties for therapists. One particular difficulty has been called vicarious or secondary traumatization (see, for example, McCann & Pearlman, 1990; Pearlman & Saakvitne, 1995), in which a therapist's assumptions about the benevolence of the world are disrupted by understanding the abuses perpetrated on patients. The brutality, callousness, sadism, and even diabolical ingenuity that characterize malevolent abuse can be difficult to comprehend and accept, especially for therapists who have no previous exposure to such experiences. Therapists may have their own posttraumatic responses to hearing about the terrible details of patients' abuse. Shock, disbelief, confusion, and even a pervasive sense of their own vulnerability can afflict therapists, who then struggle to regain their own sense of safety and stability. Such reactions are common, and clinicians must use their own personal interpersonal supports—friends, colleagues, consultants, or their own therapists—to help regain their equilibrium. Fortunately, most clinicians are generally able to adjust to even new and horrifying knowledge, to integrate such information, and even to reinstate some healthy denial and dissociation in rebuilding a new and workable set of assumptions about the world.

Overidentification and overprotection of patients are common countertransference difficulties. In addition, fascination is a particular difficulty, especially with the rather dramatic symptomatology of the multiple identities of patients with DID (Chu, 1994; Kluft, 1989a). However, the most difficult countertransference problem in working with abuse survivors may be unacknowledged therapist discomfort. The level of involvement that is necessary to work with traumatized patients and the inevitable recapitulation of abusive interpersonal relationships places significant emotional strains on therapists. In addition, the extraordinary psychological pain experienced by patients frequently causes them to be narcissistically preoccupied and unable to have a sense of the experience of others around them, including the impact of the therapy on their therapists. In relationships with patients, therapists often feel that their work and efforts are often disregarded or invalidated, and, given the slow pace of many treatments, actual gratitude on the part of patients for sometimes lengthy and extraordinary services may be long delayed.

Many patients go through episodic crises, endanger their own lives, wrestle with their intolerable conflicts and unbearable experiences, and have numerous regressions where they are unable to take responsibility for themselves or control their experiences. As a result, therapists are often placed in positions where they feel anxious, confused, and burdened. However, therapists are frequently unable to acknowledge the extent of their own discomfort or even anger with both the therapeutic process and with patients. Instead, it is usually much more ego-syntonic to acknowledge only compassion for the patients' pain and sympathy for their struggle to overcome their past abuse. Moreover, many patients give both direct and indirect messages for therapists not to become upset, frustrated, or angry. Patients perceive the all-important and sustaining interpersonal bond between them and their therapists as very fragile, and they fear they could not withstand any expression of therapists' discomfort or anger. In addition, many patients have had previous experiences with anger as out-of-control and destructive, and they see any expression of anger as inevitably leading to abuse. Many patients who are unable to integrate their own conflictual feelings are unable to see their therapists as being complex and multifaceted. Thus, any indication of frustration or anger is seen as being the therapist's primary affect toward them. Therapists' unintentional collusion with patients by not acknowledging their dysphoric feelings (even to themselves) is remarkably common.

Unacknowledged anger can inhibit appropriate therapeutic responses. For example, therapists can fail to set appropriate limits or define boundaries because they unconsciously fear that they are acting out their anger or sadism. Even in situations where therapists can acknowledge to themselves that they are angry, they may confuse primary and secondary motivations. Limit-setting in order to preserve the treatment frame is the primary motivation. Any gratification of anger or sadism that therapists may feel by confronting patients is secondary. When consulting on cases in these kinds of situations, I usually counsel therapists to be candid in acknowledging their own feelings and then to be clear to themselves that the interventions are for the primary purpose of restoring a healthy therapeutic relationship, and that if they are secretly gratified by the process they should just accept it.

Therapists' experiences of unacknowledged discomfort, frustration, and anger vary considerably, and therapists are not immune from utilizing common so-called primitive defense mechanisms. For example, although few therapists are overtly hostile, many find themselves becoming neglectful or distant. This kind of acting out is usually manifested in failure to follow through with commitments, forgetfulness concerning appointments, habitual tardiness, feeling detached or drowsy in sessions, or behaviors such as interrupting sessions to take telephone calls, excessive note taking, or scheduling appointments in an erratic or unpredictable manner.

A more common manifestation of countertransference discomfort occurs through therapists' use of reaction formation. Instead of acknowledging frustration or angry feelings about patients, therapists instead become extremely worried and concerned about patients and convinced that they need to redouble their efforts. This kind of response can be detrimental to the therapy, as therapists avoid bringing up any issues that might disturb patients and exercise a level of overprotectiveness that does not allow patients to develop psychologically. This overprotective stance is also very painful for therapists, who tend to feel anxious, enmeshed, and burdened, as in the following example:

> Dr. S., an experienced and respected therapist, consulted me for difficulties he was encountering in his work with a survivor of extreme familial neglect and physical abuse. For several years, he weathered many difficult periods, most of which were marked by the patient becoming extremely controlling concerning the nature of the therapy and the therapist's responses; in such situations there was always the implied threat of the patient killing herself. He gave me one example where the patient called him for help on her cell phone while standing on the roof of her house, threatening to jump to her death. Dr. S. found himself becoming so anxious about the patient that he worried constantly and even woke up at night with anxiety about her. He had frequent emergency appointments with the patient and called her several additional times per week to make sure she was safe.
>
> In the consultation meeting, he was highly anxious and tearful as he began to describe his fears about the patient's safety and his uncertainties about the therapy. I suggested to him that he felt burdened by the work and might be angry about it. At this point, he denied being angry. I reminded him that he had been dedicated to helping this patient for years, making sometime heroic efforts on her behalf, and that she had responded by repeatedly threatening suicide in a way that evolved into his feeling responsible for her safety—an untenable position. After being able to discuss his concerns and to acknowledge his frustration about being manipulated, Dr. S. was able to gently confront the patient on an ongoing manner about the nature of the therapy and to set some reasonable limits. After a period of some turmoil, the therapy became much more stable and contained. Dr. S.'s overall level of anxiety and sleep returned to normal.

The most painful form of countertransference reactions occur when therapists are unable to acknowledge their countertransference anger and actually project their own anger and sadism onto their patients. In the therapists' eyes, the patients then become a seemingly real and substantial threat. Not infrequently in such situations, the therapists may actually develop a mild form of posttraumatic stress disorder, complete with unwanted intrusive thoughts, nightmares and disturbed sleep, avoidant responses, and even startle responses. The therapists actually begin to feel threatened by the patients and to dread sessions or other interactions. Furthermore, the therapists feel as though they cannot abandon (escape from) the patients, but they feel impotent to make any kind of positive change in the therapy. The following personal vignette illustrates such a dilemma:

> Several years following my graduating from my residency, I undertook the treatment of a young man for what I understood to be the aftereffects of emotional and physical abuse and neglect. By that time, I had already had experience with treating complex trauma patients, and I should have been able to avoid the ensuing enmeshment. In retrospect, I was quite overdentified with him; he was about my age, was interested in the mental health field, and was a gifted artist. Over the course of several years, the usual boundaries of the therapeutic frame became eroded. In response to what seemed like legitimate needs at the time, we had meetings outside the office and formed a kind of dual relationship as both therapist-patient and quasi-friends. This made it more difficult to maintain any real sense of a treatment frame, and I responded to crisis by providing frequent sessions and taking numerous emergency telephone calls. At one point in time, the phone calls became much more frequent and changed in tone to become more entitled, angry, and demanding. I began dreading the calls and even started to jump at the sound of the telephone ring in my office—a true startle response. I began to doubt my ability to help the patient and to wonder if I could endure continuing the treatment; I fantasized that the patient would magically disappear and I would be relieved of my burden.
>
> At the point that my physical and mental health were beginning to be affected (since I had PTSD-like recurrent intrusive thoughts and disturbed sleep), I finally had some insight into the process. I realized that I had allowed the situation to become unmanageable and that I was projecting all of my anger and frustration onto the patient as if he could destroy me. I realized that it was perfectly possible for me to restore some sanity to the therapy process and that I was more than capable of providing competent treatment. Over the next several weeks, I was able to introduce some boundaries back into the therapy and to establish the necessary distance to restore some reasonable therapeutic perspective. Some time after that, it became clear that the patient's crisis situation, the intrusions into my life, and his entitlement and irritability were caused by an emerging manic episode that I had failed to recognize because of the level of my overinvolvement.

This kind of reaction by therapists, although extreme, is understandable in the context of the patient's dilemmas. It is yet another recapitulation of the patient's unresolved early abuse. In the setting of the therapeutic relationship, the patient becomes the real or imagined abuser. In response to patients' cues, therapists find themselves in enmeshed relationships in which they are highly emotionally invested and from which they feel they cannot exit. They feel dysphoric, panicky, despairing, and limited in their options and choices. In short, they have assumed the position of the abused child in a reenactment of the abuse. It is essential for therapists in this position to directly address these issues. This type of reenactment must be understood and interpreted, and patients and therapists must move back into mutually respectful, collaborative relationships.

Professional supports through ongoing consultation, attending continuing education programs, and talking with supportive colleagues are an essential part of working with patients with complex posttraumatic and dissociative disorders. Given the intensity of the patient-therapist relationship, the powerful affects related to traumatization, and the slow pace of treatment, there is often little or very intermittent gratification for therapists. Clinicians must use their professional and personal support networks to help them maintain their own equilibrium and to hone their professional skills. Especially in situations of transference-countertransference enmeshment, therapists must practice what they preach: reaching out to others for interpersonal connection and support is an essential part of human experience and is particularly necessary in times of difficulty or stress. After all, traumatized patients are often very astute in observing their therapists, and patients' dilemmas cannot be resolved until therapists are able to understand and to model how they are able to resolve relational impasses.

10

The "Impossible" Patient

Chronic Disempowerment

Even among a very symptomatic and extensively traumatized patient population, there seem to be subsets of patients who have a more difficult clinical course and whose disabilities appear to be more chronic in nature. Over many years in a hospital setting, we have observed hundreds of patients with posttraumatic and dissociative disorders resulting from childhood traumatization. All of these patients have been seriously ill and/or disabled. Many patients that we have seen have maximally utilized available treatment and have rapidly achieved stabilization of symptoms and overall improvement. In contrast, we have also seen at least two groups of patients who have had a more difficult and chronic clinical course. Patients in one of these groups have had major DSM-IV Axis I disorders in addition to posttraumatic and dissociative disorders. These comorbid disorders have included major mood disorders, psychosis, and substance abuse, resulting in complicated clinical presentations with complex differential diagnosis issues that often require prolonged treatment.

A second group of patients who have a more difficult and chronic course have a clinical presentation I have called *chronic disempowerment*. Even among patients with complex trauma-related disorders, these patients present long-standing difficulties that seem impervious to change. They seem to come to treatment with a combination of intense psychological distress and a truly entrenched and unchanging sense of despair, hopelessness, and helplessness. This group of patients represents an extraordinary clinical challenge. They are highly symptomatic and utilize extensive amounts of psychiatric and psychological care. They are prone to severe regression in treatment, which can lead to considerable morbidity and even mortality. And, they elicit strong and often negative reactions from their caregivers. Understanding chronically disempowered patients is a clinical necessity, for without expert treatment they are likely to remain "impossible" patients.

CHRONIC DISEMPOWERMENT

Generations of theorists and investigators of early childhood development have concluded that healthy psychological growth derives from appropriate parent-child attachments and interactions in a protective and nurturing environment. Good parenting requires that parents be attuned to the needs of a child, and they must interact in a way that validates the child's positive sense of self, soothes and protects the child from overwhelming stimuli, and challenges and encourages the child's developing coping capacities. Good parenting allows a child to achieve healthy and mature characterologic development including (a) a sense of self-esteem and self-efficacy, (b) a stable sense of self in relation to others, (c) a capacity for self-soothing, and (d) an ability to flexibly respond to the environment. In contrast, in our patient population, we have observed that childhood traumatization leads to (a) a sense of self as hateful and defective, (b) intense difficulties in managing relationships, (c) dependency on others for soothing, and (d) dysfunctional and rigid responses to the environment.

Many of the patients with posttraumatic and dissociative symptomatology that we see in the inpatient setting have horrific histories of childhood abuse. The effects of this kind of maltreatment on psychological development are profound. As discussed in previous chapters, early and prolonged traumatization often leads to massive disturbances in characterologic and ego development, and some of these fundamental impairments can easily evolve into a syndrome of chronic disempowerment. An ingrained sense of self as defective, helpless, and powerless perpetuates the effects of early victimization and interferes with abuse survivors' ability to take control of their lives. Moreover, profound difficulty in negotiating supportive relationships results in chronic isolation and promotes a tendency toward reenactment and revictimization. These negative thoughts and beliefs can perpetuate shame, misery, and torment long after the etiologic abuse has ended.

The concept of empowerment has become a part of the psychological literature, particularly concerning the psychological development of women. Psychologist Janet Surrey, PhD (1991), has written:

> I define psychological empowerment as: the motivation, freedom and capacity to act purposefully, with the mobilization of the energies, resources, strengths, or powers of each person through a mutual, relational process. Personal empowerment can be viewed only through the larger lens of power through connection, that is, through the establishment of mutually empathic and mutually empowering relationships. (p. 164)

In contrast to this view of empowerment, many persons who have been victims of extensive childhood abuse can be described as strikingly disempowered. Survivors of childhood traumatization often have little sense of any freedom to act in a way that asserts a sense of control or autonomy. Rather than be able to engage with others in a mutually empowering fashion, they repeatedly relate to others in ways that recapitulate abusive or exploitative past relationships or flee into dysfunctional isolation.

Views of healthy empowerment have absolutely no meaning to victims of chronic childhood traumatization. They may even cling to their sense of disempowerment as the only reality they have known. Very often, patients' disempowerment creates dissonance in the therapy when therapists assume that patients share their own assumptions about the world and relationships. When therapists assume that patients naturally feel empowered, an impasse can occur based on therapists' failure to understand their patients' deep sense of disempowerment. Patients react by becoming more resistant, distant, or angry, and therapists tend to become overwhelmed, frustrated, and blaming. Moreover, because patients only understand their own disempowered world, they may have difficulty articulating what is wrong; they simply feel confused, misunderstood, and not heard, as in the following clinical illustration.

> Janice, an attractive 27-year-old woman, sought psychotherapy after a series of failed relationships. The young and enthusiastic therapist quickly ascertained that she had a history of severe emotional abuse and neglect. Janice's mother and father routinely used her as the family scapegoat, demeaning her and blaming her for the failure of the family to get along together, calling her "stupid," "gross," and "ugly." They would punish her by refusing to speak to her for days, denying her food, and even putting her out of the house. Not surprisingly, Janice developed patterns of behavior based on her early experience. She engaged with others in a defensive and angry way, assuming they would grow to hate her. Unfortunately, this self-fulfilling prophecy resulted in her relationships often ending with the other person blaming her for all the difficulties they had experienced together. Janice also learned to punish herself for these relational failures, sometimes starving herself and even taking small overdoses of aspirin.
>
> The therapist was horrified by the history of abuse and was determined to help her patient overcome her abusive past. She tried to be positive and encouraging, urging Janice to work on social skills issues and to make practical steps toward meeting others, such as joining a dating service. Janice became progressively less responsive in therapy and began to lose weight and to neglect her grooming. When pressed to explain this behavior, she seemed to struggle for words, finally saying, "I guess I don't like myself very much." Frustrated, the therapist said, "You're going to have to try and have a more positive attitude about yourself if you're going to get anywhere!" to which Janice responded, "I knew you would come to hate me, too."

The treatment of chronically disempowered patients poses several painful dilemmas for both patients and therapists. Most therapists have only a minimal number of these so-called impossible patients in their practice but find that they create a disproportionate amount of clinical crises, personal distress, and uncomfortable countertransference responses. Certain clinical problems are commonly presented by such patients. Each of these problems must be well understood, and treatment approaches must be well conceived and skillfully implemented.

Rigid and Repetitive Reenactments

Reenactments of past abuse and past abusive relationships are particularly difficult with chronically disempowered patients and tend to be remarkably rigid and repetitive. Patients often interact with seemingly prescripted scenarios that are resistant to change. From the patient's vantage point, the reenactments feel like familiar but painful interpersonal situations. From the caregiver's point of view, the clinician may feel pulled into an interaction in which the responses seem prearranged. Such scripted scenarios can vary from repetitious discussions of despair and helplessness that seem impervious to alteration to statements that seem to demand certain responses from the therapist. Or conversely, therapists may even feel as though the patient seems to be stuck in a drama played out for the therapist as audience, sometimes not even requiring a response, as in the following example:

> Diane, a 38-year-old woman, was admitted to the hospital in crisis and was having flashbacks of sexual abuse and intense suicidal impulses. Although she was advised by her long-term therapist and inpatient treatment team to find ways to contain and stabilize her symptoms, she insisted that the only real treatment was for her to abreact some episodes of childhood abuse. Furthermore, she insisted that the only safe way this exploration could occur was for her to be in physical restraints. The staff felt that Diane should work on her controls and that restraints would only reinforce the notion that she could not control her impulses. As this conflict in treatment philosophies escalated, Diane became more angry and accused various staff members of deliberately mistreating her in order to trigger even more flashbacks of abuse.
>
> In one interaction with her therapist, she angrily recited a litany of complaints and accused the therapist and staff of malpractice and abuse. The therapist felt uncomfortable and defensive but also noticed that the patient was staring at the floor and seemed caught in a somewhat unreal prescripted scenario. The therapist said, "It feels to me as though you are talking *at* me as though I were an audience and not *to* me. I wonder if you can remember that I have tried very hard to listen to you and to try to resolve our differences, and that I am not at all interested in hurting you." Diane stopped talking abruptly, turned and looked at the therapist, and said, "Oh! That's right. I keep forgetting that you have actually been very helpful to me."

In the chronically disempowered world of the patient, change does not seem possible—neither internal change that helps the patient better adapt to the world nor change in the nature of abuse-related relationships. Hence, the patient and therapist are caught in a conundrum: the therapist attempts to promote change while the patient cannot conceive of positive change and resists any change at all. This profound resistance to change may be a key characteristic of some patients that appear impossible. Chronically disempowered patients are unable to ally with others and to use support to reach new understandings and solutions. Instead, the scenarios of childhood abuse are reenacted in displacement without substantial change in their scripts. Although much tension, despair, and rage are vented, little is changed in patients' views of themselves or the world.

Enmeshment

Reenactments of past abusive relationships frequently involve interpersonal enmeshment. In the treatment of patients who have been profoundly mistreated, therapists may need to be active and involved in a way that fosters trust and attachment. However, this type of necessary involvement has the potential for intense dependency and enmeshment. To the extent that the therapist initially is able to respond to the patient in a helpful or gratifying manner, the patient develops a deep dependency on the therapist. Patients' dependency combined with the angry and paranoid transferences that inevitably derive from past abuse often lead to intensely painful interpersonal struggles, as the therapeutic relationship becomes an arena for acting out hostile dependency. Patients may find themselves repeatedly testing and challenging the therapists to determine if they can be trusted. Repetitive and excessive efforts of therapists to reassure patients can lead to the escalation of a kind of struggle that becomes a reenactment of abusive relationships, as in the following clinical example:

> Marilyn, a young woman with a horrendous history of abandonment, neglect, and abuse, repeatedly told her therapist that she was terrified that she would be abandoned by him. This conflict was also acted out in many ways. There were many occasions (such as the therapist's vacation, change in appointment times, the therapist being late to appointments, misinterpretation of the therapist's comments) when Marilyn would panic about being abandoned. On such occasions, she would isolate herself, refusing any contact with the therapist or friends. Overwhelmed with anger, self-blame, and despair, she would act self-destructively, drinking heavily, taking overdoses of medication, and engaging in risky behavior. The therapist redoubled his efforts to reassure Marilyn and on several occasions promised never to abandon her. These promises failed to reassure her, and she engaged in increasingly serious self-destructive acts, almost as if to challenge the sincerity of the therapist's commitment.
>
> Finally, the therapist, feeling exhausted and frustrated, sought consultation. In a series of interactions with Marilyn, the therapist explained that he would continue to be committed to her, but only if the therapy was helpful. The therapist made it clear that he did not feel it was helpful to engage in a way that recapitulated the enmeshed and abusive relationships of her childhood. The therapist emphasized that Marilyn had control over the relationship and could ensure an ongoing relationship by learning to take care of herself. A very painful period ensued as Marilyn and her therapist tried to negotiate how they would relate to each other, but eventually the therapy proceeded in a more positive direction.

In work with chronically disempowered patients, management of the therapeutic relationship may be the most difficult part of therapy. Many of these patients have grown up being the target of hostile projection or profound neglect, and they may have little concept of normal functional patterns of relating. Explicit attention to the therapeutic relationship must be a priority throughout the course of the treatment, as relational issues become the most important factors in the success or failure of treatment.

One of the basic skills of dynamic therapy that has particular relevance to work with chronically disempowered patients has to do with attention to both the *content* and *process* of therapeutic interactions. The content is what the patient says, and the process is reflected by the manner in which the patient interacts. At any given point, the therapist must decide whether to respond to the content or process, whichever is more important. For the most part, responding to the content is most appropriate. However, for patients with whom anger and enmeshment become prominent in the interaction, the process of therapy must be clarified and interpreted. Often, this takes the form of a simple observation: "You seem upset about how I am responding to you. Is there something I am doing (or not doing) that is making you angry or frustrated?" If this kind of relational disruption is a frequent occurrence in the therapy, it is often wise to routinely and periodically reflect with the patient concerning the status of the therapeutic alliance: "I'd just like to take a moment to 'check in' with you. How are we doing in our work together?"

Many chronically disempowered patients have no understanding or expectation of being able to change their patterns of relating. Rather than change, their primary goals in relationships are to hold onto important nurturing relationships (particularly the relationship with the therapist), to discharge intolerable feelings such as anger, and to obtain comfort. The following clinical illustration demonstrates how both intense dependency and covert manifestations of anger result in complex, painful, and repetitive scenarios.

Carol, a 31-year-old woman with a 15-year history of psychiatric treatment and lifelong impairment, began work with her fifth therapist. Work with previous therapists had ended when she had overstepped boundaries, made suicide attempts, or, in one case, when a therapist had moved out of town (because in part, she implied, the work with Carol was too stressful). Carol had a known history of extensive neglect and intrusive abuse over the course of her childhood. She had been briefly married and had a child who was in the custody of the state social services department. She was on disability insurance. In addition to the diagnosis of PTSD, Carol also strongly hinted that she had DID, and she frequently referred to herself as "we." She had many medical difficulties, including migraine headaches, chronic fatigue syndrome, irritable bowel syndrome, and asthma.

Because of Carol's history of intrusiveness, the therapist set firm guidelines around the nature of the therapy, appointment times, and her availability. Over the first several weeks of treatment, all seemed to go well. Carol seemed surprisingly workable, and the therapist wondered if prior treatments had gone poorly simply because of a poor treatment frame and clashes in personalities.

As the therapy continued, Carol began bringing in small gifts for the therapist. Although the therapist first accepted the gifts (a collage and a small bouquet of wildflowers), she became quite uncomfortable when she was presented with a Valentine's Day card. She attempted to discuss the meaning of this card with Carol, who reacted with surprise, wounded innocence, anger, and then intense shame and guilt. The therapist emphasized the importance of boundaries, and Carol apologized for her behavior.

A similar pattern emerged concerning telephone calls. The therapist initially agreed to talk to Carol in emergencies outside the office "occasionally," although she was permitted to leave messages on the therapist's answering machine. Although initial calls were intermittent and benign, she soon began to leave numerous messages, some of which were so long as to exhaust the message capacity of the answering machine. Finally, she called the therapist in a panic several times in one week because it was "really important." When the therapist brought up the issue of limits, Carol seemed again surprised and deeply ashamed. She later left a note of apology on the windshield of the therapist's car in the clinic parking lot, which the therapist found somehow disconcerting. However, following this incident, the treatment seemed to progress reasonably well until the therapist announced she was going on vacation. In the session just before the vacation, Carol asked if the therapist was going away with her husband. When the therapist asked why Carol assumed that she (the therapist) was married, Carol initially was silent, but she eventually confessed that she had driven by the therapist's house, opened the mailbox, and looked at some letters she had found. In the shocked silence that followed, Carol hastened to add, "But I didn't open and read anything!"

When working with chronically disempowered patients, even many experienced therapists find that they have more difficulty maintaining usual boundaries and setting limits. Some of this difficulty has to do with the intensity of the therapeutic relationship and the patient's conviction that only the therapist can provide the relief that they cannot provide for themselves. This is the crux of the disempowerment. Rather than expecting that they can develop tools for self-soothing, the disempowered patient feels totally reliant on others. Patients who feel tormented by their uncertainty about relationships may seek reassurance by asking therapists to blur boundaries, maintain dual relationships, and to provide constant caretaking. Particularly in times of crisis, it may seem reasonable for therapists to extend themselves to an extraordinary degree. However, any significant alteration of the normal structure of therapy should be made with great caution. Blurred boundaries and inadequate limits will almost certainly result in the recapitulation of the lack of boundaries and limits in the patient's abusive family of origin. It is a necessary and integral part of the early phase of treatment for disempowered patients to begin to learn the ability to collaborate in treatment and to work with therapists to respect and maintain the structure of the treatment.

Control and Manipulation

Lacking the ability to engage with others in a collaborative way, chronically disempowered patients continue to rely on control and manipulation as some of the only ways that they know they can get their needs met. From the patient's viewpoint, this interactive style is familiar and adaptive; because it feels impossible to trust enough to do things *with* others, the only alternative is to do things *to* others. From the therapist's viewpoint, control and manipulation can be perceived as intentionally hostile and noxious; clinicians should remind themselves that many patients have no other experience of effective ways of getting their needs met. Although these ways of relating are understandable, they may nonetheless be extremely painful for caregivers. At times the demands on therapists may be infused with anger and entitlement, as was evident when one patient said to me, "You can't terminate with me and you can't leave me; you're stuck with me because no one else would be willing to see me at the ridiculously low fee you agreed to." Another patient who was admitted to our program told her outpatient therapist, "You better do what I say, because if you don't I'll kill myself." She enacted an extremely coercive scenario by carrying around a deadly poison on her person at all times as evidence that she was willing to execute her threat. Of course, no such way of relating is therapeutically workable, and limits must be set while pursuing whatever measures necessary to protect both the patient and the therapist. Extreme control and manipulation very often results in termination of the therapeutic relationship (as it did in the latter example while the patient was hospitalized).

Therapists' responses may also be molded in much subtler ways. One common pattern of interaction occurs when patients react by taking a victimized position whenever they are confronted with dysfunctional behavior. They may react with anger and hostility, but more often they reflexively have responses of intense shame and guilt. This kind of response can then lead to therapists avoiding necessary interventions or retreating from crucial therapeutic stances. This type of control and manipulation through chronic victimization is both common and remarkably effective, as in the following clinical illustration:

> Lorraine, a 30-year-old lesbian woman, began the Women's Treatment Program at McLean Hospital, a residential outpatient program designed to teach a variety of skills to help patients transition from inpatient hospitalization to outpatient treatment. There was, at the time, a two-month limit to participation in the program, with patients expected to meet individual behavioral goals every two weeks as a condition of remaining in the program. After the first two weeks, Lorraine had made little progress toward the goal she had set. She met with her case manager, who tried to question her about why she hadn't worked toward achieving her goal. Lorraine reacted strongly: "I know I screwed up! You'll probably tell me that I have to leave the program. I'm sorry. I'm sorry. I'm sorry." The case manager apologized for having upset her with her "demanding" inquiries and approved an additional two-week stay in the program.

Two weeks later, when again Lorraine failed to make any progress toward achieving her goals, the case manager approached her with considerable trepidation and anxiety. Lorraine responded by bursting into tears and saying, "I know I've been a failure in this program. I'm sure you have all been talking about me, and how I've been just avoiding doing the work I need to do. I know you think I'm stupid and lazy, and you probably hate me because I'm gay. I'll leave and won't bother you again." The case manager hastened to offer another extension in the program.

Fixation on the Trauma

Some chronically disempowered patients appear to be fixated on exploration of the trauma, regardless of the lack of safety and ongoing chaos in their lives. Having no sense of their own ability to gain a sense of control over their experiences, these patients see abreaction as a magical panacea for their difficulties—a cathartic process from which they will emerge somehow changed. Unfortunately, however, this kind of premature abreaction is not only overwhelming but also self-perpetuating. Predictably, the intense affects of past abuse are poorly tolerated, and patients retreat to dysfunctional solutions such as isolation and self-harming behaviors. In addition, the dissociative barriers, which previously kept traumatic memories from flooding into consciousness, are weakened. Chronically disempowered patients lack the skills to have a sense of control over these memories, and they are vulnerable to repeated intrusions of unwanted and intolerable memories and experiences. They nonetheless persist in trying to work on the memories that they are ill-equipped to tolerate.

Most chronically disempowered patients will require a very long period of preliminary work prior to active focus on past trauma. In some patients, the extended focus of treatment will remain on these basic issues for many years. The following case—which went well—illustrates the importance of sometimes deferring the focus on the trauma:

An experienced therapist, Dr. P., sought consultation for a patient he had been treating for more than 12 years. Although the treatment seemed to be going smoothly, he was concerned about the pace of the treatment. In describing the patient and the therapy, he noted, "About two years ago she started telling me about memories of sexual abuse which she had hidden until then, and about six months ago she started talking about a sense of having other 'people' inside of her, which sounds like DID. Do you think I really missed the boat?" After hearing about the extraordinary chaos of the patient's life and the long, stabilizing, and ego-supportive therapy, I felt strongly that although Dr. P. might have suspected the role of trauma and presence of dissociative symptoms at an earlier point, the treatment probably had gone in the right direction. It seemed as though this patient needed a very lengthy period of growth and stabilization before accessing traumatic material. This sense of the patient was confirmed some years subsequently, as she began to reveal a long history of intentional and malevolent sadistic abuse. It was only her well-learned coping mechanisms and her strong relational bonds with her therapist and her social support network that kept her from becoming decompensated and disorganized at that time.

Developing a primary identity as a trauma survivor may have deleterious effects with chronically disempowered patients. Such an identity may have the unintended consequences of patients' acceptance of their helplessness and victimization. More disturbingly, such patients may even develop a sense of entitlement; having been victimized they may feel that they deserve reparations. They may come to feel that they do not have to meet societal expectations in terms of functioning, and they may expect that they are due some kind of compensation for their maltreatment. Because these kind of reparations are not forthcoming from the original perpetrators of abuse, they may expect that others—including their treaters or society as a whole—should provide extra considerations in compensation for their traumatic experiences. Such expectations may be understandable, but they are rarely realistic and never fulfilled.

Inauthenticity

There are occasions where disempowered patients with a combination of chronically poor functioning, disability, and dependence present with a strong sense of inauthenticity. They have learned how to behave appropriately as psychiatric patients or therapy patients, but their responses have a kind of rote quality: "I've been working on my issues…" "I've been trying to keep myself safe…" Therapists can sometimes observe that there is no shared underlying therapeutic agenda and little real progress in treatment, but that the patients need to present the appearance of therapeutic work even though they don't feel close to being empowered enough to make changes in their lives. It can be frustrating and unproductive for therapists to engage in a kind of pseudo-therapy that continues without ever addressing the underlying real issues. Yet, therapists generally find it very difficult to address patients' inner emptiness and chronic disempowerment for fear of appearing critical and destabilizing patients' rather brittle and fragile defenses. In addition, patients' fear of losing crucial attachments leads them to nonverbally influence therapists into colluding with avoidance of these issues. However, it can be much more productive to find a way to restore some sense of authenticity. As a consultant to stalemated therapies (a role that makes it sometimes easier to promote change), I have sometimes been able to talk directly to the issues in an effort to restore some sense of authenticity:

My impression is that you feel that you have to give your therapist the sense that you think you can make progress in therapy even though you've never believed that you could do that. I don't want you to feel ashamed because I think you've come by your sense of powerlessness and despair for very understandable reasons. But, I think the reason why you continue in treatment is that the relationship with your therapist is the most important one in your life and the closest you think you can come to a real relationship. You think if you admit to your therapist that you don't think you can make progress that the therapy will end. But, I think you have legitimate problems, and it will serve you better to be able to talk candidly about what you really feel. Instead of talking about issues that you think interest your therapist and goals that are unrealistic, why not talk about what might be more possible to achieve. What do you think you can honestly accomplish? Perhaps you and your therapist could work on how you might be able to get yourself out of bed and showered by 9:00 a.m. once or twice a week? I know that doesn't seem like much, but it's a start and something real that you could work on together.

CLINICAL WORK WITH "IMPOSSIBLE PATIENTS"

The general principles of clinical practice used to treat patients with complex post-traumatic and dissociative disorders are described elsewhere in this volume; they are critically important in treating chronically disempowered patients. Some other particularly relevant elements of treatment are also essential in treating these most vulnerable patients.

Clarification of the Therapeutic Agenda

In the treatment of chronically disempowered survivors of childhood abuse, therapists' understanding of the nature of therapy may differ considerably from patients' assumptions about therapy. For example, therapists may place a high value on patients gaining a sense of mastery over their lives through better self-care, achieving control over their feelings and impulses, and learning from their experiences. In contrast, chronically disempowered patients may not be able to even conceive of developing a sense of mastery over their lives. Patients may assume that the therapy will simply help them to feel better and that their therapists should do whatever is necessary to care for them and to deal with their feelings and impulses. Given patients' assumptions about themselves as chronically victimized and powerless, it is not surprising that they assume that there must be some external locus of control in their lives.

Differences in assumptions about the agenda of therapy are remarkably commonplace in the treatment of disempowered patients. Even experienced therapists repeatedly make the mistake of implicitly assuming that treatment goals are shared. When there is not a mutually agreed-upon agenda for the therapy, impasses inevitably arise, particularly around issues such as being taken care of versus learning self-care, and impulsive tension-release versus learning to cope with dysphoric affect. It is the therapist's responsibility to provide explicit explanation and teaching to patients about the process of therapy. Furthermore, given the chronic disempowerment that patients experience, therapists must provide such psychoeducation at the beginning of the treatment and then again throughout the course of the treatment. The following clinical example illustrates some common issues concerning the treatment process:

> Judy, a 32-year-old married woman, had a long history of depression and had been treated for years with psychotherapy and medication. She was on disability and had few demands on her life, but she reported feeling overwhelmed by her family responsibilities. She began a new therapy, and it soon became clear to the therapist that she had problems related to many experiences of childhood abuse that had included intense devaluation and physical abuse. Both outside the office (as described by the patient) and within the therapy sessions, Judy would seem to reenact being victimized. She would bitterly describe how she knew that others (including the therapist) thought of her as worthless, how helpless she was to change her life, and how suicidal she felt. She was convinced that it was her fate to be abandoned (despite a 12-year marriage) and felt that she was of no importance to anyone else.
>
> The therapist would gently try to comfort Judy, empathizing with her despair, but also expressing his conviction that she was worthwhile. He would also remind her of her many accomplishments and her value to her family, helping her gain a better sense of perspective. As the therapy continued, Judy began making increasing numbers of emergency telephone calls to the therapist. Typically, she would feel panicky and overwhelmed and call the therapist saying that she was about to kill herself. The therapist responded patiently at first but soon became both frustrated and worried at the increasing frequency of the telephone calls. Finally, following some consultation, the therapist began to talk to Judy about the need to limit emergency calls. She was furious and incredulous. "What am I supposed to do when I'm going to kill myself?" she demanded. The therapist responded, "I hoped that you would use the therapy to learn to soothe yourself and to know how to cope when you feel overwhelmed and unhappy," to which Judy replied with genuine confusion, "I thought that was *your* job!"

It is inevitable that in the course of treatment the therapist will provide support and comfort to traumatized patients. Such interventions may be very differently understood by different patients. For example, patients with a greater sense of self-empowerment may implicitly understand that a therapist who provides support, validation, and caring is modeling ways of thinking and behaving that the patient can internalize (e.g. "How can I learn to provide this for myself?"). Chronically disempowered patients, however, may simply see the therapist's interventions as a substitute for the seemingly impossible work of learning self-regard, self-soothing, and self-care (e.g., "How can I get my therapist to do more of this for me?"). Moreover, because these patients may not have any real sense of interpersonal relatedness, they see learning to care for themselves only as a lonely, impossible, and unwanted task and the route to losing the critically important relationship with their therapists. This dysfunctional, albeit understandable, outlook has enormous regressive potential; as more support is provided by the therapist, the patient becomes less competent. This impasse often results in an increasing intensity of the therapy and an associated deterioration of the patient's clinical condition.

Therapists must provide ongoing psychoeducation and support to help disempowered patients understand that they must learn about self-care and mutuality in relationships. Therapists should be empathic about the difficulties that disempowered patients have in facing these tasks, and they must be prepared to repeatedly encourage patients to take a stance that will help them gain an internal sense of control. Therapy is only helpful in this context, and therapists must not collude in perpetuating patients' disempowerment through endless cycles of regressive caretaking. After all, the goal of any therapy is increased self-esteem and self-efficacy, and no therapist would knowingly participate in any therapy that increases patients' disempowerment.

Treatment Intensity and Functioning

The intensity of treatment with chronically disempowered patients should be closely monitored. There is a real danger that treatment can come to substitute for coping with the real world, and that functioning is abandoned in favor of an identity as an impaired psychiatric patient. In general, a frequency of sessions of once or twice a week is optimal. More frequent sessions are generally regressive. Although very frequent sessions encourage a sense of object constancy, they allow patients to surrender too much of their own control and coping mechanisms, and engender an interpersonal intensity that is threatening and consuming for many patients. If more frequent contact with others is needed, it should be structured as part of a therapeutic program or activities, preferably not involving the primary therapist.

An enhanced emphasis on functioning is especially important with chronically disempowered patients. Even completing very minimal tasks can be the beginning of building a sense of accomplishment and self-efficacy. Such basic efforts as getting out of bed, showering, and taking care of daily needs can be the beginning of seeing oneself as having control over one's self and the environment. Such elementary efforts may progress toward structured activities, volunteer efforts, or even paid employment. A progressive ability to function—even if not initially perceived by the patient as important—may be one of the keys to growth beyond chronic disempowerment.

Learning Relational Skills and Authenticity

As in the therapy of all severely traumatized patients, the essential interpersonal process for chronically disempowered patients is to help them establish patterns of relatedness that are mutual and collaborative. As patients repeatedly bring the reenactments of abusive interactions into the therapeutic arena, therapists must help them move toward respect and mutuality. Unfortunately, it often is a lengthy process of seemingly endless cycles of disconnection and reconnection before patients can begin to internalize a healthy model of interpersonal interactions. However, it is crucial in the treatment of chronically disempowered patients that therapists understand that corrective emotional experience involves patients learning to care for themselves in the context of supportive relationships, and not simply to be cared for by others.

Chronically disempowered patients adapt to the culture of the institutions of psychiatric treatment. They become facile in the language of therapeutic settings, and learn to talk about their "treatment," "working in therapy," and "safety." All of these terms sometimes seem to be used in going through the motions of being in therapy and to obscure the underlying agenda of seeking contact and nurturing from caregivers. However, to truly make progress in treatment, patients must learn a new kind of authenticity, acknowledging their sense of helplessness and their wish for passive dependency and gratification. Only this kind of authenticity can allow patients to begin to grow and move from their disempowered positions. Therapists must be sensitive to patients' difficulty in coming to terms with acknowledging their real-life situations and internal life, using tact rather than brutal honesty. Patients' authenticity is only gradually achieved with therapists taking a nonjudgmental and empathic stance and helping them begin to grapple with difficult and painful realities.

A common scenario often occurs with patients who are struggling to control dysfunctional and maladaptive behaviors. There are inevitably lapses of control and regression to actions (or inactions) that are counter to the goals of therapy. That is, patients frequently return to old dysfunctional behaviors that are familiar but countertherapeutic. When confronted about this regression, patients typically react primarily with intense shame and guilt that appears to be traumatically based, as if their behaviors are yet another manifestation of their defectiveness and "badness." This regression/acting out/shame/guilt cycle is not productive, as it does not allow the patient and therapist to reflect on the behaviors as being understandable albeit maladaptive and to find alternative solutions. Instead the cycle only reinforces negative self-perceptions and contributes to inauthenticity as the patient tries to suppress regressive impulses in an effort to be "good." Because the pull toward regression is not effectively processed and understood, there is a heightened likelihood that the dysfunctional behaviors will recur, perpetuating the cycle. One way to resolve this dilemma is to address it directly:

I can see by your responses that you feel bad and shamed by my observations. That is not my intent and is not useful to you. I can easily understand how you can lapse into behaviors that feel familiar, and how difficult it must be to take the risk to do things differently. I want you to leave the shame and guilt outside of this discussion. It is not helpful and only further complicates your efforts to find a solution to your problems. It is important that we understand how you have come to this point and what we can do together to make it different.

A critical and necessary trait for therapists who treat "impossible" and chronically disempowered patients is endless patience. Therapists must learn how to empathically set limits over and over again, being aware that the cycles of dysfunctional behavior rarely abate quickly and that only small incremental changes can be expected. However, lapses with regression to old behaviors or minor violations of the therapeutic contract should be tolerated only if there is progress over time toward the agreed-upon goals of treatment. The therapist is in the best position to provide productive treatment by being clear that the therapy is not only about sustaining the therapeutic relationship, but that incremental change is a prerequisite for continuing the treatment. Persistent absence of any perceived benefits in treatment or major violations of the therapeutic agreement should prompt therapists to consider whether the therapy is worthwhile, workable, or tolerable, and whether an alternative kind of clinical management is indicated.

The treatment of chronically disempowered patients represents a significant challenge to individual clinicians and to the mental health profession. Many of these patients have been so egregiously abused that they have no belief in their own self-efficacy and little ability to relate to others in ways that might help them. As a result, clinicians must exercise sensitivity and skill to find ways to engage them and to work with them in a way that will maximize the possibilities for their growth and minimize regression. In our era of limited health care resources, the treatment of chronically disempowered and traumatized patients must be closely examined. On an outpatient basis, the frequency and intensity of treatment must be carefully balanced to provide both opportunities for growth and also to limit the regressive potential of excessive caretaking. In some instances where individual therapy proves to be too regressive, alternatives such as group treatment should be considered. The utilization and nature of inpatient hospitalization must also be carefully evaluated. Although hospitalization is clearly indicated when patients are seriously at risk, inpatient treatment must emphasize stabilization and containment rather than exploration and abreaction. The inpatient setting must not become an arena for flight from impasses in outpatient therapy, for reenactment of abuse scenarios, or as a substitute for learning to live in the world. Partial hospitalization may be an attractive alternative treatment modality for some patients with a more long-term course, but much still needs to be learned about the optimal mix of structure and programming needed to work with these challenging patients.

Clinicians must be patient and respectful of chronically disempowered survivors of abuse and the psychological prisons in which they live. Even at best, the objectives of the treatment seem formidable to most patients, and the process of therapy is long and arduous. However, therapists must also insist that these patients begin to share an agenda that will help them truly take control of their lives, even in small increments. Therapists must refuse to collude in interactions that result in reenactments of abuse or revictimization. The ultimate prognosis of many chronically disempowered patients is uncertain. Although many will improve steadily with skillful treatment, others may have more long-term disability. In either case, therapists will provide good treatment if they approach therapeutic work with compassion, patience, skill, and a commitment to enhancing authentic growth while ensuring that they do no harm.

11

Good Fences Make Good Neighbors

Maintaining the Treatment Frame

The abuse of children is an inherent violation of boundaries and limits. Physical and sexual abuse clearly violate parent-child boundaries, as children are exploited for personal needs. These kinds of abuse ignore the limits of the coping capacities of children, overwhelming them repeatedly with stimuli that they are unable to tolerate. In treatment, many patients who have experienced childhood abuse will replicate the enmeshment and violation of their early experiences, breaching boundaries and challenging limits. Effective treatment must confront these recapitulations of abuse and help patients establish reasonable boundaries and limits within the therapeutic relationship, providing a safe and respectful framework for both the patient and the therapist.

Establishing a safe structure for treatment is a basic and essential part of the treatment for all patients, but it has particular relevance with patients who are survivors of severe childhood abuse (Briere, 1992; Chu, 1988, 1992c; Courtois, 2010; Davies & Frawley, 1994; Herman, 1992b; Pearlman & Saakvitne, 1995). Particularly in the early phases of therapy, many patients have frequent crisis situations, such as repeated and unpredictable reexperiences of traumatic events accompanied by despair and panic. They also experience intense impulses—often of a destructive nature—that feel compelling and overwhelming. These crisis situations often lead patients to seek increasing amounts of reassurance and time from their therapists. As the intensity of the therapeutic relationship heats up, therapists may begin to find themselves responding to frequent calls, increasing the frequency or length of sessions, and coping with intrusions into their personal lives. In these kinds of situations, therapists must understand the need for establishing safety and predictability in the therapy and must find some way of maintaining boundaries and setting appropriate limits.

ESTABLISHING THE TREATMENT FRAME

A treatment frame that incorporates the ground rules of therapy is one of the foundations of treatment. Therapists must be clear about issues such as the frequency and length of sessions, the availability of the therapist outside of the office, and the roles of both patient and therapist. The treatment frame serves somewhat different functions for therapists and for patients. Patients require a treatment frame that clarifies what they can consistently expect and count on and that ensures the safety of both parties by establishing the kind of boundaries and limits that were not a part of their early lives. Therapists must establish a treatment frame that minimizes the anxiety and stress that comes from the intensity of their professional work and protects their personal lives and privacy.

Therapists must be explicit about the treatment frame and should not assume that traumatized patients will inherently understand the norms of any relationship, let alone the special nature of the therapeutic relationship. Many patients from abusive backgrounds may not even understand the need for a treatment frame. Patients may actually invite boundary violations that feel normal to them (e.g., wanting the therapist to be more of a friend in order to feel more secure, or even inviting the therapist to engage in a sexual relationship as a way of experiencing safe intimacy). Although setting limits and establishing boundaries may be frustrating or confusing to patients, a strong treatment frame ultimately allows patients to feel safe in a relationship where the rules are mutually understood and respected.

Struggles around the treatment frame often seem to occur regarding the issue of therapist availability outside of therapy sessions. A certain amount of availability on the part of therapists is helpful, and some patients in crisis are able to make use of brief telephone contacts to feel reassured and contained until the next session. However, constant or extraordinary availability is problematic for at least three important reasons. First, escalating demands for therapists' availability ignores the very real human limitations of therapists and their legitimate need to maintain their own separate lives. Second, constant availability leads to increasing dependence on the therapist to provide reassurance rather than compelling patients to find their own internal mechanisms of containing dysphoric affects and providing self-soothing. Finally, the expectation that therapists can always provide soothing and reassurance early in therapy is unrealistic. Both patients and therapists need to accept that throughout the early phase of treatment, patients may encounter pain that may be overwhelming, and that an important aspect of therapy is learning to find nonharmful ways of managing and tolerating psychic distress.

Therapists must establish very clear limits based on both their own needs and their judgment of patients' needs and abilities. Exactly where the limits are set—within reason—is a function of what is tolerable for the therapist and what is helpful for the patient. For example, some therapists are willing to accept calls up to several times per week, whereas others are not. Some patients require someone to be available on evenings and weekends, whereas others need to be challenged to find ways of coping on their own during these times. If there is a clash between therapist and patient needs, such as the patient who needs out-of-office contact and a therapist who is not willing to be available, some other solution must be found (e.g., hotlines, a walk-in crisis center, other supports). However, the basic principle is not so much exactly where the boundaries and limits are set, but that there are clear boundaries and limits constitute a reasonable and workable treatment frame. Therapists who avoid setting and maintaining a clear treatment frame are likely to become exhausted and then either to abandon the therapy or to renege on explicit or implied promises. Although periodic renegotiation of the treatment frame is common, it is important to avoid situations where too much is promised, because retrenching is likely to result in patients feeling abandoned, betrayed, or abused. The following clinical example of my early-career dilemmas illustrates some of the relevant issues concerning limit setting:

Following my graduation from residency training, I took on the treatment of several patients with a history of sexual abuse in my private practice, many of whom were frequently in crisis. As a successful product of medical education and training, I had taken on the belief that I should be able to respond to meet the needs of my patients at any hour, day or night, even at the cost of sleep, health, mental stability, and family. I soon began to find myself awakened frequently at night by emergency phone calls, often to participate in long discussions around the issue of suicide. For example, one patient with dissociative identity disorder (DID) would sometimes call around 2 a.m. as a suicidal personality. In response to my asking why she was suicidal, she typically responded, "Because it's my job"—a response to which, at the time, I had no idea of how to counter.

Over time, I learned that just continuing to talk for about 20 minutes would result in the suicidal impulses abating, and I could get off the phone, but by then I would usually be wide awake. I learned to dread the ring of the telephone and slept poorly, expecting to be awakened and not being able to get back to sleep. The introduction of a new puppy into my household and the responsibility of getting up at dawn's first light to walk the dog brought me to the brink of physical and emotional exhaustion. Violating the teachings about not talking to patients about personal needs, I told each of my patients that I retired early and that I expected each of them to respect my sleep. I emphasized that I did not enjoy late-night calls and would permit calls for only serious emergencies after 8 p.m., and that the conversations would consist of a brief discussion about arranging immediate hospitalization.

Several of my patients became very upset at this limit. One patient retorted, "Fine! Then I'll just kill myself!" to which I responded that a condition of the therapy was for the patient to call if seriously suicidal at whatever time. Another patient became very distant and panicky, and then called later just before 8 p.m. to be reassured that I still wished to work with her. After a very stormy period of protest and anger on the part of my patients, evening and night calls decreased dramatically to only one call every few weeks. One patient later explored how she was acting out her anger by sadistically calling me repeatedly at home. Another acknowledged that the limits made it both harder and easier for her: "Since I know I can't call you, I just make myself shut down instead of fighting with myself whether or not to call."

The guidelines in this discussion may seem rather obvious, but I have known many otherwise competent and experienced therapists to make major errors in permitting egregious violations of the treatment frame. Such therapists have tried to become friends with patients, engaged in activities such as extensive touching, holding, and even bottle feeding, entered into business arrangements with patients, or even invited patients to live with them. What leads otherwise competent therapists to fail to set adequate limits and to participate in major boundary violations? Several common patterns occur. Therapists may lose their therapeutic perspective and come to believe that their only alternative is to gratify patients' demands. They may recognize patients' own limited internal resources and fail to understand the need to help patients find ways of developing coping mechanisms rather than simply filling in the gaps in their functioning. Therapists may also come to believe that survivors of childhood abuse deserve and need a radically different kind of treatment than other psychologically injured patients. They may then proceed to implement a treatment based primarily on patients' perceived needs, such as schemes to reparent or allowing unlimited regression.

Perhaps one of the more difficult scenarios that I have encountered involves therapists who have promised never to abandon the patient—no matter what the patient does. While this promise may give patients a certain amount of security, it also permits some patients to engage in uncontrolled and escalating scenarios to test the therapist's resolve, which can be in the form of appalling and sadistic reenactments of past abusive interpersonal interactions. There is little evidence that providing a kind of unconditional love is either realistic or helpful to patients. In contrast, a therapy that is based on the patient adhering to the treatment frame and achieving maximal personal growth is far more reassuring and safe. The continuing treatment must always be based not on false assurances but on the condition that the patient is able to benefit from the therapy to make progress in treatment.

Boston forensic psychiatrist Thomas Gutheil, MD (1989), has witnessed many therapeutic misadventures as an expert witness in legal cases where patients have sued their therapists for engaging in boundary violations (e.g., engaging in a sexual relationship). He has described the phenomenon of a kind of bubble that can separate the patient and therapist from the realities of the external world. Within this bubble, the therapist empathically enters the intrapsychic world of the patient, where the needs of the patient are intense and compelling. Separated from the perspective and judgment of others, the patient and therapist then proceed on a course of action that may seem to make sense within the patient's frame of reference but that lacks any kind of wider or longer-term perspective, and that almost inevitably damages both patient and therapist. Therapists in this situation are at least somewhat aware that the course of treatment that they are pursuing might be questionably regarded by other professionals, and they are often reticent about their decisions (e.g., "I know this is the right thing to do, but I'm not going to talk to anyone else about it because they wouldn't understand"). It should be a red flag when therapists find themselves thinking that they would not want their colleagues to know about the course of therapy they are pursuing with a particular patient.

Therapists who find themselves in this position should immediately seek consultation with a trusted senior clinician.

Patients' reactions to their therapists' interventions are powerful determinants of therapists' behavior. Patients' responses often seem alternately idealized (e.g., "You are the first therapist who truly understands me") and devaluing (e.g., "You have no idea what I am feeling and can't help me"). This is a pattern of so-called intermittent reinforcement that in classic operant conditioning theory is a particularly effective way of inducing compliant behaviors. The pattern of patients' responses, having both positive and negative reinforcers, is extremely effective in creating a powerful bond that can be focused around meeting patients' perceived needs. Thus, therapists may tolerate a pattern of slowly escalating demands and only become aware of the consequences when they find themselves constrained and overwhelmed by them.

The intensity of patients' experiences also promotes premature and ill-considered decision making on the part of therapists. Patients' wishes to be comforted, reassured, rescued, touched, or soothed are all too human and often intensely compelling. These real needs are often combined with an atmosphere of crisis, with the implied threat of patients decompensating or suiciding ("I can't continue to live feeling like this"), and are conducive to ill-considered decisions. Therapists should remember that predictability and consistency provide containment rather than extraordinary therapeutic interventions. In particular, touch and physical contact are very problematic with traumatized patients, and therapists should be extremely conservative regarding such matters. In general, any major changes concerning limits and boundaries should be carefully evaluated. No such decisions should be made against the therapist's better judgment because of a crisis situation. In fact, nothing in terms of the treatment frame should be changed in the midst of a crisis, because the full implications of any such change cannot be given the careful consideration that is necessary to make an appropriate decision. For example, even agreeing to something extra that is legitimate and within acceptable boundaries is almost never a short-term proposition; therapists should be aware that they are likely to be called on to continue to provide the extra intervention for *years*. Thus, changes in the treatment frame need to be fully considered and extensively discussed before being implemented. Therapists must take the responsibility for making decisions that maintain the treatment frame, keep the structure of the therapy intact, and promote patients' healthy psychological growth.

THERAPEUTIC RESPONSIBILITY

The issue of therapeutic responsibility is another area that involves boundaries and limits. The locus of responsibility for achieving treatment goals or even remaining alive may seem obvious, but it often becomes quite unclear in the roller coaster ride of the therapy of severely traumatized patients. It is a common experience for therapists who begin treating an abuse survivor to find that the direction of the therapy shifts dramatically after only a few months. For example, the therapy may begin with some general agreement that the work is to improve the quality of patients' life. However, therapists may soon find themselves in the position of attempting to convince the patient to remain in therapy or not to suicide. Clearly, some major change has occurred in the therapy. Understanding this change involves recognition of the conflicts and profound ambivalence of abuse survivors.

Abuse survivors are exposed to experiences that lead to internal psychological conflict in almost every major aspect of their lives. The intensity and circumstances of the childhood abuse leads to these seemingly irreconcilable psychological conflicts. For example, the child who is sexually abused by a parent often carries the incompatible feelings of "I love my father" and "I hate my father." The intensity of these intrapsychic conflicts leads to the use of dissociative defenses, so that the conflicted feelings can be repressed and forgotten, or even apportioned into different parts of the self as in the case of patients with DID. As discussed previously in Chapter 7, abuse survivors are also conflicted concerning self-harm. In fact, they have deeply ambivalent feelings about virtually all major issues in their lives: I am worthwhile/I am worthless, I was abused/the abuse never happened, I was loved/I was hated and exploited, I was powerless and victimized/the abuse was my fault, I can have a life/I'll never have anything, I want therapy/I'm afraid of therapy, I trust my therapist/I'm afraid of my therapist, and so on. These sorts of ambivalent feelings and beliefs are unbearably painful. Particularly when overwhelmed, it is only human for patients to ignore one side of their ambivalence.

Therapists may find themselves assuming one side of the ambivalent feelings—usually the therapeutic side. This dynamic can occur in multiple arenas resulting in the responsibility for finding solutions to impossible dilemmas being assumed by the therapist: how to or even whether to function, whether to remain alive, and even whether to continue in therapy at all, among others. Unfortunately, this dynamic allows patients to be unambivalently negative about these complex issues. The shift of therapeutic responsibility results in the therapist being placed in an untenable therapeutic position. Therapists and patients find themselves battling over these conflicts (some of which involve actual survival) rather than recognizing them as the projections of patients' intrapsychic dilemmas. Among the untoward effects of such situations are the therapist assuming additional burdens, the patient failing to grapple with critical internal conflicts, and a foundering of the therapeutic process, as illustrated in the following example:

Barbara, a woman in her late 40s, entered therapy to deal with emerging depression, hopelessness, and isolation. Despite having difficulties with coping and almost no close friends or other interpersonal supports, she took pride in having held down a good job and having functioned at a high level. However, with the retirement of her boss, Barbara felt inexplicably betrayed. She began to increasingly dwell on the emptiness in her life and her failed marriage, and to vividly recall details of a very neglectful and abusive childhood. She began to abuse alcohol on a regular basis, often becoming more depressed and calling her therapist at night for comfort and reassurance. These calls were initially brief and helpful. However, over time the calls became more frequent and less productive as she became more depressed and seriously thought about suicide. She began to push the idea of confronting her parents concerning their maltreatment of her, feeling that if they apologized that she would somehow feel healed from the aftereffects of their neglect and abuse. When her therapist pointed out the dangers of such a course of action, Barbara accused him of being overprotective. Predictably, when she convinced him to call her parents to invite them to a family meeting, they refused, plunging Barbara into more despair.

The therapist became progressively more frantic, redoubling his efforts to help Barbara move forward in her treatment. He reminded her of her past accomplishments and considerable strengths but to no avail. Barbara began to talk about quitting therapy, as she could not bear to hurt the therapist by killing herself while being treated by him. Finally, after she was found unconscious by her ex-husband after ingesting excessive amounts of tranquilizers and alcohol, she was hospitalized. The therapist was able to use the hospital staff as consultants for his dilemma. After perceiving how he was carrying the entire impetus for Barbara's treatment, he was able to approach her to renegotiate the treatment contract, saying, "I feel as though you and I have found ourselves struggling about a whole host of issues that primarily reflect your mixed feelings about them. Although *I* want you to stay in therapy and live, *my* feelings don't really matter. *You* have to make the commitment to cope with these issues, and not depend on me to provide you with the reasons to go on. If we are to continue to work together, you will have to decide that you are willing to wrestle with the issues of your own welfare, learning ways to cope instead of expecting me to always be there to convince you to live." After prolonged discussion, Barbara was able to commit to certain safety measures, including abstinence from alcohol and taking on the responsibility of working out a crisis plan. Much later on in her treatment, she was able to recognize how much she wanted the therapist to be the encouraging father she longed for and to take over and manage the burdens of her life.

Therapists need to encourage and help abuse survivors to carry the weight of their conflicts. It is not that therapists should avoid making their own stances clear (e.g., about suicide or the value of treatment), but they should help patients take on the responsibility of grappling with these issues rather than projecting them onto the patient-therapist relationship. Interventions regarding therapeutic responsibility need to be made with empathy and sensitivity, as it is all too easy for therapists to use the issue of responsibility punitively and to effectively abandon patients. Even the phase, "You need to take responsibility for . . ." can feel like a verbal cudgel if said accusingly or reproachfully. After all, these difficulties are often caused by the immense psychological distress of conflictual feelings and not knowing how to cope with them, not by lack of motivation or weak moral fiber. Therapists should demonstrate that they understand patients' dilemmas and offer their assistance in trying to work out conflicts (e.g., "I know that you have very mixed feelings about therapy. I would like to help understand both your hopes and fears about therapy rather than your feeling that I am 'making' you attend therapy.").

Obviously, the principle of expecting patients to assume primary responsibility for their lives and treatment does *not* extend to emergency situations where patients are acutely at risk of suicide or possible serious self-harm. In particular, confrontation concerning ambivalence about personal safety should *not* be made during emergency telephone contacts. In such circumstances, clinicians must do whatever is necessary for the patient's safety and welfare (e.g., hospitalization). Once safety is assured, the issue can then be directly addressed in subsequent face-to-face meetings. In fact, therapeutic responsibility should be the primary issue discussed until some resolution is reached.

Another area of therapeutic responsibility that abuse survivors often have difficulty maintaining concerns basic interpersonal relatedness. Abuse survivors often have histories of being exploited and blamed. This difficulty may be recapitulated in the therapy, as such patients may have little understanding of their personal responsibility in the therapeutic relationship and may exploit and blame their therapists for any difficulties they encounter. Compounding this circumstance is the valid therapeutic view that the therapy is primarily for the patient's benefit, and the therapist's needs should only minimally interfere with the process. As a result, therapists may fail to set limits on behaviors that are not acceptable as a part of any workable interpersonal relationship, overlooking the need for patients to appropriately control their responses and interactions. Patients should recognize that they must share the commitment to the relationship and to the therapeutic process, the commitment to try to resolve interpersonal difficulties, and the commitment to maintain shared therapeutic goals. The following example illustrates this issue:

> I was consulted by Dr. J. concerning a crisis in her treatment of Patty, a 44-year-old single woman with an extensive early abuse history. After three years of therapy, Patty began to despair of ever achieving closeness with others. Despite considerable gains in self-care and vocational matters, she still experienced intense fear when trying to make friends or function in social situations. In therapy she became increasingly angry, until virtually every session was a combination of stony silence and diatribes about the inadequacies of the therapist and the therapy: "I don't know what you expect of me. *You* have a life and a husband and a baby and house. *I* have nothing! I *hate* you for that! You think this therapy is so great. What has it done for me? My life is over. I'm in a lot of pain and I have to pay attention to giving myself the relief that I need. You think I should continue to live but you don't have to live my life! You just want me to go on suffering. Well, see if you can stop me. I can kill myself whenever *I* choose!"

Dr J. tolerated Patty's anger for many sessions. She recalled that during a period of her own personal therapy she had been quite angry at her therapist, and that expressing this anger had allowed her to eventually achieve important insights on how she had felt unheard by her parents. However, Patty's angry attacks seemed to only intensify and not to result in any new insights or gains. After hearing the story, I observed that the patient was caught up in a functionally psychotic transference. That is, she had lost the ability to understand that Dr. J. was not actually the source of her difficulties (unlike Dr. J.'s experience in her own therapy where she was aware that her therapist was fundamentally helpful). Patty was so consumed by her rage that she was effectively destroying the therapy. I made several suggestions about setting limits on the patient's behavior, essentially about finding empathic and supportive ways to say, "Cut it out."

Dr. J. subsequently was able to say to Patty: "I understand that you are truly tortured. However, I cannot allow you to continue to attack me. I think you have forgotten that I have spent years trying to help you and that I am not your enemy. Even though you feel tormented, you still are in a relationship with me, and we *both* have a responsibility for maintaining our relationship. You have frequently asked me not to abandon you. You now seem to be saying that you have the right to destroy and abandon our relationship. We cannot have a workable therapy if I'm constantly on the defensive or terrified that you might kill yourself." Patty responded with genuine surprise, saying, "I didn't know therapists had feelings!" She managed to control her attacks (initially with reluctance) and was later able to examine how she repeatedly found herself angrily challenging persons in her life with whom she felt the most vulnerable.

One other issue involving therapeutic responsibility has arisen as attitudes have shifted from widespread disbelief about patients' reports of childhood abuse to sometimes too-easy acceptance of *any* such reports. Patients have sometimes asked therapists to validate or deny the reality of their past abuse when patients do not have adequate information to make such a determination. It seems quite appropriate for a therapist to acknowledge or even raise the issue of abuse when the history seems relatively clear, but given the vagaries concerning the nature of traumatic memory, it is difficult to respond to all inquires of "Do you believe me?" In situations where patients are uncertain about the reality of past events or when memories are clearly not credible, therapists should respond to these inquiries by acknowledging only the painfulness of uncertainty and being able to know the realities of what actually happened. Patients and therapists together should assume the responsibility of sifting through known facts, possible occurrences, fantasies, and conjectures until such time as patients can be reasonably clear about their own personal realities. See Chapter 5 for a more detailed discussion of this complex issue.

THE MODEL OF EMPATHIC CONFRONTATION[1]

Patients with trauma-based disorders frequently have worthwhile ideas concerning the course of their therapy, guided by a kind of internal roadmap. However, as discussed throughout this book, it is also common for patients to advocate unwise treatment strategies or to cling to very dysfunctional but ingrained behaviors. For example, patients may vigorously advocate for premature abreactive work without having established the psychotherapeutic foundations for safe exploration. Similarly, patients may insist that they have no control over their posttraumatic and dissociative symptoms, may persist in self-destructive, revictimizing, or risk-taking behavior, or may demand inordinate therapist availability and reassurance that result in boundary violations. When such issues emerge in psychotherapy, patients often manifest extraordinary resistance to change. After all, many of the dysfunctional patterns of behavior have long served as coping mechanisms, and no matter how unpleasant, are more familiar than the well-intentioned but unknown treatment course advocated by therapists.

Setting limits on patients' dysfunctional behavior involves confrontation and is often an extremely difficult task. Patients with severe childhood abuse and a lifetime's experience of abandonment and betrayal may have a tenuous sense of alliance with their therapists. Hence, therapists often hesitate to confront patients even with important therapeutic issues because they fear patients' likely reactions of withdrawal, anger, and regressive and self-destructive behavior. However, confrontation of unsafe and/or dysfunctional patterns *must* be a part of the therapy, not only to guide the therapy in a positive direction, but also to prevent the therapist from becoming an unwitting enabler of continued destructive behavior.

Confrontation in psychotherapy has a long tradition of being an important part of psychodynamic treatment—to clarify resistances in therapy and to facilitate change (see, for example, Greenson, 1967; Mann, 1973; Myerson, 1973). Written in an era before acceptance of trauma as an important common etiology of adult psychopathology, two papers by two of my former teachers and supervisors—noted psychoanalysts Daniel Buie, MD, and Gerald Adler, MD—described the uses and misuses of confrontation in the treatment of borderline patients (Adler & Buie, 1972; Buie & Adler, 1972). These papers are still highly applicable to work with some traumatized patients. For example, confrontation was seen as sometimes necessary to help patients recognize "(1) the real danger in certain relationships; (2) the real danger in action used as a defense mechanism; and (3) the real danger in action used for discharge of impulses and feelings" (Buie & Adler, 1972, p. 101). The authors felt that confrontation of patients' denial allows the therapist "(1) to help the patient become aware of his impulses, so that he need not be subject to action without warning; (2) to help him gain temporary relief through abreaction; and (3) to help him gain a rational position from which he

---

[1]Portions of this section were adapted from the article, "Empathic Confrontation in the Treatment of Childhood Abuse Survivors, Including a Tribute to the Legacy of Dr. David Caul" (Chu, 1992a).

can exert self-control or seek help in maintaining control" (Buie & Adler, 1972, p. 103). In discussing the misuses of confrontation, the authors stressed patients' vulnerability to harm from confrontation caused by their propensity to feel abandoned, their intense impulses and inadequate defenses, and their tenuous capacity to form a working alliance. They noted that the therapist can misuse confrontation caused by countertransference "rage and envy when he feels he must rescue his helpless, demanding patient and then finds his efforts met by increasing demands and regression" (Adler & Buie, 1972, p. 109).

Many of the observations noted here are surprisingly apt in the context of the sometimes decidedly nonpsychoanalytic treatment of survivors of childhood abuse. However, it is a normative experience that clinicians find it difficult to implement confrontation in the psychotherapy of patients with severe childhood abuse. The need for confrontation may be obvious, such as danger to the patient, therapist, or therapeutic relationship, or behaviors that are out of control or sabotage the therapy. Although most persons find confrontation and conflict uncomfortable, therapists may be extremely reluctant to confront patients either because of countertransference difficulties (Chu, 1992a; Comstock, 1991) or the simple concern that confrontation will be misunderstood and make patients feel abandoned and betrayed. In fact, therapeutic confrontations are almost *always* initially misunderstood, but patience in reiterating concern for the patient and for the therapy often allows the confrontation to eventually be heard and understood as intended. I have proposed a model of *empathic confrontation* that offers a way of intervening that is effective in helping patients ally with therapists in a direction that is positive and therapeutically sound.

When making a confrontation, the demonstration of empathy for the patient's position is absolutely essential. With survivors of extensive childhood trauma, particularly early in the therapeutic process, it should never be assumed that firm therapeutic alliance exists. Early in treatment, patients experience a sense of disconnection routinely between sessions, and sometimes repetitively within sessions, especially when there is a sense of disagreement between the patient and therapist. Feeling disconnected, patients sometimes actively push away a dangerous sense of vulnerable intimacy and retreat to views of the therapist as threatening or abusive. Thus, if no connection is established *immediately prior* to making a confrontation, the patient is compelled to hear the intervention as simply an attempt of the therapist to control, abuse, exploit, or deprive the patient.

The model of empathic confrontation is based on the need to establish empathic resonance as a part of making a confrontation or other intervention that is painful to the patient (Chu, 1992a). That is, it is crucial to reestablish some sense of alliance before saying something that has the potential for making the patient feeling attacked, defensive, guilty, or shamed. In practical terms, empathic confrontation often takes the form of a statement in two parts. The first part strongly communicates that the therapist understands the patient's position, feelings, and experience. This can often be done in a few sentences. The second part (often connected to the first part by a "but" or "however") contains the confrontation concerning the patient's behavior. Two examples are illustrated here:

> Kay, a 24-year-old woman who had been brutally sexually abused throughout much of her childhood, chronically cut herself on her arms and legs with a razor. She tended to cut herself whenever she was overwhelmed with feelings, particularly when angry or ashamed. Despite the urgings of her therapist, she continued to self-mutilate, claiming that she found the cutting helpful and that only her therapist found it objectionable. Moreover, Kay argued convincingly that the cutting was not intended to be lethal and that she had no other ways to cope with her feelings. Her therapist gently confronted her on this behavior, saying, "I understand that you don't want to give up cutting yourself, and that the cutting has helped you survive. In fact, your cutting yourself has been an ingenious solution when you didn't have anyone else to rely on. However, unless you begin to work together with me on this, you will not find other ways to deal with your feelings, and your therapy will not be successful."
>
> Kay responded by angrily accusing her therapist of trying to control her, to which the therapist responded, "I know that it has been crucial for you to have a sense of your own control in your life, especially when others have hurt you. I know you have often been controlled by other people, but I'm asking you to do something that will be helpful in your therapy, not to do something my way." After some discussion, Kay was able to acknowledge the need to find a way to control her cutting and noted, "When people used to try to get me to stop, I always felt that they thought I was bad and didn't want anything to do with me."
>
> Cheryl, a 35-year-old woman with DID, was hospitalized because of frequent flashbacks of horrendous childhood abuse. In the hospital she continued to be out of control, frequently having flashbacks late in the evening, during which she was so agitated that she needed to be physically restrained. When asked to control her behavior she angrily claimed to have no control over the flashbacks, and, in fact, didn't remember them since *she*, Cheryl, wasn't "out." Her therapist said, "I know that it feels as though the flashbacks just take over and that you have no control. I also understand that you feel very separate from the other parts of you that were out of control. I know it is a core issue of your difficulties to feel alienated from the other parts of you. However, unless you can work very hard with me to *begin* to establish some control, and to communicate with your other parts, the therapy will not work, and neither I nor the hospital will be able to help you." After a period of angry denial, Cheryl was observed to be exercising extraordinary efforts to maintain control, pace the therapy, and promote internal communication.

The work with adult survivors of severe childhood abuse can sometimes be extremely challenging. It is crucial that therapists maintain attitudes that are empathic but also based on solid psychotherapeutic tenets, such as maintaining a solid treatment frame and confronting patients' dysfunctional behaviors. I formulated my model of empathic confrontation on the work of a pioneer in the treatment of patients with DID, the late David Caul, MD (see Chu, 1992a, for more examples of his work), who once wrote:

The therapist should be willing to exhibit appropriate respect for the patient... —respect, not indulgence. Respect does not preclude firmness and insistence on working together for progress. Respect does not preclude normal differences in feelings of the therapist with recognition that a wide variety of feelings toward the therapist will be forthcoming, especially early in therapy.... There has to be an element of cooperation that is woven as a thread throughout the course of therapy. The fact that a patient keeps coming back for sessions may be the main indication (even if unspoken) of cooperation by the patient. The therapist should always be willing to listen and accept suggestions and workable ideas. Sometimes it is difficult for a therapist to acknowledge the exquisitely sensitive nature of this "two-way street." Continue to emphasize the fact that productive therapy will require some sort of partnership between the parties.... The therapist should be able to distinguish between candor and sometimes cruel hostility. Remember that these people are very sensitive and very vulnerable. I suppose candor might be described as being truthful in addition to being caring, considerate, and concerned. The therapist should not be afraid to appropriately admit that there are difficulties in the treatment and should attempt to openly discuss them. All attempts should be made to do this in a positive way and to relate it to the therapy, and not direct it toward the patient.... It will remain for the therapist to use whatever energies there are toward good judgment and careful consideration in providing therapy for this phenomenon that is of such magnitude that it will require all the help that we can get. (Chu, 1992a, pp. 101–102).

PART III
Special Topics in Treatment of Complex Trauma-Related Disorders

12

The Rational Treatment of Dissociative
Identity Disorder[1]

Over the past three decades, professional awareness has increased dramatically concerning dissociation as a response to childhood trauma. As a consequence, many more patients have been diagnosed as suffering from dissociative identity disorder (DID) and related disorders. The accurate diagnosis of DID and similar dissociative disorders certainly has proved to be of benefit to many patients. However, in many instances, the particular nature of DID and dissociative symptoms appears to have led some professionals to engage in therapeutic practices that are largely ineffective or misguided. Over more than 20 years of consulting with therapists, I repeatedly have observed the difficulties that even competent and experienced therapists have in understanding and treating DID and dissociative disorder patients. Many of these difficulties are generic to patients with complex PTSD and are described elsewhere in this volume. This discussion examines the specific areas of difficulty commonly encountered with patients with DID and dissociative disorders.

The manifestations of DID are often dramatic and difficult to manage. The switching of personalities, the dissociative and amnestic barriers, and the complexity of internal psychic structures and identity are often bewildering to clinicians when they first encounter DID. In addition, the periodic intrusions of posttraumatic reexperiencing phenomena, including flashbacks, nightmares, overwhelming affect, and even somatic sensations, lead a sense of chronic instability. Furthermore, comorbid characterologic difficulties including patients' intense interpersonal disturbances, affective instability, and impulsive and self-destructive behavior add to the sense of ongoing crisis and chaos. In this context, many clinicians seem to ignore many of the established principles of traditional psychotherapy and engage in practices that appear to respond to the immediate clinical situation, but may be ill-advised in terms of the therapeutic process.

DID and the difficulties that are suffered by patients who have histories of severe childhood abuse sometimes *do* require therapists to make thoughtful modifications of certain psychotherapeutic techniques. However, most of the treatment of DID involves

---

[1] Portions of this chapter were adapted from the article, "The Rational Treatment of Multiple Personality Disorder" (Chu, 1994).

using the same traditional interventions used in the psychotherapy of all patients. Therapists should adhere to the basic principles of psychotherapy that have been established and proven as effective over generations of patient-therapist interactions. Not to do so can and does result in potential therapeutic impasses and negative outcomes. Treatments that are not founded on traditional psychotherapeutic principles risk becoming out of control and detrimental, not only to patients but to their therapists as well.

This chapter focuses specifically on the treatment of patients with DID and those similar, severe dissociative disorders that do not quite meet the criteria for DID—patients who experience themselves as fragmented but retain a single identity and/or do not have amnesia between personalities, for example, dissociative disorder, not otherwise specified (DDNOS). This discussion is intended as a practical guide to the management of adult patients and focuses on four areas of therapeutic difficulty that are common in the treatment of DID and related dissociative disorders: (1) etiology and diagnosis, (2) treatment goals and staging, (3) understanding severe dissociative disorders as system of personalities or self-states representing a fragmented sense of self within a single person, and (4) working with patients who have DID without undue focus on DID phenomenology. For more details and discussion concerning the treatment of DID, see *Guidelines for Treating Dissociative Identity Disorder in Adults, 3rd Revision* (International Society for the Study of Trauma and Dissociation, 2011) and *Guidelines for the Evaluation and Treatment of Dissociative Symptoms in Children and Adolescents* (International Society for the Study of Dissociation, 2004), available through the ISSTD and published in the *Journal of Trauma & Dissociation*. There are also numerous papers in the scientific literature concerning the treatment of DID and allied disorders—many of which are cited in this chapter—as well as several comprehensive texts for professionals (Dell & O'Neil, 2009; Michelson & Ray, 1996; Putnam, 1989; Ross, 1997; Vermetten, Dorahy, & Spiegel, 2007), and one written for patients with DID and the significant others in their lives (Haddock, 2001).

ISSUES CONCERNING ETIOLOGY AND DIAGNOSIS

Severe and prolonged traumatic experiences, especially early in childhood, can lead to the development of discrete, personified behavioral states (i.e., rudimentary alternate personalities) that compartmentalize intolerable traumatic memories, affects, sensations, beliefs, or behaviors. Elaboration and further structuring of these rudimentary alternate personalities occurs over time through a variety of developmental and symbolic mechanisms, resulting in the characteristics of the specific alternate personalities. The personalities may vary in complexity and sense of separateness as the child grows into adulthood (Kluft, 1984; Putnam, 1997). DID develops during the course of childhood and almost never derives from adult-onset trauma (unless it is superimposed on preexisting childhood trauma and latent or dormant fragmentation). Kluft (1984) has offered a four-factor theory for the development of DID: (1) the capacity for dissociation, (2) precipitating traumatic experiences that overwhelm the child's nondissociative coping capacity,

(3) specific psychological structuring of the DID alternate personalities, and (4) perpetuating factors such as lack of soothing and restorative experiences, which necessitate individuals to find their own ways of moderating distress.

As with any clinical presentation, evidence of DID must be carefully examined in terms of differential diagnosis. Specifically, patients must be examined for evidence of DSM-IV criteria (APA, 1994) for DID, including naturalistically occurring internal separate states, dissociative barriers between states, and amnesia. Etiologic issues concerning the necessary traumatic antecedents must be carefully considered. It should be determined whether there are comorbid conditions such as another Axis I diagnosis of an affective or psychotic disorder, substance abuse, an eating disorder, or somatization, and Axis II disorders such as borderline personality disorder. The possibility of self-induced elaboration of symptoms or iatrogenic factors should be considered, and embellished dissociative features, factitious or malingered DID should be ruled out; for a discussion of the latter issues, see Chapter 15.

DSM-IV criteria for DID require the following four essential features (APA, 1994, p. 487):

A. The presence of two or more distinct identities or personality states (each with its own relatively enduring pattern of perceiving, relating to, and thinking about the environment and self).
B. At least two of these personalities or personality states recurrently take control of the person's behavior.
C. Inability to recall important personal information that is too extensive to be explained by ordinary forgetfulness.
D. [The above symptoms are] not due to the direct effects of a substance (e.g., blackouts or chaotic behavior during alcohol intoxication) or a general medical condition (e.g., complex partial seizures).

A variety of terms have been developed to describe the DID patient's subjective sense of self-states or identities. Commonly used terms include *personality, personality state, self-state, alter, alter personality, alternate identity,* and *part* among others. Because the DSM-IV (APA, 1994) generally uses the term *alternate personality* and because of the traditional use of this term in describing DID, this term is used in this discussion.

Psychiatrist Richard Kluft, MD (1996), perhaps the most preeminent investigator of DID over the past three decades, has described some of the classic presenting features of naturalistically occurring DID:

> The personalities' overt differences and disparate self-concepts may be striking. They may experience and represent themselves as being different ages, genders, races, religions, and sexual orientations; they may experience themselves as having different appearances and/or hold discrepant values and belief systems. Their awareness of one another may range from complete to nil. Directionality

of knowledge is almost always found among some alters, such that alter A knows of doings of B, but B is unaware of the activities of A.... Differences in handwriting and handedness, voice and vocabulary, accents and speech patterns, and even preferred languages are encountered. Their facial expressions and movement characteristics, both when neutral and affectively engaged, may show impressive and rather consistent differences.... The classic host personality, which usually... presents for treatment, nearly always bears the legal name and is depressed, anxious, somewhat neurasthenic, compulsively good, masochistic, conscience-stricken, constricted hedonically, and suffers both psychophysiological symptoms and time loss and/or time distortion. While no personality types are inevitably present, many are encountered quite frequently: childlike personalities..., protectors, helper-advisors, inner self-helpers..., personalities with distinctive affective states, guardians of memories and secrets, memory traces..., inner persecutors..., anesthetic personalities..., expressers of forbidden pleasures..., avengers..., defenders or apologists for the abusers, those based on lost love objects and other introjects and identifications, specialized encapsulators of traumatic experiences and powerful affects, very specialized personalities, and those... that preserve the idealized potential for happiness, growth, and the healthy expression of feelings.... (pp. 345–346)

Kluft (2009) has cautioned that dramatic presentations are actually unusual, and that "only 6% make their DID obvious on an ongoing basis" (p. 600). Clinically apparent symptoms are only seen intermittently, sometimes referred to as moments of visibility or "windows of diagnosability" (Kluft, 1991b; Loewenstein, 1991). Instead of showing visibly distinct alternate identities, the typical patient with DID presents a polysymptomatic mixture of dissociative and PTSD symptoms that are embedded in a matrix of ostensibly non-trauma-related symptoms such as depression, anxiety, panic attacks, substance abuse, somatoform symptoms, eating-disordered symptoms, and so forth (Dell, 2006b). The prominence of these latter, highly familiar symptoms often misleads clinicians to diagnose *only* the comorbid symptoms as the primary condition. When this happens, the patient may undergo a long and often unsuccessful treatment for both the undiagnosed DID and the other comorbid symptoms (Putnam et al., 1986).

Despite the lack of obvious evidence of separate internal identities, careful clinical interviewing and thoughtful differential diagnosis can usually lead to the correct diagnosis of DID (Coons, 1984). As discussed in Chapter 3, every diagnostic interview should inquire about a history for trauma and screen for dissociative symptoms. At a minimum, the patient should be asked about episodes of amnesia and depersonalization/derealization, and if these are present, the clinician should inquire about identity confusion and identity alteration. Other useful inquiries include questions about hearing voices (usually heard inside the head and not attributable to psychosis) (Putnam, 1991), passive-influence symptoms such as "made" (i.e., that do not feel attributable to the self) thoughts, emotions, or behaviors (Dell, 2009; Kluft, 1987a), and somatoform dissociative symptoms (Nijenhuis, 1999). Psychiatrist Richard Loewenstein, MD (1991), has published a comprehensive office mental status examination that inquires about many symptoms of DID, including evidence of amnesia, alternate personalities, autohypnotic phenomena, PTSD, somatoform dissociation, and affective symptoms. The diagnostic measures described in Chapter 3 may also be helpful for clinicians who are not familiar with the interviewing techniques and questions that elicit evidence of dissociative disorders.

In addition to the symptomatic expression of dissociative fragmentation, patients with severe dissociative disorders almost universally have historical evidence of trauma (Kluft, 1985d; Putnam, 1985, 1997; Ross, 1997) and long-standing dissociative symptoms. Particularly early in treatment, these patients have a reluctance to discuss, acknowledge, or reveal both evidence of internal separateness and past histories of traumatization, because the nature of their difficulties is based on the need to distance and disavow such experiences. There is frequently one-way amnesia between personalities, with the host personality having the least knowledge of other personalities. Given that the patient most often presents as the host early in treatment, the patient is frequently unable to confirm the presence of other parts of the self. Moreover, if the traumatization is caused by abuse or victimization, there is universally deep shame, guilt, and a wish to hide these experiences from others. Any clinical presentations that do not have these characteristics should be examined closely for evidence of an atypical dissociative disorder that requires modifications of treatment, another psychiatric diagnosis masquerading as a dissociative disorder, or a factitious or malingered dissociative disorder (see Chapter 15; Brick & Chu, 1991; Chu, 1991a; Kluft, 1987c; Thomas, 2001 for a more detailed discussion of the latter issue).

Comorbid diagnoses must be recognized. As discussed elsewhere in this book, any prominent Axis I diagnosis must be actively treated before instituting treatment for a dissociative disorder. Disorders such as depression, bipolar disorder, or psychoses will inevitably exacerbate and perpetuate any existing dissociative symptoms. Major substance abuse, eating disorders, or somatization should also be an initial focus for stabilization. Borderline personality disorder is diagnosed in up to 70% of the DID population (Boon & Draijer, 1993a; Dell, 1998; Ellason, Ross, & Fuchs, 1996). Axis II disorders such as borderline personality disorder must be recognized, as the patient's deficits in affect tolerance, behavior control, and relational ability will have an enormous impact on the emphasis and pacing of treatment.

TREATMENT GOALS AND STAGING

The goal of treatment for DID is integrated functioning. The term *integration* is used here to denote progressively greater coordination and harmony among the alternate personalities. Kluft (1993) describes integration as

[An] ongoing process of undoing all aspects of dissociative dividedness that begins long before there is any reduction in the number or distinctness of the identities, persists through their fusion, and continues at a deeper level even after the identities have blended into one. It denotes an ongoing process in the tradition of psychoanalytic perspectives on structural change. (p. 109)

Fusion refers to the merger of two or more alternate personalities, resulting in the patient's perception of their joining together, completely surrendering a sense of subjective separateness. Thus, progressive integration is the goal of therapy throughout the treatment process, whereas fusion occurs in the latter stages of treatment, usually in the middle and late phases.

Many experts in the treatment of DID advocate complete fusion as the most stable treatment outcome (e.g., Kluft, 1993), resulting in a full merger of all personality states. Early in treatment, most patients with DID have a strong investment in the separateness of the alternate personalities, seeing them as separate and autonomous entities. They have difficulty in perceiving any value in merging the identities, seeing this as destructive or annihilating rather than a joining of forces. As the treatment proceeds and individual characteristics and jobs or functions of the personalities become less differentiated, patients often become more amenable to some type of unification. However, such complete merger or fusion may not be possible for all patients with DID for a variety of reasons, including ongoing situational stress, extensive comorbidity of other psychiatric difficulties, or continuing narcissistic investment in the alternate identities. The ultimate pragmatic solution is a maximal level of cooperative and integrated functioning, even if complete fusion is not possible for a given patient. Psychiatrist David Caul, MD, once remarked (as quoted in Kluft, 1985c, p. 3), "It seems to me that after treatment you want a functional unit, be it a corporation, a partnership, or a one-owner business."

Perhaps the most common difficulty in the treatment of patients with DID has to do with failure to stage the treatment and pace the therapy. Kluft (1989a) has observed:

A common experience of the sophisticated therapist is to have difficulties with regards to issues of dosage in treating DID. The patient often experiences therapy as a guided tour of his or her personal hell without anesthesia. When a therapist fails to pace the treatment to the tolerance of the patient, the patient may become overwhelmed over and over. (p. 88)

All of the caveats concerning work with patients with complex PTSD are particularly relevant to patients with DID and similar disorders. Premature efforts to abreact past traumatic events generally result only in regression and retraumatization. Therapists treating patients with DID should be aware of and respect the need for establishing the necessary and proper psychotherapeutic foundations before engaging in exploratory and abreactive work. The major principles in treating severely traumatized patients are described elsewhere in this volume, including the SAFER model, which calls for the development of skills concerning *self-care* and *symptom control, acknowledgment* (but not extensive exploration) of traumatic antecedents, *functioning*, appropriate *expression of affect*, and maintaining collaborative and supportive *relationships*, as a preliminary stage before exploratory work. The profound difficulties that patients with DID often have in establishing a sense of safety and mastering the various tasks of early phase therapy may mandate a very long period of preliminary work before active focus on the etiologic abuse.

Failure to adequately pace treatment is also seen in premature attempts at integration and fusion. All too often, therapists and patients try to shortcut the treatment process by attempting fusion of personalities before adequate working through the underlying conflicts and traumatic events that led to their dissociation. Such misguided efforts have sometimes entailed strenuous efforts by therapists in the form of prolonged sessions and special techniques. These fusions usually either quickly disintegrate, or new personalities emerge to take on the functions of those who had been merged. Patients and therapists who are invested in this kind of practice often seem to persist in working in this manner, convinced that the next fusion will result in therapeutic gains and stability. Unfortunately, there is usually only a downhill spiral of regression, chaos, and exacerbated symptomatology.

WORKING WITH ALTERNATE PERSONALITIES

In DID, the alternate personality system is frequently organized and internally logical. The alternate personalities have failed to integrate with the presenting host personality because they hold knowledge, conflictual beliefs, unacceptable feelings, or memories of traumatic events that the host personality disavows and denies. The host is generally depleted and emotionally numb as a result and is usually amnestic for the experience of the other personalities. To the extent that the host disavows the other personalities, they generally become more autonomous in their function and self-perception. Effective therapy focuses on the alternate personality system as a whole rather than on specific personalities. In other words, the patient is comprised of *all* of the personalities, not just the host. Although this may seem obvious, it is all too easy to collude with a patient who, presenting as the host, does not acknowledge that the disavowed alternate personalities are part of the self. It is part of the psychoeducational process for patients with DID that all personality states (particularly the host personality) must begin to understand, accept, and communicate with all other relevant parts of the alternate personality system. Moreover, the patient as a whole must accept accountability for the behaviors of all of the alternate personalities.

Denial and disavowal of a unitary identity is not seen just in the host. For example, some alternate personalities deny that they share the same body as the other personalities, even to the extent of insisting that self-injury would not affect them. It is not unusual for angry persecutory personalities to talk about killing off the host or other personalities as a way of going off and finding their "real" bodies. Although this may appear to be delusional, it is actually a characteristic of DID patients' trance logic. When such logic endangers patients' safety, it is important to confront it directly: "I know you feel that this body isn't yours and that you won't die if you induce one of the others to commit suicide, but I must tell you that I am certain that you would also die."

Effective treatment of DID almost always requires interacting and communicating with the alternate personalities. As a minimal sense of safety is established in the therapy, it is usually quite easy for a therapist to access the alternate personalities, for example, saying, "I need to speak directly with whatever parts have been engaged in self-harming activities." However, there is one particular common trap through which the host can maintain the appearance of working in therapy, but can continue to remain to disavow the presence and meaning of the other personalities. In this scenario, the therapist is induced to contact and communicate with the other personalities—for example, to deal with difficult personalities or to hear about past traumas—while the host goes away and is amnestic for the experience. Little is accomplished in this scenario in terms of sharing experiences between personality states. It is often much more therapeutically effective to ask the host personality to internally communicate with the other personalities. For example, the patient can be asked to listen inside to hear what the other personalities have to say, or the therapist may suggest that the personalities engage in inner conversations with one another to communicate information or negotiate important issues. The therapist may insist that "all parts who need to know should listen" when crucial matters are being discussed, or can *talk through* to communicate with alternate personalities relevant to the current clinical issues. Although it is sometimes necessary for the therapist to first work with certain alternate personalities, this should only be a transition for the host to eventually assume the central role in internal communication.

The development of internal cooperation and co-consciousness between personalities is an essential part of early phase treatment that then continues into the middle phase. The therapist must emphasize the adaptive role and validity of all personalities and encourage the host to find adaptive ways to accommodate the wishes and needs of all personalities. In general, work with alternate personalities should occur as they appear naturalistically in relation to current clinical issues. However, if there are immediate safety issues or therapeutic impasses related to specific personalities, it may be essential to directly make contact with the alternate personalities associated with these difficulties.

One particular area of difficulty in the early treatment phases concerns how the alternate personalities emerge. Often after the acknowledgment of the existence of DID, personality switching begins to escalate with the appearance of an increasing array of different personalities, the most common sequence being first child parts, then depressed/suicidal and angry/self-destructive personalities. Therapists may soon find the process out of control as patients present a veritable parade of personalities, as they emerge to vent their feelings or to tell their stories to the therapist, but do not promote any interpersonality communication or co-consciousness. Moreover, the compartmentalized experience of the personalities sometimes results in denial of a sense of interpersonal vulnerability, and patients will prematurely expose intensely private aspects of themselves. They will then experience negative therapeutic reactions after showing aspects of themselves that then induce shame, repugnance, or fear. The following clinical example illustrates this scenario:

> Cathy, a 23-year-old patient with DID, entered therapy with a long history of interpersonal instability and several failed past therapies. In the therapy hours, she was very cautious about exposing herself to her therapist, aware that she was not yet ready to cope with forming an intense attachment. However, outside of the office she began to write in a journal that she gave to her therapist to read. In the journal, various personalities began expressing strong feelings about the therapy and therapist, and began disclosing details of past abuse. Over the course of several weeks, Cathy began to appear markedly more frightened in the session, and she was either mute or made angry verbal attacks toward the therapist. The therapy became stalemated. The therapist finally realized that Cathy was exposing too much about herself in the journal and was feeling very vulnerable, and that she could not tolerate having her writings discussed in the sessions. Cathy and her therapist then agreed that the journal writing be limited in amount and that the content would be restricted to only material that could be discussed in sessions. There was an immediate improvement in her clinical condition, and the therapy then proceeded in a useful manner.

Early in the evolution of treatment models for DID, some authors have advocated the process of mapping the system of alternate personalities (Kluft, 1993; Putnam, 1989; Ross, 1989); that is, identifying personality states and clarifying their relationships to each other. This technique should only be used when it is clinically appropriate to do so, and therapists should realize that it is often only quite late in the treatment course that a reasonably complete understanding of the personality system is known. In fact, it is normative for therapists to have only a very incomplete knowledge of the patient's alternate personality system and to lack a detailed chronology of the patient's history until well into the treatment. The practice of actively eliciting personalities (sometimes assisted by hypnotic interventions) for the purpose of mapping—especially when patients are very reluctant to bring them into the therapy—is potentially destructive. Therapists can appropriately help patients overcome resistance, but the psychological dissection of patients with DID is an extremely questionable practice. After all, when working with other types of patients, most therapists would not consider extensive exploration of hidden and vulnerable aspects of the patient until therapeutically appropriate.

As patients with DID progress into the middle phase of treatment and begin the process of active work on traumatic memories, the need for separate personalities diminishes. Memories and feelings that were previously dissociated into different parts of the self are brought together and integrated. As with other survivors of severe childhood trauma, realizing the extent of personal losses and mourning what happened (or did not happen) become the central themes of the therapy. As traumatic experiences are worked through, the alternate personalities may experience themselves (and appear to the therapist) as less separate and distinct. Spontaneous and/or facilitated fusions among alternate personalities may occur in which personalities join together to have the subjective experience of becoming unified. Some therapists use *fusion rituals*—hypnotic or guided imagery interventions that mark a transition to a different sense of identity— to facilitate this process (see Kluft, 1993, for a fuller discussion). It is important not to see fusion as a way of promoting integration, with fusion rituals "merely formaliz[ing] the subjective experience of the work that therapy has already accomplished...." (Kluft, 1993, p. 120).

In the late phase of DID treatment, patients make additional gains in internal co-operation, coordinated functioning, and integration. As with other severely traumatized patients, they begin to achieve a more solid and stable sense of self and to relate better to others and to the outside world. Patients with DID may continue to fuse alternate personalities. As they become less fragmented, they have fewer posttraumatic and dissociative symptoms, may better understand their past history, and cope more effectively with current problems. There is less of a focus on the past traumas, more interaction with the external world, and an enhanced ability to plan for the future.

TREATING THE DID SYSTEM

The sometimes bewildering presentation of many patients with DID may be confusing to therapists who are unfamiliar with dissociative disorders. Which personalities should be part of the treatment? How many personalities should be involved in a given therapy session? Is it necessary to call personalities forward into the therapy? Many of these kinds of questions can be answered by imagining how a DID presentation would appear in a nondissociative patient. For example, most therapists understand the model of intrapsychic conflict. Patients with DID manage conflict through segregating the conflicting views, feelings, or knowledge into separate identities. Thus, an understanding of the inherent conflicts in a given situation will determine which personalities are involved and must be in working through a current dilemma. At any given time in the therapy of patients with DID, the therapist should be working with a relatively small number of personalities who represent the current issues and conflicts to be resolved. The particular personalities working in the therapy will change as conflicts are resolved and the therapeutic process progresses. The following clinical example may illustrate these principles:

> Marjorie, a 35-year-old married nurse, entered therapy for treatment of sexual dysfunction and depression. Over the first few months of treatment, it became clear that she had the diagnosis of DID. She had a long history of periods of amnesia with evidence of having done things she could not explain, and abrupt changes in her mood, appearance, and functioning reported by her husband, as well as a known history of brutal childhood abuse. Marjorie had

been able to deny the significance of her symptoms and background until her therapist began to gently inquire about them. Several alternate personalities emerged in treatment, including childlike personalities who asked to be able to play with toys in the therapy room "because we were never allowed to play when we lived with our parents." Over the course of a few weeks, the therapist played with the child personalities in therapy, and no adult personalities appeared except at the very end of sessions when they seemed confused and disoriented.

Finally, Marjorie's husband called the therapist to complain that Marjorie was on probation at her job because of her absenteeism, that she had been very withdrawn, passive, and needy at home, and that she had driven off the road coming home from a therapy session (presumably because a child personality had emerged while she was driving). After some consideration, the therapist realized that she had unwittingly permitted the patient to focus on only gratification of her unmet childhood need to be cared for, at the cost of attending to the demands of work and adult functioning. Moreover, the increased intimacy with the therapist seemed to have brought up defenses that interfered with Marjorie's ability to engage in and tolerate intimacy in her marriage. The therapist then tried to explain the situation to the child personalities, and despite their tearful recriminations, insisted that adult personalities appear regularly in sessions and use the time to solve problems concerning the current realities of Marjorie's life. Balance seemed to be restored to both the therapy and her outside life. In retrospect, the therapist recognized the clinical situation as a DID version of fairly straightforward regression.

In a similar way, common issues such as addressing interpersonal concerns, coping with stress and impulse control, maintaining functioning, and expressing dysphoric affects, among many others, will be manifested by the various personalities that hold the relevant affects, attitudes, experience, information, and abilities concerning the issues.

Therapists treating patients with DID commonly find themselves highly involved (and sometimes overinvolved) in the emotional experience of their patients. As with other patients who have fundamental problems with basic trust, their difficulty with maintaining a sense of interpersonal connection and their vulnerability to feeling abandoned and abused often makes it necessary for therapists to be more active in the therapeutic relationship in demonstrating their empathic understanding of patients' experience. This necessary level of involvement has some potential untoward effects in that therapists are vulnerable to becoming so empathically identified with their patients that they lose therapeutic perspective about the personalities. With patients with DID, it is a particular risk that therapists become so attuned to patients' sense of internal fragmentation that they accept the patients' various alternate personalities as virtually independent, autonomously functioning entities. In this situation, therapists begin to treat the personalities themselves, rather than treating the whole system of personalities, as in the following clinical example:

> Stacie, a 32-year-old woman with DID, progressed well in her therapy for over a year. She struggled to understand her diagnosis and worked productively with her therapist to develop appropriate skills to stabilize her life. She began to have more of a sense of an internal personality who she called the Evil Father. The host, Stacie, was terrified of this personality, who appeared to be angry and persecutory, and who apparently "made" her lacerate her arms and genitals. The therapist was similarly alarmed by this personality, who seemed to be the personification of Stacie's sadistic and abusive father. The therapist tried to help Stacie with strategies to block the behaviors of this personality, but to no avail. Finally, the therapist used a hypnotic intervention and managed to induce the Evil Father to emerge in a session. This personality did emerge and insisted that he needed to "teach" the other personalities to behave through his actions. The therapist tried to point out the destructiveness of his behavior and urged him to cease such behavior. Stacie then returned and reported amnesia for the previous several minutes. That evening, she again lacerated herself, and the Evil Father wrote a threatening note in Stacie's journal challenging the therapist to try and control his actions.

This kind of interaction ignores the psychological validity of the father introject, as well as the functioning of the personalities as part of a system. It also assumes that the therapist (rather than the patient) should primarily have the omnipotent position of dealing with difficult alternate personalities, a task that is both inappropriate and therapeutically untenable.

The outcome of these kinds of clinical dilemmas depends on the therapist's ability to understand the psychodynamic underpinnings of the clinical presentation, to help the patient negotiate the resolution of the inherent conflict, and to insist on the active involvement and collaboration of the patient. In working with so-called difficult alternate personalities, the therapist must understand the psychological development and role of each of the personalities and must respect the validity of each personality. The whole personality system must work toward the resolution of conflict that the difficult personality represents, because the conflict made the dissociative splitting of identity necessary. Finally, the therapist should engage other personalities in working with the difficult personality.

The conceptual model of family/systems theory (Bowen, 1966) is of great assistance in negotiating difficult DID dilemmas. In family/systems theory, the family as a whole is seen as the patient rather than any particular family member being the identified patient. For example, in a family situation involving an acting-out adolescent, the family as a whole is asked to look at family conflicts rather than focusing on the adolescent. Are there issues between parents or other family members, or projective identification from parents, or major disturbances in other family members that are covertly driving the acting-out behavior? The family as a whole takes on the responsibility of understanding, resolving, and containing the behaviors of each family member. In patients with DID, family/systems theory is applicable to the *internal* family of alternate personalities or identities. Using this framework, there are no bad personalities, only personalities that are compelled to behave in a particular way because of past events and in reaction to or to compensate for the actions and behaviors of other parts of the personality system. Increased internal communication, collaboration, and empathy are the key elements of this kind of family/systems work with patients with DID.

The psychopathological process in DID depends on the separation of apparently irreconcilable conflicts through fragmentation into alternate personalities. Hence, patients are understandably resistant to increase internal communication, because this process intensifies awareness of intrapsychic conflict. As a result, patients are generally uncomfortable about promoting co-consciousness, and they often will not provide the primary impetus for resolution of intrapsychic conflict. However, the therapist can provide reasons for increasing communication, can suggest safe mechanisms for doing so, and can point out potential positive gains and the negative consequences of not doing so. In the previous case about Stacie, the impasse was resolved as follows:

> Following consultation, the therapist approached Stacie somewhat differently. She said to her, "I know that you are frightened of the Evil Father who seems to represent much of what you've hated about your father. However, you must begin to understand that this Evil Father is part of you. I know you will find this hard to accept, but this part of you actually helped you survive by becoming like your father." The therapist went on to underscore the survival value of identification with the aggressor, as well as the potential value of being able to express aggression, albeit in a more controlled manner. The therapist then suggested a type of bargain or truce: "If I help you to understand this part of yourself that you are so frightened of, I would like to ask that the Evil Father stop hurting your body. I have no way of forcing this to happen, but if you, Stacie, are willing to work hard at accepting and understanding, perhaps your safety can be maintained."
>
> When the Evil Father emerged, the therapist said, "I know you have played an important role in Stacie's life in the past, and that you are upset at not being recognized. I will work with the other parts of you so that they will acknowledge you and will begin to bear the burden of your angry feelings. I hope you understand that some of the threats you have made and the destructive behavior are not necessary or productive, and if you can work together with me and the other parts of yourself, we may be able to avoid more extreme measures such as hospitalization." After a considerable period of negotiation, internal stability was restored.

It is not always necessary to have relevant underlying personalities actually emerge in the therapy as in the previous example. The technique of talking through to underlying personalities can be very useful in allowing the patient the control of when to expose previously hidden parts. All that is usually required is for the therapist to make it clear that he or she is addressing all parts that are relevant to the situation (e.g., "It is very important that all parts involved in the current problem listen to what I have to say."). Sometimes, therapists can communicate by talking through with personalities who are reluctant to emerge in sessions. For example, in the previous situation, the therapist might have talked about the importance of the Evil Father with the host personality, Stacie, emphasizing his role in her life: "I hope that the Evil Father will listen to what I have to say and know that I understand his important role in your life and all he has done to protect you." This is heard throughout the personality system and often results in the persecutory personality emerging to make the acquaintance of the therapist, albeit sometimes leading with suspicion and mistrust: "I don't believe you care about me! Stay the hell away from us!"—a persecutor personality's version of "Hello."

The DID patient's perception of separate personalities with different characteristics, such as age, gender, and appearance, has been thought to be an autohypnotic trance phenomenon. Thus, hypnotic interventions may be particularly effective with patients with DID. Guided imagery and formal trance induction can facilitate many interventions in working with patients with DID, particularly in managing symptoms and accessing experiences and personalities as appropriate. It is worthwhile for therapists to have some training in hypnotherapy, if only to understand altered states of mind and trance logic. The use of formal trance can be helpful but is not necessary to treat DID, and many hypnotic techniques that do not involve trance induction are useful. For example, the technique of hypnotic suggestion can be used to facilitate new skills: "I want you to take a moment and sit quietly and listen inside. I think it's likely that you may be able to hear what other important parts of you have to say." An attitude of calm assurance (even if the therapist is uncertain of what to do) assists in the effectiveness of this type of intervention.

Though all parts of the patient with DID must participate and cooperate in the therapy, the host personality has a special role, a concept that has been called the "centrality of the host." It a major goal of the therapy to have the host personality achieve an awareness and understanding of the other personalities that have been disavowed, and to increasingly achieve control over the executive functioning of the entire personality system. However, this can only be achieved by having the host personality acknowledge the painful and overwhelming thoughts, feelings, knowledge, and memories that are held by the other personalities that have previously been disavowed. In almost all instances when an impasse is reached in patients with DID, it is caused by the resistance of the host to understand and accept the unacknowledged alternate personalities and what they represent. To the extent that these personalities remain disavowed, they begin to take on more autonomous functioning.

Somewhat paradoxically, if the host personality is able to begin to acknowledge and accept disavowed personalities, they can be more controlled and integrated into the self as a whole—somewhat analogous to the adage, "Keep your friends close and your enemies even closer." However, it can be difficult to get the host personality's cooperation in acknowledging realities that have been disavowed and disowned. Psychoeducation plays a major role in this kind of therapeutic work, and I have sometimes used stories and analogies as a way of teaching patients what needs to occur in the therapeutic process. For example, in trying to work out internal cooperation with persecutory personalities, I often tell patients the following story:

> I'd like to tell you something about me that might help you understand your current dilemma. It's a story that's partly true and partly pretend (and I'll tell you what parts are true and what parts I've made up). When I was a child, I was a very good child, generally obedient, polite, and well-behaved as my parents required. My next-door neighbor, Paul, was my best friend, and he was a good kid too, but he was definitely more adventurous, mischievous, and outspoken. Paul was the one who induced me into playing games like spying on our neighbors, stealing strawberries and tomatoes from neighborhood gardens, and playing telephone games such as randomly calling numbers and pretending to be a long-distance operator (only to hang up giggling uncontrollably).
>
> When I was in the 6th grade, I had Mrs. Turner as my teacher. She had the well-deserved reputation as the strictest and scariest teacher in the middle school. She tolerated no misbehavior, and we students met her expectations—except on one occasion when she had to be away and we had a substitute teacher. Released (temporarily) from Mrs. Turner's repressive control, we behaved badly and could not be controlled from talking to each other, passing notes, and throwing spitballs. The next day, when Mrs. Turner returned, she was furious, informing the class that she was *very* disappointed in our behavior and that she would enter an adverse note in each student's *permanent* record. I was terrified, envisioning a future when I would apply to college or try to get a job only to be turned down because of this note in my record.
>
> Unlike me, Paul was highly amused and had a plan of action. After we went back to his house that day, he called Mrs. Turner at home and yelled, "Rabbits! Rabbits! Rabbits! You old bag!" into the phone and hung up. I was both appalled and highly gratified. Now, let's imagine that as Paul and I grew up, he took on this role of protecting and defending me, perhaps even more aggressively to the point of being chronically angry and rude. And let's imagine that when we were teenagers that I said to Paul, "I know we've been friends for a long time, but you've really become an angry, unpleasant, and difficult guy. I don't want to be friends with you and I don't want you around me anymore." What do you think my friend Paul might have been feeling at that point?

Patients almost always understand that Paul would have been hurt and angry—at *me*. And they almost always understand the analogy that their persecutor personalities have played a similar role in their lives but have been rejected and have become retaliatory. And they almost always understand the need to acknowledge the critical significance of the persecutory personalities and to begin the process of reconciliation.

Psychologist Ruth Blizard, PhD, has written eloquently about the dilemmas of working with persecutory personalities (1997, 2001). Her 1997 paper offers a sophisticated and pragmatic approach to treating abuser alternate personalities:

> Abuser alters present a dilemma in the treatment of adults with dissociative identity disorder, because they often undermine the therapy as well as re-abuse the patient. They are paradoxical because they were created to help the child survive abuse, and continue to do so by abusing the self. They were often modeled after an abusive primary caretaker to whom the child was attached.... By understanding how abuser alters function to maintain attachment, contain overwhelming memories, and protect against abuse, therapists can better engage abuser alters in a therapeutic alliance. Empathy, cognitive reframing, and gentle paradoxical techniques can help host and abuser personalities become more empathic toward one another, develop common purpose, and begin integrating. (p. 246)

The crisis in the former country of Yugoslavia in the 1980s offers an interesting analogy to the DID system. Under authoritarian rule of president Josip Broz Tito, the many different ethnic factions in Yugoslavia functioned as a single entity, albeit with considerable repression of personal freedom for its citizens. This political situation is not unlike some trauma survivors who function in a state of rigid control in a chronic benumbed state. However, when the control breaks down, there is an irreversible fragmentation similar to the reemergence of the Balkan States following the death of Tito and the collapse of Communist Europe. Yugoslavia was fractured into Serbia, Slovenia, Croatia, Bosnia-Herzegovina, and Macedonia with renewed conflicts, warfare, and genocide. Peacemaking efforts with these states of the former Yugoslavia failed utterly, and an uneasy truce was only restored when the warring parties agreed to a truce with NATO forces acting only to facilitate their agreements. In a similar fashion, no therapeutic efforts can bring about internal agreements within the conflicted personality systems of patients with DID unless the whole patient is clearly motivated to do so.

Work with personalities who present as young children often brings a different kind of vulnerability to making errors in psychotherapy. Therapists are frequently confronted with situations in which child alternate personalities ask to be cared for, held, or nurtured by the therapist. Some child personalities are able to present in such a believable and disarming manner that the therapist sometimes loses sight of the fact that the child personalities exist as only a part of an adult patient. In fact, these child identities are personifications of the patient as a child—not actual children. As psychologist Sheila Shusta-Hochberg, PhD (2004), has described, treating these identities as if they are real children carries the real danger of allowing them to become fixated in childlike identities, as well as overall regression and impasses in the therapy. I do not use special ways of talking and relating to child personalities. I use a normal adult conversational tone and my usual vocabulary. If the child personalities do not understand me, I suggest that they "ask inside" for help. In this way, I try to model the expectation that they are to grow and develop. It is also critically important that family and friends who are aware of the child personalities do not overly nurture them. Although significant others—and the other internal identities—should have respect for their psychological validity and their contributions to the whole person, child personalities will not grow and mature simply with a simplistic focus on meeting their needs and wishes.

Therapists should keep in mind that child personalities need to conform to the constraints of reality, including the reality that the patient must function as an adult for the most part outside of the therapy, and usually in therapy sessions as well. Child personalities cannot rely on their therapists as the primary source of gratification and nurturing. In practical experience it seems inevitable that therapists have some role in providing care for the child personalities of the patient. However, any such nurturing should be viewed only as modeling to help patients begin to take care of themselves. Extensive reparenting schemes are always ill-advised and countertherapeutic. Any kind of reparenting should come predominantly from within the patient, with adult person-alities taking on this responsibility. Promoting internal soothing and nurturing is often difficult, as the adult personalities in patients with DID are often resistant to internal caretaking of child personalities. After all, early abusive experiences often seem to have resulted in patients having to disavow and dissociate their identities as children and their legitimate childhood needs. Often, the DID system reinforces this separation. For ex-ample, it is common to find angry and persecutory personalities who punish child per-sonalities in order to "teach" them that it isn't safe to trust others. Therapists must insist that adult personalities begin to have empathy for the distress of internal child parts and to care for and internally nurture them as part of learning self-care and self-soothing.

The intense ambivalence of childhood abuse survivors about important issues (e.g., wanting to live/wanting to die, wanting to trust/fearing relationships, remembering the past/blocking out the past) may be apportioned to the various personalities in patients with DID, with dissociated parts holding radically different views and feelings. It is all too easy for therapists to forget that they are dealing with only a part of their patient at any given time, and not to consider the omnipresent internal ambivalence and conflict. Thus, therapists may find themselves understanding the patient with a very narrow perspective and advocating certain stances that are at odds with the patient's interests as a whole. This kind of situation is frequently aggravated by the patient's understandable wish to disavow conflict and ambivalence, as in the following example:

> Anita, the host personality of a patient with DID, began arguing persuasively for more aggressive exploration of past traumatic experiences. The therapist had the sense that exploration was premature and was reluctant to pursue such a course. Anita became angry and accused the therapist of blocking her psychological healing, of not wanting to hear about her abuse, and of not being able to handle

the stressful emotions associated with the abuse. Although he denied this, the therapist began to wonder if this were true. However, after some thought he said to Anita, "I know you feel strongly that you want to deal with the abusive events of your childhood. However, are you aware that there may be other parts of you who would almost certainly be completely overwhelmed by these memories, and that other parts of you would be frightened and angry by talking about secrets at this point? I will be much more comfortable working on the memories when you have much better internal communication and an overall better sense of safety and stability."

The transference-countertransference dilemmas discussed in Chapter 9 are heightened in the treatment of severe dissociative disorders because the diverse and conflicting feelings are held in the different personalities and, at any given time, are not readily apparent. For example, it is common for the DID patient's system of personalities to view the therapist as a savior, a perfect parent, a demanding disciplinarian, a harsh critic, a dangerous and devious enemy, and an incompetent and useless helper, among others. In understanding these patients' transferential feelings, the motto should be: "What you see is *never* all you get." In her workshops, trauma expert, Kathy Steele, MN, CS, advises that in situations of positive transference, the therapist should accept and not interpret the transference, but understand it as often being appeasement-based and deriving from the intense need to remain attached to the therapist. Positive transference is often followed by negative transference, a situation in which Steele advises therapists to stay attuned and grounded, to "step aside" from the intensity of patients' feelings, to modulate one's intensity in responding, to help contain patients' affect, and to be genuine and honest in discussing the relational situation.

In the treatment of patients with DID, increasing internal communication through promoting co-consciousness is a crucial task. The amnestic and dissociative barriers are significant liabilities. These barriers not only preclude a sense of continuous awareness but also predispose patients and therapists to make decisions and act without awareness of the full range of patients' thoughts and feelings. Thus, even from the beginning of treatment, the therapist must encourage and reinforce the relationship of various personalities to the personality system as a whole (e.g., "I know you have the experience of just going away, but I want to encourage you to stay and feel painful feelings, or to try and stay close when other parts of you emerge.").

In addition to standard interventions that encourage sharing information among personalities, a variety of techniques can be used to promote communication across the alternate personality system. The use of a journal in which all personalities can write can be helpful when used with appropriate structure (e.g., what can/can't be written, agreement on where it is kept, commitments not to hide or destroy it, etc.). Internal communication can also be encouraged through specialized techniques, for example, Fraser's Dissociative Table Technique (Fraser, 2003), a hypnotic intervention in which the various personalities can visualize themselves sitting around a conference table and negotiating conflictual issues. The patients must see themselves as a kind of family system (albeit dysfunctional) that must find a way to act in concert and in harmony without exploiting, scapegoating, or attempting to destroy any member of the family. Of course, the need for helping the DID family system to achieve some sense of cohesion and harmony is particularly urgent, because ultimately this family cannot literally separate or split up.

DID PHENOMENOLOGY

DID is a disorder that can be dramatic in its presentation and can be a fascinating phenomenon. Even to sophisticated professionals, DID is striking as a model of the human psyche. In DID, one sees the separation of psychic structures, where hypothesized phenomena such as introjects and the punitive superego present as distinct entities. DID is also a model for understanding how overwhelming life events affect the human mind and how dissociative mechanisms can provide at least temporary adaptive protection. In addition, the dramatic changeability of patients with DID and their stories of tragic victimization arouse the interest of virtually all persons. However, excessive fascination or preoccupation with DID phenomenology can also have several untoward effects. Sensing their therapists' interest, patients may become invested in prolonging their dysfunctional symptomatic presentation or may even play up the differences in the manifestations of their personalities.

Therapists' overt fascination with DID phenomenology clearly leads to considerable secondary gain for patients in terms of maintaining their therapists' attention. The clinicians who, in past years, have appeared on television or radio talking about their patients with DID, have written books with their patients, or have featured their patients in research or teaching may have allowed their patients to develop and solidify a primary identity as patients with DID, which is far from an ideal outcome. However, even more subtle preoccupation with the phenomenon of DID can sidetrack or obscure the main work of the psychotherapy, as in the following example:

Katie, a 21-year-old woman with DID, was admitted to the hospital. The outpatient therapist informed the inpatient team that the patient had a total of 76 alternate personalities. He was able to describe the personalities in detail, citing differences in appearance, age, gender, mannerisms, and other characteristics. Katie showed frequent and precipitous personality switches on the ward, and she was generally out of control with flashbacks and other dissociative symptoms. The inpatient treatment team introduced a treatment regimen to help the patient achieve a sense of control over her behavior. As her behavior stabilized, it became clearer that Katie had focused on her personalities as a way of ignoring (and hiding from her therapist) her continued frequent contacts with her father who had been a perpetrator of abuse. She and her outpatient therapist were urged to focus on issues of personal and psychological safety, as opposed to a focus on the manifestations of DID. Although both Katie and the therapist were somewhat resistant to this idea, they were eventually able to find a way to work with the patient's personalities in the context of rational overall treatment goals.

There is considerable evidence against the notion of iatrogenesis of DID in patients who do not already have dissociative symptoms (see Chapter 15 for more discussion of this topic). However, patients who do have dissociative symptoms, but who do not have DID, may consciously or unconsciously exaggerate their symptoms. Particularly in settings such as inpatient milieus and outpatient groups, an identity as a patient with DID, with distinct, well-defined, and dramatic symptomatology, may seem appealing. Therapists must help patients to understand and cope with existing symptomatology, and they must not even subtly encourage patients toward developing a greater degree of dissociation. For example, therapists should not label ego-state phenomena (Watkins & Watkins, 1997) as alternate personalities. Therapists should use unifying language consistent with the least degree of fragmentation that the patient is able to accept (e.g., "part" or "aspect" being preferable to "personality" or "person"). Overall, careful attention to the patient's needs as a whole should be a priority, with the clear therapeutic intent of decreasing the level of dissociative fragmentation.

There are some particular issues concerning the names of personalities. For the most part, it is necessary and useful to use the names that the various alternate personalities have already adopted for themselves. However, therapists should avoid naming of personalities who do not already have names as this promotes more separateness. Instead, unnamed personalities can be referred to according to their characteristics or roles (e.g., "the one who deals with the parents" or "the part who goes to work"). It is permissible, however, to agree with the patient to change pejorative personality names. For example, in the previous clinical illustration of Stacie, it might have turned out that the Evil Father eventually self-identified as a 14-year-old girl who had to defensively take on a persecutory role. As the need for this role diminished, perhaps her name could have been changed to something similar but more benign, such as Evie.

Specialized treatment modalities that have been useful in DID treatment have been described in a variety of papers and texts. However, the use of any specialized treatment modality or intervention should conform to the following criteria: (a) the use of any treatments must adhere to the general principles of understanding and treating traumatized patients; (b) clinicians must be skilled in any modality utilized (e.g., hypnosis, expressive therapy, sensorimotor therapy, EMDR); and (c) principles of good psychotherapy must be respected. Clinicians must be clear that a majority of the interventions used in the treatment of DID and complex dissociative disorders involve the same fundamental skills that are used with all patients. Only a relatively few specialized perspectives and interventions are essential in the treatment of patients with DID.

In summary, the successful treatment of patients with DID depends on a thoughtful and rational approach. As with all severely traumatized patients, patients with DID must be encouraged to build solid coping skills before moving on to abreaction and eventual integration. Premature abreaction has little value other than venting dysphoric affect. Until patients can control dysfunctional behavior, tolerate intense affect, and maintain good collaborative relationships, they cannot work through traumatic events, so premature abreaction is largely retraumatizing. Therapists must also respect the need to proceed carefully in the process of uncovering personalities. DID patients' intense interpersonal vulnerability should be respected, and therapists should use good clinical judgment to guide the therapeutic process.

The rational treatment of DID must always primarily focus on the treatment of the *patient* who has DID and not on the personalities or on DID phenomenology. The various personalities should be acknowledged, and therapists need to be skillful in working with them. However, the various personalities must always be considered as part of an overall family system, and the goals of the work should be toward increased communication, cooperation, and integration. Therapists should keep in mind that excessive fascination or preoccupation with DID may interfere with patients' treatment or even encourage the development of further fragmentation.

Dr. David Caul once observed, "Therapists should always remember that good basic psychotherapy is the first order of treatment regardless of any specific diagnosis" (Chu, 1992a, p. 101). This sage advice should be heeded by all therapists involved in the treatment of dissociative disorders. The treatment of patients who have survived profound childhood abuse is a challenging task for even experienced therapists, and the difficulties these patients present have the potential to lead to serious pitfalls and impasses. However, good clinical judgment and the use of sound psychotherapeutic practices permit rational and productive treatment for even the most challenging patients with DID.

13

Managing Crisis

Acute Care and Hospitalization

Severely traumatized patients maintain a tenuous homeostasis between numbing and intrusion, control and dyscontrol, and interpersonal connection and alienation. They often have brittle defenses that shatter in the face of stress or changes in the external environment. Current stresses or losses may plunge patients into isolation, despair, and suicidal impulses. Reminders of a past traumatic event may result in powerful intrusive symptomatology. In addition, even effective therapeutic efforts may actually increase symptomatology, as patients feel intensely vulnerable and panicked over fears of being abandoned, hurt, or violated. Changes in the patient's external environment are frequent precipitants for decompensation. The loss of critical relationships or important external supports, either temporarily or permanently, can precipitate a crisis. The vacation of a therapist, the breakup or deterioration of a relationship (even a dysfunctional relationship), the sudden lack of availability or loss of an important person (or a pet), or the ending of a job or other regular sustaining activity are frequent causes for decompensation. When patients are at risk for serious harm, or become so symptomatic that they are unable to function, they may need acute psychiatric care. Traditionally, such care has been provided in a hospital setting but is now sometimes also provided in residential or partial hospital settings.

Traumatized patients experience one particular personal dilemma that merits special emphasis. Patients' flight into isolation from others results in a profound experience of aloneness. Although such a course may seem safest to patients, it leaves them with only themselves—and their self-hate. Behind many complicated scenarios of decompensation in traumatized patients lies a simple formulation. Patients who are left alone with their own self-blame and self-loathing often turn to self-destructive activities or other dysfunctional behaviors as a way of alleviating an intolerable internal experience.

ASSESSMENT AND FORMULATION

It is always crucial to evaluate psychiatric decompensation in patients with complex PTSD and dissociative disorders in the context of psychosocial issues and the patient's external environment. Given the common formulation of psychosocial stressors resulting in increased symptomatology and dysfunctional attempts to cope, comprehensive treatment must be focused not only on the symptomatology but also on ameliorating the stressors that precipitated decompensation. That is, there is an important difference between accurate diagnosis and a formulation of the patient's current situation. Clinicians should understand the patient in terms of background, symptoms, strengths and vulnerabilities, and the circumstances that led to the current difficulties. For example, a patient may present with symptoms such as traumatic nightmares or flashbacks. In addition to attempts to contain and alleviate these symptoms, attention must also be directed toward their precipitants—for example, the loss of an important supportive relationship or the presence of a current abusive relationship that repetitively destabilizes the patient. The following case illustrates some of the complexities of assessment:

> Lucy, a 27-year-old married woman with dissociative identity disorder (DID), was admitted to the hospital in crisis. Internally, she heard the voice of a persecutor personality who threatened to hurt her. She also was having nearly constant flashbacks of sexual molestation that occurred when she was a teenager. Lucy was initially uncommunicative on the unit and had to be physically restrained on two occasions when she was having flashbacks and began banging her head into a wall. She reacted angrily to the restraints and accused staff members of being abusive. She managed to convince her inpatient therapist that she needed to work through her adolescent rapes. However, after a week of tumultuous and frightening abreactions, Lucy actually appeared to be more regressed and was acutely suicidal.
>
> As her treatment did not appear to be helping Lucy, the treatment team conducted a careful review of her circumstances. It was eventually ascertained that an incident of somewhat aggressive sexual contact with her husband before admission had been very frightening to her. Lucy had told her outpatient therapist about this in the next session, after which the therapist announced he would be going on vacation. The acute symptoms began at this point. In reviewing the events prior to admission, it was clear that the patient had been triggered by the sexual interaction with her husband, which was then compounded by the vacation (perceived as abandonment) by the therapist. In view of this information, the treatment team shifted approaches. The outpatient therapist was brought in as part of the treatment team, and the husband was engaged in a series of couples meetings to negotiate safety at home. On the unit, active efforts were made to help Lucy with grounding techniques to control her florid dissociative symptoms. Aftercare arrangements were a focus of the treatment, and Lucy was discharged without incident after a few days.

A focus on both the current symptoms and the dynamics of their underlying cause is particularly important when working with patients with complex PTSD and dissociative disorders. Their intriguing and shifting presentations may often hide the ordinary realities that cause their current distress. In many ways, such therapeutic difficulties are not surprising. After all, posttraumatic and dissociative defenses are utilized to distance and disavow stressful experiences; the psychological gain is in *not* attending to them. However, any successful resolution of a crisis situation will necessitate both symptomatic control and restoration of a safe and stable external environment.

Another area of importance is the ongoing outpatient treatment. Acute intensive treatment such as hospitalization offers the opportunity for consultation to the ongoing treatment. Although acute care may be routinely necessary for unstable patients who are receiving thoughtful, sophisticated, and competent therapy, some hospitalizations are precipitated when therapy is poorly conceived or implemented. Consultations must be performed with great sensitivity, as there appear to be particular characteristics of severely traumatized patients and their therapy that normatively result in painful clinical dilemmas (see Chapters 9 and 10; Chu, 1988; Davies & Frawley, 1994; Kluft, 1988; Pearlman & Saakvitne, 1995), and even well-meaning and competent therapists can fall into difficult clinical traps. As a result, clinicians who provide the long-term, ongoing therapy can find themselves beleaguered, emotionally drained, and uncertain, and defensive about what they are doing. Issues regarding the pacing of the therapy, transference-countertransference binds, defining treatment goals, setting limits, and maintaining boundaries are all common dilemmas in ongoing treatment. Given that patients generate similar dynamics and reenact similar scenarios in both the inpatient and outpatient settings, the inpatient treaters are in a unique position to be able to empathize with the dilemmas posed by the patient and to consult with the outpatient therapist. If this kind of consultation is done sensitively, supportively, and effectively, the beneficial effects of inpatient hospitalization on the patient's treatment may extend well beyond the hospital stay.

DIAGNOSTIC ISSUES

Hospitalization offers the opportunity to reassess the accuracy of a patient's diagnosis. In some instances, the failure of the outpatient treatment to contain the patient derives from interventions that do not take into account a hidden underlying condition (e.g., a presentation that appears to be trauma-related but is actually caused by an undiagnosed mood disorder or psychosis, or vice versa). Inpatient treaters have a unique opportunity to tease out how various presentations mimic the symptoms of others or obscure their expression.

The differential diagnosis of posttraumatic disorders from mood disorders can be subtle. Time-limited assessment of patients in an office setting may fail to distinguish between traumatized patients and those with more biologically based major depression. Patients who feel subjectively depressed, hopeless, and helpless on the basis of complex trauma-related issues may present in office appointments in a way that is similar to nontraumatized depressed patients with many of the classic vegetative signs of major depression: lack of energy, motivation, and interest; guilty and suicidal thoughts; and appetite and sleep disturbances (Chu, Dill, & Murphy, 2000). On an inpatient unit, some interesting differences between trauma-related dysphoria and a major depressive episode may emerge. For example, although patients with trauma-related dysphoria may appear quite classically depressed in interviews with the unit staff, they might be observed to be animated and engaged in interactions with other patients in ways that are uncharacteristic for classic major depression.

There can be confusion about differentiating the symptoms of bipolar disorder from those of severe dissociative disorders such as DID. The switches in self-states often seen in severe dissociative disorders may mimic the mood changes of bipolar disorder. In general, the state switches of dissociative disorders are much more frequent and abrupt than the mood changes in bipolar disorder—even in so-called rapid-cycling bipolar disorder. In addition, although in some cases of DID personalities that appear grossly disorganized or hypomanic can emerge, there is rarely the kind of sustained energized, grandiose, and delusional presentation that is characteristic of true mania. And, although sleep disturbance is common in both posttraumatic and dissociative disorders, total sleep time is maintained at a minimum of four to five hours per night on average. Sleep disturbances that persist at levels less than two or three hours per night are more consistent with mania or hypomania, particularly in the presence of high energy upon awakening. In the hospital setting, actual sleep times can be observed to differentiate between patients' subjective reports (e.g., "I didn't sleep more than an hour all night") and the nursing observations of several hours of interrupted sleep.

As discussed in Chapters 2 and 3, symptoms of some posttraumatic and dissociative disorders may also mimic psychotic symptomatology. Our study of adult psychiatric patients (Chu & Dill, 1990) demonstrated a correlation between childhood abuse experiences and an elevated level of psychotism on the Minnesota Multiphasic Personality Inventory (MMPI), which might be explained by the observations of some investigators that symptoms such as hallucinations and even Schneiderian first-rank symptoms of schizophrenia frequently occur in severe dissociative disorders (Dell, 2009; Kluft, 1987a). Recurrent "brief reactive psychoses" should be examined as to whether they might be better understood as posttraumatic flashbacks or dissociative state switches. Intense visual, auditory, somatic, and olfactory illusions or hallucinations are frequent components of flashbacks, and auditory hallucinations are common in severe dissociative disorders as parts of the self talk internally to other dissociative self-states. Differential diagnosis concerning auditory hallucinations may be sharpened by the characteristics of the hallucinations. Dissociative hallucinations almost always are heard as coming from inside the head and are generally recognized as a familiar set of voices over time. Psychotic auditory hallucinations tend to be more bizarre (e.g., voices from the radio or TV), heard from both inside and outside the head, and variable over time.

Differential diagnosis is further complicated in situations where there is true co-morbidity (i.e., two or more disorders), not simply one disorder mimicking another. Very often, the patient will present with pronounced posttraumatic or dissociative symptoms rather than clear evidence of the other disorder. One hypothesis for this kind of presentation is that because PTSD and dissociative disorders are responses to stress, the onset of another disorder such as a mood disorder or acute psychosis creates high levels of psychological stress, thus increasing the posttraumatic or dissociative responses. In virtually all situations in which there is true comorbidity of an Axis I disorder, such as a mood disorder or psychosis, the trauma-related disorder has *secondary* importance in the hierarchy of treatment. The following case illustrates this principle:

Peter, a 36-year-old married attorney, was admitted to a unit specializing in the treatment of psychosis. The presenting symptoms included long periods where he appeared to be in a trance—staring off into space, his mouth some-times moving (apparently speaking unheard words)—from which he could be aroused only with difficulty. Though he was a highly functional individual in both his work and socially, his functioning had progressively deteriorated, having difficulty performing his job and becoming increasingly isolated at home. Peter's outpatient treaters had believed him to be quietly psychotic and arranged for him to be admitted to the psychosis specialty unit. Once he was admitted, the unit staff thought his presentation was atypical for psychotic disorder and asked me to evaluate him for possible PTSD or a dissociative disorder.

When I interviewed Peter, I found him to be a quiet, soft-spoken young man who was well organized and articulate. I asked him about his internal experience when he was observed in the trance-like state, and to my surprise he admitted that he actually induced those states deliberately. All throughout his life, he had the ability to retreat to a pleasurably numb, depersonalized state whenever he felt under stress simply by relaxing deeply and visually focusing on his folded hands; he had clearly taught himself autohypnosis. He recalled doing this as a young child when he hid in his room during screaming, drunken bat-tles between his parents that occurred frequently until they divorced when he was 10 years old. In the months leading up to the hospitalization, he had been self-inducing trance more frequently as he found himself having less energy to do his work and be with his family. He felt tired all the time, and although he was not hungry, he had gained 20 pounds and was sleeping 10 to 12 hours per night. He felt badly about what his situation was doing to his family and had thought of suicide, but instead retreated to his trance states as a way of not act-ing on his self-destructive impulses. With this history, I made the diagnosis of underlying major depression, which was subsequently successfully treated with medication.

HOSPITAL PRACTICE FOR TRAUMA-RELATED DISORDERS[1]

Specialized inpatient units dedicated to the treatment of trauma and/or dissociative disorders may be particularly effective in helping patients in crisis. These programs are often able to do more than stabilization and crisis management, providing specialized diagnostic evaluations and trauma-focused training in symptom management and the skills that are necessary for treatment and personal growth. However, the treatment of complex PTSD and most cases of DID and similar dissociative disorders should be within the capabilities of most general inpatient psychiatric units if certain treatment principles and clinical practices are observed and implemented.

The complex posttraumatic and dissociative symptoms of traumatized patients are often difficult and challenging problems to professionals who work in inpatient settings. In addition, the atmosphere of crisis and the involvement of many members of the inpatient treatment team usually complicate an already complex treatment. In order for treatment to be productive, the philosophy and structures of inpatient hospitalization must be clearly understood, and some of the potential pitfalls that seem to be part of the treatment of severely traumatized patients should be anticipated and addressed.

Therapeutic Philosophy

A general acceptance of trauma-related disorders is essential for the successful hospital treatment of patients with posttraumatic and dissociative disorders. Program leadership with hospital administrative support is necessary to provide the resources for the sometimes intensive treatment interventions (Kluft, 1991a; Ross, 1997). In addition, the risks involved in treating patients who are chronically self-destructive and impulsive must be understood by the hospital's clinical administration and the risk management department. The senior clinical staff of the unit—specifically including the program director, medical director, and/or nurse manager (different hospitals have variations in the configuration of roles)—must be supportive and knowledgeable about the treatment of trauma-related disorders. Without such support, the treatment team will be unable to sustain the treatment approaches and staff cohesion that are necessary for productive treatment. The professionals on the treatment team who provide the psychotherapy for individual patients must also have a high level of acceptance about trauma-related disorders as well as sophistication about treatment. In the case of DID, it is less essential for each member of the staff to have a high level of expertise concerning the diagnosis, as

---

[1] I would like to acknowledge the contributions of Karen Terk, MS, RN, who has been my colleague for nearly 25 years and co-founded the Trauma and Dissociative Disorders Program at McLean Hospital with me. Her extraordinary clinical skills and intuition and her common-sense approach formed the basis for the treatment philosophy and interventions that are described in this chapter. She was the primary architect for many innovations in nursing practice for patients with complex PTSD and dissociative disorders.

long as there is agreement to pursue a unified and coherent treatment approach (Kluft, 1991a; Steinmeyer, 1991). This kind of approach is crucial, as the potential for conflicts in the treatment teams of patients with DID is high. In fact, without active efforts to maintain a unified and coherent treatment approach, it is common for the treatment to founder as the treatment team begins to reflect the projected internal fragmentation of the patient.

In addition to the acceptance of the diagnosis, the therapeutic milieu must place a high value on respect and collaboration, as opposed to authoritarian attitudes and control. In actual practice, this type of philosophy is extremely difficult to maintain. The out-of-control behaviors of many traumatized patients often invite more than the limit setting needed to stabilize the treatment. Too often, inpatient units respond to patients' dysfunctional behaviors with an ever-increasing array of rigid rules and policies that eventually make any kind of flexibility or collaboration impossible. Basic unit rules concerning important treatment issues are essential, but care should be exercised to avoid the tendency to collude with patients' compulsion to reenact the abusive relationships of their childhoods in the milieu. Especially because inpatient protocols to maintain patient safety can be experienced as controlling and intrusive, special care must be exercised to allow patients to maintain as much personal dignity and autonomy as is possible and appropriate to their clinical status.

Interpersonal relationships should have a high value in the treatment of traumatized patients. In addition to relationships between patients and their treatment teams, important relationships include those among patients, as well as outside relationships such as those involving community therapists, families, spouses, partners, and other persons who provide social support. The treatment of traumatized patients should include all of the important individuals in the patient's outside life. Specifically, anyone living with and interacting with the patient should be involved in the treatment, and the unit should make active efforts to involve community therapists and to foster and maintain outside therapeutic relationships.

Personal responsibility should be a hallmark in the philosophy of inpatient treatment of patients with posttraumatic and dissociative disorders. Before admission, patients are frequently overwhelmed by the burdens of maintaining control, such as refraining from impulsive and self-destructive behavior and modulating symptomatology. To some patients, being in the hospital often may seem to be a welcome relief from having to stay in control and an opportunity to let down their defenses. This often results in their letting go of personal responsibility and placing hospital staff in the position of taking care of them. This shift of therapeutic responsibility is untenable, and patients must be willing to assume as much personal responsibility as possible during their hospitalizations. It is unworkable and regressive for the inpatient staff to have to take full responsibility for such issues as personal safety and behavioral control. Patients should be expected to monitor their own capabilities and seek out help should they need it. Simply put, it is impossible for the staff to keep all patients from harming themselves all of the time without some element of cooperation and shared responsibility from the patients.

Psychoeducation

Psychoeducation about the process of treatment is extremely important in the inpatient treatment of patients with complex PTSD and dissociative disorders. In particular, patients must learn and understand how to pace the therapeutic work. Virtually all traumatized patients who are admitted to inpatient settings are in early phases of their treatment, and some are attempting to do destabilizing abreactive work before building adequate psychotherapeutic foundations. In some cases, patients are flooded with memories and are spilling their recollections in therapy—sometimes even if their therapists are urging containment. In other cases, patients—and sometimes with the support of their therapists—have been attempting to purge themselves of their abusive childhood experiences long before they have built up the requisite relational skills and coping capacities that make productive abreaction possible. The task for most hospitalized patients with complex PTSD and dissociative disorders is to learn how to maintain control—letting go and letting down defenses is very rarely a problem.

Current accepted models of treatment staging (see the treatment model described at length in Chapter 6) emphasize that safety, containment, and stabilization are prerequisites for abreaction of trauma, which will most likely occur outside of a hospital setting. Any attempts at abreaction of past traumatic experiences during episodes of acute care must be approached cautiously. A very few patients who have mastered the tasks of early phase treatment may benefit from a circumscribed amount of abreactive therapy in the hospital. However, this kind of work should be limited in scope and carefully monitored, because patients are prone to becoming once again overwhelmed. There are common clinical situations where patients must be able to discuss some of the memories of past abuse, because not to do so would create only more problems. In these kinds of situations, the patient and the hospital staff must share the burden of limiting the extent of work about the traumatic material and must avoid the trap of believing that just one more piece of abreactive work would result in full resolution of the current difficulties. In past years, elective hospitalization has been used to support patients in later phases of treatment during particularly difficult abreactions (Kluft, 1991a; Sakheim, Hess, & Chivas, 1988). This kind of support has often been very helpful to patients while working through horrendous past experiences. However, given the economic realities of the health care environment, such elective admissions are likely to become increasingly rare.

Limits and Boundaries

Although authoritarian attitudes and controlling stances are not productive in the treatment of patients with posttraumatic and dissociative disorders, clear limits and boundaries are essential to minimize regression and foster therapeutic growth. Limits and boundaries are crucial to help preserve the treatment frame, to help patients exercise control of dysfunctional behaviors, and to maintain the hospital therapeutic milieu.

Limits and boundaries are particularly important given the intensity of involvement between traumatized patients and staff. These patients often require a high level of involvement with staff members, because problems such as managing reexperiencing phenomena and personality switching often requires considerable time and effort. The mistrust with which traumatized patients approach relationships may require some additional involvement on the part of staff members in order to help patients feel safe. However, the extent of staff involvement needs to have realistic limitations both to prevent staff exhaustion as well as to encourage patients to learn to meet some of their own needs for care and reassurance.

Out-of-control behaviors should not be tolerated in patients with PTSD and dissociative disorders, including repetitive self-harming or self-destructive behaviors, verbal abuse or violence, and prolonged abreactions. Patients should be expected to conform their behavior to unit norms as a condition of their treatment. Placing limits on patients puts the burden on them to find alternate ways of expressing themselves and to contain posttraumatic and dissociative symptoms to appropriate settings. Patients must begin to work with the treatment team around achieving these goals. Intermittent lapses in control are inevitable because of the nature of patients' difficulties and are expectable and understandable. However, lapses caused by patients' failure to strive for control are not therapeutically acceptable.

Dissociative Disorder Issues

The characteristics of inpatients with dissociative disorders predispose their treatment to particular difficulties. As Putnam (1989) noted:

> Once a patient is admitted, perceptions of the hospital can change dramatically and rapidly. Within a short time, most [DID patients] will have alters emerge who experience the hospital as a frightening and traumatizing place. Normal hospital procedures and routines, such as medications, milieu activities, privilege status, pass restrictions, and other unit rules are perceived as coercive and traumatizing. (p. 272)

Patients with complex PTSD who have difficulty building supportive alliances often engage with hospital staff in a way that reenacts the control struggles and abuses of their childhoods. In addition, patients with DID may also project their internal fragmentation onto various staff members, resulting in a particularly intense form of "staff splitting" (Braun, 1993; Putnam, 1989; Steinmeyer, 1991). Some staff will be viewed as hostile and abusive, whereas others will be seen as nurturing and understanding. This problem is sometimes aggravated by the tendency of staff to have markedly differing views of patients with DID (Kluft, 1991a). Some staff may view the diagnosis skeptically, whereas others may be overly accepting of patients' difficulties in controlling switching and maintaining control.

The initial assessment of patients with dissociative symptoms is crucial, particularly for patients with DID symptoms. Historically, relatively few patients were admitted to hospitals with a diagnosis of DID. However, in recent years, it has become necessary to determine both when a patient has DID and when a patient does *not* have DID. It is also important to distinguish between patients with full-blown DID and the many patients who have a lesser degree of dissociation or some other kind of posttraumatic disorder. After all, treatment should be designed to decrease dissociative symptoms and should not reinforce dissociative symptoms that are consciously or unconsciously exaggerated. Clinicians also should consider the possibility of factitious or malingered DID, particularly in a forensic context or where there is compelling secondary gain (see Chapter 15; Brick & Chu, 1991; Chu, 1991a; Coons & Milstein, 1994; Kluft, 1987c; Thomas, 2001 for further discussion of this issue).

All therapeutic work with DID patients must be approached as work with a single (although fragmented) person rather than with individual personalities. During a time of crisis such as hospitalization, all work with personalities should emphasize conflict resolution and stabilization. The patient's cooperation must be obtained in this venture, and hospital staff must encourage and reinforce interpersonality communication, understanding, and acceptance. Patients with DID must not learn that having DID makes them special—after all, an identity even as a special psychiatric patient is far from optimal. Furthermore, even though the hospital environment buffers patients with DID from some of the demands of the outside environment, they do need to exercise some control to respond to routine demands of their surroundings. Psychiatrist Colin Ross, MD (1997), has some excellent practical suggestions:

> We expect our patients to follow regular ward guidelines and procedures. They do not have special rooms, they eat with other patients, and the consequences for unacceptable conduct are generally the same as for other patients. (p. 368)

Ross suggests that out-of-control switching should not be allowed on the unit milieu and that child alternate personalities should generally be allowed to have executive control only in psychotherapy. As a general rule, patients with DID are expected to conform to the usual adult standards of behavior in the public areas of the hospital unit.

Nursing Practice

Hospitalized patients with histories of severe traumatization often are very fearful that they will be subject to excessive control and mistreatment. In a hospital setting, members of the nursing staff bear the brunt of this mistrust because of their role in monitoring and managing the milieu, and their inherent authority and control over patients' daily lives. Thus, nursing staff have a major responsibility for establishing and maintaining a therapeutic alliance with patients. The staff should have a sophisticated understanding of the effects of early abuse and should be able to empathize with the difficulties experienced by patients. They should be able to project the therapeutic attitudes of acceptance and respect. They should be skilled in bridging mistrust during control struggles and in setting limits and establishing boundaries. The negotiation of the therapeutic alliance begins at the time of admission, when issues such as privileges, rooming arrangements, and unit rules are areas of potential conflict. Patients should be treated respectfully, but patients must also respect the judgments of the staff and the real limitations of the hospital environment. For example, attempts should be made to accommodate the patient in terms of comfort and privacy (e.g., room location or room-mate), but nursing staff also must be allowed to consider and weigh the clinical needs of all patients and to make decisions based on their assessments. Similarly, patients with DID should be accorded the respect of being called what they choose. However, it is an unrealistic expectation that every staff member consistently recognize (or even remember) each patient's different alternate personalities (Kluft, 1991a).

During a hospitalization, many traumatized patients experience distress from intrusive reexperiencing of past abuse. Patients suffer with overwhelming affects such as despair, panic, and rage, and they may have impulses to flee, strike out, or hurt themselves. Effective nursing interventions are critical. Daily structure can be helpful for patients who are experiencing intrusive symptoms such as flashbacks and nightmares. Planned activities as well as rest and recuperation are important components of a daily structure. Emotional support and medication should be provided as necessary. It is helpful if the hospital setting has flexible rules about sleep and rest. Many patients are afraid of sleeping at night in a darkened room (especially if their abuse occurred at night). The use of nightlights should be permitted, and patients should be allowed to get out of bed and sit quietly in an area close to staff for brief periods. Patients may need to sleep for brief periods during the day if they did not get sufficient sleep during the previous night, although nursing staff should be careful not to allow patients to completely reverse their sleep/wake cycles.

The management of flashbacks and other forms of traumatic reexperiencing involves the use of grounding techniques (see Chapter 8 for further discussion of grounding techniques and Benham, 1995, concerning nursing practice). Patients may find it helpful for a staff member to approach them and maintain contact with them until the flashback is over. Staff members should let the patients know that they are there and orient the patients to time and place. Staff members may need to speak firmly and give specific instructions to help anchor the patients in the here-and-now. The following clinical example illustrates some common grounding techniques:

Ellen, a 26-year-old woman with DID, was found huddled in her closet shortly after admission. She appeared quite frightened and refused to speak to the nurse who found her, and instead stared at the wall while sucking her thumb. The nurse said, "You look very frightened and very young. You seem to be reliving something very frightening. My name is Sally, and I am a nurse in this hospital. I am here to help you, and I will not let you be hurt. I'd like you to try to understand that you are safe. I'd like you to try to look at me and remember that you know me as a safe person. I'd like you to try to look around you, and to feel yourself here with your feet on the floor, and to remember that you are safe in the hospital." Ellen was able to engage with the nurse and was able to calm down and emerge from the closet. She was observed closely until she could begin to talk about her distress and reengage in the milieu.

The psychoeducation that patients receive on how to manage their symptoms often occurs through nursing interventions in the milieu. Nursing staff are often the principal teachers of grounding techniques and other ways to help patients achieve control of dissociative symptoms and to pace the process of abreaction. They can help patients who are overwhelmed by past abusive events by encouraging containment of painful memories to therapy sessions. In addition to grounding techniques, nursing staff can use nonverbal means (e.g., imagery such as visualizing shutting the door on memories until therapy sessions). When patients become flooded, they can be encouraged to use artwork or journals for brief periods and then put them away.

Nursing staff are in the unique position of being with patients during periods of crisis—often in the evening or at night. During such times they have the opportunity to reinforce important messages such as, "It wasn't your fault that you were hurt." Nursing staff are able to participate in helping patients achieve crucial skills in self-care and self-soothing by maintaining adequate food and fluid intake, accessing medical attention, or simply taking a warm bath, reading, watching television, or going on a brisk walk. Nursing staff also have the critical task of helping patients utilize other people during periods of crisis, especially by making contact with them and encouraging patients to trust their support.

Individual Therapy and Case Management

Individual therapy or case management is critical in the treatment of complex patients with posttraumatic and dissociative conditions. The individual therapist or case manager can be a central figure in formulating a dynamic understanding of the patient's difficulties and implementing a productive treatment plan. Therapists or case managers should be given the autonomy and authority to make important decisions about and with the patient during an acute care episode. Patients often are able to better tolerate hospitalization when decisions that affect them are made by someone who has taken the time to develop a trusting relationship, rather than when decisions are based on inflexible and rigid unit rules.

If possible, patients should be provided with individual therapy during their hospital course, as some therapeutic gains are best realized in an individual trusting relationship. Therapists or case managers also are able to provide services such as specific interventions (e.g., negotiations between alternate personalities in a patient with DID), liaison with outpatient professionals, family work, and aftercare planning. The individual therapy should be well integrated into the remainder of the inpatient treatment, and the work should pursue treatment goals that are consistent with the overall treatment plan. Although individual treatment is valuable, much of the therapy during the course of a hospitalization is derived not only from individual therapists but also through contact with many other members of the hospital staff, especially nursing staff.

Ongoing contact with outside treaters should be encouraged as practical and appropriate, and the community therapist should be involved as much as possible as part of the inpatient treatment team. Often, covert problems in the ongoing therapy become apparent during an inpatient hospitalization. For example, if a patient consistently appears destabilized following sessions with the outside therapist, it can be an opportunity to examine what processes are occurring that should be reexamined and potentially changed. Unacknowledged ambivalence about the therapy can also become apparent, as in the following example:

> Sarah Jane, a 41-year-old woman with DID, was admitted to the hospital because of increased suicide risk. Although she seemed to be managing well at work and at home with her husband and three children, several of her alternate personalities had left messages for her therapist threatening to kill or harm herself and to warn the therapist to "keep your nose out of our business." In discussions with various hospital staff members, Sarah Jane talked about her ongoing treatment, and an interesting split developed between various staff members concerning opinions about the community therapist. Sarah Jane described how helpful the work with her therapist had been and how flexible the therapist could be, responding to emergencies, extending session time, and even occasionally meeting outside the office around specific community-based tasks. While some staff members felt that the ongoing therapy was useful and helpful, others voiced the opinion that the outside therapist was "just crazy" and was, at a minimum, allowing violations of the treatment frame and overgratifying the patient. The therapist was able to attend a brief meeting with members of the inpatient treatment team, where she described her perspective of the treatment, and it appeared that all alterations in the usual boundaries of therapy had been carefully considered and discussed (even utilizing the resources of a consultant to the therapy). It then became clear that the split in the opinions of the staff was primarily a reflection of Sarah Jane's ambivalence about the therapist, probably based on her sense of vulnerability as she began to share sensitive information about her life and feelings. The therapist saw this as an opportunity to address those issues in the ongoing treatment.

Group Treatment

The use of verbal groups in the acute care of traumatized patients has been controversial. Although group treatment for posttraumatic disorders has a long tradition (van der Kolk, 1993), the use of groups with dissociative disorders has been discouraged (Kluft, 1991a; Putnam, 1989). In clinical practice, certain kinds of verbal groups are regressive, whereas others appear to be more helpful. Traditional process-oriented psychotherapy groups that focus on relationships within the group and psychoanalytically based groups that tend to mobilize intense affect are contraindicated because they are far too overwhelming for patients who have intense relational difficulties and affective instability. Groups that encourage or permit the discussion or details of past abusive experiences are also countertherapeutic because patients often are triggered by other patients' stories into reexperiencing their own trauma.

Verbal groups that are focused on particular tasks appear to be quite useful for many traumatized patients. Some of these groups deal with current symptomatology and the effects of past experiences but explicitly do not permit detailed discussion of past abuse. These groups have a psychoeducational and skills-training focus and discuss ways of coping with posttraumatic and dissociative symptoms, expressing and containing intense feelings, controlling impulses, finding ways to remain functional, and making and sustaining relationships. Some cognitive-behavioral groups (e.g., assertiveness training, relaxation, or anger management groups) or gender-related groups (e.g., women's issues) can also be helpful. Finally, the role of groups that involve activities is enormously valuable. Certain rehabilitation-oriented or expressive groups can be extremely helpful for patients who are regressed or who struggle to use verbal modalities. Their self-esteem can be enhanced by accomplishing concrete goals, and they can express intense nonverbal feelings and impulses in art, music, or movement. Recreational activities are a welcome relief from the heavy burdens of psychotherapeutic work and are a good reminder that treatment is intended to improve the quality of patients' lives, not to consume them.

Both inside and outside the hospital, some patients with complex PTSD and DID can make good use of 12-step groups such as AA, NA, or Al-Anon when addressing comorbid substance abuse problems. However, involvement in 12-step incest survivor groups or self-help groups for trauma patients are generally contraindicated, because their process and content are unregulated, resulting in emotional flooding and other psychological distress. In some of these groups, there are not adequate structures concerning boundaries between group members, and there is the potential for enmeshed, intrusive, and/or exploitative relationships.

Family Work

Inpatient hospitalization often brings family issues into the treatment arena. Current families and other persons who are part of the patient's social support system almost always should be involved in the treatment. Spouses or partners simply may need support and education. Often, however, significant relationship problems exist, ranging from a partner who reenacts abusive or neglectful relationships, or conversely, a partner who is overinvolved, overfascinated, and/or overprotective. Significant others often need counseling and advice concerning the delicate balance of being sensitive and involved with their partners who have complex PTSD or DID, but also understanding they should not enable dysfunctional behavior. Spouses or partners sometimes need to be reminded of their appropriate roles and that they should never function as an adjunctive therapist.

Children in the home should be assessed as to whether they are at risk as a result of the patient's difficulties. Although many traumatized patients are exemplary parents, others are extremely overprotective, involve their children in the transgenerational cycle of abuse, or neglect them through self-absorption in their own difficulties (Kluft, 1987b). In the hospital setting, staff members have an obligation to report any clear evidence of neglect or abuse of patients' minor children to the local or state child protective agency. If this needs to occur, it should generally be done with the full involvement of the patient (and partner or spouse) in the context of providing the needed additional supports for appropriate parental functioning.

In situations where there is a history of childhood abuse, contact with families of origin is extremely problematic. Sometimes when the patient can be sure of a positive response from a family member (e.g., a supportive brother or sister), disclosure can be appropriate and helpful. However, premature disclosure of the abuse secret to family members is destabilizing to families' equilibrium and can often result in the family closing ranks around the denial of the abuse and essentially ostracizing the patient. Most experts in the field of treatment of childhood abuse survivors suggest that disclosure and confrontation of a perpetrator should occur only when it is the patient's clear choice, and relatively late in treatment—not during episodes of decompensation and acute care (Courtois, 2010; Herman, 1981; MacFarlane & Korbin, 1983; Schatzhow & Herman, 1989).

Seclusion and Restraint

Despite the potential for reenacting traumatic abuse, there may be times when seclusion or restraint is necessary to prevent self-harm to patients with complex PTSD and dissociative disorders. For example, if a patient is unable to stop head-banging or other forms of self-harm, physical intervention may be necessary. Of course, seclusion or restraint is used only when other alternatives—verbal, behavioral, or pharmacologic interventions, or increased monitoring such as constant observation—have been ineffective. Seclusion or restraint is usually very upsetting not just to the patient involved but also to other patients who feel tenuous and fear loss of control. In situations where these interventions are necessary, care must be exercised to deal with the effect on the inpatient milieu and other specific patients who may be destabilized as a result.

In recent years, in conjunction with the efforts of many state mental health departments, many hospital systems have instituted initiatives to minimize or even eliminate the use of seclusion and restraint. Training staff to use de-escalation and crisis prevention measures, to sometimes allow patients to win control struggles, to encourage time-outs, and to never use restraint and seclusion as punishment has often resulted in dramatic decreases in the frequency and duration of these interventions. Careful planning in advance can be helpful in working with patients to develop crisis plans or personal safety plans that involve various interventions to avoid seclusion and restraint. These interventions may include listing personal posttraumatic triggers and individualized measures that provide reassurance, soothing, and a sense of safety. Medications for anxiety and/or agitation, such as benzodiazepines or neuroleptics, can be part of the plan.

In the early years of the development of treatment models for DID, the use of voluntary physical restraints to control a violent alternate personality while a patient worked through trauma was proposed. This type of intervention is clinically inappropriate because it neglects patients' responsibility in controlling their own actions and violates the regulations of the mental health departments of many states.

Staff Support

Working with traumatized patients requires considerable personal involvement on the part of staff. Staff members must be willing to extend themselves to empathize with patients and to struggle with them to overcome their difficulties. This can be a psychologically exhausting task. Sometimes just sitting with someone who is reliving trauma may be difficult for staff members who may have to confront their own dysphoric feelings or who are reminded of their own painful past experiences. In addition, patients bring their intense emotions into the treatment arena and even reenact the abusive relationships in the hospital setting. The anger and rage that often results from childhood abuse may be overwhelmingly intense, and patients may displace their anger onto hospital staff.

Hospitalized patients with PTSD and dissociative disorders are often in crisis. Difficult situations that are common in the hospital include episodes of self-destructive behaviors. These may include suicide gestures or attempts, self-harming activities, substance abuse, eating problems, violence, and out-of-control behaviors that may require restraint and even actual flight from the hospital. All of these kinds of crises create high levels of anxiety, anger, and guilt in hospital staff. Commonly, staff feel that they should have been able to prevent crises from happening, and they question whether they are competent to treat these patients. They also can become upset or withdrawn, feeling violated when patients act out against themselves or others and anxious about being held responsible for the patients' destructive behavior.

Given that the treatment of traumatized patients subjects hospital staff to significantly stressful experiences, it is essential that there be a supportive environment for all staff, particularly for nursing staff. An important component of support is staff empowerment. For example, staff members must be given the authority to make decisions in their area of expertise and must be supported and guided in their work. In order for staff to encourage patients' growth, they must also be validated and empowered. This model of empowerment of staff must have the full cooperation of the clinical leadership and administrative staff associated with the unit.

Hospital staff must be given permission by the unit leadership to express the feelings that are engendered by work with traumatized patients. In addition to positive feelings, staff commonly experience exhaustion, frustration, anger, and even dislike. Such feelings must be expressed in a responsible manner, as opposed to being acted out in the milieu. Staff must learn to differentiate anger about patients' behavior from dislike for patients themselves. Even when staff actually dislike patients, they must find appropriate ways to express their feelings privately so that they can continue to work with patients with a nonjudgmental and empathic approach. Staff must also be given the opportunity to express their anger and fear. In order to maintain a safe and supportive milieu, staff must be able to set limits on inappropriate behavior and cannot be immobilized by their anger or worry excessively about retraumatizing patients. In fact, one common reason for failure to set appropriate limits is staff members' fear that they are acting out their feelings of anger and sadism.

Periodic staff meetings open to all staff are essential to maintain unit functioning. Although some of the meeting may be used for unit or hospital business, there should always be an opportunity for staff to discuss the feelings generated by working with patients. Just as it is important to provide education for patients about their illness and symptoms, it is necessary to provide adequate education for staff. Staff members must learn that it is normal for them to sometimes feel abused, burned out, or depleted, and how to support each other. Staff members must also learn about the process of the treatment so they understand and appreciate the importance of the work they are doing, how it helps patients, and how it affects them. It is part of the job of unit leadership to provide a sense of mission that can guide and inspire the work of the unit staff.

Informal availability of senior staff is perhaps one of the most important ways to support and reassure staff. If all therapists and senior clinical staff leave the unit at the earliest opportunity, nursing staff are left feeling burdened and unsupported. It is very helpful if senior staff are consistently available to nursing staff (even for brief periods) to help with problem solving and to actually intervene and provide informal supervision and role modeling. Formal supervision for all staff is also helpful, and staff should constantly be given the opportunity to learn more about their work and the treatment of patients with complex PTSD and dissociative disorders.

The principles and practices outlined in this discussion are easier to maintain on specialty units dedicated to the treatment of patients with posttraumatic or dissociative disorders. However, patients with trauma-related disorders can be successfully treated on general, mixed-diagnosis psychiatric units. On general psychiatric units, individualized treatment plans must be implemented for traumatized patients, as their treatment may differ significantly from the treatment of other patients. For example, a psychotic patient may need more control and structure from staff, whereas a trauma patient may need to be more engaged in collaborative treatment planning. A treatment team that is particularly knowledgeable about PTSD and dissociative disorders and clear leadership around treatment issues are helpful on a general psychiatric unit.

Many other kinds of patients can be treated with traumatized patients. However, two groups of psychiatric patients do not seem to mix well with them. Highly agitated, acutely psychotic, and intrusive patients may be extremely difficult for patients who may be reminded of abuse from frightening and unpredictable individuals. Patients who are sexual predators are also often problematic, sometimes frightening traumatized patients, but sometimes engaging them in seductive and abusive reenactments.

The hospitalization of patients with complex PTSD and dissociative disorders often appears to magnify the normative difficulties of outpatient treatment. However, a well-grounded understanding of the principles of treatment, clear and compassionate interventions, and measures to sustain the treaters can make the inpatient treatment a productive and growth-enhancing experience for both patients and staff.

14

Psychopharmacology for Trauma-Related Disorders[1]

For most of the symptoms of complex PTSD and dissociative disorders, pharmacotherapy is not the primary treatment modality. However, as an adjunctive modality, the careful pharmacological treatment of patients with trauma-related disorders can be of considerable benefit. Perhaps because of the extreme dysphoria and multiple symptoms of these disorders, the use of medications is very common. Typically, pharmacotherapy for trauma-related disorders targets the autonomic hyperarousal symptoms of PTSD, but given the cycle of intrusive symptoms and hyperarousal triggering each other, pharmacologic treatment also often appears to be effective for the intrusive thoughts, flashbacks, and nightmares of PTSD. Medication is also used for the symptoms of depression, anxiety, agitation, mood lability, and sleep disturbance that often accompany PTSD and dissociative disorders. Although many medications have been used for trauma-related symptomatology, relatively few studies have demonstrated clear and consistent efficacy, so their use remains mostly empirical in nature (and informed consent with patients should reflect this information). This chapter discusses the pragmatic use of various classes of medication in trauma-related disorders and reviews the relevant literature and theory behind their use.

ANTIDEPRESSANT MEDICATIONS

The evidence base for the pharmacotherapy of PTSD includes randomized controlled trials, open trials, and case reports. The evidence concerning efficacy is strongest for the selective serotonin reuptake inhibitor (SSRI) antidepressants. The only two FDA-approved medications for the treatment of PTSD are sertraline (Zoloft) and paroxetine (Paxil). However, many other antidepressants have been empirically used and studied. Table 14.1 summarizes controlled studies that have shown efficacy for antidepressants in the treatment of PTSD (not included are open trials, case reports, and studies that showed no efficacy).

[1] In this chapter, following the usual convention, the generic names for drugs are in lower case, while the first letter of brand names are capitalized.

Table 14.1   Controlled Studies of Antidepressants in PTSD

Study	Antidepressant	N	Population
Frank, Kosten, Giller, & Dan, 1988	imipramine/phenelzine	34	combat
Kosten, Frank, Dan, McDougle, & Giller, 1991	imipramine/phenelzine	60	combat
Davidson et al., 1990	amitriptyline	60	combat
Van der Kolk, Dreyfuss et al., 1994	fluoxetine	31	mixed
Connor, Sutherland, Tupler, Malik, & Davidson, 1999	fluoxetine	53	combat
Brady et al., 2000	sertraline	187	civilian
Davidson, Rothbaum, van der Kolk, Sikes, & Farbel, 2001	sertraline	208	civilian
Marshall, Beebe, Oldham, & Zaninelli, 2001	paroxetine	365	civilian
Tucker et al., 2001	paroxetine	307	civilian
Davidson et al., 2003	mirtazapine	48	mixed

Although the evidence base for the efficacy of antidepressants in PTSD appears solid, their usefulness in clinical practice is not so clear. Patients with complex PTSD and dissociative disorders do not seem to respond robustly to these agents, perhaps because the study populations had lesser degrees of trauma exposure, less chronicity, and fewer comorbid conditions. Another explanation may be that there is so much comorbidity in complex PTSD that patients subjectively remain intensely symptomatic even if the antidepressant agents are somewhat effective in treating the PTSD and affective symptoms. This may be why, in everyday practice, patients often report a modest improvement in their overall symptoms but rarely experience a remission of either PTSD or anxiety/depressive symptoms. Thus, when approaching the subject of medication, clinicians should caution patients that they may feel a modest rather than dramatic improvement. The doses of antidepressant medications should be tailored to the needs and responses of individual patients but are in the same general range as when these agents are used for depression or anxiety.

ANTIPSYCHOTIC MEDICATIONS

Neuroleptic or antipsychotic medications have long been used in complex PTSD patients in clinical settings to treat agitation, overactivation, and intrusive PTSD symptoms, as well as for chronic anxiety, insomnia, and irritability, but until recently, they have not been studied for these uses. Particularly because PTSD and dissociative disorder patients do not have true psychosis, and because antipsychotic medications have serious side effects such as tardive dyskinesia (a potentially irreversible movement disorder) and adverse

Table 14.2   Studies of Antipsychotic Medications in PTSD

Study	Antipsychotic	Type	N	Population
Bartzokis, Lu, Turner, Mintz, & Saunders, 2005	risperidone	controlled	48	combat
Hamner, Faldowski et al., 2003	risperidone	controlled	40	combat
Reich, Winternitz, Hennen, Watts, & Stanculescu, 2004	risperidone	controlled	19	civilian
Kozarić-Kovačić, Pivac, Mück-Šeler, & Rothbaum, 2005	risperidone	open	26	combat
Stein, Kline, & Matloff, 2002	olanzapine	controlled	19	combat
Petty et al., 2001	olanzapine	open	30	combat
Hamner, Deitsch, Brodrick, Ulmer, & Lorberbaum, 2003	quetiapine	open	18	combat
Filteau, Leblanc, & Bouchard, 2003	quetiapine	open	5	mixed
Ahearn, Mussey, Johnson, Krohn, & Krahn, 2006	quetiapine	open	15	combat
Kozarić-Kovačić & Pivac, 2007	quetiapine	open	53	combat

metabolic effects (leading to obesity and elevations in blood levels of fasting glucose, triglycerides, and cholesterol), clinicians have been reluctant to acknowledge the extent to which these agents have been used in trauma-related disorders. The newer atypical antipsychotic medications—introduced in the 1990s—have been a welcome addition to options for pharmacologic treatment of PTSD because of their lower extrapyramidal and anticholinergic side effects, which make them much more acceptable to patients. However, these new agents have proved to have some risk of tardive dyskinesia, and some have the same adverse metabolic effects as older-generation antipsychotics, especially olanzapine (Zyprexa), which is associated with significant weight gain and metabolic changes in many patients. In recent years, a flurry of studies have demonstrated the usefulness of antipsychotic medications for PTSD as shown in Table 14.2 (included are controlled studies and open trials, but not case reports and studies that showed no efficacy).

The Reich et al. (2004) study of risperidone (Risperdal) is of particular interest, as the study population was a group of women with chronic PTSD related to childhood physical, sexual, verbal, or emotional abuse. The change in PTSD symptoms was related to reduction of intrusive symptoms and hyperarousal, not the numbing symptoms. Although to date there are no controlled trials of quetiapine (Seroquel), the outcomes from the open label studies have been extremely promising, with substantial decreases in PTSD symptoms across large percentages of the study populations, in some cases in all three categories of symptoms—intrusion, numbing, and autonomic arousal. In another investigation related to the Hamner et al. (2003) study, quetiapine was effective in reducing PTSD-related sleep disturbances.

In clinical practice, risperidone and quetiapine have been the primary antipsychotic agents used for complex PTSD. They are generally given at bedtime in doses that are considerably less than when used for the treatment of active psychosis: risperidone 0.5 mg to 2 mg, and quetiapine 50 mg to 200 mg. The target symptoms are improved sleep and reduced anxiety on the following day. If necessary, this regimen can be supplemented by a small morning dose and as-needed doses of quetiapine during the day; risperidone is not recommended for as-needed dosing because severe orthostatic drops in blood pressure sometimes lead to an increased risk of falls.

ANTIANXIETY AND SEDATIVE/HYPNOTIC MEDICATIONS

Benzodiazepines—so-called minor tranquilizers, the class that includes lorezepam (Ativan), clonazepam (Klonapin), diazepam (Valium), chlordiazepoxide (Librium), and alprazolam (Xanax)—are widely prescribed for PTSD patients despite a complete absence of controlled studies that show efficacy for trauma-related symptomatology. Only one open trial suggested that clonazepam is helpful for control of posttraumatic symptoms in patients with dissociative identity disorder (DID) (Loewenstein, Hornstein, & Farber, 1988). Despite this lack of evidence of efficacy, in one study of hospitalized combat veterans with PTSD, 45% with no substance abuse history and 26% with a substance abuse history received these medications (Kosten, Fontana, Semyak, & Rosenheck, 2000). Benzodiazepines appear to be commonly used for panic attacks, agitation, chronic anxiety, and sleep disturbances that accompany trauma-related disorders. However, if at all possible, benzodiazepines should be used acutely rather than routinely, as they carry the risks of tolerance and habituation, and their disinhibiting properties may potentiate acting on destructive impulses and behavioral dyscontrol. If tolerance to benzodiazepines develops, the use of risperidone or quetiapine in low doses may be a better alternative. Patients' anxiety usually cannot be completely resolved, but medication can help reduce panic so that patients are then able to work psychologically.

Disturbed sleep also is quite common in traumatized patients. As described in Chapter 2, patients are likely to be too anxious to fall asleep (despite feeling tired) and to wake up repeatedly with high anxiety and/or nightmares. Some patients may be fearful at night because of recall of nighttime abuse, and in some patients with DID, alternate personalities may engage in nocturnal activities. Sleep problems are most effectively addressed in the overall framework of the treatment, for example, using cognitive-behavioral strategies, relaxation, and guided imagery to cope with anxiety and PTSD-related reactivity at night. Proper sleep hygiene (getting out of bed and staying awake during the day) may be of some help, as are other practical measures such as getting adequate exercise. In patients with DID, specific focused strategies can be used for fearful personalities, and to negotiate within the system of alternate personalities to control those who are active at night. Used in the context of environmental and psychotherapeutic interventions, the judicious use of medications for sleep may be helpful.

The regular use of benzodiazepines for sleep is usually of limited effectiveness over time. Other sedative-hypnotic medications can be used for sleep problems in patients with complex PTSD, especially for patients with substance abuse histories or who grow tolerant to benzodiazepines. Trazodone, a sedating antidepressant, has been used in doses of 50 mg to 200 mg. In one study of combat veterans, trazodone in this dose range was given for sleep problems (Warner, Dorn, & Peabody, 2001); a substantial majority of patients had improvement in traumatic nightmares, sleep latency (difficulty falling asleep), and midsleep awakening. The more recently introduced non-benzodiazepine hypnotics zolpidem (Ambien) and eszopiclone (Lunesta) appear to be reasonable alternatives to benzodiazepines with reduced risk of habituation, and the negative effects of long-term use appear to be minimal at this point. Other sedative-hypnotic medications, such as the antihistamines diphenhydramine (Benadryl) and hydroxyzine (Vistaril), the antidepressant mirtazapine (Remeron), and low-dose tricyclic antidepressants, may be used for sleep problems in traumatized populations. In general, the barbiturates and chloral hydrate should generally be avoided in complex PTSD and dissociative disorder patients because of their propensity to become addictive and their potential to be lethal if taken in excess.

ANTIADRENERGIC MEDICATIONS

Antiadrenergic agents (traditionally used to manage cardiac arrhythmias and for hypertension) have been increasingly used in recent years to block the autonomic overactivation that is induced by traumatic experiences. This has proved to be a particularly interesting area of inquiry, as theoretically the use of such agents in the period immediately following traumatic events might block the effects of the catecholamine response that appears to play a major role in the development of PTSD (see Chapter 5 for a discussion of the role of catecholamines in traumatic memory). Two early noncontrolled studies of the beta-adrenergic antagonist (beta blocker) propranolol were promising in demonstrating symptomatic improvement in adults and children with PTSD (Famularo, Kinscherff, & Fenton, 1988; Kolb, Burris, & Griffiths, 1984). In two more recent controlled studies, when propranolol was given for a period shortly after traumatic events, participants developed significantly less physiologic reactivity although no fewer of the other symptoms of PTSD (Pitman et al., 2002; Vaiva et al., 2003). It appears that although propranolol is not the hoped-for agent that would block the development of PTSD, it may eventually have some role in ameliorating the physiologic effects of trauma.

Studies of another group of antiadrenergic agents that act in the alpha-adrenergic system appear to have more promise. Early studies of clonidine, an alpha-2 agonist, showed some promise in treating PTSD (Kinzie & Leung, 1989; Kolb et al., 1984). But more recently, prazosin, an alpha-1 antagonist, has received more attention and has been used clinically to treat traumatic nightmares and the sleep disturbances and other symptoms of PTSD. Two controlled studies have demonstrated clear efficacy for this use (Raskind et al., 2007; Raskind et al., 2003). Prazosin is usually begun as an evening

Table 14.3 Open-Label Studies of Mood Stabilizers in PTSD

Study	Mood Stabilizer	N	Population
Kitchner & Greenstein, 1985	lithium	5	combat
van der Kolk, 1983	lithium	14	combat
Lipper et al., 1986	carbamazepine	10	combat
Fesler, 1991	valproate	16	combat
Clark, Canive, Calais, Qualls, & Tuason, 1999	valproate	13	combat
Berlant & van Kammen, 2002	topiramate	35	civilian
Bremner et al., 2005	phenytoin	12	mixed

dose of 1 mg to 3 mg and can be increased to 15 mg daily as an evening dose or in divided doses. In clinical practice for PTSD, it has been primarily used for treating traumatic nightmares at relatively modest doses—3 mg at night and 1 mg to 3 mg in the morning, although in the Raskind et al. studies, it was used around the 10 mg dose level.

MOOD STABILIZING MEDICATIONS

The use of mood stabilizers in the treatment of PTSD has received considerable attention in the scientific literature, based on the idea that limbic structures that process emotions in the brain may be sensitized by traumatic experiences, lowering the threshold for their responsiveness to environmental cues, especially reminders of the trauma (Post, Weiss, Smith, Li, & McCann, 1997). In theory, mood stabilizers could raise the threshold for activation and lead to symptom reductions in trauma patients (Keck, McElroy, & Friedman, 1992). A limited number of open-label trials (Table 14.3) have shown beneficial effects of various mood-stabilizing agents (not included are case reports and studies that showed no efficacy).

There are also case studies and anecdotal accounts of the use of gabapentin (Neurontin) for PTSD. In terms of practical clinical use, lithium and phenytoin (Dilantin) are rarely used, and carbamazepine (Tegretol), valproate in the form of divalproex (Depakote), and topiramate (Topomax) are generally used only empirically when mood swings and affective lability are prominent clinical features.

AN ALGORITHM FOR THE PHARMACOLOGIC TREATMENT OF TRAUMA PATIENTS

I am indebted to D. Bradford Reich, MD, a skilled clinical and research psychiatrist, who worked for many years providing acute hospital-based care in the Trauma and Dissociative Disorders Unit at McLean Hospital. Over time, he was able to develop a practical system of pharmacologic interventions for use with complex trauma patients with a wide array of posttraumatic, dissociative, anxiety, and mood problems. The algorithm that I present here is largely based on his work, with modifications from my own practice:

1. First treat any comorbid major depression, bipolar disorder, psychosis, or ADHD.

2. Tailor psychopharmacologic treatment toward target symptoms (e.g., anxiety, sleep difficulties, depression, intrusive symptoms, and overactivation) rather than the PTSD diagnosis.

3. If there is no history or risk of substance abuse, begin treatment with a benzodiazepine for anxiety, agitation, or overactivation.

4. If there is comorbid substance abuse or if a benzodiazepine is not effective, consider quetiapine (Seroquel) or risperidone (Risperdal) for anxiety, agitation, overactivation, or the intrusive symptoms of PTSD. Begin with a small bedtime dose and increase as necessary and/or add a morning dose.

5. Consider an SSRI antidepressant for symptoms of depression or the numbing/avoidant symptoms of PTSD. If there is no response or only a partial response, consider a tricyclic or MAOI antidepressant.

6. Hypnotics such as trazodone, zolpidem (Ambien), and eszopiclone (Lunesta) may alleviate difficulty falling asleep or midsleep awakening, but they rarely relieve nightmares. Fear of falling asleep because of nightmares or flashbacks may interfere with any pharmacotherapy.

7. Antihistamines such as hydroxyzine (Vistaril) or diphenhydramine (Benadryl) may be useful for sleep or sedation in patients with histories of substance abuse or tolerance to other agents.

8. Alpha adrenergic agents (e.g., prazosin or clonidine) may be useful for nightmares, sleep disturbance, and flashbacks; hypotension may limit the usefulness of these agents. Begin these agents as a low bedtime dose and increase as necessary and/or add a morning dose.

9. The various mood stabilizers may be useful for affective lability. Topiramate (Topomax) may be useful for nightmares, sleep disturbance, flashbacks, or intrusive memories; cognitive side effects may limit its usefulness. Gabapentin (Neurontin) can be a benign agent for treating agitation.

10. Conventional antipsychotic agents such as chlorpromazine (Thorazine) or thioridazine (Mellaril) in low to moderate doses may be useful for agitation in patients who have not responded to atypical antipsychotic agents or other medications.

11. Some patients quickly develop tolerance and may need to be switched between classes of medication.

12. Any exacerbation of PTSD is usually associated with a psychosocial stressor that must be addressed if pharmacotherapy is to be effective.

PRESCRIBING FOR COMPLEX PTSD AND DISSOCIATIVE DISORDER PATIENTS

Medications may be effective in relieving particular target symptoms in patients with complex PTSD and dissociative disorders, but they do not generally have a major impact on the overall clinical syndrome. Partial responses to many different medications are common (i.e., lots of medications each help a little). Thus, there is the danger of polypharmacy in this patient population, where an incremental number of different medications—in different classes or even multiple medications in the same class—are prescribed over time. This problem is even more pronounced when patients become very invested in their medications, believing that each one is helpful for a specific problem. Unfortunately, with such regimens, the effectiveness of each medication may become unclear. It also may be impossible to ascertain all possible drug-drug interactions, and there may be adverse cumulative effects of multiple medications (e.g., producing chronic sedation or decreased mental acuity). Although it is not unusual for patients with complex trauma-related syndromes to be on multiple medications, periodic reassessment and simplification of medication regimens is often advisable.

Patients with complex PTSD and dissociative disorders commonly have variations in their moods and symptoms from day to day, or even over the course of a single day. It is generally ineffective for the prescribing clinician to try to medicate these kind of transient changes. Rather, some overall assessment of symptoms over time—and in the case of patients with DID, across personalities—is usually more productive. In addition, effective psychotherapy involving skills training in affect regulation, grounding, and management of PTSD and dissociative symptoms may be more effective than medication.

There are interesting issues with patients with DID concerning the differences in perceived effects of medications on the various alternate personalities. Various personalities may report different responses to the same medications or may even claim to be able to block medication effects. This phenomenon is likely a result of the different levels of physiologic activation in different personality states, or of the personalities' subjective experience, rather than actual differential physiologic effects of the medications.

The ability of patients with DID to hold conflicting views and attitudes across the personality system enables some unusual forms of compliance problems with medications. For example, ambivalence about taking medication may result in some personalities "tricking" other personalities into believing that medications have (or have not) been taken when the reverse situation is actually the case, or some personalities hiding or throwing away medication. Because of problems with amnesia, there is also the risk of too much medication being taken when one personality takes a dose of medication, unaware that another personality has already taken the scheduled dose. Of course, medications may be inappropriately used by certain personalities as tools for punishing other identities or to attempt suicide. It is incumbent on the prescribing clinician to negotiate these thorny issues with patients with DID to ensure that medications are taken properly and safely (e.g., "In order for me to prescribe these medications, I must have assurance from all parts that they will be used as intended, and never as a way of hurting any part.").

Finally, given the complexity and the frequent disability of complex PTSD and dissociative disorder patients, the prescribing clinician is often part of a team of treaters, unless the prescriber is both psychopharmacologist and therapist. Careful coordination of responsibilities and communication between team members is essential, lest the treaters take on conflicting roles, which is a particular liability in treating patients with DID, where various members of the team identify with the disparate views, attitudes, and beliefs of the various alternate personalities. Even in situations where various team members have a role in the psychotherapy of patients, a lead clinician should have the responsibility to oversee the therapeutic activities of all team members. Lack of coordination concerning interventions and treatment goals, failures of communication, and a sense of dysfunctional isolation are all too often experienced in the team treatment of patients who are dysfunctional and fragmented, and the amelioration of these problems provides a model for the internal integration and healing of these patients.

15

Controversies and Future Directions in the
Field of Trauma and Dissociation

Ever since the introduction of dissociative identity disorder (DID)—then called multiple personality disorder—into the DSM-III (American Psychiatric Association) in 1980, controversy has swirled around the nature and the validity of this diagnosis (in parallel to the controversy about the occurrence and validity of traumatic amnesia). Some prominent authors who are skeptical about the validity of the DID diagnosis have proposed a sociocognitive model through which DID is thought to be caused by clinicians who believe strongly in the diagnosis and who covertly mold patients to enact the symptoms of DID (McHugh, 1992; Merskey, 1992; Piper, 1997). According to this model,

> DID is a socially constructed condition that results from the therapist's cueing (e.g., suggestive questioning regarding the existence of possible alternate personalities), media influences (e.g., film and television portrayals of DID), and broader sociocultural expectations regarding the presumed clinical features of DID. For example, some proponents of the sociocognitive model believe that the release of the book and film *Sybil* in the 1970s played a substantial role in shaping conceptions of DID in the minds of the general public and psychotherapists. (Lilienfeld & Lynn, 2003, p. 117)

From my perspective, I find most of these assertions absurd. I have made the definitive diagnosis of DID in dozens of patients and have no special interest in promoting that diagnosis. In fact, I have also determined on many occasions that patients do not have DID, or that they have been misdiagnosed with DID (Chu, 1991a). I also find authentic DID presentations to be credible and their symptomatic expressions to be consistent with patients' trauma histories. Treatment outcome research has demonstrated that patients with DID are responsive to treatment (Brand, Classen, Zaveri, & McNary, 2009)—quite the opposite from what one would expect if the DID was essentially a shared delusion between patients and their therapists.

Despite some defensiveness about dissociative disorders and the validity of reports of recovered memory of childhood abuse, professionals in the trauma and dissociation field have reexamined their understanding of basic concepts related to childhood traumatization. As the dust begins to clear, ample evidence supports the validity of dissociation and dissociative disorders. Moreover, the link between dissociative pathology and childhood trauma is clear. However, evidence also shows a variety of alternative mechanisms that can explain some cases of dissociation and related symptoms, such as amnesia and recovered memory. Even those professionals who accept trauma-related dissociation must also understand that some dissociative presentations may derive from etiologies other than trauma.

PSEUDO-DISSOCIATION

Although dissociative symptoms occur frequently in psychiatric patients, not all dissociation is DID, and in fact, only approximately 20% of patients with clinically significant levels of dissociative symptoms appear to have DID (Chu & Dill, 1990; Ross et al., 1991). Hence, it is important *not* to treat patients with lesser levels of dissociation as though they have DID. In general, no clear evidence shows that authentic DID can be iatrogenically created *de novo* by suggestion, contagion, or hypnosis in adult persons who do not have some preexisting dissociative capacity or history of trauma (Brown, Frischholz, & Scheflin, 1999; Gleaves, 1996; Loewenstein, 2007; Ross, Norton, & Fraser, 1989). However, patients with lesser degrees of dissociation can be pushed into DID-like presentation by naïve or overzealous therapists (Chu, 1991a; Kluft, 1996). Or, pseudo-dissociation can result from extremely poor therapeutic practices, as in the following clinical illustration that occurred many years ago:

> Michelle, a 19-year-old college student, sought treatment for depression in a program for the treatment of personality disorders. After approximately two months of treatment, I was asked to see her in consultation to evaluate the possibility of a dissociative disorder. To my surprise, Michelle spoke easily of her various "alters," naming and describing many of them. Upon being asked how she knew she had these "alters," she replied, "I know this program is about personality disorders and I figured I must have multiple personalities. I was up several nights just finding my personalities and naming them!" When I carefully asked about the possibility of childhood abuse, Michelle said, "I know I wasn't treated very nicely when I was a kid, but I don't remember being sexually abused. However, my therapist says that I must have amnesia for the abuse, and that my sexual abuse is the reason I am so afraid of men and sex."

Although I am convinced that this kind of suggestive clinical practice is far from the norm, especially in the current era, I have seen remarkably misguided efforts where therapists seem to be fixated on finding sexual abuse and evidence of dissociation. Treatment must be carefully directed toward evaluating what is known about the patient and moving the patient toward reducing internal fragmentation and dissociation. Therapists must be very cautious about conjectures of presumed abuse and any activities or interventions that tend to reinforce or elaborate internal states.

Frequent difficulties with pseudo-dissociation appear to arise from patients who erroneously come to believe that they have DID. Some of these patients do have some level of dissociative experiences and some have trauma in their backgrounds. Others seem to suffer primarily from severe personality disorders with intense identity diffusion and internal emptiness. For many of these patients, the DID diagnosis appears to become a focus for their lives. Even in the initial stages of treatment, they embrace the diagnosis and often speak of themselves as "multiple," using the pronoun "we," and referring to their "alters." Some patients arrive at the conclusion that they have DID because the description of different internal self-states resonates with aspects of their own experience. To others, it may seem appealing to adopt a diagnosis that has a dramatic presentation and draws attention to themselves. Others seem to assume the diagnosis to explain why their impulses or behaviors are out of their control, and point to their "multiplicity" as a way of disavowing responsibility for their actions. In any case, if the DID diagnosis is inappropriate, it is detrimental to treatment. To the extent to which patients cling to a false DID identity, the treatment of the true underlying difficulties is not possible. Furthermore, to the extent that pseudo-DID patients use the diagnosis to disavow out-of-control behaviors, improvement in impulse control and stabilization is unlikely.

The clinical implications of these pseudo-DID presentations are varied. For patients who have *some* dissociation, acceptance of their internal experience is important, and treatment can then be directed in a way that helps them reduce both the internal sense of fragmentation and their emphasis on the DID. However, for patients who have nondissociative disorders but believe they have DID, other interventions may be necessary. In situations where a previous therapy was focused on the misdiagnosis of DID, but the patient is not invested in the diagnosis, it may be simple and effective to suggest that the patient has entered into a new phase of treatment and the "DID" will rapidly resolve. However, in cases where the belief in DID is central to the patient's identity, gentle but direct confrontation may be necessary. As painful as this process may be for both patient and therapist, it avoids putting the therapist in the position of colluding with a false diagnosis and working on issues that are unrelated to the central problems.

Some psychologically healthier persons appear to use DID as a metaphor. That is, they can identify internal parts of themselves that feel poorly integrated with their primary identities (e.g., an inner child). For the most part, these patients are able to easily recognize that all internal parts are components of a single self, and they readily assume responsibility for their inner selves and their behavior. Although efforts to clarify these patients' sense of self are important, there is rarely the need to confront or change the way they understand themselves. For the most part, such patients move easily into internal empathy, cooperation, and self-care, and the identity of having separate internal identities is given up when it no longer serves a useful purpose. The following clinical example illustrates the use of DID as a metaphor:

Nancy, a 35-year-old married nurse, was well aware of having grown up in a family that routinely victimized her. She recalled her childhood as a painful period in which she was treated as the family maid and nanny, caring for her parents and younger siblings. She was viewed with contempt by her mother and regularly brutalized by her alcoholic and psychotic father. During the course of treatment, she also uncovered clear memories of near-murderous abuse, including being thrown out of a window that explained current radiologic evidence of old healed fractures of her arm, ribs, and skull. Although she understood that she had been abused, Nancy had difficulty believing that she had not brought on the abuse by bad behavior or inadequate completion of her assigned tasks, and she was able to have little compassion for herself. However, as the therapy progressed, she began to have awareness of a very young part of her that continued to experience intense pain related to her childhood abuse. She named this part Little Nancy and began to talk about and relate to this part of herself almost as if it were a separate self. She began to have increasing compassion for her younger self, particularly after a brief hypnotic session in which Big Nancy visualized Little Nancy as physically bowed under the weight of adult responsibilities and overwhelming shame and humiliation. This intervention marked a turning point in Nancy being able to accept herself as a whole, letting down her stoic defenses, understanding her childhood experiences, and being better able to care for herself.

Neurologic presentations that resemble DID are uncommon but not rare. Some investigators have linked dissociative phenomena to neurologic abnormalities such as temporal lobe or complex partial seizures (Mesulam, 1981; Schenk & Bear, 1981). Although so-called soft findings on neurologic examination and EEG and MRI abnormalities are present in many traumatized patients (Teicher et al., 1997), patients with neurologically based dissociation may have clearer positive findings, particularly on neuropsychological testing. Of particular note in these presentations is long-standing pervasive depersonalization and derealization. Any difficulties with memory are largely the result of difficulties with focused attention and encoding rather than true amnesia. A known history of abuse or traumatization is often not present. A clinical example follows:

Stephanie, a 27-year-old college graduate, was admitted to a trauma program because of long-standing difficulties with dissociative symptoms. She had struggled with a severe learning disability for most of her life, but she was able to complete college through much work and self-discipline. However, she continued to suffer with chronic depersonalization and derealization, as well as difficulties retaining information. A therapist had questioned the possibility of DID, and although there was no known history of trauma, Stephanie had begun to have dreams of "some kind of sexual abuse." A neurologic evaluation and an awake EEG failed to reveal any abnormalities, but neuropsychological testing showed findings consistent with right brain dysfunction, and an MRI scan of the brain revealed a one-centimeter cyst in the right temporal lobe. Stephanie was advised to seek treatment that would address her style of learning and processing information, and would help her become grounded in states that minimized the depersonalization and derealization.

FACTITIOUS OR MALINGERED DID

As with any other diagnosis that captures public and professional attention, DID may be simulated. Information about DID is widespread, and as noted by Spanos and colleagues (Spanos, Weekes, & Lorne, 1985):

> When given the appropriate inducements, enacting the multiple personality role is a relatively easy task. . . . Following the rules for being a multiple means remembering which experiences, behavior, and preferences go with Identity A and which go with Identity B. (p. 372)

In my experience with hundreds of cases of DID, the deliberate simulation of this disorder, while not common, is far from rare. Such a possibility should be carefully considered in the differential diagnosis of possible DID patients, both as malingering in forensic settings (Coons, 1991) and as factitious disorder in clinical settings (Brick & Chu, 1991; Chu, 1991a; Coons & Milstein, 1994; Kluft, 1987c; Thomas, 2001).

How can a clinician approach the task of sorting through potential fiction? In addition to the careful examination of presenting features, Kluft (1987c) suggested other areas of differences between true DID patients and malingerers. For example, malingerers generally were unable to manifest consistent alternate personalities over time in terms of memory, affect, and personal characteristics. Malingerers were generally unconvincing about any evidence of dividedness in the distant past. Malingerers did not have histories of prior unsuccessful treatments. Malingerers tended to have stereotyped good/bad identities, whereas true DID cases commonly showed a "tetrad configuration of depleted host, persecutors, traumatized alters, and protectors" (p. 112). True DID patients rarely "played up" their symptoms and tended to "minimize public manifestations of their disorder" (p. 112).

Psychiatrist Ann Thomas, MD (2001), extended Kluft's work by proposing 12 clinical observations that suggested factitious disorder or malingering in 18 cases that she studied, including the following:

> [1] having a score above 60 on the Dissociative Experiences Scale (DES), [2] reporting dissociative symptoms inconsistent with the reporting on the DES, [3] being able to tell a chronological life story and to sequence temporal events,

[4] using the first person over a range of affect, [5] being able to express strong negative affect, [6] bringing "proof" of a dissociative diagnosis to the consultation, [7] having told persons other than close confidants about the alleged abuse or alleged dissociative diagnosis, [8] reporting alleged abuse that was inconsistent with the medical or psychiatric history or volunteering allegations of cult or ritualized abuse, [9] telling of alleged abuse without accompanying shame, guilt, or suffering, [10] having been involved in community self-help groups, [11] not having symptoms of co-morbid posttraumatic stress disorder, and [12] having obvious secondary gain in having a dissociative diagnosis. (p. 59)

Thomas noted that the patients with factitious DID that she studied had a minimum of eight of the twelve characteristics, whereas genuine DID patients had no more than three.

A somewhat more complicated presentation of factitious DID appears to be a form of Munchausen Syndrome, in which the patient seems to be deliberately fabricating medical and/or psychiatric symptoms with the motivation of remaining in the role of patient. A related syndrome of Munchausen Syndrome By Proxy is manifested by the patient seeming to mold others (most often the patient's children) into having medical or psychiatric difficulties. The underlying psychiatric disorder is almost always a severe personality disorder with borderline and narcissistic features, often based on a history of pervasive childhood deprivation. Often there are both psychological and physical symptoms, as in the following clinical illustration:

Dottie, a 42-year-old nurse and mother of two, was being treated for several psychiatric and medical difficulties. She had a known history of childhood trauma and at various times had been given the diagnoses of PTSD, DID, major depression, and bipolar disorder. Over years she had alternated between periods of reasonable functioning and other periods when she required either medical or psychiatric hospitalization. Dottie had received many different kinds of treatment, including intensive individual psychotherapy, medication, and electroconvulsive therapy. No interventions seemed to bring about lasting improvement.

During one hospitalization for depression, Dottie appeared almost cheerful but intimated that she "knew" her "alters" were planning to kill her. Indeed, the presumed "alters" did talk with her therapist about their rage at being suppressed and their homicidal plans, precipitating a series of suicide precautions. One morning, Dottie appeared very ill. An intensive workup revealed that she had a severe urinary tract infection, and she was transported to a medical unit for treatment. While packing Dottie's clothes, an alert member of the nursing staff spotted a urinary catheter. When confronted by hospital staff, Dottie was evasive, but she did not deny that she had used the catheter to introduce contaminated material into her bladder. On the medical unit, Dottie told the staff that she had multiple personalities and that one of her "alters" was trying to kill her through this method. Dottie also reported that her children had serious problems. Taking one of the nurses into her confidence, she reported that her 14-year-old daughter had DID and that her 10-year-old son was suicidal—a clear manifestation of Munchausen Syndrome By Proxy.

One final twist concerning factitious DID has been seen in the legal arena. There are situations in which patients convince their therapists and other treaters that they have DID, but they later recant the DID and the associated history of abuse. Subsequently, they move on to situations that do not give them sufficient attention, and then go on to accuse their treaters of malpractice and of having implanted false memories of abuse. It is sadly ironic that these patients are accusing others of having believed the very behaviors that they so diligently tried to portray, and that the accusations prolong the attention on them that they pathologically crave.

THE RITUAL ABUSE CONTROVERSY

Ritual abuse (i.e., the systematic and malevolent abuse of children by organized groups of perpetrators involved in cult activities) emerged as an issue in the late 1980s. Many patients, especially those with DID, reported extensive childhood victimization in satanic cults and even adult involvement in such activities. Many clinicians came to believe, based on the reports of their patients, in an organized international underground network of cult participants, many of who were involved in satanism. Canadian psychiatrist George Fraser, MD, edited a well-balanced book on the subject, *The Dilemma of Ritual Abuse* (Fraser, 1997), and succinctly described the common themes of the ritual abuse stories (pp. vii–viii):

> Perverted physical, psychological, and sexual abuse of children and adults is reported in groups frequently claiming or pretending to worship Satan.
> Mind coercion techniques, including terror and isolation, are reportedly used to obtain compliance, discourage defection, and ensure future obedience, allegiance, and secrecy.
> Enforced membership lasts for many years, lasting ideally for life.
> Members may believe themselves wedded or committed to Satan and unable to escape his ever-watchful eye.
> There is obedience to a hierarchy of leadership. Leaders are often called priests or priestesses.
> Ceremonies are said to include the ingestion of blood and urine obtained from humans or animals.
> Human sacrifices allegedly occur, and human body parts may be disposed of in ritualized cannibalistic ceremonies.

Inbreeding and the subsequent desecration of the fetus or newborn are reported. In other cases, some infants are supposedly groomed as future leaders or recruiters.

Members may come from all strata of society. Multigenerational familial participation is said to be common.

Sexual orgies, including pedophilia, promiscuity, and bestiality, reportedly take place. Frequently these acts are done under the influence of mind-altering chemicals. These acts may be filmed for future sale in the pornographic market.

Ceremonies supposedly occur on major Christian feast days or on days relating to natural planetary phases, such as the summer solstice or the cycles of the moon.

Substantial numbers of patients reported such activities in the mid- to late 1980s, primarily among those who were already being treated for recovered memories of childhood abuse and for dissociative disorders. The initial reaction of the professionals who were treating such patients was that a horrific new form of childhood abuse had been discovered. However, some clinicians and academics in the mental health community—from both within and outside the trauma field—voiced skepticism about the factual basis of these recollections (see, for example, Ganaway, 1989), eventually helping to fuel the false memory movement. Much has appeared in the literature concerning the validity of ritual abuse, including books that generally support its existence (Ross, 1995; Sakheim & Devine, 1992) and those that do not accept it as objective reality, understanding it more as a sociological phenomenon (Richardson, Best, & Bromley, 1991; Victor, 1993).

Although the reality of ritual abuse continues to be the subject of heated debate, such activities are now not generally seen as widespread or pervasive, and the genesis of the ritual abuse stories is still unclear. Greaves (1992) offered a number of possible explanations. In addition to the possibility that some accounts are accurate, Greaves discussed the possibility that they are the result of screen memories, urban legends, contamination, contagion, propagation of rumors, or the result of a collective unconscious. Another theory suggests that ritual abuse stories have their basis in some other kind of actual occurrences that were deliberately distorted by abusers (e.g., the simulated killing and dismemberment of a doll being understood by a young child as actual murder).

Screen memories that mask even more distressing realties, displacement or distortions of memory, or elaboration are certainly components of some recall of ritual abuse; Kluft (1997b) provides some excellent clinical examples from his own practice. Contamination and contagion effects are likely causes as well. Some authors (e.g., Greaves, 1992) have noted that ritual abuse stories began to proliferate following the publication of a sensationalistic and religious account of satanic abuse titled *Michelle Remembers* (Smith & Pazder, 1980), although there is little evidence that this work was widely distributed or read. Contagion was certainly a major factor in the late 1980s in specialized inpatient programs, where stories of having been ritually abused were quite common.

Cultural phenomena and collective unconscious human processes have also been suspected as the genesis of ritual abuse memories. It appears too coincidental that the ritual abuse stories share much in common with accounts of alien abduction, where persons believe that they have been held captive and subjected to systematic bodily and sexual intrusions. Similar stories of captivity, murder, and even cannibalism are found in the folklore of many cultures—dark stories such as those found in fairy tales (e.g., Hansel and Gretel) that fascinate, thrill, and horrify children. The common themes may well originate in the human unconscious, representing deep fears and fantasies that become elaborated in culturally acceptable ways.

Despite the skepticism about the validity of accounts of satanic ritual abuse, psychologist David Sakheim, PhD (1996), has pointed out that organized, sadistic, and malevolent abuse is known to occur and is not rare. Although there is no concrete evidence about the existence of the phenomenon of organized transgenerational satanic cults, there is no question that rituals are practiced by neo-satanic churches, self-styled satanic cults, and dabblers and solitary satanists. There have been well-documented instances of activities involving adherents to satanism that involve criminal abduction, rape, and murder that have been fully investigated and confirmed by law enforcement officials.

In addition to occult, solitary, or homegrown satanic activities, there is also well-documented evidence of the systematic abuse and exploitation of children and young adults through child pornography and child prostitution rings and human trafficking activities. Shocking news stories appear periodically of organized and individual criminal activities that occur *sub rosa* in ordinary neighborhoods and locales, but the memory of these occurrences fades rapidly in our collective need to deny their reality. These realities are consistent with our experience that a substantial number of patients seem to have severe and persistent PTSD and complex dissociative disorders based on systematic and deliberate traumatization. While the perpetrating individuals and groups may be isolated rather than part of a widespread conspiracy, the egregious victimization of children results in massive devastation of the self and in ongoing florid and disabling posttraumatic and dissociative symptomatology.

While adherents to the belief in organized ritual abuse have advocated special treatment techniques—deprogramming or even ill-advised exorcism rituals, the serious psychiatric symptomatology and disability of patients who may have been the victims of deliberate and sadistic abuse require even more careful and conservative treatment. Patients who have undergone truly malevolent abuse are the most shattered, vulnerable, and precarious, and the injunction "to do no harm" has priority. With his usual eloquence, Kluft (1997b) has written:

> The patient alleging ritualistic abuse poses an enormous clinical challenge. We can meet that challenge best by marshaling the cumulative wisdom of psychotherapeutic practice and relevant scientific findings and bringing them to bear with compassion and circumspection in these unusual and trying circumstances. (p. 61)

NOT ALL DISSOCIATIVE IDENTITY DISORDERS ARE THE SAME

Although it appears absurd to believe that DID and other severe dissociative disorders can be created through a sociocognitive model where no underlying dissociation exists, it seems likely that the precise symptoms of dissociation can be molded through cultural expectations. How else does one explain the high prevalence of conversion disorders and relatively few cases of DID at the beginning of the 20th century and the opposite proportions 100 years later? It appears that the dissociative effects of trauma can take a variety of different forms depending on cultural norms. Though I disagree with the conclusions of Lilienfeld and Lynn's statement concerning the role of the film and book versions of *Sybil* (Babbin & Petrie, 1976; Schreiber, 1973) in creating false DID syndromes, I don't question that they helped to shape how patients experience their dissociation and what clinicians expect to see in severely dissociative patients. In addition, whatever the most common naturalistically occurring form of severe dissociation might be, I imagine it may well be similar to the syndrome suffered by Shirley Ardell Mason, the real "Sybil."

Given the idea that some dissociative symptomatology may be somewhat malleable, it behooves clinicians to not superimpose any particular model of symptoms on patients. In another famous DID case described in *The Three Faces of Eve* (Thigpen & Cleckley, 1957) and the autobiographical accounts of Chris Costner Sizemore (the real name of "Eve") (Sizemore, 1989; Sizemore & Pittillo, 1977), there was a rather different presentation of personalities. The Thigpen and Cleckley account chronicles the story of the original three personalities—Eve White, Eve Black, and Jane—and ends with their integration. Sizemore tells a quite different story. For many years, various clusters of personalities emerged after the integration of the original three personalities. Usually as a result of some personal crisis, the existing cluster of personalities would disappear, and a new cluster would emerge until there was a final, more stable integration.

Cases of severe dissociative disorders are not all uniform in their symptomatic expression, and not all cases of DID are static and unchanging in their level of dissociation over time. Because dissociation is a stress-responsive phenomenon, it is not surprising that dissociative symptoms can be exacerbated by internal or external stressors. I have observed many cases in which there were multiple identities and more amnesia during a period of crisis, and less clear fragmentation and little amnesia when the crisis resolved. In one unusual case, a patient had the sudden onset of quite distinct and separate personalities following electroconvulsive therapy (ECT) for her depression (Ellison, Chu, & Henry, 2000). Before the ECT, she reported a history of severe childhood physical and sexual abuse, much of which had been confirmed by other family members. She described long-standing dissociative symptoms, including depersonalization, derealization, and amnesia for some childhood experiences, but no distinct personalities. After the ECT, the patient appeared to be somewhat hypomanic and manifested identities that were distinctive and consistent, bearing names and well-defined characteristics.

This sudden, fully elaborated appearance of DID symptoms rapidly resolved less than three weeks later, and the patient's level of dissociative symptoms returned to the pre-ECT level. In this case, I believe that the physiologic stress from the ECT and the psychological stress of the hypomania induced an exacerbation of the existing dissociative symptoms, and the DID-like symptoms resolved with the effective treatment of the hypomania.

I have had the privilege of working with a bright and articulate woman with DID or DDNOS over the past 25 years. She clearly has a dissociative disorder with numerous split-off identities, but she has had a very atypical presentation, which I describe here.

Ruth was a well-spoken, pleasant woman in her 40s when she came to see me in the mid-1980s. Tall, with flowing white hair, she had a rather intense (but also detached and intellectualized) way of speaking and relating. A self-taught computer expert, Ruth described herself as an "alien being" who shared nothing in common with the rest of humankind, had no bonds with others, and was happiest when she didn't have to interact with anyone. From her own research, she had correctly concluded that she had a dissociative disorder. Although over the years I have not seen dramatic state switches, Ruth has reported numerous named and unnamed internal identities that communicate with her (e.g., "I'm hearing someone inside really disagreeing with what I'm saying" and "I don't know who that was that was talking to you"). Ruth's dissociative disorder most likely stemmed from a prolonged period in her early childhood when she was in a small children's residential center, where she was being treated for a chronic infection. She had not been expected to survive, but after nearly four years she eventually recovered. Ruth has never had visual or verbal memories of anything that happened at the residential center, but she has clear implicit recall of the experience in terms of feelings of horror, terror and panic, and intense bodily sensations of tingling, burning, and the "creepy crawlies."

In the early years of our work together, Ruth's internal experience was quite chaotic with unwanted powerful thoughts and feelings emerging at various times, which she sometimes could only control by using what she metaphorically called "the plunger." She has always had a deeply felt sense of her internal world that she experienced in dynamic and nonverbal ways. Most of the time, she felt disconnected with others. However, on occasion, she resonated deeply with writings, lectures, photographs or films, and on rare occasions in direct conversations; she once wrote to a colleague: "It made a great deal of difference to be able to talk with someone who understands, on a deep level, many aspects of my mindset and the non-symbolic nature of the way my cognitive webs form and evolve. When I start attempting to articulate things that I experience in non-linear, multi-perspective forms most people are polite but dismissive. You listened, really listened, and engaged with the space I've been trying to actualize for 30 years."

In addition to her skills in programming and hypertext, Ruth has been certain that she is fundamentally a mathematician, fascinated not with the mechanics and algorithms of numbers, but with their music, meaning, and structure. Despite having almost no training and no advanced skills in mathematics, she is able to relate to academic mathematicians at the university where she works, sharing a common language and feel for the subject. Ruth also has studied many ways of trying to access her internal world. In addition to psychotherapy with me, she is quite expert in Buddhist meditative practices and has pursued several mind-body practices that give her glimpses of different aspects of herself and allow greater expression of her emotions and ideas. She has also had interests in various artistic activities, including drawing and painting, which she has avidly pursued.

Periodically, early in our years together, Ruth would have a massive internal decompensation in response to serious life stresses, where her internal world collapsed into disorganization. She would gradually reconstitute in a significantly different internal configuration, with changes in the characteristics of identities and with certain identities having more prominence and others becoming submerged and sealed away. Although these meltdowns have almost completely abated in recent years, she would still have remarkable discontinuity in her sense of self and access to her inner resources. For example, there were times when she would be feverishly engrossed in her art, only to have no interest in it at all a week later. Ruth's passion for math was sometimes deeply buried and at other times at the forefront of her consciousness. She was both amazingly associative, capable of dizzying and complex patterns of thought, and profoundly dissociative, being completely unable to access certain feelings and knowledge that were previously available to her.

Ruth has made extraordinary improvements over the years. Her progressive integration has been slow and subtle as she has struggled to live in what used to feel like a completely foreign world. She still has clear and separate identities, but there is markedly improved functioning as a whole system, and the discontinuities and difficulties in access are much diminished. She has slowly been able to allow herself to feel more related to others, although she is still happiest with solitude. She continues the process of mourning what she has lost because of her dissociation and is moving toward even greater integration, as she has begun the process of owning some of the internal identities as integral parts of herself.

FUTURE DIRECTIONS IN THE FIELD OF
TRAUMA AND DISSOCIATION

In laying out diagnostic and treatment principles for the treatment of complex PTSD and dissociative disorders, this book has recounted the story of the growth of awareness, interest, and controversy in these areas over the past 30 years. This story is just beginning. There is much to be understood and accomplished over the coming years and decades. In terms of diagnosis, there needs to be increasing sophistication about the subtypes of trauma-related disorders. Similar to other areas in psychiatry, many of the diagnoses that we use are broad categories that do not distinguish between common variants that have differing symptomatic manifestations and require somewhat different treatment approaches. For example, as I conclude the process of writing this edition, the lead article in the *American Journal of Psychiatry* describes a dissociative subtype of PTSD (Lanius et al., 2010) that is primarily characterized by symptoms of dissociation in the wake of prolonged traumatic experiences (e.g., chronic childhood trauma or combat experiences). In contrast to forms of PTSD where intrusive symptoms such as flashbacks and nightmares predominate, in the dissociative subtype of PTSD, emotions are excessively inhibited in response to recall of traumatic memories, leading to a subjective disengagement from the emotional content of the traumatic memory through depersonalization and derealization responses. Based on studies of brain activation in dissociative PTSD and borderline personality disorder, the authors hypothesized that a hyperinhibition of limbic regions by prefrontal areas occurs in situations of excessive emotional stimulation. There are enormous implications for the findings. As I wrote in an accompanying editorial to the paper (Chu, 2010):

> Lanius et al.'s identification of the dissociative subtype of PTSD may offer a rational explanation for one of the major controversies in the field of trauma psychiatry. Many of the empirically based studies that examine clinical treatment of PTSD show that exposure therapy is an effective treatment. That is, treatments that use deliberate reexposure to trauma-related stimuli (e.g., trauma scripts) are thought to result in desensitization of the trauma response and to aid in integration of the traumatic events into ordinary experience. Lanius et al. note that some authors have speculated that overmodulated responses to trauma-related stimuli may prevent the necessary full engagement in exposure. However, there may also be a protective function for the dissociation of memories, affect, and meaning for persons with chronic traumatization. By passing this protective function may result in persons becoming overwhelmed by reliving the trauma and finding that once again that they cannot tolerate, make sense of, or cope with their experiences. Persons with complex PTSD seem to respond better to the phase-oriented treatments that were developed in the 1990s, which focus on building better functioning in multiple domains prior to grappling directly with traumatic memories. The differences between the subtypes of PTSD may well account for the variations seen in disparate traumatized populations. (p. 617)

The publication of the new DSM-5 is expected in 2013, and the current proposed revisions are now public and being debated. There are relatively minor changes in the proposed diagnostic criteria for PTSD and dissociative disorders (American Psychiatric Association, 2010a, 2010b). For example, dissociative fugue is subsumed as a subtype of dissociative amnesia, and the definition of identity disruption in DID includes the experience of possession in order to reduce the use of DDNOS. However, the existing DSM-IV nosology and categories are largely intact, not addressing the issue of the very common real-world manifestations of chronic traumatization such as complex PTSD. Similarly, PTSD and acute stress disorder remain in the Anxiety Disorders category, despite some discussion about whether trauma-related disorders (including some of the dissociative disorders) should be grouped together.

In terms of treatment, there also needs to be an increased level of sophistication regarding the assessment of patients, including an understanding of prognosis, and the application of treatment models and treatment modalities. Several authors have offered their understanding of the factors that influence treatment prognosis (Boon, 1997; Horevitz & Loewenstein, 1994; Kluft, 1994, 1997a; Simon, 1999; van der Kolk, 2002). And now a new paper (Baars et al., 2011) reports on research regarding prognosis, confirming many of the impressions of these authors; a large group of expert clinicians were found to be in agreement that particular patient characteristics are impediments to more complete and successful treatments: lack of motivation, lack of healthy relationships, lack of healthy therapeutic relationships, lack of internal and external resources, severe Axis I or Axis II comorbidity, difficulties with attachment, and self-destructiveness. These findings will help clinicians to appropriately assess and understand specific patients in terms of treatment staging and realistic expectations for improvement. Simply put, the effects of severe and chronic traumatization are varied, so the treatments for patients should reflect this complexity. Clinicians must be flexible in their thinking and not too rigidly apply theoretical and treatment models that are based only on limited experience or presumptive bias.

Treating patients with complex PTSD and dissociative disorders requires the flexibility to apply the appropriate methods of treatment for specific patients depending on their internal and external resources and on the characteristics of their difficulties. Several alternative treatment modalities have been used with considerable clinical success for traumatized patients. Hypnosis has a long history of utility in treatment, and eye movement desensitization and reprocessing (EMDR) has applicability to the treatment of complex PTSD and dissociative disorders if appropriate modifications are made in its use (Beere, 2009; Fine & Berkowitz, 2001; Forgash & Knipe, 2008; Gelinas, 2003; Paulsen, 2008; Twombly, 2005). Newer modalities such as sensorimotor psychotherapy (Ogden et al., 2006) and internal family systems therapy (Schwartz, 1997) have been well received by the clinical community, but more time and experience is necessary to assess their efficacy with the severely traumatized patient population.

Going forward, more and different treatment interventions will be developed, but clinicians need to use them only with proper training and only as appropriate for the treatment of specific patients and not as a substitute for solid clinical practices. Even with new developments, treatment of the severely traumatized population will continue to require skill, sophistication, and patience. It is probably accurate to predict that although the trauma field will have new approaches to treating complex posttraumatic and dissociative disorders, no new interventions will offer dramatic shortcuts to the time and care that is necessary to provide optimal treatment.

There are diverse unanswered questions in the field of trauma psychiatry and future research that will play a critical role in the understanding and treatment of traumatized patients. For example, although several papers have been published concerning the issue of sexuality in patients who have histories of extensive childhood sexual abuse (see, for example, the articles in Chu & Bowman, 2002), there have been no systematic studies of sexual orientation, gender identity and sexual adaptation in this patient population. It seems likely that early sexual abuse must profoundly affect adult sexual identity and practices. Research is needed to understand the apparently high prevalence of gay and lesbian sexual abuse survivors, how early sexual trauma can result in hyposexuality or hypersexuality, and how early frightening sexual experiences are transformed and adapted into healthy sexual functioning. Such research is critical in order to help patients address a crucial domain in their lives that is generally too little discussed and remains shrouded in secrecy and shame.

There are other areas worth studying that may be more personally uncomfortable. We in the trauma field should also be interested in understanding the perpetrators of childhood sexual abuse, despite our reflexive revulsion concerning them that is based on the harm they have inflicted on our patients. For example, there is evidence that pedophilia—sexual attraction to minor children—is not particularly uncommon in the normal adult male population (Hall, Hirschman, & Oliver, 1995). The causes of pedophilia are not well established and may have genetic or hormonal influences, and they may be related to issues around socialization and early attachments. There is currently little evidence of a link between pedophilia and having been sexually abused (Garland & Dougher, 1990). There is also scant evidence that those with pedophilic traits are routinely at risk to perpetrate sexual abuse. Presumably, most adults who experience sexual attraction to children—especially those who are also attracted to adults—do not act on their impulses and find ways to sublimate them. What distinguishes those with pedophilic traits and those who actually molest children or become serial offenders? What can the professional community do to identify and help those who are at risk to sexually offend? There is only rudimentary research in this taboo area, which has the potential to yield important information in the prevention of child sexual abuse.

In more traditional areas of study, more is needed to assist clinicians to understand what processes in treatment actually help patients. Many of the interventions that we use have not been tested. Dalenberg's (2000) book, *Countertransference and the Treatment of Trauma*, is an illuminating exception to this, where her clinical experience combined with analysis of transcripts of therapy sessions and experimental studies provides insights into what is helpful in psychotherapy. Dalenberg's empirical work contradicts some traditional tenets of therapy; for example, that the therapist should always withhold personal reactions or not admit mistakes. Her psychotherapy research has shown that an owned mistake can be a building block for trust (Dalenberg, 2004). Appropriate disclosures of therapists' feelings and reactions (particularly if they are already obvious) and a willingness to discuss personal limitations advance the therapeutic process as patients come to trust therapists' honesty and authenticity. As Dalenberg (2000) has observed, "It is a central task of trauma therapy for therapists to present themselves as objects that can be clung to, rejected, and returned to without punishment" (p. 230).

Too little is written about what to actually say and do in therapy sessions. While the scientific literature is replete with valuable research findings and academic discussions of theory and treatment, there are few publications of the actual process of psychotherapy itself. Much of what we clinicians do in the important day-to-day work with patients has been passed down through oral tradition in supervision, consultation, and workshops, or has been learned through personal experience. Case reports, case series, and clinical discussions with actual examples of the processes and dialogs used in therapy rarely appear in the literature. Experienced and accomplished psychotherapists need to both study and write about what they do, in order to pass down their wisdom and expertise to others who struggle with uncertainty and isolation in their clinical practice, and to future generations of clinicians.

The clinical and academic communities involved with trauma treatment have a responsibility to continue to educate the public and our governmental institutions about the effects of psychological trauma. It has been an interesting development that although U.S. governmental officials and the American public have been sympathetic and supportive of the military troops in the long conflicts in Afghanistan and Iraq, there have been repeated accounts about the lack of anticipation concerning the effects of combat trauma and the much higher than expected levels of posttraumatic syndromes of impairment and dysfunction. For example, in a comprehensive analysis of more than 13,000 questionnaires from Iraqi war veterans, researchers found prevalence rates of PTSD ranging from 21% to 31% and rates of depression ranging from 11% to 16%, with high comorbidity concerning alcohol misuse and aggression (Thomas et al., 2010). Given what we in the trauma field have learned about the impact of traumatic events, there should have been less surprise about the high incidence of PTSD and the associated problems of depression, substance use, disruption of family structures, and even suicide in returning veterans of these conflicts. Although we in the professional community see ourselves primarily as clinicians, teachers, and researchers, we—and our professional associations—have an important role in educating others and assuring that proper attention and resources are allocated to the victims of trauma and victimization.

This book began by tracing the pendulum swings of societal and professional belief in the existence and effects of childhood abuse. However, an even wider acceptance of dissociation and traumatically based disorders is just the beginning of understanding the complexities of posttraumatic and dissociative symptoms and trauma-related adaptations. Those of us who study and treat patients with DID and pathological dissociation have developed a healthy respect for the complexities of these difficulties. We have learned that severe dissociative presentations and reports of abuse can result from a variety of different circumstances. Certainly, trauma-related cases of DID and dissociation are prevalent in patient populations, and our understanding of the relationship between childhood trauma and adult dissociation is now based on both empirical research and theoretical models. However, we must also acknowledge that apparent DID and dissociative symptoms may sometimes emerge from very different circumstances. Those of us who treat and study trauma-related disorders must now integrate multiple views of dissociation.

Some very wise mental health professionals have passionately argued about dissociation and particularly about DID, reminiscent of John Godfrey Saxe's (1851) satirical poem entitled "The Blind Men and Elephant"—his version of an Indian fable, possibly attributable to Mualana Jalaluddin Rumi, a 13th-century Afghani mystic. In this fable, six learned blind men of Indostan went to study the elephant. Each felt only a part of the elephant and concluded that the elephant must be like the part he touched; that is, like a wall (the elephant's side), spear (tusk), snake (trunk), tree (leg), fan (ear), or rope (tail). Each blind wise man was convinced that he was correct and persisted in his views.

This fable has its analogy in our present-day controversy over the nature of dissociative phenomena. Although views of traumatically based dissociative phenomena may have more general validity, we are like the learned but foolish blind men of Indostan if we understand our initial ideas and our own early clinical experiences to be the *only* valid interpretation of all that we observe. This verse (Chu, 1997a), adapted from Saxe's satirical poem, perhaps may serve as a reminder that the important and serious work with traumatized patients requires honesty, flexibility, integrity, and humor.

The Blind Men and the "Elephant"
(with apologies to John Godfrey Saxe)

Six men who had great expertise
In the human mind,

Went to see some Multiples,
To see if they could find

What circumstances might have led
To the symptoms of this kind.

The First, a learned specialist
In trauma most abstruse,

Saw clearly that traumatic pasts
Of patients was no ruse.

Cried he, "It's clear that Multiples
Have always had abuse!"

The Second, an able therapist
Of noted mastery,

Hearing tales of devilish doings,
Said, "It's no mystery

That Multiples have likely had
A cult-ish history!"

The Third, a scholar of repute,
Said, "Multiples conform

To their treaters expectations
And the cultural norm.

They're grand hysterics who conceal
Their conflicts 'neath a storm!"

The Fourth, a famed psychiatrist
Who knew biology

Said, "What these Multiples are like
Is mighty clear to me.

I don't acknowledge that they are
Occurring naturally."

The Fifth, a teacher of renown,
Was skeptical at best:

"These Multiples are feigning woe
To see if they can wrest

Attention from their therapists;
Impairment is their quest!"

The Sixth, a legal-minded sage
Saw conspiracy

'Tween therapists and Multiples
To form false memory:

"They think that their 'abuse' should have
A legal remedy!"

And so these men of mental health
Disputed loud and long,

Each in his own opinion
Exceeding stiff and strong.

And each was partly in the right,
And all in part were wrong.

Afterword: Why We Do This Work[1]

The challenges involved in clinical work with traumatized and dissociative patients are sometimes all too clear. Many of us who treat survivors of childhood abuse find our practices flooded with persons who have suffered devastating victimization and who present for treatment with a nightmarish mix of problems that may include out-of-control dissociative and posttraumatic symptoms, depression, chronic anxiety, self-mutilation, continuous suicidal impulses, substance abuse and eating disorders, enormous self-hate, intense aloneness, and pervasive mistrust of others. Furthermore, having grown up in abusive environments, our patients almost inevitably reenact the interpersonal battle-grounds of their family relationships with us. They recreate scenarios of victimization, betrayal, and abandonment, sometimes through exceedingly unpleasant mechanisms including control, manipulation, and exploitation that mirror their childhood experiences. Perhaps the most dysphoric experience of working with our patients concerns the empathy and involvement that is necessary for their treatment. To be effective, we must often feel the unbearable and explosive torment that constitutes the daily experience of those who we seek to help.

Many of us entered the field of mental health with considerable naïveté. We wanted to help others through involving ourselves in their lives. We felt if we could only be good enough for our patients through exercising kind and thoughtful care that they would respond with positive growth and healing. Moreover (although we may not have admitted this), we hoped that patients would see us as compassionate, sensitive, and supportive, and would reward us with their respect, appreciation, and gratitude. Confronted with the realities of clinical practice, we soon learned that none of this was likely to occur quickly, and most of us developed strong skills in delayed gratification. We learned that the paths we follow with our patients is often long, painful, and not always in our control. Some of these paths are exceeding difficult, and it is only through patience and

---

[1] Adapted from a column in the Newsletter of the International Society for the Study of Dissociation (Chu, 1997b).

endurance that patients are able to perceive that their fleeting moments of peace and happiness are beginning to mesh into a stable fabric of true recovery.

Why, then, do we do this work? Undoubtedly, some reasons are personal. Many of us have had our own painful experiences of feeling lost, victimized, or disenfranchised. We identify with our patients (hopefully not too strongly) and we use our own experiences (hopefully not too prominently) in our work. And, of course, there is the element of fascination—that all-too-human trait that underlies our intense interest in stories of appalling human misfortune. However, many of us who survive and even thrive in this field rely on three areas of gratification. The first is skill. We learn to help those who are terribly damaged by their experiences. We are forced to examine the essential elements of what actually helps persons heal from victimization. We learn how to help patients cope with uncontrollable and overwhelming symptoms. We develop the skills around changing profoundly negative personal beliefs and assisting patients in building a new sense of identity. We learn (often the hard way) about maintaining therapeutic perspective and therapeutic neutrality, limits and boundaries, and the structure of treatment. We develop a high level of interpersonal skills in negotiating complicated and painful interactions with patients, learning how to combine empathy with confrontation, and providing both understanding and the imperative to change. We justifiably can take pride in having the ability to treat those who others see as too difficult and too damaged to help.

The second area of gratification is personal growth and wisdom. We are changed from our work with traumatized patients. We learn some vital truths about human beings—many negative traits certainly, but also about the indomitable human spirit and the ability to struggle against extraordinary odds to achieve fulfillment. We learn how we all depend on our connections with others and the value of a sense of community. We are tested to find meaning where there seems to be none, and learn about the value of patience, introspection, and perseverance. Through our work we are exposed to our own intense and uncomfortable feelings, such as helplessness, panic, and isolation, and even anger, hatred, and sadism. In integrating these feelings we learn self-acceptance. We achieve some wisdom about what we can do and what we cannot do, and in the process come to a better self-understanding of our own strengths and limitations.

The third area from which we derive gratification is the pleasure and satisfaction of having some of our patients actually get better—eventually. They develop a healthy and positive sense of themselves, and they become ever more skilled in dealing with their lives. Having been able to acknowledge their past traumatization and having found ways to engage with others despite having been victimized, some of our patients achieve a striking depth of character that has been forged through overcoming adversity. We are an essential part of this process of healing from trauma. One patient described this well:

> It has been an incredibly long journey. I'm a different person than I used to be. When I was young and in such pain, I didn't know there was any other world. I thought I knew everything, but I didn't know anything. I only knew my pain. It has taken so many years to dismantle the negative and destructive structures of

my life so that I could have the chance to rebuild my life on solid foundations. I now know that I'm a good and decent person. I like myself and other people, and I know how to deal with the world—perhaps even better than people that haven't had to go through what I've gone through. I not only *exist* in life, but I actually *live* my life. I know you will say that I have been primarily responsible for getting better. I agree, but I am certain that I couldn't have done it without you. You believed in me, you listened to me, you put up with me, and you stood by me. Your being there for me has helped me become someone that I never dreamed I could become. You will always be a part of me and I will always carry you with me.

That is why we do this work.

Appendix 1: The Dissociative Experiences Scale (DES and DES-T)

In 1986, Drs. Eve Bernstein Carlson and Frank W. Putnam (based at the time at the National Institutes of Mental Health) introduced a scale called the Dissociative Experiences Scale (DES), which made it possible to quantify the level of dissociative symptoms in individual patients (Bernstein & Putnam, 1986). The level of these symptoms were elevated in patients with trauma-related disorders such as PTSD and dissociative disorders, but they were not substantially elevated in patients with other psychiatric and neurologic disorders (including temporal lobe epilepsy in which depersonalization and derealization are markedly elevated but with only small elevations in pervasive amnesia). The Dissociative Experiences Scale (DES) consists of 28 items that describe common dissociative experiences. Each individual item asks about the percentage of time (from 0% to 100%) that a particular dissociative symptom is experienced. The overall DES score is the average of all the individual scores. Although the DES was designed as a research instrument, it is an excellent source for clinical inquiries concerning dissociative symptoms and a good clinical screening tool for determining the possible presence of trauma-related disorders. Scores of 20 or more are consistent with various kinds of posttraumatic or dissociative disorders. Median DES scores for participants in the original study were:

	N (%)	Median Scores
Participants scoring at or above the median scores for		
Normals	81 (83%)	4.28
Agoraphobia	71 (72%)	7.38
Schizophrenia	32 (33%)	20.63
PTSD	24 (24%)	31.30
Dissociative identity disorder	6 (6%)	57.10

Two versions of the DES exist. The original DES-I asks respondents to make slash marks on a 100-mm line estimating the percentage of time that they have the specific dissociative experience (the score for each item is the nearest 5-mm point, e.g., 0, 5, 10, etc.). The DES-II asks respondents to circle a percentage number (e.g., 0%, 10%, 20%... 100%) indicating the frequency that they experience the dissociative symptom (Bernstein & Putnam, 1993). The DES-II has the same reliability and validity as the original DES and is presented here for its ease in completing and scoring.

There are three subscales of the DES that can be useful in teasing apart the various components of respondents' dissociative experiences for clinical or research purposes (Bernstein & Putnam, 1993). The amnestic dissociation subscale includes items 3, 4, 5, 6, 8, 10, 25, and 26. The absorption and imaginative involvement subscale includes items 2, 14, 15, 16, 17, 18, 20, 22, and 23. The depersonalization and derealization subscale includes items 7, 11, 12, 13, 27, and 28. Scores for the subscales can be calculated by dividing the sum of the item scores divided by the number of items in each subscale.

The Dissociative Experiences Scale Taxon (DES-T; Waller & Ross, 1997) is an eight-item subscale of the full-scale DES. The format is the same as the full-scale DES, with each item scored on a scale from 1 to 100 and the overall score being the mean of the eight items. The DES-T distinguishes pathological dissociation more accurately than does the full-scale DES, with a cutoff score of 20 capturing nearly 90% of cases of DID and DDNOS.

DISSOCIATIVE EXPERIENCES SCALE II

This questionnaire consists of 28 questions about experiences you have had in your daily life. We are interested in how often you have had these experiences. It is important, however, that your answers show how often these experiences happen to you when you *are not* under the influence of alcohol or drugs. To answer the questions, please determine to what degree the experience described in the question applies to you and circle the appropriate number to show what percentage of the time you have had the experience.

Example: 0%   10   20   (30)   40   50   60   70   80   90   100%

1. Some people have the experience of driving a car and suddenly realizing that they don't remember what has happened during all or part of the trip. Circle a number to show what percentage of the time this happens to you.

   0%   10   20   30   40   50   60   70   80   90   100%

2. Some people find that sometimes they are listening to someone talk and they suddenly realize that they did not hear part or all of what was just said. Circle a number to show what percentage of the time this happens to you.

   0%   10   20   30   40   50   60   70   80   90   100%

3. Some people have the experience of finding themselves in a place and having no idea how they got there. Circle a number to show what percentage of the time this happens to you.

    0%   10   20   30   40   50   60   70   80   90   100%

4. Some people have the experience of finding themselves dressed in clothes that they don't remember putting on. Circle a number to show what percentage of the time this happens to you.

    0%   10   20   30   40   50   60   70   80   90   100%

5. Some people have the experience of finding new things among their belongings that they do not remember buying. Circle a number to show what percentage of the time this happens to you.

    0%   10   20   30   40   50   60   70   80   90   100%

6. Some people sometimes find that they are approached by people that they do not know who call them by another name or insist that they have met them before. Circle a number to show what percentage of the time this happens to you.

    0%   10   20   30   40   50   60   70   80   90   100%

7. Some people sometimes have the experience of feeling as though they are standing next to themselves or watching themselves do something, and they actually see themselves as though they were looking at another person. Circle a number what percentage of the time this happens to you.

    0%   10   20   30   40   50   60   70   80   90   100%

8. Some people are told that they sometimes do not recognize friends or family members. Circle a number to show what percentage of the time this happens to you.

    0%   10   20   30   40   50   60   70   80   90   100%

9. Some people find that they have no memory for some important events in their lives (for example, a wedding or graduation). Circle a number to show what percentage of the important events in your life you have no memory for.

    0%   10   20   30   40   50   60   70   80   90   100%

10. Some people have the experience of being accused of lying when they do not think that they have lied. Circle a number to show what percentage of the time this happens to you.

    0%   10   20   30   40   50   60   70   80   90   100%

11. Some people have the experience of looking in a mirror and not recognizing themselves. Circle a number to show what percentage of the time this happens to you.

    0%   10   20   30   40   50   60   70   80   90   100%

12. Some people sometimes have the experience of feeling that other people, objects, and the world around them are not real. Circle a number to show what percentage of the time this happens to you.

    0%   10   20   30   40   50   60   70   80   90   100%

13. Some people sometimes have the experience of feeling that their body does not seem to belong to them. Circle a number to show what percentage of the time this happens to you.

    0%   10   20   30   40   50   60   70   80   90   100%

14. Some people have the experience of sometimes remembering a past event so vividly that they feel as if they were reliving that event. Circle a number to show what percentage of the time this happens to you.

    0%   10   20   30   40   50   60   70   80   90   100%

15. Some people have the experience of not being sure whether things that they remember happening really did happen or whether they just dreamed them. Circle a number to show what percentage of the time this happens to you.

    0%   10   20   30   40   50   60   70   80   90   100%

16. Some people have the experience of being in a familiar place but finding it strange and unfamiliar. Circle a number to show what percentage of the time this happens to you.

    0%   10   20   30   40   50   60   70   80   90   100%

17. Some people find that when they are watching television or a movie they become so absorbed in the story that they are unaware of other events happening around them. Circle a number to show what percentage of the time this happens to you.

    0%   10   20   30   40   50   60   70   80   90   100%

18. Some people sometimes find that they become so involved in a fantasy or daydream that it feels as though it were really happening to them. Circle a number to show what percentage of the time this happens to you.

    0%   10   20   30   40   50   60   70   80   90   100%

19. Some people find that they sometimes are able to ignore pain. Circle a number to show what percentage of the time this happens to you.

    0%   10   20   30   40   50   60   70   80   90   100%

20. Some people find that they sometimes sit staring off into space, thinking of nothing, and are not aware of the passage of time. Circle a number to show what percentage of the time this happens to you.

    0%   10   20   30   40   50   60   70   80   90   100%

21. Some people sometimes find that when they are alone they talk out loud to themselves. Circle a number to show what percentage of the time this happens to you.

    0%   10   20   30   40   50   60   70   80   90   100%

22. Some people find that in one situation they may act so differently compared to another situation that they feel almost as if they were two different people. Circle a number to show what percentage of the time this happens to you.

    0%   10   20   30   40   50   60   70   80   90   100%

23. Some people sometimes find that in certain situations they are able to do things with amazing ease and spontaneity that would usually be difficult for them (for example, sports, work, social interactions, etc.). Circle a number to show what percentage of the time this happens to you.

    0%   10   20   30   40   50   60   70   80   90   100%

24. Some people sometimes find that they cannot remember whether they have done something or have just thought about doing that thing (for example, not knowing whether they have just mailed a letter or have just thought about mailing it). Circle a number to show what percentage of the time this happens to you.

    0%   10   20   30   40   50   60   70   80   90   100%

25. Some people sometimes find evidence that they have done things that they do not remember doing. Circle a number to show what percentage of the time this happens to you.

    0%   10   20   30   40   50   60   70   80   90   100%

26. Some people sometimes find writings, drawings, or notes among their belongings that they must have done but cannot remember doing. Mark the line to show what percentage of the time this happens to you.

    0%   10   20   30   40   50   60   70   80   90   100%

27. Some people sometimes find that they hear voices inside their head which tell them to do things or comment on things that they are doing. Circle a number to show what percentage of the time this happens to you.

    0%   10   20   30   40   50   60   70   80   90   100%

28. Some people sometimes feel as if they are looking at the world through a fog so that people and objects appear far away or unclear. Circle a number to show what percentage of the time this happens to you.

    0%   10   20   30   40   50   60   70   80   90   100%

DISSOCIATIVE EXPERIENCES SCALE TAXON

This questionnaire consists of eight questions about experiences you have had in your daily life. We are interested in how often you have had these experiences. It is important, however, that your answers show how often these experiences happen to you when you *are not* under the influence of alcohol or drugs. To answer the questions, please determine to what degree the experience described in the question applies to you and circle the appropriate number to show what percentage of the time you have had the experience.

Example: 0%   10   20   (30)   40   50   60   70   80   90   100%

1. Some people have the experience of finding themselves in a place and having no idea how they got there. Circle a number to show what percentage of the time this happens to you.

   0%   10   20   30   40   50   60   70   80   90   100%

2. Some people have the experience of finding new things among their belongings that they do not remember buying. Circle a number to show what percentage of the time this happens to you.

   0%   10   20   30   40   50   60   70   80   90   100%

3. Some people sometimes have the experience of feeling as though they are standing next to themselves or watching themselves do something and they actually see themselves as though they were looking at another person. Circle a number what percentage of the time this happens to you.

   0%   10   20   30   40   50   60   70   80   90   100%

4. Some people are told that they sometimes do not recognize friends or family members. Circle a number to show what percentage of the time this happens to you.

   0%   10   20   30   40   50   60   70   80   90   100%

5. Some people sometimes have the experience of feeling that other people, objects, and the world around them are not real. Circle a number to show what percentage of the time this happens to you.

   0%   10   20   30   40   50   60   70   80   90   100%

6. Some people sometimes have the experience of feeling that their body does not seem to belong to them. Circle a number to show what percentage of the time this happens to you.

   0%   10   20   30   40   50   60   70   80   90   100%

7. Some people find that in one situation they may act so differently compared to another situation that they feel almost as if they were two different people. Circle a number to show what percentage of the time this happens to you.

   0%   10   20   30   40   50   60   70   80   90   100%

8. Some people sometimes find that they hear voices inside their head which tell them to do things or comment on things that they are doing. Circle a number to show what percentage of the time this happens to you.

   0%   10   20   30   40   50   60   70   80   90   100%

Appendix 2: The Somatoform Dissociation Questionnaire (SDQ-20 and SDQ-5)[1]

The 20-item Somatoform Dissociation Questionnaire (SDQ-20; Nijenhuis et al., 1996) evaluates the severity of somatoform dissociation. The SDQ-20 items were derived from a pool of 75 items describing clinically observed somatoform dissociative symptoms that in clinical settings had appeared upon activation of particular dissociative parts of the personality and that could not be medically explained. The items pertain to both negative (e.g., analgesia) and positive dissociative phenomena (e.g., site-specific pain).

Each individual item asks about the frequency that a particular somatoform dissociative symptom is experienced using a Likert 5-point scale, ranging from "1 = this applies to me NOT AT ALL" to "5 = this applies to me EXTREMELY." The respondent is also asked to indicate whether a physician has connected the symptom or bodily experience with a physical disease. In clinical practice the relevant item score can be adjusted to "1" when physical disease is indicated, the medical diagnosis has been checked with the physician who assigned it, and this diagnosis seems valid. The SDQ-20 score, which may range from 20 to 100, is obtained by sum of the individual item scores.

The SDQ-20 discriminates between dissociative identity disorder, dissociative disorder NOS, somatoform disorders, and other psychiatric diagnostic categories. Scores over 30 are significant for the presence of somatoform dissociation. In studies using this scale, most patients with DID scored over 50, most of those with DDNOS scored over 40, and most of those with somatoform disorders scored over 30.

The five-item SDQ-5 was derived from the SDQ-20, and includes the items 4, 8, 13, 15, and 18. The five items as a group discriminated best between patients with dissociative disorders and nondissociative psychiatric comparison patients. The scores can range from 5 to 25. Scores over 8 indicate significant somatoform dissociation and a probable dissociative disorder. Nearly all dissociative disorder patients score over 11.

[1]From "The Scoring and Interpretation of the SDQ-20 and SDQ-5" (Nijenhuis, 2010).

The versions of the SDQ that follow are for use by clinicians who are interested in assessing their patients for somatoform dissociation. If used for research purposes, standard demographic information is also gathered including age, sex, marital status and years of education.

SDQ-20

This questionnaire asks about different physical symptoms or body experiences, which you may have had either briefly or for a longer time. Please indicate to what extent these experiences apply to you *in the past year*. For each statement, please circle the number in the first column that best applies to YOU.

The possibilities are:
    1 = this applies to me NOT AT ALL
    2 = this applies to me A LITTLE
    3 = this applies to me MODERATELY
    4 = this applies to me QUITE A BIT
    5 = this applies to me EXTREMELY

If a symptom or experience applies to you, please indicate whether a *physician* has connected it with a *physical disease*. Indicate this by circling the word YES or NO in the column "Is the physical cause known?" If you circle YES, please write the physical cause (if you know it) on the line.

Example:

Sometimes	Extent to which the symptom or experience applies to you	Is the physical cause known?
My teeth chatter	1 2 3 4 5	NO YES, namely _____
I have cramps in my calves	1 2 3 4 5	NO YES, namely _____

If you have circled a 1 in the first column (i.e., This applies to me NOT AT ALL), you do NOT have to respond to the question about whether the physical cause is known. On the other hand, if you circle 2, 3, 4, or 5, you MUST circle NO or YES in the "Is the physical cause known?" column.

Please do not skip any of the 20 questions. Thank you for your cooperation.

Here are the questions:
    1 = this applies to me NOT AT ALL
    2 = this applies to me A LITTLE
    3 = this applies to me MODERATELY
    4 = this applies to me QUITE A BIT
    5 = this applies to me EXTREMELY

Sometimes	Extent to which the symptom or experience applies to you					Is the physical cause known?
1. I have trouble urinating	1	2	3	4	5	NO YES, namely _____
2. I dislike tastes that I usually like (Women: at times *other than* during pregnancy or monthly periods)	1	2	3	4	5	NO YES, namely _____
3. I hear sounds from nearby as if they were coming from far away	1	2	3	4	5	NO YES, namely _____
4. I have pain while urinating	1	2	3	4	5	NO YES, namely _____
5. My body, or a part of it, feels numb	1	2	3	4	5	NO YES, namely _____
6. People and things look bigger than usual	1	2	3	4	5	NO YES, namely _____
7. I have an attack that resembles an epileptic seizure	1	2	3	4	5	NO YES, namely _____
8. My body, or a part of it, are insensitive to pain	1	2	3	4	5	NO YES, namely _____
9. I dislike smells I usually like	1	2	3	4	5	NO YES, namely _____
10. I feel pain in my genitals (at times *other than* sexual intercourse)	1	2	3	4	5	NO YES, namely _____
11. I cannot hear for a while (as if I am deaf)	1	2	3	4	5	NO YES, namely _____
12. I cannot see for a while (as if I am blind)	1	2	3	4	5	NO YES, namely _____
13. I see things around me differently than usual (for example, as if looking through a tunnel, or merely seeing part of an object)	1	2	3	4	5	NO YES, namely _____
14. I am able to smell much *better* or *worse* (even though I do not have a cold)	1	2	3	4	5	NO YES, namely _____
15. It is as if my body, or part of it, has disappeared	1	2	3	4	5	NO YES, namely _____

1 = this applies to me NOT AT ALL
2 = this applies to me A LITTLE
3 = this applies to me MODERATELY
4 = this applies to me QUITE A BIT
5 = this applies to me EXTREMELY

16. I cannot swallow, or can only   1   2   3   4   5   NO   YES, namely _____
    swallow with great difficulty

17. I cannot sleep for nights   1   2   3   4   5   NO   YES, namely _____
    on end, but remain very
    active during the day

18. I cannot speak (or only   1   2   3   4   5   NO   YES, namely _____
    with great effort) or I can
    only whisper

19. I am paralyzed for a while   1   2   3   4   5   NO   YES, namely _____

20. I grow stiff for a while   1   2   3   4   5   NO   YES, namely _____

© Nijenhuis, Van der Hart & Vanderlinden, Assen-Amsterdam-Leuven

SDQ-5

This questionnaire asks about different physical symptoms or body experiences, which you may have had either briefly or for a longer time. Please indicate to what extent these experiences apply to you *in the past year.* For each statement, please circle the number in the first column that best applies to YOU.

The possibilities are:
    1 = this applies to me NOT AT ALL
    2 = this applies to me A LITTLE
    3 = this applies to me MODERATELY
    4 = this applies to me QUITE A BIT
    5 = this applies to me EXTREMELY

If a symptom or experience applies to you, please indicate whether a *physician* has connected it with a *physical disease.* Indicate this by circling the word YES or NO in the column "Is the physical cause known?" If you circle YES, please write the physical cause (if you know it) on the line.

Example:

Sometimes	Extent to which the symptom or experience applies to you	Is the physical cause known?
My teeth chatter	1 2 3 4 5	NO YES, namely _____
I have cramps in my calves	1 2 3 4 5	NO YES, namely _____

If you have circled a 1 in the first column (i.e., This applies to me NOT AT ALL), you do NOT have to respond to the question about whether the physical cause is known. On the other hand, if you circle 2, 3, 4, or 5, you MUST circle NO or YES in the "Is the physical cause known?" column.

Please do not skip any of the 20 questions. Thank you for your cooperation.

Here are the questions:

1 = this applies to me NOT AT ALL
2 = this applies to me A LITTLE
3 = this applies to me MODERATELY
4 = this applies to me QUITE A BIT
5 = this applies to me EXTREMELY

Sometimes	Extent to which the symptom or experience applies to you					Is the physical cause known?
1. I have pain while urinating	1	2	3	4	5	NO YES, namely _____
2. My body, or a part of it, are insensitive to pain	1	2	3	4	5	NO YES, namely _____
3. I see things around me differently than usual (for example, as if looking through a tunnel, or merely seeing part of an object)	1	2	3	4	5	NO YES, namely _____
4. It is as if my body, or part of it, has disappeared	1	2	3	4	5	NO YES, namely _____
5. I cannot speak (or only with great effort) or I can only whisper	1	2	3	4	5	NO YES, namely _____

Appendix 3: The Multidimensional Inventory of Dissociation (MID)

The Multidimensional Inventory of Dissociation (MID; Dell, 2006a, 2006b) is a multi-scale diagnostic instrument that is designed to comprehensively assess the entire domain of dissociative phenomena. The MID has a breadth of coverage that is greater than the brief self-report instruments and structured interviews for dissociation. The MID is a 218-item instrument with 168 dissociation items and 50 validity items. It is written at a seventh-grade reading level. The MID uses an 11-point Likert scale format that is anchored by *Never* and *Always*, and takes approximately 30 to 90 minutes to complete. The MID and its Excel-based scoring program[1] generates both scale scores and categorical diagnoses (i.e., DID, DDNOS, PTSD, and severe borderline personality disorder). The MID measures 23 dissociative symptoms and six response sets, which serve as validity scales (i.e., defensiveness, emotional suffering, rare symptoms, attention-seeking behavior, factitious behavior, and a severe borderline personality disorder index). The MID's 168 dissociation items have 12 first-order factors (i.e., self-confusion, angry intrusions, dissociative disorientation, amnesia, distress about memory problems, subjective experience of the presence of alternate personalities, derealization/depersonalization, persecutory intrusions, trance, flashbacks, body symptoms, circumscribed loss of remote autobiographical memory) and one second-order factor: pathological dissociation.

The MID has two scoring systems: total score and severe dissociation score. Total score ranges between 0 and 100. A score of 30 and above is considered a cutoff mark indicative of probable dissociative psychopathology, whereas a score of 10 and below is considered an indication of a low level of dissociation. Severe dissociation scores are based on empirically determined pass/fail cutoff scores for 23 dissociative symptoms. MID severe dissociation scores range from 0 to 168. In one study (Dell, 2006b) of 220

---

[1] Available from Paul F. Dell, PhD, Trauma Recovery Center, 1709 Colley Avenue, Suite 312, Norfolk, VA 23517; PFDell@aol.com.

DID cases, the mean total score was 50.6 and the mean severe dissociation score was 124. The average DID patient had 20.2 of the 23 symptoms. MID scores significantly discriminate among four groups: DID, dissociative disorder not otherwise specified (DDNOS) Example 1 (symptoms similar to DID that do not meet the full criteria for this disorder, e.g., no distinct personality states or no amnesia), mixed psychiatric, and nonclinical controls.

MID 6.0: MULTIDIMENSIONAL INVENTORY OF DISSOCIATION V. 6.0

Instructions: How often do you have the following experiences when you are not under the influence of alcohol or drugs? Please circle the number that best describes you. Circle a "0" if the experience never happens to you; circle a "10" if it is always happening to you. If it happens sometimes, but not all the time, circle a number between 1 and 9 that best describes how often it happens to you.

Never   0 1 2 3 4 5 6 7 8 9 10   Always

1.	While watching TV, you find that you are thinking about something else.	0 1 2 3 4 5 6 7 8 9 10
2.	Forgetting what you did earlier in the day.	0 1 2 3 4 5 6 7 8 9 10
3.	Feeling as if your body (or certain parts of it) are unreal.	0 1 2 3 4 5 6 7 8 9 10
4.	Having an emotion (for example, fear, sadness, anger, happiness) that doesn't feel like it is "yours."	0 1 2 3 4 5 6 7 8 9 10
5.	Things around you suddenly seeming strange.	0 1 2 3 4 5 6 7 8 9 10
6.	Hearing the voice of a child in your head.	0 1 2 3 4 5 6 7 8 9 10
7.	Having pain in your genitals (for no known medical reason).	0 1 2 3 4 5 6 7 8 9 10
8.	Having another personality that sometimes "takes over."	0 1 2 3 4 5 6 7 8 9 10
9.	Hearing yourself talk, but you don't feel that you are choosing the words that are coming out of your mouth.	0 1 2 3 4 5 6 7 8 9 10
10.	Forgetting errands that you had planned to do.	0 1 2 3 4 5 6 7 8 9 10
11.	Feeling that your mind or body has been taken over by a famous person (for example, Elvis Presley, Jesus Christ, Madonna, President Kennedy, etc.).	0 1 2 3 4 5 6 7 8 9 10
12.	Trying to make someone jealous.	0 1 2 3 4 5 6 7 8 9 10
13.	Feeling as if close friends, relatives, or your own home seems strange or foreign.	0 1 2 3 4 5 6 7 8 9 10
14.	Reliving a traumatic event so vividly that you totally lose contact with where you actually are (that is, you think that you are "back there and then").	0 1 2 3 4 5 6 7 8 9 10

15. Having difficulty swallowing (for no known medical reason).   0 1 2 3 4 5 6 7 8 9 10

16. Having trance-like episodes where you stare off into space and lose awareness of what is going on around you.   0 1 2 3 4 5 6 7 8 9 10

17. Being puzzled by what you do or say.   0 1 2 3 4 5 6 7 8 9 10

18. Seeing images of a child who seems to "live" in your head.   0 1 2 3 4 5 6 7 8 9 10

19. Being told of things that you had recently done, but with absolutely no memory of having done those things.   0 1 2 3 4 5 6 7 8 9 10

20. Thoughts being imposed on you or imposed on your mind.   0 1 2 3 4 5 6 7 8 9 10

21. Pretending that something upsetting happened to you so that others would care about you (for example, being raped, military combat, physical or emotional abuse, sexual abuse, etc.).   0 1 2 3 4 5 6 7 8 9 10

22. Strong thoughts in your head that "come from out of nowhere."   0 1 2 3 4 5 6 7 8 9 10

23. Having blank spells or blackouts in your memory.   0 1 2 3 4 5 6 7 8 9 10

24. Not remembering what you ate at your last meal—or even whether you ate.   0 1 2 3 4 5 6 7 8 9 10

25. Feeling like you're only partially "there" (or not really "there" at all).   0 1 2 3 4 5 6 7 8 9 10

26. Your mind being controlled by an external force (for example, microwaves, the CIA, radiation from outer space, etc.).   0 1 2 3 4 5 6 7 8 9 10

27. Having no feeling at all in your body (for no known medical reason).   0 1 2 3 4 5 6 7 8 9 10

28. Feeling divided, as if you have several independent parts or sides.   0 1 2 3 4 5 6 7 8 9 10

29. Nobody cares about you.   0 1 2 3 4 5 6 7 8 9 10

30. Hearing voices in your head that argue or converse with one another.   0 1 2 3 4 5 6 7 8 9 10

31. "Losing" a chunk of time and having a total blank for it.   0 1 2 3 4 5 6 7 8 9 10

32. Strong feelings of emotional pain and hurt that come from out of nowhere.   0 1 2 3 4 5 6 7 8 9 10

33. While reading, you find that you are thinking about something else.   0 1 2 3 4 5 6 7 8 9 10

34. Having strong impulses to do something, but the impulses don't feel like they belong to you.   0 1 2 3 4 5 6 7 8 9 10

35. Feeling empty and painfully alone.   0 1 2 3 4 5 6 7 8 9 10

36. Feeling mechanical or not really human.   0 1 2 3 4 5 6 7 8 9 10

37. Things around you feeling unreal.   0 1 2 3 4 5 6 7 8 9 10

38. Pretending that you have a physical illness in order to get sympathy for example, flu, cancer, headache, having an operation, etc.).   0 1 2 3 4 5 6 7 8 9 10

39. Not being able to see for a while (as if you are blind) (for no known medical reason).   0 1 2 3 4 5 6 7 8 9 10

40. Feeling that the color of your body is changing.   0 1 2 3 4 5 6 7 8 9 10

41. Feeling split or divided inside.   0 1 2 3 4 5 6 7 8 9 10

42. Hearing a voice in your head that tries to tell you what to do.   0 1 2 3 4 5 6 7 8 9 10

43. Finding things at home (for example, shoes, clothes, toys, toilet articles, etc.), that you don't remember buying.   0 1 2 3 4 5 6 7 8 9 10

44. Feeling very detached from your behavior as you "go through the motions" of daily life.   0 1 2 3 4 5 6 7 8 9 10

45. Feeling mad.   0 1 2 3 4 5 6 7 8 9 10

46. Being unable to remember who you are.   0 1 2 3 4 5 6 7 8 9 10

47. Talking to others about how you have been hurt or mistreated.   0 1 2 3 4 5 6 7 8 9 10

48. Being in a familiar place, but finding it strange and unfamiliar.   0 1 2 3 4 5 6 7 8 9 10

49. Feeling uncertain about who you really are.   0 1 2 3 4 5 6 7 8 9 10

50. "Coming to" in the middle of a conversation with someone and having no idea what you and that person have been talking about; you didn't even know that you were having a conversation.   0 1 2 3 4 5 6 7 8 9 10

51. Talking to others about very serious traumas that you have experienced.   0 1 2 3 4 5 6 7 8 9 10

52. Your thoughts being broadcast so that other people can actually hear them.   0 1 2 3 4 5 6 7 8 9 10

53. Being told that there were times when you did not recognize friends or family members (for example, asking your spouse or friend, "Who are you?").   0 1 2 3 4 5 6 7 8 9 10

54. Being rejected by others.   0 1 2 3 4 5 6 7 8 9 10

55. Feeling the presence of an old man inside you who wants to read his newspaper or go to the bathroom.   0 1 2 3 4 5 6 7 8 9 10

56. Being unable to remember your name, or age, or address.   0 1 2 3 4 5 6 7 8 9 10

57. Your moods changing so rapidly that you don't know what you are going to feel from one minute to the next.   0 1 2 3 4 5 6 7 8 9 10

58. Feeling that other people, objects, or the world around you are not real.   0 1 2 3 4 5 6 7 8 9 10

59.	Being angry that your life is ruined.	o 1 2 3 4 5 6 7 8 9 10
60.	Being paralyzed or unable to move (for no known medical reason).	o 1 2 3 4 5 6 7 8 9 10
61.	Hearing a voice in your head and, at the same time, seeing an image of that "person" or of that voice.	o 1 2 3 4 5 6 7 8 9 10
62.	Nobody understands how much you hurt.	o 1 2 3 4 5 6 7 8 9 10
63.	Exaggerating the symptoms of a physical illness (that you genuinely have) in order to get sympathy or attention (for example, flu, cold, headache, fever, pain, etc.).	o 1 2 3 4 5 6 7 8 9 10
64.	Finding yourself lying in bed (on the sofa, etc.) with no memory of how you got there.	o 1 2 3 4 5 6 7 8 9 10
65.	Being impulsive.	o 1 2 3 4 5 6 7 8 9 10
66.	Being so bothered by flashbacks that it was hard to get out of bed and face the day.	o 1 2 3 4 5 6 7 8 9 10
67.	Not remembering large parts of your childhood after age 5.	o 1 2 3 4 5 6 7 8 9 10
68.	Not being able to keep friends.	o 1 2 3 4 5 6 7 8 9 10
69.	Feeling disconnected from everything around you.	o 1 2 3 4 5 6 7 8 9 10
70.	Having to "stretch the truth" to get your doctor's (or therapist's) concern or attention.	o 1 2 3 4 5 6 7 8 9 10
71.	Not being able to hear for awhile (as if you are deaf) (for no known medical reason).	o 1 2 3 4 5 6 7 8 9 10
72.	Feeling like you are often different from yourself.	o 1 2 3 4 5 6 7 8 9 10
73.	Feeling the pain of never being really special to anyone.	o 1 2 3 4 5 6 7 8 9 10
74.	Suddenly "waking up" in the middle of doing something (that you were completely unaware you were doing) (for example, vacuuming the carpet, cooking dinner, spanking the children, driving the car, etc.).	o 1 2 3 4 5 6 7 8 9 10
75.	Hurting yourself so that someone would care or pay attention.	o 1 2 3 4 5 6 7 8 9 10
76.	Finding things in your shopping bags, which you don't remember buying.	o 1 2 3 4 5 6 7 8 9 10
77.	People think that you live "in a world of your own."	o 1 2 3 4 5 6 7 8 9 10
78.	Feeling that pieces of your past are missing.	o 1 2 3 4 5 6 7 8 9 10
79.	Immediately forgetting what other people tell you.	o 1 2 3 4 5 6 7 8 9 10
80.	Not being sure about what is real (and what is unreal) in your surroundings.	o 1 2 3 4 5 6 7 8 9 10

81. Being so bothered by flashbacks that it is hard to function at work (or it is hard to carry out your daily responsibilities).   0 1 2 3 4 5 6 7 8 9 10

82. Having difficulty walking (for no known medical reason).   0 1 2 3 4 5 6 7 8 9 10

83. Switching back and forth between feeling like an adult and feeling like a child.   0 1 2 3 4 5 6 7 8 9 10

84. Hearing a voice in your head that wants you to hurt yourself.   0 1 2 3 4 5 6 7 8 9 10

85. When something upsetting happens, you go blank and lose a chunk of time.   0 1 2 3 4 5 6 7 8 9 10

86. After a nightmare, you wake up and find yourself not in bed (for example, on the floor, in the closet, etc.).   0 1 2 3 4 5 6 7 8 9 10

87. Not being able to remember something, but feeling that it is "right on the tip of your tongue."   0 1 2 3 4 5 6 7 8 9 10

88. Making decisions too quickly.   0 1 2 3 4 5 6 7 8 9 10

89. Feeling very confused about who you really are.   0 1 2 3 4 5 6 7 8 9 10

90. Feeling that important things happened to you earlier in your life, but you cannot remember them.   0 1 2 3 4 5 6 7 8 9 10

91. Standing outside of your body, watching yourself as if you were another person.   0 1 2 3 4 5 6 7 8 9 10

92. Feeling as if you were looking at the world through a fog so that people and objects felt far away or unclear.   0 1 2 3 4 5 6 7 8 9 10

93. Seeing or talking with others who have the same disorder that you have.   0 1 2 3 4 5 6 7 8 9 10

94. Having seizures for which your doctor can find no reason.   0 1 2 3 4 5 6 7 8 9 10

95. Going into trance so much (or for so long) that it interferes with your daily activities and responsibilities.   0 1 2 3 4 5 6 7 8 9 10

96. Thinking about how little attention you received from your parents.   0 1 2 3 4 5 6 7 8 9 10

97. Hearing a lot of noise or yelling in your head.   0 1 2 3 4 5 6 7 8 9 10

98. Hearing voices, which come from unusual places (for example, the air conditioner, the computer, the walls, etc.), that try to tell you what to do.   0 1 2 3 4 5 6 7 8 9 10

99. Words just flowing from your mouth as if they were not in your control.   0 1 2 3 4 5 6 7 8 9 10

100. Listening to someone and realizing that you did not hear part of what he/she said.   0 1 2 3 4 5 6 7 8 9 10

101. Sudden strong feelings of anger that seem to come from out of nowhere.   0 1 2 3 4 5 6 7 8 9 10

102. Feeling that there are large gaps in your memory.   0 1 2 3 4 5 6 7 8 9 10

103. Feeling as if you are two different people: one who is going through the motions of daily life and the other who is just watching.   0 1 2 3 4 5 6 7 8 9 10

104. Feeling that your surroundings (or other people) were fading away or disappearing.   0 1 2 3 4 5 6 7 8 9 10

105. Having traumatic flashbacks that make you want to inflict pain on yourself.   0 1 2 3 4 5 6 7 8 9 10

106. Going into trance for hours.   0 1 2 3 4 5 6 7 8 9 10

107. Feeling like some of your behavior isn't really "yours."   0 1 2 3 4 5 6 7 8 9 10

108. Finding something that has been done (for example, the lawn mowed, the kitchen painted, a task at work completed, etc.), that you don't remember doing, but knowing that you must be the one who did it.   0 1 2 3 4 5 6 7 8 9 10

109. Forgetting where you put something.   0 1 2 3 4 5 6 7 8 9 10

110. Having dreams that you don't remember the next day.   0 1 2 3 4 5 6 7 8 9 10

111. Desperately wanting to talk to someone about your pain or distress.   0 1 2 3 4 5 6 7 8 9 10

112. Feeling the presence of an angry part in your head that tries to control what you do or say.   0 1 2 3 4 5 6 7 8 9 10

113. Your mind blocking or going totally empty.   0 1 2 3 4 5 6 7 8 9 10

114. Feeling like time slows down or stops.   0 1 2 3 4 5 6 7 8 9 10

115. Bad memories coming into your mind and you can't get rid of them.   0 1 2 3 4 5 6 7 8 9 10

116. Drifting into trance without even realizing that it is happening.   0 1 2 3 4 5 6 7 8 9 10

117. Words come out of your mouth, but you didn't say them; you don't know where those words came from.   0 1 2 3 4 5 6 7 8 9 10

118. Hearing voices crying in your head.   0 1 2 3 4 5 6 7 8 9 10

119. Suddenly finding yourself standing someplace and you can't remember what you have been doing before that.   0 1 2 3 4 5 6 7 8 9 10

120. Something in your mind interferes when you think about things that you "shouldn't" think.   0 1 2 3 4 5 6 7 8 9 10

121. Daydreaming.   0 1 2 3 4 5 6 7 8 9 10

122. Being able to remember very little of your past.   0 1 2 3 4 5 6 7 8 9 10

123. Not recognizing yourself in the mirror.   0 1 2 3 4 5 6 7 8 9 10

124. Feeling hurt.   0 1 2 3 4 5 6 7 8 9 10

125. Reexperiencing body sensations from a past traumatic event.   0 1 2 3 4 5 6 7 8 9 10

126. Part of your body (for example, arm, leg, head, etc.) seems to disappear and doesn't reappear for several days.   0 1 2 3 4 5 6 7 8 9 10

127. When something upsetting starts to happen, you "go away" in your mind.   0 1 2 3 4 5 6 7 8 9 10

128. Telling others about your psychological disorder(s).   0 1 2 3 4 5 6 7 8 9 10

129. When you are angry, doing or saying things that you don't remember (after you calm down).   0 1 2 3 4 5 6 7 8 9 10

130. Exaggerating the symptoms of a psychological illness (that you genuinely have) in order to get sympathy or attention (for example, depression, bulimia, posttraumatic stress disorder, memory blackouts, being suicidal, etc.).   0 1 2 3 4 5 6 7 8 9 10

131. Being able to do something really well one time, and then not being able to do it at all at another time.   0 1 2 3 4 5 6 7 8 9 10

132. Being unable to recall something, then something "jogs" your memory and you remember it.   0 1 2 3 4 5 6 7 8 9 10

133. Feeling like you are "inside" yourself, watching what you are doing.   0 1 2 3 4 5 6 7 8 9 10

134. Not being able to remember important events in your life (for example, your wedding day, the birth of your child, your grandmother's funeral, taking your final exams, etc.).   0 1 2 3 4 5 6 7 8 9 10

135. Feeling distant or removed from your thoughts and actions.   0 1 2 3 4 5 6 7 8 9 10

136. Things around you seeming to change size or shape.   0 1 2 3 4 5 6 7 8 9 10

137. Having traumatic flashbacks that make you want to die.   0 1 2 3 4 5 6 7 8 9 10

138. Feeling that you have multiple personalities.   0 1 2 3 4 5 6 7 8 9 10

139. Being bothered by how much you "trance out."   0 1 2 3 4 5 6 7 8 9 10

140. Hearing a voice in your head that calls you names (for example, wimp, stupid, whore, slut, bitch, etc.).   0 1 2 3 4 5 6 7 8 9 10

141. Suddenly realizing that hours have gone by and not knowing what you were doing during that time.   0 1 2 3 4 5 6 7 8 9 10

142. Having to go back and correct mistakes that you made.   0 1 2 3 4 5 6 7 8 9 10

143. Poor memory causing serious difficulty for you.   0 1 2 3 4 5 6 7 8 9 10

144. Feeling that your vision was suddenly sharper or that colors suddenly seemed more vivid or more intense.   0 1 2 3 4 5 6 7 8 9 10

145. Reliving a past trauma so vividly that you see it, hear it, feel it, smell it, etc.   0 1 2 3 4 5 6 7 8 9 10

146. Your thoughts and feelings are so changeable that you don't understand yourself.   0 1 2 3 4 5 6 7 8 9 10

147. Going into trance several days in a row.   0 1 2 3 4 5 6 7 8 9 10

148. Not feeling together, not feeling whole.   0 1 2 3 4 5 6 7 8 9 10

149. Having other people (or parts) inside you who have their own names.   0 1 2 3 4 5 6 7 8 9 10

150. Discovering that you have changed your appearance (for example, cut your hair, or changed your hairstyle, or changed what you are wearing, or put on cosmetics, etc.) with no memory of having done so.   0 1 2 3 4 5 6 7 8 9 10

151. Thoughts coming into your mind that you cannot stop.   0 1 2 3 4 5 6 7 8 9 10

152. Being told about things that you did that you don't remember doing and would never do (for example, swearing like a sailor, being very mad, acting like a young child, or being very sexual).   0 1 2 3 4 5 6 7 8 9 10

153. Having trance-like episodes during which you see yourself being taken into a spaceship and experimented on by aliens.   0 1 2 3 4 5 6 7 8 9 10

154. Being bothered or upset by how much you forget.   0 1 2 3 4 5 6 7 8 9 10

155. Exaggerating something bad that once happened to you (for example, rape, military combat, physical or emotional abuse, sexual abuse, mistreatment by our spouse, etc.) in order to get attention or sympathy.   0 1 2 3 4 5 6 7 8 9 10

156. Reliving a traumatic event so totally that you think that a present-day person is actually a person from the trauma (for example, being home with your partner, suddenly reliving being raped by your alcoholic uncle, and actually thinking that your partner is your uncle; that is, you see your uncle in front of you instead of seeing your partner).   0 1 2 3 4 5 6 7 8 9 10

157. Thinking about nothing.   0 1 2 3 4 5 6 7 8 9 10

158. Feeling like you are not the same kind of person all the time.   0 1 2 3 4 5 6 7 8 9 10

159. Hearing a voice in your head that wants you to die.   0 1 2 3 4 5 6 7 8 9 10

160. Suddenly finding yourself somewhere odd at home (for example, inside the closet, under a bed, curled up on the floor, etc.) with no knowledge of how you got there.   0 1 2 3 4 5 6 7 8 9 10

161. Feeling as if there is something inside you that takes control of your behavior or speech.   0 1 2 3 4 5 6 7 8 9 10

162. Totally forgetting how to do something that you know very well how to do (for example, how to drive, how to read, how to use the computer, how to play the piano, etc.). 0 1 2 3 4 5 6 7 8 9 10

163. Hearing a voice in your head that keeps talking about AIDS and homosexuals. 0 1 2 3 4 5 6 7 8 9 10

164. Feeling that part of your body is disconnected (detached) from the rest of your body. 0 1 2 3 4 5 6 7 8 9 10

165. Wishing you knew why you feel and behave the way you do. 0 1 2 3 4 5 6 7 8 9 10

166. Hearing sounds from nearby as if they were coming from far away (for no known medical reason). 0 1 2 3 4 5 6 7 8 9 10

167. Going into trance and being possessed by a spirit or demon. 0 1 2 3 4 5 6 7 8 9 10

168. Having snapshots of past trauma that suddenly flash in your mind. 0 1 2 3 4 5 6 7 8 9 10

169. Feeling no pain (when you should have felt pain) (for no known medical reason). 0 1 2 3 4 5 6 7 8 9 10

170. Discovering that you have a significant injury (for example, a cut, or a burn, or many bruises) and having no memory of how it happened. 0 1 2 3 4 5 6 7 8 9 10

171. Hearing a voice in your head that calls you a liar or tells you that certain events never happened. 0 1 2 3 4 5 6 7 8 9 10

172. Feeling as if part of your body (or your whole body) has disappeared. 0 1 2 3 4 5 6 7 8 9 10

173. Suddenly finding yourself somewhere (for example, at the beach, at work, in a nightclub, in your car, etc.) with no memory of how you got there. 0 1 2 3 4 5 6 7 8 9 10

174. Feeling that there is another person inside you who can come out and speak if it wants. 0 1 2 3 4 5 6 7 8 9 10

175. Being willing to do or say almost anything to get somebody to feel that you are "special." 0 1 2 3 4 5 6 7 8 9 10

176. Having nightmares about a trauma from your past. 0 1 2 3 4 5 6 7 8 9 10

177. People noticing your blank stare and the fact that you are "gone." 0 1 2 3 4 5 6 7 8 9 10

178. Being pleased by the concern and sympathy of others when they hear about the traumas that you have suffered. 0 1 2 3 4 5 6 7 8 9 10

179. "Coming to" and finding that you have done something you don't remember doing (for example, smashed something, cut yourself, cleaned the whole house, etc.). 0 1 2 3 4 5 6 7 8 9 10

180. Having thoughts that don't really seem to belong to you.   0 1 2 3 4 5 6 7 8 9 10

181. Having pain while urinating (for no known medical reason).   0 1 2 3 4 5 6 7 8 9 10

182. Switching back and forth between feeling like a human and feeling like a member of some other species (for example, a cat, a dog, a squirrel, etc.).   0 1 2 3 4 5 6 7 8 9 10

183. Having "tunnel vision" (where your visual field narrows down to just a tunnel) (for no known medical reason).   0 1 2 3 4 5 6 7 8 9 10

184. Having difficulty staying out of trance.   0 1 2 3 4 5 6 7 8 9 10

185. Your mood changing rapidly without any reason.   0 1 2 3 4 5 6 7 8 9 10

186. Discovering that you have attempted suicide, but having no memory of having done it.   0 1 2 3 4 5 6 7 8 9 10

187. Finding things that you must have written (or drawn), but with no memory of having done so.   0 1 2 3 4 5 6 7 8 9 10

188. Suddenly feeling very small, like a young child.   0 1 2 3 4 5 6 7 8 9 10

189. Suddenly not knowing how to do your job.   0 1 2 3 4 5 6 7 8 9 10

190. Feeling as if there is a struggle going on inside of you about who you really are.   0 1 2 3 4 5 6 7 8 9 10

191. Your body suddenly feeling as if it isn't really yours.   0 1 2 3 4 5 6 7 8 9 10

192. Being bothered by flashbacks for several days in a row.   0 1 2 3 4 5 6 7 8 9 10

193. Being confused or puzzled by your emotions.   0 1 2 3 4 5 6 7 8 9 10

194. Not remembering what happens when you drive a familiar route in your car.   0 1 2 3 4 5 6 7 8 9 10

195. Distinct changes in your handwriting.   0 1 2 3 4 5 6 7 8 9 10

196. Very strong feelings (for example, fear, or anger, or emotional pain and hurt) that suddenly go away.   0 1 2 3 4 5 6 7 8 9 10

197. Looking in the mirror and seeing someone other than yourself.   0 1 2 3 4 5 6 7 8 9 10

198. Some thoughts are suddenly "taken away from you."   0 1 2 3 4 5 6 7 8 9 10

199. Hearing a voice in your head that tells you to "shut up."   0 1 2 3 4 5 6 7 8 9 10

200. People telling you that you sometimes act so differently that you seem like another person.   0 1 2 3 4 5 6 7 8 9 10

201. Switching back and forth between feeling like a man and feeling like a woman.   0 1 2 3 4 5 6 7 8 9 10

202. Having another part inside that has different memories, behaviors, and feelings than you do.   0 1 2 3 4 5 6 7 8 9 10

203. Feeling that your feet or hands (or other parts of your body) have changed in size.   0 1 2 3 4 5 6 7 8 9 10

204. There were times when you "came to" and found pills or a razor blade (or something else to hurt yourself with) in your hand.   0 1 2 3 4 5 6 7 8 9 10

205. Finding writings at your home in handwriting that you don't recognize.   0 1 2 3 4 5 6 7 8 9 10

206. Having flashbacks of poor episodes of your favorite TV show.   0 1 2 3 4 5 6 7 8 9 10

207. Hearing a voice in your head that calls you no good, worthless, or a failure.   0 1 2 3 4 5 6 7 8 9 10

208. Having a very angry part that "comes out" and says and does things that you would never do or say.   0 1 2 3 4 5 6 7 8 9 10

209. Feeling like some of your thoughts are removed from your mind – by some force or by some other part of you.   0 1 2 3 4 5 6 7 8 9 10

210. Feeling a struggle inside you about what to think, how to feel, what you should do.   0 1 2 3 4 5 6 7 8 9 10

211. Not remembering where you were the day before.   0 1 2 3 4 5 6 7 8 9 10

212. Feeling that another part or entity inside you tries to stop you from doing or saying something.   0 1 2 3 4 5 6 7 8 9 10

213. Wishing that someone would finally realize how much you hurt.   0 1 2 3 4 5 6 7 8 9 10

214. More than one part of you has been reacting to these questions.   0 1 2 3 4 5 6 7 8 9 10

215. Feeling the presence of an angry part in your head that seems to hate you.   0 1 2 3 4 5 6 7 8 9 10

216. Hearing a voice in your head that is soothing, helpful, or protective.   0 1 2 3 4 5 6 7 8 9 10

217. Things in your home disappear or get moved around (and you don't know how this is happening).   0 1 2 3 4 5 6 7 8 9 10

218. Noticing the presence of a child inside you.   0 1 2 3 4 5 6 7 8 9 10

Author Index

Subject Index

Hesse, Erik
See also attachment
Adult Attachment Interview; 66
Himber, Judith
self-cutting treatment strategies; 131
therapeutic alliance role in
treatment of self-harming
behaviors; 134
hippocampus
neuronal degeneration,
glucocorticoid impact on; 100
histories
trauma, validation strategies;
101–104
Holocaust
dissociation of evil in perpetrators
of; 46
as source of traumatic amnesia, in
adults; 88
hopelessness
See depression; despair
as complex PTSD symptom; 36
hormones
ACTH (adrenocorticotropic
hormone)
homeostasis maintenance role; 98
stress response sensitivity; 99
catecholamines
memory impact of different
levels; 98–99
response; 250
stress-related neurohormone;
98–99
CRF (corticotropin-releasing
factor); 98
endogenous opioids; 98–100, 113,
132
glucocorticoids; 98, 100
dopamine; 98
HPA (hypothalamic-pituitary-
adrenal) axis; 98–99
stress-related; 98
hospitalization
See also crisis/crises
acceptance of trauma-related
diagnosis, importance, in
hospital treatment; 233
crisis management; 228–245
general psychiatric units, patient
mixture issues; 244–245
outside relationships, importance
of; 234
partial
acute care provision in; 228
as alternative to individual
therapy; 189
practices; 233–245
disadvantages of rigid rules and
policies; 234, 239
dissociative disorder issues;
236–247
family work; 241–242
group treatment; 240–241
individual therapy and case
management; 239–240

limits and boundaries; 235–236
nursing practice; 237–239
psychoeducation; 235
seclusion and restraint; 242–243
staff support; 243–245
therapeutic philosophy; 233–234
retraumatization fear; 140
host personality
See also alternate personalities/
identities
centrality of, in DID therapy;
220–221
facilitating communication with
alternate personalities; 213
role and characteristics, in DID;
213
hostility
See also anger; emotions/emotional
as abused role manifestation, in
trauma therapy; 168
control and manipulation by
patients perceived as; 182
and dependency, in chronically
disempowered patients; 179
therapeutic withholding interpreted
as, by trauma patients;
163–164
as therapist reaction, in reenactment
dynamics of trauma therapy;
168
how-to
See clinical strategies and
suggestions; therapist(s)
Howell, Elizabeth
history of dissociation in
psychoanalytic thinking; 46
**HPA (hypothalamic-pituitary-
adrenal) axis**
homeostasis maintenance role,
PTSD role; 98–99
response, impact of age on; 100
stress response sensitivity; 99
hydroxyzine (Vistaril); 250, 252
hyperarousal symptoms
See also anxiety; hypervigilence;
irritability; sleep disturbances;
startle responses
in complex PTSD; 32
panic attacks, neurobiology of; 99
in PTSD; 55
DSM-IV criteria; 29
hypermnesia; 105
See also amnesia; memory(s)
in chronically traumatized children;
34
pervasive amnesia vs.; 105
hypervigilence; 55
See also complex PTSD
(posttraumatic stress disorder);
hyperarousal symptoms; PTSD
(posttraumatic stress disorder)
in complex PTSD; 32
in DSM-IV PTSD criteria; 29
neurobiology of; 99
war-related; 5

hypnosis/hypnotic
See also adjunctive therapies
as alternative complex PTSD
treatment modality; 268
autohypnotic trance phenomenon,
alternate personalities as; 220
dissociation relationship to; 49
interventions, in management of
posttraumatic and dissociative
symptoms; 156
irrelevance in percentage of
corroborated memories of
childhood sexual abuse; 92
medications; 249–250
role in middle phase treatment; 124
therapy, use with DID therapy; 226
trauma research on; 15
hypochondriasis
See also somatic/somatization
trauma relationship; 25
**hypothalamic-pituitary-adrenal
(HPA) axis**
homeostasis maintenance role,
PTSD role; 98–99
stress response sensitivity; 99
hysteria
See also disorders
as dissociation form; 42
Freud's theories; xiv
history of relationship to trauma; 24

iatrogenic factors
consideration in differential
diagnosis of dissociative
disorders; 209
dissociative symptoms exaggeration
potential; 226, 256
lack of evidence for DID creation
by; 256
idealization
as abused role manifestation, in
trauma therapy; 168
identity
See also DID (dissociative identity
disorder); self-perceptions
alteration in, DSM-IV, definition; 49
confusion and alteration, diagnostic
instruments; 64
impact of abuse on; xiii
primary, as trauma survivor,
negative consequences of; 184
self, establishing positive, as
fundamental skill; 109
stable sense of, in normal
dissociation; 47
illustrations of clinical presentations
See clinical examples
imaginary/imagined/imaginative
abandonment, DSM-IV borderline
personality disorder criteria; 72
absorption/involvement; 49
interviewing skills and sample
questions; 62–63
abuser, countertransference issue;
173

References

Adler, G. (1985). *Borderline psychopathology and its treatment.* New York, NY: Jason Aronson.

Adler, G., & Buie, D. (1972). The misuses of confrontation in the treatment of borderline personality. *International Journal of Psychoanalytic Psychotherapy, 1*(3), 109–120.

Afifi, T. O., Enns, M. W., Cox, B. J., Asmundson, G. J. G., Stein, M. B., & Sareen, J. (2008). Population attributable fractions of psychiatric disorders and suicide ideation and attempts associated with adverse childhood experiences. *American Journal of Public Health, 98,* 946–952.

Ahearn, E. P., Mussey, M., Johnson, C., Krohn, A., & Krahn, D. (2006). Quetiapine as an adjunctive treatment for post-traumatic stress disorder: An 8-week open-label study. *International Clinical Psychopharmacology, 21,* 29–33.

Ainsworth, M. D. S., Blehar, M. C., Waters, E., & Wall, S. (1978). *Patterns of attachment: A psychological study of the strange situation.* Hillsdale, NJ: Lawrence Erlbaum.

American Psychiatric Association. (1952). *Diagnostic and statistical manual of mental disorders.* Washington, DC: Author.

American Psychiatric Association. (1968). *Diagnostic and statistical manual of mental disorders, edition II.* Washington, DC: Author.

American Psychiatric Association. (1980). *Diagnostic and statistical manual of mental disorders, edition III.* Washington, DC: Author.

American Psychiatric Association. (1994). *Diagnostic and statistical manual of mental disorders, edition IV.* Washington, DC: Author.

American Psychiatric Association. (2000). *Statement on therapies focused on memories of childhood physical and sexual abuse.* Washington, DC: Author.

American Psychiatric Association. (2010a). American Psychiatric Association DSM-5 development, 309.81 posttraumatic stress disorder. Retrieved May 15, 2010, from http://www.dsm5.org/ProposedRevisions/Pages/proposedrevision.aspx?rid=165

American Psychiatric Association. (2010b). American Psychiatric Association DSM-5 development, dissociative disorders. Retrieved June 10, 2010, from http://www.dsm5.org/ProposedRevisions/Pages/DissociativeDisorders.aspx

American Psychological Association. (1994). *Interim report of the APA working group on investigation of memories of childhood abuse.* Washington, DC: Author.

American Psychological Association. (1996). *Final report of the working group on investigation of memories of child abuse.* Washington, DC: Author.

Amir, M., Kaplan, Z., Efroni, R., & Kotler, M. (1999). Suicide risk and coping styles in posttraumatic stress disorder patients. *Psychotherapy and Psychosomatics, 68*(2), 76–81.

Appelbaum, P. S., Uyehara, L. A., & Elin, M. R. (Eds.). (1997). *Trauma and memory: Clinical and legal controversies.* New York, NY: Oxford University Press.

Australian Psychological Association. (1994). *Guidelines relating to the reporting of recovered memories.* Sydney, Australia: Author.

Baars, E. W., Van der Hart, O., Nijenhuis, E. R. S., Draijer, N., Glas, G., & Chu, J. A. (2011). Predicting stabilizing treatment outcomes for complex posttraumatic stress disorder and dissociative identity disorder: An expertise-based prognostic model. *Journal of Trauma & Dissociation, 11, 12,* 67–87.

Babbin, J. (Producer), & Petrie, D. (Director). (1976). *Sybil* [motion picture]. USA: Warner Home Video.

Bagley, C., & Ramsey, R. (1986). Sexual abuse in childhood: Psychosocial outcomes and implications for social work. *Social Work Practice in Human Sexuality, 4,* 33–47.

Baker, D. G., West, S. A., Nicholson, W. E., Ekhator, N. N., Kasckow, J. W., Hill, K. K., Bruce, A. B., Orth, D. N., & Geracioti, T. D., Jr. (1999). Serial CSF corticotropin-releasing hormone levels and adrenocorticoid activity in combat veterans with posttraumatic stress disorder. *American Journal of Psychiatry, 156,* 585–588.

Barach, P. M. (1991). Multiple personality disorder as an attachment disorder. *Dissociation, 4*(3), 117–123.

Barsky, A. J. (1996). Hypochondriasis: Medical management and psychiatric treatment. *Psychosomatics, 37,* 48–56.

Barsky, A. J., Wool, C., Barnett, M. C., & Cleary, P. D. (1994). Histories of childhood trauma in adult hypochondriacal patients. *American Journal of Psychiatry, 151,* 397–401.

Bartzokis, G., Lu, P., Turner, J., Mintz, J., & Saunders, C. S. (2005). Adjunctive risperidone in the treatment of chronic combat-related posttraumatic stress disorder. *Biologic Psychiatry, 57,* 474–479.

Bass, E., & Davis, L. (1988). *The courage to heal: A guide for women survivors of child sexual abuse.* New York, NY: Collins Living.

Becker-Blease, K. A., Deater-Deckard, K., Eley, T., Freyd, J. J., Stevenson, J., & Plomin, R. (2004). A genetic analysis of individual differences in dissociative behaviors in childhood and adolescence. *Journal of Child Psychology and Psychiatry, 45,* 522–532.

Beecher, C. E., & Stowe, H. B. (1869). *American women's home.* New York, NY: J. B. Ford.

Beere, D. (2009). An EMDR protocol for dissociative identity disorder (DID). In M. Luber (Ed.), *Eye movement desensitization and reprocessing (EMDR) scripted protocols: Special populations* (pp. 387–425). New York, NY: Springer.

Beitchman, J. H., Zucker, K. J., Hood, J. E., da Costa, G. A., Akman, D., & Cassavia, E. (1992). A review of the long-term effects of child sexual abuse. *Child Abuse & Neglect, 16,* 101–118.

Ben-Yaacov, Y., & Amir, M. (2004). Posttraumatic symptoms and suicide risk. *Personality and Individual Differences, 36,* 1257–1264.

Benham, E. (1995). Coping strategies: A psychoeducational approach to post-traumatic symptomatology. *Journal of Psychosocial Nursing & Mental Health Services, 33*(6), 30–35.

Berlant, J., & van Kammen, D. P. (2002). Open-label topiramate as primary or adjunctive therapy in chronic civilian posttraumatic stress disorder: A preliminary report. *Journal of Clinical Psychiatry, 63,* 15–20.

Bernstein, E. M., & Putnam, F. W. (1986). Development, reliability, and validity of a dissociation scale. *Journal of Nervous and Mental Disease, 174,* 727–734.

Bernstein, E. M., & Putnam, F. W. (1993). An update on the dissociative experiences scale. *Dissociation, 6,* 16–27.

Blizard, R. A. (1997). Therapeutic alliance with abuser alters in DID: The paradox of attachment to the abuser. *Dissociation, 10,* 246–254.

Blizard, R. A. (2001). Masochistic and sadistic ego states: Dissociative solutions to the dilemma of attachment to an abusive caretaker. *Journal of Trauma & Dissociation, 2*(4), 37–58.

Bonanno, G. A. (2004). Loss, trauma, and human resilience. *American Psychologist, 59*(1), 20–28.

Boon, S. (1997). The treatment of traumatic memories in DID: Indications and contra-indications. *Dissociation, 10*, 65–79.

Boon, S., & Draijer, N. (1993a). The differentiation of patients with MPD or DDNOS from patients with cluster B personality disorder. *Dissociation, 150*(6), 126–135.

Boon, S., & Draijer, N. (1993b). Multiple personality disorder in the Netherlands: A clinical investigation of 71 patients. *American Journal of Psychiatry, 150*, 489–494.

Bowen, M. (1966). The use of family theory in clinical practice. *Comprehensive Psychiatry, 7*, 345–374.

Bowlby, J. (1969). *Attachment and loss I: Attachment*. London, England: Hogarth Press.

Bowlby, J. (1973). *Attachment and loss II: Separation anxiety and anger*. London, England: Hogarth Press.

Bowlby, J. (1980). *Attachment and loss III: Loss, sadness and depression*. London, England: Hogarth Press.

Brady, K., Pearlstein, T., Asnis, G. M., Baker, D., Rothbaum, B., Sikes, C. R., & Farfel, G. M. (2000). Efficacy and safety of sertraline treatment of posttraumatic stress disorder: A randomized controlled trial. *Journal of the American Medical Association, 283*, 1837–1844.

Brand, B. L., Classen, C. C., Zaveri, P., & McNary, S. (2009). A review of dissociative disorders treatment studies. *Journal of Nervous and Mental Disease, 197*, 646–654.

Brandchaft, B., & Stolorow, R. D. (1987). The borderline concept: An intersubjective viewpoint. In J. Grotstein, M. F. Solomon, & J. A. Long (Eds.), *The borderline patient* (pp. 103–126). Hillsdale, NJ: The Analytic Press.

Braun, B. G. (1986). Issues in the psychotherapy of multiple personality disorder. In B.G. Braun (Ed.), *Treatment of multiple personality disorder* (pp. 1–28). Washington, DC: American Psychiatric Press.

Braun, B. G. (1988). The BASK model of dissociation. *Dissociation, 1*(1), 4–23.

Braun, B. G. (1993). Aids to the treatment of multiple personality disorder on a general psychiatric unit. In R. P. Kluft & C. G. Fine (Eds.), *Clinical perspectives on multiple personality disorder* (pp. 155–175). Washington, DC: American Psychiatric Press.

Braun, B. G., & Sachs, R. G. (1985). The development of multiple personality disorder: Predisposing, precipitating, and perpetuating factos. In R. P. Kluft (Ed.), *Childhood antecedents of multiple personality* (pp. 37–64). Washington, DC: American Psychiatric Press.

Bremner, J. D., Krystal, J. H., Southwick, S. M., & Charney, D. S. (1996a). Noradrenergic mechanisms in stress and anxiety. I. Preclinical studies. *Synapse, 23*, 28–38.

Bremner, J. D., Krystal, J. H., Southwick, S. M., & Charney, D. S. (1996b). Noradrenergic mechanisms in stress and anxiety. II. Clinical studies. *Synapse, 23*, 39–51.

Bremner, J. D., Mletzko, T., Welter, S., Quinn, S., Williams, C., Brummer, M., Siddiq, S., Reed, L., Heim, C. M., & Nemeroff, C. B. (2005). Effects of phenytoin on memory, cognition and brain structure in post-traumatic stress disorder: A pilot study. *Journal of Psychopharmacology, 19*, 159–165.

Bremner, J. D., Randall, P., Vermetten, E., Staib, L., Bronen, R. A., Mazure, C., Capelli, S., McCarthy, G., Innis, R. B., & Charney, D. S. (1997). Magnetic resonance imaging–based measurement of hippocampal volume in posttraumatic stress disorder related to childhood physical and sexual abuse: A preliminary report. *Biologic Psychiatry, 41*, 23–32.

Bremner, J. D., Randall, P. R., Scott, T. M., Bronen, R. A., Delaney, R. C., Seibyl, J. P., Southwick, S. M., McCarthy, G., Charney, D. S., & Innis, R. B. (1995). Magnetic resonance imaging–based measurement of hippocampal volume in posttraumatic stress disorder. *American Journal of Psychiatry, 152*, 973–981.

Brenner, I. (2001). *Dissociation of trauma: Theory, phenomenology, and technique*. Madison, CT: International Universities Press.

Breslau, N., Davis, G. C., Andreski, P., & Peterson, E. (1991). Traumatic events and posttraumatic stress disorder in an urban population of young adults. *Archives of General Psychiatry, 48*, 216–222.

Brewin, C. R., Andrews, B., & Valentine, J. D. (2000). Meta-analysis of risk factors for posttraumatic stress disorder in trauma-exposed adults. *Journal of Consulting and Clinical Psychology, 68*, 748–766.

Brick, S. S., & Chu, J. A. (1991). The simulation of multiple personalities: A case report. *Psychotherapy, 28*, 267–272.

Briere, J. (1992). *Child abuse trauma: Theory and treatment of the lasting effects.* New York, NY: Sage.

Briere, J., & Conte, J. (1993). Self-reported amnesia for abuse in adults molested as children. *Journal of Traumatic Stress, 6,* 21–31.

Briere, J., & Elliott, D. M. (2003). Prevalence and psychological sequelae of self-reported childhood physical and sexual abuse in a general population sample of men and women. *Child Abuse & Neglect, 27,* 1205–1222.

Briere, J., & Runtz, M. (1987). Post sexual abuse trauma: Data and implications for clinical practice. *Journal of Interpersonal Violence, 2,* 367–379.

Briere, J., & Runtz, M. (1990). Differential adult symptomatologies associated with three types of child abuse histories. *Child Abuse & Neglect, 14,* 357–364.

Briere, J., & Spinazzola, J. (2005). Phenomenology and psychological assessment of complex posttraumatic states. *Journal of Traumatic Stress, 18,* 401–412.

British Psychological Society. (1995). *Recovered memories: The report of the working party of the British Psychological Society.* East Leicester, England: Author.

Bromberg, P. M. (1998). *Standing in the spaces: Essays on clinical process, trauma, and dissociation.* Hillsdale, NJ: Analytic Press.

Brown, D. (1995). Pseudomemories: The standard of science and the standard of care in trauma treatment. *American Jounral of Clinical Hypnosis, 37*(3), 1–24.

Brown, D., Scheflin, A. W., & Hammond, D. C. (1998). *Memory, trauma treatment, and the law.* New York, NY: W. W. Norton.

Brown, D., Scheflin, A. W., & Whitfield, C. L. (1999). Recovered memories: The weight of the evidence in science and in the courts. *Journal of Psychiatry & Law, 27,* 5–156.

Brown, D. P., & Fromm, E. (1986). *Hypnotherapy and hypnoanalysis.* Hillsdale, NJ: Lawrence Erlbaum.

Brown, D. W., Frischholz, E. J., & Scheflin, A. W. (1999). Iatrogenic dissociative identity disorder: An evaluation of the scientific evidence. *Journal of Psychiatry & Law, 27,* 549–638.

Brown, G. R., & Anderson, B. (1991). Psychiatric morbidity in adult inpatients with childhood histories of sexual and physical abuse. *American Journal of Psychiatry, 148,* 55–61.

Brown, R., & Kulick, J. (1977). Flashbulb memories. *Cognition, 5,* 73–99.

Brown, R. J., Schrag, A., & Trimble, M. R. (2005). Dissociation, childhood interpersonal trauma, and family functioning in patients with somatization disorder. *American Journal of Psychiatry, 162,* 899–905.

Brown, W. (1919). Hypnosis, suggestion and dissociation. *British Medical Journal, 191,* 734–736.

Browne, A., & Finkelhor, D. (1986). Impact of child sexual abuse: A review of the research. *Psychology Bulletin, 99,* 66–77.

Bryer, J. B., Nelson, B. A., Miller, J. B., & Krol, P. A. (1987). Childhood sexual and physical abuse as factors in adult psychiatric illness. *American Journal of Psychiatry, 144,* 1426–1430.

Buck, O. D. (1983). Multiple personality as a borderline state. *Journal of Nervous and Mental Disease, 171,* 62–65.

Buie, D., & Adler, G. (1972). The uses of confrontation in the treatment of borderline personality. *International Journal of Psychoanalytic Psychotherapy, 1*(3), 90–108.

Burgess, A. W. (2008). Famous and not so famous cases of a forensic psychiatric nurse. Paper presented at the McLean Hospital Grand Rounds, Belmont, MA.

Burgess, A. W., Baker, T., & Hartman, C. R. (1996). Parents' perceptions of their children's recovery 5 to 10 years following day-care abuse. *Scholarly Inquiry for Nursing Practice, 10*(1), 75–92.

Burgess, A. W., Groth, A. N., Holmstrom, L. L., & Sgroi, S. M. (1978). *Sexual assault of children and adolescents.* Lexington, MA: Lexington Books.

Burgess, A. W., & Hartman, C. R. (2005). Children's adjustment 15 years after daycare abuse. *Journal of Forensic Nursing, 1*(2), 73–83.

Burgess, A. W., & Holmstrom, L. L. (1974). Rape trauma syndrome. *American Journal of Psychiatry, 131,* 981–986.

Cahill, L., Prins, B., Weber, M., & McGaugh, J. L. (1994). ß-adrenergic activation and memory for emotional events. *Nature, 371*, 702–704.

Cameron, C. (1994). Women survivors confronting their abusers: Issues, decisions and outcomes. *Journal of Child Sexual Abuse, 3*, 7–35.

Carmen, E. H., & Rieker, P. P. (1989). A psychosocial model of the victim-to-patient process: Implications for treatment. *Psychiatric Clinics of North America, 12*, 431–444.

Carmen, E. H., Rieker, P. P., & Mills, T. (1984). Victims of violence and psychiatric illness. *American Journal of Psychiatry, 141*, 378–383.

Ceci, S. J., & Huffman, M. L. C. (1997). How suggestible are preschool children? Cognitive and social factors. *Journal of the American Academy of Child and Adolescent Psychiatry, 36*, 948–958.

Ceci, S. J., Huffman, M. L. C., Smith, E., & Loftus, E. W. (1994). Repeatedly thinking about non-events: Source misattributions among preschoolers. *Consciousness and Cognition, 3*, 388–407.

Charney, D. S., Deutch, A. Y., Krystal, J. H., Southwick, S. M., & Davis, M. (1993). Psychobiologic mechanisms of posttraumatic stress disorder. *Archives of General Psychiatry, 50*, 294–305.

Cheit, R. E. (2010). The recovered memory project. Retrieved May 23, 2010, from http://www.brown.edu/Departments/Taubman_Center/Recovmem/index.html

Christianson, S.-Å., & Loftus, E. (1987). Memory for traumatic events. *Applied Cognitive Psychology, 1*, 225–239.

Chu, J. A. (1988). Ten traps for therapists in the treatment of trauma survivors. *Dissociation, 1*(4), 24–32.

Chu, J. A. (1991a). On the misdiagnosis of multiple personality disorder. *Dissociation, 4*, 200–204.

Chu, J. A. (1991b). The repetition compulsion revisited: Reliving dissociated trauma. *Psychotherapy, 28*, 327–332.

Chu, J. A. (1992a). Empathic confrontation in the treatment of childhood abuse survivors, including a tribute to the legacy of Dr. David Caul. *Dissociation, 5*, 98–103.

Chu, J. A. (1992b). The revictimization of adult women with histories of childhood abuse. *Journal of Psychotherapy Practice and Research, 1*, 259–269.

Chu, J. A. (1992c). The therapeutic roller coaster: Dilemmas in the treatment of childhood abuse survivors. *Journal of Psychotherapy Practice and Research, 1*, 351–370.

Chu, J. A. (1994). The rational treatment of multiple personality disorder. *Psychotherapy, 31*, 94–100.

Chu, J. A. (1997a). The president's message, March 1997. *The International Society for the Study of Dissociation News, 15*(2), 2–3.

Chu, J. A. (1997b). The president's message, September 1997. *International Society for the Study of Dissociation News, 15*(4), 1–2.

Chu, J. A. (2010). Posttraumatic stress disorder: Beyond DSM-IV. *American Journal of Psychiatry, 167*, 615–617.

Chu, J. A., & Bowman, E. S. (2000). Trauma and dissociation: 20 years of study and lessons learned along the way. *Journal of Trauma & Dissociation, 1*(1), 5–20.

Chu, J. A., & Bowman, E. S. (Eds.). (2002). *Trauma and sexuality: The effects of childhood sexual, physical, and emotional abuse on sexual identity and behavior*. New York, NY: Haworth Press.

Chu, J. A., & Dill, D. L. (1990). Dissociative symptoms in relation to childhood physical and sexual abuse. *American Journal of Psychiatry, 147*, 887–892.

Chu, J. A., Dill, D. L., & Murphy, D. E. (2000). Depressive symptoms and sleep disturbance in adults with histories of childhood abuse. *Journal of Trauma & Dissociation, 1*(3), 87–99.

Chu, J. A., Frey, L. M., Ganzel, B. L., & Matthews, J. A. (1999). Memories of childhood abuse: Dissociation, amnesia and corroboration. *American Journal of Psychiatry, 156*, 749–755.

Chu, J. A., Matthews, J. A., Frey, L. M., & Ganzel, B. (1996). The nature of traumatic memories of childhood abuse. *Dissociation, 9*, 2–17.

Clark, R. D., Canive, J. M., Calais, L. A., Qualls, C. R., & Tuason, V. B. (1999). Divalproex in posttraumatic stress disorder: An open-label clinical trial. *Journal of Traumatic Stress, 12*, 395–401.

Clary, W. F., Burstein, K. J., & Carpenter, J. S. (1984). Multiple personality and borderline personality disorders. *Psychiatric Clinics of North America, 7*, 89–99.

Cloitre, M., Tardiff, K., Marzuk, P. M., Leon, A. C., & Portera, L. (1996). Childhood abuse and subsequent sexual assault among female inpatients. *Journal of Traumatic Stress, 9*, 473–482.

Coid, J., Petruckevitch, A., Feder, G., Chung, W.-S., Richardson, J., & Moorey, S. (2001). Relation between childhood sexual and physical abuse and risk of revictimisation in women: A cross-sectional survey. *Lancet, 358*, 450–454.

Cole, W. G., & Loftus, E. F. (1979). Incorporating new information into memory. *American Journal of Psychology, 3*, 413–425.

Comstock, C. M. (1991). Counter-transference and the suicidal multiple personality patient. *Dissociation, 4*, 25–35.

Connor, K. M., Sutherland, S. M., Tupler, L. A., Malik, M. L., & Davidson, J. R. (1999). Fluoxetine in posttraumatic stress disorder: Randomised, double-blind study. *British Journal of Psychiatry, 175*, 17–22.

Connors, M. E., & Morse, W. (1993). Sexual abuse and the eating disorders: A review. *International Journal of Eating Disorders, 13*, 1–11.

Coons, P. M. (1984). The differential diagnosis of multiple personality disorder: A comprehensive review. *Psychiatric Clinics of North America, 7*, 51–67.

Coons, P. M. (1991). Iatrogenesis and malingering of multiple personality disorder in the forensic evaluation of homicide defendants. *Psychiatric Clinics of North America, 14*, 757–768.

Coons, P. M. (1994). Confirmation of childhood abuse in child and adolescent cases of multiple personality disorder and dissociative disorder not otherwise specified. *Journal of Nervous and Mental Disease, 182*, 461–464.

Coons, P. M., Cole, C., Pellow, T. A., & Milstein, V. (1990). Symptoms of posttraumatic stress and dissociation in women victims of abuse. In R. P. Kluft (Ed.), *Incest-related syndromes of adult psychopathology* (pp. 205–226). Washington, DC: American Psychiatric Press.

Coons, P. M., & Milstein, V. (1994). Factitious or malingered multiple personality disorder: Eleven cases. *Dissociation, 7*, 81–85.

Courtois, C. A. (1988). *Healing the incest wound: Adult survivors in therapy.* New York, NY: W. W. Norton.

Courtois, C. A. (1999). *Recollections of sexual abuse: Treatment principles and guidelines.* New York, NY: W. W. Norton.

Courtois, C. A. (2010). *Healing the incest wound: Adult survivors in therapy* (2nd ed.). New York, NY: W. W. Norton.

Courtois, C. A., & Ford, J. D. (Eds.). (2009). *Treating complex traumatic stress disorders.* New York, NY: Guilford Press.

Courtois, C. A., Ford, J. D., & Cloitre, M. (2009). Best practices in psychotherapy for adults. In C. A. Courtois & J. D. Ford (Eds.), *Treating complex traumatic stress disorders* (pp. 82–103). New York, NY: Guilford Press.

Crabtree, A. (1992). Dissociation and memory: A two-hundred-year perspective. *Dissociation, 5*, 150–154.

Crook, L. S., & Dean, M. C. (1999). "Lost in a shopping mall"—A breach of professional ethics. *Ethics & Behavior, 9*(1), 39–50.

Da Costa, J. M. (1871). On irritable heart: A clinical study of a form of functional cardiac disorder and its consequences. *American Journal of Medical Sciences, 61*, 17–52.

Dalenberg, C. J. (1996). Accuracy, timing and circumstances of disclosure in therapy of recovered and continuous memories of abuse. *Journal of Psychiatry and Law, 24*, 229–275.

Dalenberg, C. J. (2000). *Countertransference and the treatment of trauma.* Washington, DC: American Psychological Association.

Dalenberg, C. J. (2004). Maintaining the safe and effective therapeutic environment in the context of distrust and anger: Countertransference and complex trauma. *Psychotherapy: Research, Practice, Training, 71*, 438–447.

Dalenberg, C. J. (2006). Recovered memory and the Daubert criteria: Recovered memory as professionally tested, peer reviewed, and accepted in the relevant scientific community. *Trauma, Violence & Abuse, 7,* 274–310.

Dalenberg, C. J., & Palesh, O. G. (2004). Relationship between child abuse history, trauma, and dissociation in Russian college students. *Child Abuse & Neglect, 28,* 461–474.

Dallam, S. J. (2002). Crisis or creation? A systematic examination of "false memory syndrome." *Journal of Child Sexual Abuse, 9*(3/4), 9–36.

Davidson, J. R., Weisler, R. H., Butterfield, M. I., Casat, C. D., Connor, K. M., Barnett, S., & van Meter, S. (2003). Mirtazapine vs. placebo in posttraumatic stress disorder: A pilot trial. *Biologic Psychiatry, 53,* 188–191.

Davidson, J. R. T., & Fairbank, J. A. (1993). The epidemiology of posttraumatic stress disorderr. In J. R. T. Davidson & E. B. Foa (Eds.), *Posttraumatic stress disorder: DSM-IV and beyond* (pp. 147–169). Washington, DC: American Psychiatric Press.

Davidson, J. R. T., Hughes, D., Blazer, D., & George, L. K. (1991). Posttraumatic stress disorder in the community: An epidemiological study. *Psychological Medicine, 21,* 1–19.

Davidson, J. R. T., Kudler, H. S., Smith, R., Mahoney, S. L., Lipper, S., Hammett, E., Saunders, W. B., & Cavenar, J. (1990). Treatment of posttraumatic stress disorder with amitriptyline and placebo. *Archives of General Psychiatry, 47,* 259–266.

Davidson, J. R. T., Rothbaum, B. O., van der Kolk, B. A., Sikes, C. R., & Farbel, G. M. (2001). Multi-center, double-blind comparison of sertraline and placebo in the treatment of posttraumatic stress disorder. *Archives of General Psychiatry, 58,* 485–492.

Davies, J. M., & Frawley, M. G. (1994). *Treating the adult survivor of childhood sexual abuse: A psychoanalytic perspective.* New York, NY: Basic Books.

Davis, M. (1992). The role of the amygdala in fear and anxiety. *Annual Review of Neuroscience, 15,* 353–375.

de Yong, M. (1982). Self-injurious behavior in incest victims: A research note. *Child Welfare, 61,* 577–584.

Dell, P. F. (1998). Axis II pathology in outpatients with dissociative identity disorder. *Journal of Nervous and Mental Disease, 186,* 352–356.

Dell, P. F. (2006a). The multidimensional inventory of dissociation (MID): A comprehensive measure of pathological dissociation. *Journal of Trauma & Dissociation, 7*(2), 77–106.

Dell, P. F. (2006b). A new model of dissociative identity disorder. *Psychiatric Clinics of North America, 29,* 1–26.

Dell, P. F. (2009). The phenomena of pathological dissociation. In P. F. Dell & J. A. O'Neil (Eds.), *Dissociation and the dissociative disorders: DSM-V and beyond* (pp. 225–238). New York, NY: Routledge.

Dell, P. F., & O'Neil, J. A. (Eds.). (2009). *Dissociation and the dissociative disorders: DSM-V and beyond.* New York, NY: Routledge.

Desai, S., Arias, I., Thompson, M. P., & Basile, K. C. (2002). Childhood victimization and adult victimization assessed in a nationally representative sample of women and men. *Violence and Victims, 17,* 639–653.

Donaldson, M. A., & Gardner, R. (1985). Diagnosis and treatment of traumatic stress among women after childhood incest. In C. Figley (Ed.), *Trauma and its wake* (pp. 356–377). New York, NY: Brunner/Mazel.

Dutton, D., & Painter, S. L. (1981). Traumatic bonding: The development of emotional attachments in battered women and other relationships of intermittent abuse. *Victimology, 6,* 139–155.

Dutton, M. A., Burghardt, K. J., Perrin, S. G., Chrestman, K. R., & Halle, P. M. (1994). Battered women's cognitive schemata. *Journal of Traumatic Stress, 7,* 237–255.

Eich, J. E., & Metcalfe, J. (1989). Mood dependent learning for internal versus external events. *Journal of Experimental Psychology: Learning, Memory and Cognition, 15,* 443–455.

Ellason, J. W., Ross, C. A., & Fuchs, D. L. (1996). Lifetime Axis I and II comorbidity and childhood trauma history in dissociative identity disorder. *Psychiatry, 59,* 255–266.

Elliott, D. M., & Briere, J. (1995). Posttraumatic stress associated with delayed recall of sexual abuse: A general population study. *Journal of Traumatic Stress, 8,* 629–647.

Ellison, J. M., Chu, J. A., & Henry, M. E. (2000). Transient dissociative identity disorder after electroconvulsive therapy. *Journal of Electroconvulsive Therapy, 16,* 314–316.

Erdelyi, M. H. (1985). *Psychoanalysis: Freud's cognitive psychology.* New York, NY: Free Press.

Erdelyi, M. H. (1990). Repression, reconstruction, and defense: History and integration of the psychoanalytic and experimental frameworks. In J. Singer (Ed.), *Repression and dissociation: Implications for personality theory, psychopathology, and health* (pp. 1–31). Chicago, IL: The University of Chicago Press.

Erickson, E. (1968). *Identity, youth and crisis.* New York, NY: W. W. Norton.

Eriksen, C. (1952). Defense against ego threat in memory and perception. *Journal of Abnormal and Social Psychology, 3,* 253–256.

Eriksen, C. (1953). Individual differences in defensive forgetting. *Journal of Experimental Psychology, 44,* 442–443.

Everill, J. T., & Waller, G. (1995). Reported sexual abuse and eating psychopathology: A review of the evidence for a causal link. *International Journal of Eating Disorders, 18,* 1–11.

Fairburn, C. G., Doll, H. A., Welch, S. L., Hay, P. J., Davies, B. A., & O'Connor, M. E. (1998). Risk factors for binge eating disorder: A community-based, case-control study. *Archives of General Psychiatry, 55,* 425–432.

Famularo, R., Kinscherff, R., & Fenton, T. (1988). Propranolol treatment for childhood posttraumatic stress disorder. *American Journal of Diseases of Children, 142,* 1244–1247.

Favazza, A., DeRosario, L., & Conteiro, K. (1989). Self-mutilation and eating disorders. *Suicide and Life-Threatening Behavior, 19,* 352–361.

Feldman-Summers, S., & Pope, K. S. (1994). The experience of "forgetting" childhood abuse: A national survey of psychologists. *Journal of Consulting and Clinical Psychology, 62,* 636–639.

Ferenczi, S. (1949). Confusion of tongues between the adult and the child. *International Journal of Psychoanalysis, 30,* 225–231.

Fergusson, D. M., Horwood, L. J., & Lynskey, M. T. (1996). Childhood sexual abuse and psychiatric disorders in young adulthood: Part II: Psychiatric outcomes of sexual abuse. *Journal of the American Academy of Child and Adolescent Psychiatry, 35,* 1365–1374.

Fesler, F. A. (1991). Valproate in combat-related posttraumatic stress disorder. *Journal of Clinical Psychiatry, 52,* 361–364.

Filteau, M. J., Leblanc, J., & Bouchard, R. H. (2003). Quetiapine reduces flashbacks in chronic posttraumatic stress disorder. *Canadian Journal of Psychiatry, 48,* 282–283.

Fine, C. G. (1990). The cognitive sequelae of incest. In R. P. Kluft (Ed.), *Incest-related syndromes of adult psychopathology* (pp. 161–182). Washington, DC: American Psychiatric Press.

Fine, C. G., & Berkowitz, A. S. (2001). The wreathing protocol: The imbrication of hypnosis and EMDR in the treatment of dissociative identity disorder and other maladaptive dissociative responses. *American Journal of Clinical Hypnosis, 43,* 275–290.

Fink, D., & Golinkoff, M. (1990). Multiple personality, borderline personality disorder, and schizophrenia: A comparative study of clinical features. *Dissociation, 3,* 127–134.

Finkelhor, D. (1994). The international epidemiology of child sexual abuse. *Child Abuse & Neglect, 18,* 409–417.

Finkelhor, D., & Browne, A. (1985). The traumatic impact of child sexual abuse: A conceptualization. *American Journal of Orthopsychiatry, 55,* 530–541.

Finkelhor, D., Hotaling, G., Lewis, I. A., & Smith, C. (1990). Sexual abuse in a national survey of adult men and women: Prevalence, characteristics and risk factors. *Child Abuse & Neglect, 14,* 19–28.

Fleming, J., Mullen, P. E., Sibthorpe, B., Attewell, R., & Bammer, G. (1998). The relationship between childhood sexual abuse and alcohol abuse in women: A case-control study. *Addiction, 93,* 1787–1798.

Foa, E. B., Steketee, G., & Rothbaum, B. O. (1989). Behavioral/cognitive conceptualizations of posttraumatic stress disorder. *Behavior Therapy, 20,* 155–176.

Follette, V. M., Polusny, M. A., Bechtle, A. E., & Naugle, A. E. (1996). Cumulative trauma: The impact of child sexual abuse, adult sexual abuse, and spouse abuse. *Journal of Traumatic Stress, 9,* 25–35.

Folsom, V., Krahn, D., Nairn, K., Gold, L., Demitrack, M. A., & Silk, K. R. (1993). The impact of sexual and physical abuse on eating disordered and psychiatric symptoms: A comparison of eating disordered and psychiatric inpatients. *International Journal of Eating Disorders, 13,* 249–257.

Foote, B., Smolin, Y., Kaplan, M., Legatt, M. E., & Lipschitz, D. (2006). Prevalence of dissociative disorders in psychiatric outpatients. *American Journal of Psychiatry, 163,* 623–629.

Foote, B., Smolin, Y., Neft, D. I., & Lipschitz, D. (2008). Dissociative disorders and suicidality in psychiatric outpatients. *Journal of Nervous and Mental Disease, 196,* 29–36.

Forgash, C., & Knipe, J. (2008). Integrating EMDR and ego state treatment for clients with trauma disorders. In C. Forgash & M. Copeley (Eds.), *Healing the heart of trauma and dissociation with EMDR and ego state therapy* (pp. 1–60). New York, NY: Springer.

Frank, J. B., Kosten, T. R., Giller, E. L., & Dan, E. (1988). A randomized clinical trial of phenelzine and imipramine for posttraumatic stress disorder. *American Journal of Psychiatry, 145,* 1289–1291.

Fraser, G. A. (2003). Fraser's "dissociative table technique" revisited, revised: A strategy for working with ego states in dissociative disorders and ego-state therapy. *Journal of Trauma & Dissociation, 4*(4), 5–28.

Fraser, G. A. (Ed.). (1997). *The dilemma of ritual abuse: Cautions and guides for therapists.* Washington, DC: American Psychiatric Press.

Freud, S. (1893–1895/1955). Studies on hysteria. In J. Strachey (Ed.), *The standard edition of the complete psychological works of Sigmund Freud* (Vol. II). London, England: Hogarth Press.

Freud, S. (1896/1966). The aetiology of hysteria. In J. Strachey (Ed.), *The standard edition of the complete psychological works of Sigmund Freud* (Vol. III, pp. 191–221). London, England: Hogarth Press.

Freud, S. (1900/1935). The interpretation of dreams. In J. Strachey (Ed.), *The standard edition of the complete psychological works of Sigmund Freud* (Vols. IV & V). London, England: Hogarth Press.

Freud, S. (1920/1955). Beyond the pleasure principle. In J. Strachey (Ed.), *The standard edition of the complete psychological works of Sigmund Freud* (Vol. XVIII, pp. 7–64). London, England: Hogarth Press.

Freyd, J. (1994). Betrayal trauma: Traumatic amnesia as an adaptive response to childhood abuse. *Ethics & Behavior, 4,* 307–329.

Freyd, J. (1996). *Betrayal trauma: The logic of forgetting childhood abuse.* Cambridge, MA: Harvard University Press.

Friedman, M. J., Jalowiec, J., McHugo, G., Wang, S., & McDonagh, A. (2007). Adult sexual abuse is associated with elevated neurohormone levels among women with PTSD due to childhood sexual abuse. *Journal of Traumatic Stress, 20,* 611–617.

Frueh, B. C., Turner, S. M., & Beidell, D. C. (1995). Exposure therapy for combat-related PTSD: A critical review. *Clinical Psychology Review, 15,* 799–817.

Ganaway, G. K. (1989). Historical versus narrative truth: Clarifying the role of exogenous trauma in the etiology of multiple personality disorder and its variants. *Dissociation, 2,* 205–220.

Garland, R. J., & Dougher, M. J. (1990). The abused/abuser hypothesis of child sexual abuse: A critical review of theory and research. In J. Feierman (Ed.), *Pedophilia: Biosocial dimensions* (pp. 488–509). New York, NY: Springer-Verlag.

Gelinas, D. (2003). Integrating EMDR into phase-oriented treatment for trauma. *Journal of Trauma & Dissociation, 4*(3), 91–135.

Gelinas, D. J. (1983). The persisting negative effects of incest. *Psychiatry, 46,* 312–332.

Gidycz, C. A., Coble, C. N., Latham, L., & Layman, M. J. (1993). Sexual assault experiences in adulthood and prior victimization experiences. *Psychology of Women Quarterly, 17,* 151–168.

Gleaves, D. H. (1996). The sociocognitive model of dissociative identity disorder: A reexamination of the evidence. *Psychological Bulletin, 120*(1), 42–59.

Gleaves, D. H., Smith, S. M., Butler, L. M., & Spiegel, D. (2004). False and recovered memories in the laboratory and clinic: A review of experimental and clinical evidence. *Clinical Psychology: Science and Practice, 11*(1), 3–28.

Gold, S. N. (2000). *Not trauma alone: Therapy for child abuse survivors in family and social context.* Philadelphia, PA: Brunner/Routledge.

Gold, S. N., Elhai, J. D., Rea, B. D., Weiss, D., Masino, T., Morris, S. L., & McInich, J. (2001). Contextual treatment of dissociative identity disorder: Three case studies. *Journal of Trauma & Dissociation, 2*(4), 5–36.

Gold, S. N., Hughes, D., & Hohnecker, L. (1994). Degrees of repression of sexual abuse memories. *American Psychologist, 49*, 441–442.

Gold, S. R., Sinclair, B. B., & Balge, K. A. (1999). Risk of sexual revictimization: A conceptual model. *Aggression and Violent Behavior, 4*, 457–470.

Grabe, H. J., Spitzer, C., & Freyberger, H. J. (1999). Relationship of dissociation to temperament and character in men and women. *American Journal of Psychiatry, 156*, 1811–1813.

Graf, P., & Schacter, D. L. (1985). Implicit and explicit memory for new associations in normal and amnesic subjects. *Journal of Experimental Psychology: Learning, Memory and Cognition, 11*, 501–518.

Greaves, G. (1992). Alternative hypotheses regarding claims of satanic cult activity: A critical analysis. In D. K. Sakheim & S. E. Devine (Eds.), *Out of darkness: Exploring satanism and ritual abuse* (pp. 45–72). New York, NY: Lexington Books.

Green, B. L. (1994). Psychosocial research in traumatic stress: An update. *Journal of Traumatic Stress, 7*, 341–362.

Greene, E., Flynn, M. S., & Loftus, E. F. (1982). Inducing resistance to misleading information. *Journal of Verbal Learning and Verbal Behavior, 21*, 207–219.

Greenson, R. (1967). *The technique and practice of psychoanalysis.* New York, NY: International Universities Press.

Greenwald, E., Leitenberg, H., Cado, S., & Tarran, M. J. (1990). Childhood sexual abuse: Long-term effects on psychological and sexual functioning in a nonclinical and nonstudent sample of adult women. *Child Abuse & Neglect, 14*, 503–513.

Grilo, C. M., & Masheb, R. M. (2001). Childhood psychological, physical, and sexual maltreatment in outpatients with binge eating disorder: Frequency and associations with gender, obesity, and eating-related psychopathology. *Obesity Research, 9*, 320–325.

Grinker, R. R., Werble, B., & Drye, R. (1968). *The borderline syndrome: A behavioral study of ego functions.* New York, NY: Basic Books.

Gross, T., & WHYY-FM (Producers). (1989). *Interview with Julia Child* [Fresh Air]. Washington, DC: National Public Radio.

Grunebaum, H. U., & Klerman, G. L. (1967). Wrist slashing. *American Journal of Psychiatry, 124*, 527–534.

Gudjonsson, G. G. (1992). *The psychology of interrogations, confessions and testimony.* New York, NY: John Wiley & Sons.

Gunderson, J. G., & Chu, J. A. (1993). Treatment implications of past trauma in borderline personality disorder. *Harvard Review of Psychiatry, 1*, 75–81.

Gunderson, J. G., Frank, A., Ronningstam, E. R., Wachter, S., Lynch, F., & Wolf, P. J. (1989). Early discontinuance of borderline patients from psychotherapy. *Journal of Nervous and Mental Disease, 177*, 38–42.

Gunderson, J. G., & Singer, M. T. (1975). Defining borderline patients: An overview. *American Journal of Psychiatry, 132*, 1–10.

Gutheil, T. G. (1989). Borderline personality disorder—boundary violations, and patient-therapist sex: Medicolegal pitfalls. *American Journal of Psychiatry, 146*, 597–602.

Haddock, D. B. (2001). *The dissociative identity disorder sourcebook.* New York, NY: McGraw-Hill.

Hall, G. C. N., Hirschman, R., & Oliver, L. L. (1995). Sexual arousal and arousability to pedophilic stimuli in a community sample of normal men. *Behavior Therapy, 26*, 681–694.

Hall, R. C. W., Tice, L., Beresford, T. P., Wooley, B., & Hall, A. K. (1986). Sexual abuse in patients with anorexia and bulimia. *Psychosomatics, 30,* 73–79.

Hamner, M. B., Deitsch, S. E., Brodrick, P. S., Ulmer, H. G., & Lorberbaum, J. P. (2003). Quetiapine treatment in patients with posttraumatic stress disorder: An open trial of adjunctive therapy. *Journal of Clinical Psychopharmacology, 23,* 15–20.

Hamner, M. B., Faldowski, R. A., Ulmer, H. G., Frueh, B. C., Huber, M. G., & Arana, M. G. (2003). Adjunctive risperidone treatment in post-traumatic stress disorder: A preliminary controlled trial of effects on comorbid psychotic symptoms. *International Clinical Psychopharmacology, 18,* 1–8.

Hastings, T., & Kern, J. M. (1994). Relationship between bulimia, childhood sexual abuse, and family environment. *International Journal of Eating Disorders, 15,* 103–111.

Helzer, J. E., Robins, L. N., & McEvoy, L. (1987). Post-traumatic distress in the general population. *New England Journal of Medicine, 317,* 1630–1634.

Hemingway, R. B., & Reigle, T. G. (1987). The involvement of endogenous opiate systems in learned helplessness and stress-induced analgesia. *Psychopharmacology, 93,* 353–357.

Henderson, J. L., & Moore, M. (1944). The psychoneurosis of war. *New England Journal of Medicine, 230,* 273–279.

Herman, J. L. (1981). *Father-daughter incest.* Cambridge, MA: Harvard University Press.

Herman, J. L. (1992a). Complex PTSD: A syndrome in survivors of prolonged and repeated trauma. *Journal of Traumatic Stress, 5,* 377–391.

Herman, J. L. (1992b). *Trauma and recovery: The aftermath of violence from domestic abuse to political terror.* New York, NY: Basic Books.

Herman, J. L., & Harvey, M. R. (1997). Adult memories of childhood trauma: A naturalistic clinical study. *Journal of Traumatic Stress, 10,* 557–571.

Herman, J. L., Perry, J. C., & van der Kolk, B. A. (1989). Childhood trauma in borderline personality disorder. *American Journal of Psychiatry, 146,* 490–495.

Herman, J. L., Russell, D., & Trocki, K. (1986). Long-term effects of incestuous abuse in childhood. *American Journal of Psychiatry, 143,* 1293–1296.

Herman, J. L., & Schatzhow, E. (1987). Recovery and verification of memories of childhood sexual trauma. *Psychoanalytic Psychology, 4*(1), 1–14.

Herman, J. L., & van der Kolk, B. A. (1987). Traumatic antecedents of borderline personality disorder. In B. A. van der Kolk (Ed.), *Psychological trauma* (pp. 111–127). Washington, DC: American Psychiatric Press.

Herzog, D. B., Staley, J. E., Carmody, S., Robbins, W. M., & van der Kolk, B. A. (1993). Childhood sexual abuse in anorexia nervosa and bulimia nervosa: A pilot study. *Journal of the American Academy of Child and Adolescent Psychiatry, 32,* 962–966.

Hesse, E. (1999). The adult attachment interview: Historical and current perspectives. In J. Cassidy & P. R. Shaver (Eds.), *Handbook of attachment* (pp. 395–433). New York, NY: Guilford Press.

Himber, J. (1994). Blood rituals: Self-cutting in female psychiatric patients. *Psychotherapy, 31,* 620–631.

Hoch, P., & Cattel, J. (1959). The diagnosis of pseudoneurotic schizophrenia. *Psychiatric Quarterly, 33,* 17–43.

Holmes, D. S. (1974). Investigation of repression: Differential recall of material experimentally or naturally associated with ego threat. *Psychological Bulletin, 81,* 632–653.

Holmes, D. S. (1990). Evidence for repression: An examination of 60 years of research. In J. Singer (Ed.), *Repression and dissociation: Implications for personality theory, psychopathology, and health* (pp. 85–102). Chicago, IL: The University of Chicago Press.

Horevitz, R., & Loewenstein, R .J. (1994). The rational treatment of multiple personality disorder. In S. J. Lynn & J. Rhue (Eds.), *Dissociation: Clinical and theoretical perspectives* (pp. 289–316). New York, NY: Guilford Press.

Horovitz, R. P., & Braun, B. G. (1984). Are multiple personalities borderline? *Psychiatric Clinics of North America, 7,* 69–88.

Horowitz, M. J. (1986). *Stress response syndromes* (2nd ed.). Northvale, NJ: Jason Aronson.

Howell, E. F. (2005). *The dissociative mind*. Hillsdale, NJ: Analytic Press.

Hunter, E. C. M., Phillips, M. L., Chalder, T., Sierra, M., & David, A. S. (2003). Depersonalisation disorder: A cognitive–behavioural conceptualisation. *Behaviour Research and Therapy, 41,* 1451–1467.

Huppert, J. D., Moser, J. S., Gershuny, B. S., Riggs, D. S., Spokas, M., Filip, J., Hajcak, G., Parker, H. A., Baer, L., & Foa, E. B. (2005). The relationship between obsessive-compulsive and posttraumatic stress symptoms in clinical and non-clinical samples. *Journal of Anxiety Disorders, 19,* 127–136.

Hyman, I. E., & Pentland, J. (1996). The role of mental imagery in the creation of false childhood memories. *Journal of Memory and Language, 35,* 101–117.

Hyman, I. E., Troy, T. H., & Billings, F. J. (1995). False memories of childhood experiences. *Applied Cognitive Psychology, 9,* 181–197.

Ibarra, P., Bruehl, S. P., McCubbin, J. A., Carlson, C. R., Wilson, J. F., Norton, J. A., & Montgomery, T. B. (1994). An unusual reaction to opioid blockade with naltrexone in a case of post-traumatic stress disorder. *Journal of Traumatic Stress, 7,* 303–309.

International Society for the Study of Dissociation. (2004). Guidelines for the evaluation and treatment of dissociative symptoms in children and adolescents. *Journal of Trauma & Dissociation, 5*(3), 119–150.

International Society for the Study of Trauma and Dissociation. (2011). Guidelines for treating dissociative identity disorder in adults, 3rd rev. *Journal of Trauma & Dissociation, 12,* in press.

Jaffe, R. (1968). Dissociative phenomena in former concentration camp inmates. *International Journal of Psychoanalysis, 49,* 310–312.

James, J., & Meyerding, J. (1977). Early sexual experience and prostitution. *American Journal of Psychiatry, 134,* 1381–1385.

Janet, P. (1907). *The major symptoms of hysteria*. New York, NY: Macmillan.

Jang, K. L., Paris, J., Zweig-Frank, H., & Livesley, W. J. (1998). Twin study of dissociative experience. *Journal of Nervous and Mental Disease, 186,* 345–351.

Janoff-Bulman, R. (1992). *Shattered assumptions: Towards a new psychology of trauma*. New York, NY: Free Press.

Jatzko, A., Rothenhöfer, S., Schmitt, A., Gaser, C., Demirakca, T., Weber-Fahr, W., Wessa, M., Magnotta, V., & Braus, D. F. (2006). Hippocampal volume in chronic posttraumatic stress disorder (PTSD): MRI study using two different evaluation methods. *Journal of Affective Disorders, 94,* 121–126.

Jordan, J. V., Kaplan, A. G., Miller, J. B., Stiver, I. P., & Surrey, J. L. (Eds.). (1991). *Women's growth in connection: Writings from the Stone Center*. New York, NY: Guilford Press.

Kardiner, A. (1941). *The traumatic neuroses of war*. New York, NY: Hoeber.

Keane, T. M., Fairbank, J. A., Caddell, J. M., & Zimering, R. T. (1989). Implosive (flooding) therapy reduces symptoms of PTSD in Vietnam combat veterans. *Behavior Therapy, 20,* 245–260.

Keck, P. E., McElroy, S. L., & Friedman, L. M. (1992). Valproate and carbamazepine in the treatment of panic and posttraumatic stress disorders, withdrawal states, and behavioral dyscontrol syndromes. *Journal of Clinical Psychopharmacology, 12*(1 Suppl.), 36–41.

Kendler, K. S., Bulick, C. M., Silberg, J., Hettema, J. M., Myers, J., & Prescott, C. A. (2000). Child sexual abuse and adult psychiatric and substance use disorders in women. *Archives of General Psychiatry, 57,* 953–959.

Kernberg, O. F. (1967). Borderline personality disorder. *Journal of the American Psychoanalytic Association, 15,* 641–685.

Kernberg, O. F. (1968). The treatment of patients with borderline personality organization. *International Journal of Psychoanalysis, 49,* 600–619.

Kernberg, O. F. (1970). A psychoanalytic classification of character pathology. *Journal of the American Psychoanalytic Association, 18,* 800–822.

Kernberg, O. F. (1984). *Severe personality disorders: Psychotherapeutic strategies*. New Haven, CT: Yale University Press.

Kessler, R. C., Berglund, P., Delmer, O., Jin, R., Merikangas, K. R., & Walters, E. E. (2005). Lifetime prevalence and age-of-onset distributions of DSM-IV disorders in the national comorbidity survey replication. *Archives of General Psychiatry, 62*, 593–602.

Kessler, R. C., Sonnega, A., Bromet, E., Hughes, M., & Nelson, C. B. (1995). Posttraumatic stress disorder in the national comorbidity study. *Archives of General Psychiatry, 52*, 1048–1060.

Khantzian, E. J. (1997). The self-medication hypothesis of substance use disorders: A reconsideration and recent applications. *Harvard Review of Psychiatry, 4*, 231–244.

Kinsey, A. C., Pomeroy, W. B., & Martin, C. E. (1948). *Sexual behavior in the human male.* Philadelphia, PA: W. B. Saunders.

Kinsey, A. C., Pomeroy, W. B., Martin, C. E., & Gebhard, P. H. (1953). *Sexual behavior in the human female.* New York, NY: W. B. Saunders.

Kinzie, J. D., & Leung, P. (1989). Clonidine in Cambodian patients with posttraumatic stress disorder. *Journal of Nervous and Mental Disease, 177*, 546–550.

Kirby, J. S., Chu, J. A., & Dill, D. L. (1993). Severity, frequency, and age of onset of physical and sexual abuse as factors in the development of dissociative symptoms. *Comprehensive Psychiatry, 34*, 258–263.

Kirmayer, L. J., & Carroll, J. (1987). A neurobiological hypothesis on the nature of chronic self-mutilation. *Integrative Psychiatry, 5*, 212–213.

Kitchner, I., & Greenstein, R. (1985). Low-dose lithium carbonate in the treatment of posttraumatic stress disorder: Brief communication. *Military Medicine, 150*, 378–381.

Kluft, R. P. (1984). Treatment of multiple personality disorder: A study of 33 cases. *Psychiatric Clinics of North America, 7*, 9–29.

Kluft, R. P. (1985a). Childhood multiple personality disorder: Predictors, clinical findings and treatment results. In R. P. Kluft (Ed.), *Childhood antecedents of multiple personality* (pp. 167–196). Washington, DC: American Psychiatric Press.

Kluft, R. P. (1985b). The natural history of multiple personality disorder. In R. P. Kluft (Ed.), *Childhood antecedents of multiple personality* (pp. 197–238). Washington, DC: American Psychiatric Press.

Kluft, R. P. (1985c). The treatment of multiple personality disorder (MPD): Current concepts. *Directions in psychiatry, 5*(4), 3–9. New York, NY: Hatherleigh.

Kluft, R. P. (Ed.). (1985d). *Childhood antecedents of multiple personality disorder.* Washington, DC: American Psychiatric Press.

Kluft, R. P. (1986). Personality unifcation in multiple personality disorder: A follow-up study. In B. G. Braun (Ed.), *Treatment of multiple personality disorder* (pp. 29–60). Washington, DC: American Psychiatric Press.

Kluft, R. P. (1987a). First-rank symptoms as a diagnostic clue to multiple personality disorder. *American Journal of Psychiatry, 144*, 293–298.

Kluft, R. P. (1987b). The parental fitness of mothers with multiple personality disorder: A preliminary study. *Child Abuse and Neglect, 11*, 273–280.

Kluft, R. P. (1987c). The simulation and dissimulation of multiple personality disorder. *American Journal of Clinical Hypnosis, 30*, 104–118.

Kluft, R. P. (1988). On giving consultations to therapists treating multiple personality disorder: Fifteen years' experience—Part I (diagnosis and treatment). *Dissociation, 1*(3), 23–29.

Kluft, R. P. (1989a). Iatrogenic creation of new alter personalities. *Dissociation, 2*, 83–91.

Kluft, R. P. (1989b). Treating patients sexually exploited by a previous therapist. *Psychiatric Clinics of North America, 12*, 483–500.

Kluft, R. P. (1990a). Incest and subsequent revictimization: The case of therapist-patient sexual exploitation, with a description of the sitting duck syndrome. In R. P. Kluft (Ed.), *Incest-related syndromes of adult psychopathology* (pp. 263–287). Washington, DC: American Psychiatric Press.

Kluft, R. P. (Ed.). (1990b). *Incest-related syndromes of adult psychopathology.* Washington, DC: American Psychiatric Press.

Kluft, R. P. (1991a). The hospital treatment of multiple personality disorder. *Psychiatric Clinics of North America, 14*, 695–719.

Kluft, R. P. (1991b). Multiple personality disorder. In A. Tasman & S. M. Goldfinger (Eds.), *American Psychiatric Press review of psychiatry* (Vol. 10, pp. 161–188). Washington, DC: American Psychiatric Press.

Kluft, R. P. (1993). Clinical approaches to the integration of personalities. In R. P. Kluft & C. G. Fine (Eds.), *Clinical perspectives on multiple personality disorder* (pp. 101–134). Washington, DC: American Psychiatric Press.

Kluft, R. P. (1994). Treatment trajectories in multiple personality disorder. *Dissociation, 1*, 63–76.

Kluft, R. P. (1995). The confirmation and disconfirmation of memories of abuse in dissociative identity disorder patients: A naturalistic study. *Dissociation, 8*, 253–258.

Kluft, R. P. (1996). Dissociative identity disorder. In L. K. Michelson & W. J. Ray (Eds.), *Handbook of dissociation: Theoretical, empirical, and clinical perspectives* (pp. 337–366). New York, NY: Plenum Press.

Kluft, R. P. (1997a). On the treatment of traumatic memories: Always? Never? Sometimes? Now? Later? *Dissociation, 10*, 80–90.

Kluft, R. P. (1997b). Overview of the treatment of patients alleging that they have suffered ritualized or sadistic abuse. In G. A. Fraser (Ed.), *The dilemma of ritual abuse: Cautions and guides for therapists.* Washington, DC: American Psychiatric Press.

Kluft, R. P. (2009). A clinician's understanding of dissociation: Fragments of an acquaintance. In P. F. Dell & J. A. O'Neil (Eds.), *Dissociation and the dissociative disorders: DSM-V and beyond* (pp. 599–624). New York, NY: Routledge.

Kluft, R. P., & Fine, C. G. (Eds.). (1993). *Clinical perspectives on multiple personality disorder.* Washington, DC: American Psychiatric Press.

Knight, R. (1958). Borderline states. *Bulletin of the Menninger Clinic, 17*, 1–12.

Kobasa, S. C., Maddi, S. R., & Kahn, S. (1982). Hardiness and health: A prospective study. *Journal of Personality and Social Psychology, 42*, 168–177.

Koenen, K. C., Stellman, S. D., Sommer, J. F., & Stellman, J. M. (2008). Persisting posttraumatic stress disorder symptoms and their relationship to functioning in Vietnam veterans: A 14-year follow-up. *Journal of Traumatic Stress, 21*, 49–57.

Koenig, L. J., & Clark, H. (2004). Sexual abuse of girls and HIV infection among women: Are they related? In L. J. Koenig, L. S. Doll, A. O'Leary, & W. Pequegnat (Eds.), *From child sexual abuse to adult sexual risk: Trauma, revictimization, and intervention* (pp. 69–92). Washington, DC: American Psychological Association.

Kolb, J. E., & Gunderson, J. G. (1990). Review of Kernberg, O. F., Selzer, M. A., Koenisberg, H. W., Carr, A. C., & Appelbaum, A. H., Psychodynamic psychotherapy of borderline patients. *International Review of Psychoanalysis, 17*, 513–516.

Kolb, L. C. (1987). A neuropsychological hypothesis explaining posttraumatic stress disorders. *American Journal of Psychiatry, 144*, 989–995.

Kolb, L. C., Burris, B., & Griffiths, S. (1984). Propranolol and clonidine in the treatment of chronic posttraumatic stress of war. In B. A. van der Kolk (Ed.), *Posttraumatic stress disorder: Psychological and biological sequelae* (pp. 97–107). Washington, DC: American Psychiatric Press.

Kosten, T. R., Fontana, A., Semyak, M. J., & Rosenheck, R. (2000). Benzodiazepine use in posttraumatic stress disorder among veterans with substance abuse. *Journal of Nervous and Mental Disease, 188*, 454–459.

Kosten, T. R., Frank, J. B., Dan, E., McDougle, C. J., & Giller, E. L. (1991). Pharmacotherapy for posttraumatic stress disorder using phenelzine or imipramine. *Journal of Nervous and Mental Disease, 179*, 366–370.

Kotler, M., Iancu, I., Efroni, R., & Amir, M. (2001). Anger, impulsivity, social support, and suicide risk in patients with posttraumatic stress disorder. *Journal of Nervous and Mental Disease, 189*, 162–167.

Kozarić-Kovačić, D., & Pivac, N. (2007). Quetiapine treatment in an open trial in combat related post-traumatic stress disorder with psychotic features: An open trial. *International Journal of Neuropsychopharmacology, 10,* 253–261.

Kozarić-Kovačić, D., Pivac, N., Mück-Šeler, D., & Rothbaum, B.O. (2005). Risperidone in psychotic combat related posttraumatic stress disorder: An open trial. *Journal of Clinical Psychiatry, 66,* 922–927.

Kramer, T. H., Buckhout, R., Fox, P., Widman, E., & Tusche, B. (1991). Effects of stress on recall. *Applied Cognitive Psychology, 5,* 483–488.

Krystal, J. H., Bennett, A., Bremner, J. D., Southwick, S. M., & Charney, D. S. (1996). Recent developments in the neurobiology of dissociation. In L. K. Michelson & W. J. Ray (Eds.), *Handbook of dissociation: Theoretical, empirical, and clinical perspectives* (pp. 183–190). New York, NY: Plenum Press.

Kubie, L. S. (1943). Manual of emergency treatment for acute war neuroses. *War Medicine, 4,* 582–599.

Kuch, K., & Cox, B. (1992). Symptoms of PTSD in 124 survivors of the Holocaust. *American Journal of Psychiatry, 149,* 337–340.

Kulka, R. A., Schlenger, W. E., Fairbank, J. A., Hough, R. L., Jordan, B. K., Marmar, C. R., & Weiss, D. S. (1990). *Trauma and the Vietnam war generation: Report of findings from the national Vietnam veterans readjustment study.* New York, NY: Brunner/Mazel.

Kumar, G., Pepe, D., & Steer, R. A. (2004). Adolescent psychiatric inpatients' self-reported reasons for cutting themselves. *Journal of Nervous and Mental Disease, 192,* 830–836.

Langeland, W., & Hartgers, C. (1998). Child sexual and physical abuse and alcoholism: A review. *Journal of Studies on Alcohol, 59,* 336–348.

Lanius, R. A., Vermetten, E., Loewenstein, R. J., Brand, B., Schmahl, C., Bremner, J. D., & Spiegel, D. (2010). Emotion modulation in PTSD: Clinical and neurobiological evidence for a dissociative subtype. *American Journal of Psychiatry, 167,* 640–647.

Le Doux, J. E. (1992). Emotion as memory: Anatomical systems underlying indelible neural traces. In S.-Å. Christianson (Ed.), *The handbook of emotion and memory* (pp. 269–287). Hillsdale, NJ: Lawrence Erlbaum.

Lebowitz, L., Harvey, M. R., & Herman, J. L. (1993). A stage-by-dimension model of recovery from sexual trauma. *Interpersonal Violence, 8,* 378–391.

Lemieux, A., & Coe, C. (1993). Abuse-related posttraumatic stress disorder: Evidence for chronic neuroendocrine activation in women. *Psychosomatic Medicine, 57,* 105–115.

Lewis, D., Yeager, C., Swica, Y., Pincus, J., & Lewis, M. (1997). Objective documentation of child abuse and dissociation in 12 murderers with dissociative identity disorder. *American Journal of Psychiatry, 154,* 1703–1710.

Lilienfeld, S. O., & Lynn, S. J. (2003). Dissociative identity disorder: Multiple personalities, multiple controversies. In S. O. Lilienfeld, S. J. Lynn, & J. M. Lohr (Eds.), *Science and pseudoscience in clinical psychology* (pp. 109–142). New York, NY: Guilford Press.

Liman, D. (Director and Producer), Crowley, P. (Producer), & Gladstein, R. N. (Producer). (2002). *The Bourne Identity* [motion picture]. USA: Universal Pictures.

Linehan, M.M. (1993). *Cognitive behavioral treatment of borderline personality disorder.* New York, NY: Guilford Press.

Liotti, G. (1992). Disorganized/disoriented attachment in the etiology of dissociative disorders. *Dissociation, 5*(4), 196–204.

Liotti, G. (2004). Trauma, dissociation, and disorganized attachment: Three strands of a single braid. *Psychotherapy: Theory, Research, Practice, Training, 41,* 472–486.

Lipper, S., Davidson, J. R., Grady, T. A., Edinger, J. D., Hammett, E. B., Mahorney, S. L., & Cavenar, J. O. J. (1986). Preliminary study of carbamazepine in post-traumatic stress disorder. *Psychosomatics, 27,* 849–854.

Lipton, A. (1999). Recovered memory in the courts. In S. Taub (Ed.), *Recovered memories of child sexual abuse: Psychological, social and legal perspectives on a contemporary mental health controversy* (pp. 165–210). Springfield, IL: Charles C. Thomas.

Lochner, C., du Toit, P. L., Zungu-Dirway, N., Marais, A., van Kradenburg, J., Seedat, S., Niehaus, D. J., & Stein, D. J. (2002). Childhood trauma in obsessive-compulsive disorder, trichotillomania, and controls. *Depression and Anxiety, 15*, 66–68.

Loewenstein, R. J. (1990). Somatoform disorders in victims of incest and child abuse. In R. P. Kluft (Ed.), *Incest-related syndromes of adult psychopathology* (pp. 75–112). Washington, DC: American Psychiatric Press.

Loewenstein, R .J. (1991). An office mental status examination for complex chronic dissociative symptoms and multiple personality disorder. *Psychiatric Clinics of North America, 14*, 567–604.

Loewenstein, R. J. (2007). Dissociative identity disorder: Issues in the iatrogenesis controversy. In E. Vermetten, M. Dorahy, & D. Spiegel (Eds.), *Traumatic dissociation* (pp. 275–299). Washington, DC: American Psychiatric Press.

Loewenstein, R. J., Hornstein, N., & Farber, B. (1988). Open trial of clonazepam in the treatment of posttraumatic stress symptoms in multiple personality disorder. *Dissociation, 1*(3), 3–12.

Loftus, E. (1979). Reacting to blatantly contradictory information. *Memory and Cognition, 7*, 368–374.

Loftus, E. F. (1993). The reality of repressed memories. *American Psychologist, 48*, 518–537.

Loftus, E. F., Korf, N. L., & Schooler, J. W. (1989). Misguided memories: Sincere distortions of reality. In J. C. Yuille (Ed.), *Credibility assessment* (pp. 155–173). Norwell, MA: Kluwer Academic.

Loftus, E. F., Miller, D. G., & Burns, H. J. (1978). Semantic integration of verbal information into visual memory. *Journal of Experimental Psychology: Human Learning and Memory, 4*, 19–31.

Loftus, E. F., Polonsky, S., & Fullilove, M. T. (1994). Memories of childhood sexual abuse. *Psychology of Women Quarterly, 18*, 64–84.

Ludolph, P. S., Westen, D., Misle, B., Jackson, A., Wixon, J., & Wiss, F. C. (1990). The borderline diagnosis in adolescents: Symptoms and developmental history. *American Journal of Psychiatry, 147*, 470–476.

Luxenberg, T., Spinazzola, J., & van der Kolk, B. A. (2001). Complex trauma and disorders of extreme stress (DESNOS) diagnosis, Part I: Assessment. *Directions in Psychiatry, 21*(21), 373–393. Long Island City, NY: Hatherleigh.

Lynn, S. J., & Ruhe, J. W. (1986). The fantasy-prone person: Hypnosis, imagination, and creativity. *Journal of Personality and Social Psychology, 51*, 404–408.

Lyons-Ruth, K., & Jacobvitz, C. (1999). Unresolved loss, relational violence, and lapses in behavioral and attentional strategies. In J. Cassidy & P. R. Shaver (Eds.), *Handbook of attachment: Theory, research and clinical applications* (pp. 89–111). New York, NY: Guilford Press.

Lyons-Ruth, K., Yellin, C., Helnick, S., & Atwood, G. (2005). Expanding the concept of unresolved mental states: Hostile/helpless states of mind on the adult attachment interview are associated with disrupted mother-infant communication and infant disorganization. *Developmental Psychopathology, 17*, 1–23.

MacFarlane, K., & Korbin, J. (1983). Confronting the incest secret long after the fact: A family study of multiple victimization with strategies for intervention. *Child Abuse & Neglect, 7*, 225–240.

MacMillan, H. L., Fleming, J. E., Trocmé, N., Boyle, M. H., Maria Wong, M., Racine, Y. A., Beardslee, W. R., & Offord, D. R. (1997). Prevalence of child physical and sexual abuse in the community: Results from the Ontario health supplement. *Journal of the American Medical Association, 278*, 131–135.

Maes, M., Lin, A., Bonaccorso, S., van Hunsel, F., Van Gastel, A., Delmeire, L., Biondi, M., Bosmans, E., Kenis, G., & Scharpé, S. (1998). Increased 24-hour urinary cortisol excretion in patients with posttraumatic stress disorder and patients with major depression, but not in patients with fibromyalgia. *Acta Psychiatrica Scandinavica, 98*, 328–335.

Mahler, M. S. (1971). A study of the separation-individuation process and its possible application to borderline phenomena in the psychoanalytic situation. *Psychoanalytic Study of the Child, 26*, 403–424.

Mahler, M. S. (1972). Rapprochement subphase of the separation-individuation process. *Psychoanalytic Quarterly, 41*, 487–506.

Main, M., & Hesse, E. (1990). Parents' unresolved traumatic experiences are related to infant disorganized attachment status: Is frightened and/or frightening parental behavior the linking mechanism? In M. T.

Greenberg, D. Cicchetti, & E. M. Cummings (Eds.), *Attachment in the preschool years* (pp. 161–182). Chicago, IL: The University of Chicago Press.

Main, M., & Solomon, J. (1990). Procedures for identifying infants as disorganized/disoriented during the Ainsworth strange situation. In M. T. Greenberg, D. Cicchetti, & M. Cummings (Eds.), *Attachment in the preschool years: Theory, research, and intervention* (pp. 121–160). Chicago, IL: The University of Chicago Press.

Mann, J. (1973). Confrontation as a mode of teaching. In G. Adler & P. G. Myerson (Eds.), *Confrontation in psychotherapy* (pp. 39–48). New York, NY: Science House.

Manosevitz, A., Fling, S., & Prentice, N. M. (1977). Imaginary companions in young children: Relationships with intelligence, creativity and writing ability. *Journal of Child Psychology and Psychiatry, 18*, 73–78.

Marmer, S. S. (1991). Multiple personality: A psychoanalytic perspective. *Psychiatric Clinics of North America, 14*, 677–693.

Marmer, S. S., & Fink, D. (1994). Rethinking the comparison of multiple personality disorder and borderline personality disorder. *Psychiatric Clinics of North America, 17*, 743–771.

Marshall, R. D., Beebe, K. L., Oldham, M., & Zaninelli, R. (2001). Efficacy and safety of paroxetine treatment for chronic PTSD: A fixed-dose, placebo-controlled study. *American Journal of Psychiatry, 158*, 1982–1988.

Mason, J. W., Wang, S., Riney, S., Charney, D. S., & Southwick, S. M. (2001). Psychogenic lowering of urinary cortisol levels linked to increased emotional numbing and a shame-depressive syndrome in combat-related posttraumatic stress disorder. *Psychosomatic Medicine, 63*, 387–401.

Masterson, J. (1972). *Treatment of the borderline adolescent: A developmental approach.* New York, NY: Wiley-Interscience.

Mathews, C. A., Kaur, N., & Stein, M. B. (2008). Childhood trauma and obsessive-compulsive symptoms. *Depression and Anxiety, 25*, 742–751.

Matthews, J. A., & Chu, J. A. (1997). Psychodynamic therapy for patients with early childhood trauma. In P. S. Appelbaum, L. A. Uyehara, & M. R. Elin (Eds.), *Trauma and memory: Clinical and legal controversies* (pp. 316–343). New York, NY: Oxford University Press.

McCann, I. L., & Pearlman, L. A. (1990). Vicarious traumatization: A contextual model for understanding the effects of trauma on helpers. *Journal of Traumatic Stress, 3*, 131–149.

McFall, M. E., Murburg, M. M., Roszell, D. K., & Veith, R. C. (1989). Psychophysiologic and neuroendocrine findings in posttraumatic stress disorder: A review of theory and research. *Journal of Anxiety Disorders, 3*, 243–257.

McGaugh, J. L. (1989). Involvement of hormonal and neuromodulatory systems in the regulation of memory storage. *Annual Review of Neuroscience, 12*, 255–287.

McGaugh, J. L. (1992). Affect, neuromodulatory systems and memory storage. In S.-Å. Christianson (Ed.), *The handbook of emotion and memory* (pp. 245–267). Hillsdale, NJ: Lawrence Erlbaum.

McGaugh, J. L., Introini, I. B., & Castellano, C. (1993). Involvement of opioid peptides in learning and memory. In A. Herz (Ed.), *Opioids II* (pp. 429–447). New York, NY: Springer-Verlag.

McHugh, P. R. (1992). Psychiatric misadventures. *The American Scholar, 61*, 497–510.

Merckelbach, H., à Campo, J., Hardy, S., & Giesbrecht, T. (2005). Dissociation and fantasy proneness in psychiatric patients: A preliminary study. *Comprehensive Psychiatry, 46*, 181–185.

Merskey, H. (1992). The manufacture of personalities: The production of multiple personality disorder. *British Journal of Psychiatry, 160*, 327–340.

Mesulam, M. M. (1981). Dissociative states with abnormal temporal lobe EEG: Multiple personality and the illusion of possession. *Archives of Neurology, 38*, 178–181.

Michaels, L. (Producer), & Wilson, D. (Director). (1978). *The French chef* [TV show; Saturday Night Live, Season 4, Episode 8]. USA: National Broadcasting Corporation.

Michelson, L. K., & Ray, W. J. (Eds.). (1996). *Handbook of dissociation: Theoretical, empirical, and clinical perspectives.* New York, NY: Plenum Press.

Miller, A. (1983). *For your own good: Hidden cruelty in child-rearing and the roots of violence*. New York, NY: Farrar, Straus and Giroux.

Miller, R. (1979). Development from one to two years: Language acquisition. In J. Noshpitz (Ed.), *Basic handbook of child psychiatry* (pp. 127–144). New York, NY: Basic Books.

Milner, B. (1962). Les troubles de la memoire accompagnant des lesions hippocampiques bilaterales. In P. Passouant (Ed.), *Physiologie de l'hippocampe* (pp. 257–272). Paris, France: Centre National de la Recherche Scientifique.

Mullen, P. E., Martin, J. L., Anderson, J. C., Romans, S. E., & Herbison, G. P. (1996). The long-term impact of the physical, emotional and sexual abuse of children: A community study. *Child Abuse & Neglect*, *20*, 7–22.

Myerson, P. G. (1973). The meanings of confrontation. In G. Adler & P. G. Myerson (Eds.), *Confrontation in psychotherapy* (pp. 21–38). New York, NY: Science House.

Najavits, L. M. (2002). *Seeking safety: A treatment manual for PTSD and substance abuse*. New York, NY: Guilford Press.

Najavits, L. M. (2004). Treatment of posttraumatic stress disorder and substance abuse: Clinical guidelines for implementing seeking safety therapy. *Alcoholism Treatment Quarterly*, *22*, 43–62.

Najavits, L. M., Weiss, R. D., & Shaw, S. R. (1997). The link between substance abuse and posttraumatic stress disorder in women: A research review. *American Journal of Addictions*, *6*(4), 273–283.

National Public Radio (Producer). (1996). *Recovered memory debate still incites disagreement* [Morning Edition]. Washington, DC: National Public Radio.

National Victim Center, Crime Victims Research and Treatment Center. (1992). *Rape in America: A report to the nation*. Arlington, VA: National Victim Center.

Neisser, U., & Harsch, N. (1992). Phantom flashbulb: False recollections of hearing news about the *Challenger*. In E. Winograd & U. Neisser (Eds.), *Affect and accuracy in recall* (pp. 9–31). New York, NY: Cambridge University Press.

Nelson, E. C., Heath, A. C., Madden, P. A. F., Cooper, M. L., Dinwiddie, S. H., Bucholz, K. K., Glowinski, A., McLaughlin, T., Dunne, M. P., Statham, D. J., & Martin, N. G. (2002). Association between self-reported childhood sexual abuse and adverse psychosocial outcomes: Results from a twin study. *Archives of General Psychiatry*, *59*, 139–145.

Nijenhuis, E. R. S. (1999). *Somatoform dissociation: Phenomena, measurement, and theoretical issues*. Assen, The Netherlands: Van Gorcum.

Nijenhuis, E. R. S. (2000). Somatoform dissociation: Major symptoms of dissociative disorders. *Journal of Trauma & Dissociation*, *4*(1), 7–32.

Nijenhuis, E. R. S. (2010). The scoring and interpretation of the SDQ-20 and SDQ-5. *Activitas Nervosa Superior*, *52*(1), 24–28.

Nijenhuis, E. R. S., Spinhoven, P., Van Dyck, R., Van der Hart, O., & Vanderlinden, J. (1996). The development and the psychometric characteristics of the somatoform dissociation questionnaire (SDQ-20). *Journal of Nervous and Mental Disease*, *184*, 688–694.

Ofshe, R. J. (1992). Inadvertent hypnosis during interrogation: False confession due to dissociative state, misidentified multiple personality and the satanic cult hypothesis. *International Journal of Clinical and Experimental Hypnosis*, *40*, 125–126.

Ofshe, R. J., & Singer, M. T. (1994). Recovered-memory therapy and robust repression: Influence and pseudomemories. *International Journal of Clinical and Experimental Hypnosis*, *42*, 391–410.

Ogata, S. N., Silk, K. R., Goodrich, S., Lohr, N. E., Westen, D., & Hill, E. M. (1990). Childhood sexual and physical abuse in adult patients with borderline personality disorder. *American Journal of Psychiatry*, *147*, 1008–1013.

Ogden, P., Minton, K., & Pain, C. (2006). *Trauma and the body: A sensorimotor approach to psychotherapy*. New York, NY: W. W. Norton.

Ozer, E. J., Best, S. R., Lipsey, T. L., & Weiss, D. S. (2003). Predictors of posttraumatic stress disorder and symptoms in adults: A meta-analysis. *Psychological Bulletin*, *129*, 52–71.

Paul, T., Schroeter, K., Dahme, B., & Nutzinger, D. O. (2002). Self-injurious behavior in women with eating disorders. *American Journal of Psychiatry, 159*, 408–411.

Pauls, D. L., Mundo, E., & Kennedy, J. L. (2002). The pathophysiology and genetics of obsessive-compulsive disorder. In K. L. Davis, D. Charney, J. T. Coyle, & C. Nemeroff (Eds.), *Neuropsychopharmacology: The fifth generation of progress* (pp. 1609–1619). Philadelphia, PA: Lippincott Williams & Wilkins.

Paulsen, S. (2008). Treating dissociative identity disorder with EMDR, ego state therapy and adjunct approaches. In C. Forgash & M. Copeley (Eds.), *Healing the heart of trauma and dissociation with EMDR and ego state therapy* (pp. 141–179). New York, NY: Springer.

Pearlman, L. A., & Saakvitne, K. W. (1995). *Trauma and the therapist: Countertransference and vicarious traumatization in psychotherapy with incest survivors*. New York, NY: W. W. Norton.

Pearson, M. L. (1997). Childhood trauma, adult trauma, and dissociation. *Dissociation, 10*(1), 58–62.

Pekala, R. J., Angelini, F., & Kumar, V. K. (2006). The importance of fantasy-proneness in dissociation: A replication. *Contemporary Hypnosis, 18*, 204–214.

Pelcovitz, D., van der Kolk, B. A., Roth, S., Mandel, F., Kaplan, D., & Resick, P. (1997). Development of a criteria set and a structured interview for disorders of extreme stress (DESNOS). *Journal of Traumatic Stress, 10*, 3–16.

Perry, B. D. (1999). Memories of states: How the brain stores and retrieves traumatic experience. In J. Goodwin & R. Attias (Eds.), *Splintered reflections: Images of the body in trauma* (pp. 9–38). New York, NY: Basic Books.

Peterson, R. G. (1994). Comment on Loftus. *American Psychologist, 49*, 443.

Petty, F., Brannan, S., Casada, J., Davis, L. L., Gajewski, V., Kramer, G. L., Stone, R. C., Teten, A. L., Worchel, J., & Young, K. A. (2001). Olanzapine treatment for post-traumatic stress disorder: An open-label study. *International Clinical Psychopharmacology, 16*, 331–337.

Piaget, J. (1962). *Plays, dreams and imitation in childhood*. New York, NY: W. W. Norton.

Piper, A. (1997). *Hoax & reality: The bizarre world of multiple personality disorder*. Northvale, NJ: Jason Aronson.

Pitman, R. K., & Orr, S. P. (1990). Twenty-four hour urinary cortisol and catecholamine excretion in combat-related stimuli in posttraumatic stress disorder. *Biologic Psychiatry, 27*, 245–247.

Pitman, R. K., Sanders, K. M., Zusman, R. M., Healy, A. R., Cheema, F., Lasko, N. B., Cahill, L., & Orr, S. P. (2002). Pilot study of secondary prevention of posttraumatic stress disorder with propranolol. *Biologic Psychiatry, 15*, 189–192.

Pitman, R. K., van der Kolk, B. A., Orr, S. P., & Greenberg, M. S. (1990). Naloxone-reversible analgesic response to combat related stimuli in posttraumatic stress disorder: A pilot study. *Archives of General Psychiatry, 47*, 541–544.

Polster, M. R., Nadel, L., & Schacter, D. L. (1991). Cognitive neuroscience analyses of memory: A historical perspective. *Journal of Cognitive Neuroscience, 3*, 95–116.

Pomeroy, W. B. (1976, November). A new look at incest. *Penthouse Forum*, p. 10.

Pope, H. G., & Hudson, J. I. (1995). Can memories of child sexual abuse be repressed? *Psychological Medicine, 25*, 121–126.

Pope, H. G., Hudson, J. I., Bodkin, J. A., & Oliva, P. (1998). Questionable validity of 'dissociative amnesia' in trauma victims. *British Journal of Psychiatry, 172*, 210–215.

Pope, K. (1996). Memory, abuse, and science: Questioning claims about the false memory syndrome epidemic. *American Psychologist, 51*, 957–974.

Post, R. M., Weiss, S. R., Smith, M., Li, H., & McCann, U. (1997). Kindling versus quenching: Implications for the evolution and treatment of posttraumatic stress disorder. *Annals of the New York Academy of Sciences, 821*, 285–295.

Pribor, E. F., & Dinwiddie, S. H. (1992). Psychiatric correlates of incest in childhood. *American Journal of Psychiatry, 149*, 53–56.

Pribor, E. F., Yutzy, S. H., Dean, T., & Wetzel, R. D. (1993). Briquet's syndrome, dissociation, and abuse. *American Journal of Psychiatry, 150*, 1507–1511.

Purcell, D. W., Malow, C. D., Dolezal, C., & Carbello-Diéguez, A. (2004). Sexual abuse of boys: Short- and long-term associations and implications for HIV infection. In L. J. Koenig, L. S. Doll, A. O'Leary, & W. Pequegnat (Eds.), *From child sexual abuse to adult sexual risk: Trauma, revictimization, and intervention* (pp. 93–114). Washington, DC: American Psychological Association.

Putnam, F. W. (1985). Dissociation as a response to extreme trauma. In R. P. Kluft (Ed.), *Childhood antecedents of multiple personality* (pp. 65–97). Washington, DC: American Psychiatric Press.

Putnam, F. W. (1989). *The diagnosis and treatment of multiple personality disorder.* New York, NY: Guilford Press.

Putnam, F. W. (1990). Disturbances of 'self' in victims of childhood sexual abuse. In R. P. Kluft (Ed.), *Incest-related syndromes of adult psychopathology* (pp. 113–132). Washington, DC: American Psychiatric Press.

Putnam, F. W. (1991). Dissociative phenomena. In A. Tasman & S. M. Goldfinger (Eds.), *Review of psychiatry* (Vol. 10, pp. 145–160). Washington, DC: American Psychiatric Press.

Putnam, F. W. (1997). *Dissociation in children and adolescents.* New York, NY: Guilford Press.

Putnam, F. W., Carlson, E. B., Ross, C. A., Anderson, G., Clark, P., Torem, M., Bowman, E. S., Coons, P. M., Chu, J. A., Dill, D. L., Loewenstein, R. J., & Braun, B. G. (1996). Patterns of dissociation in clinical and non-clinical samples. *Journal of Nervous and Mental Disease, 184,* 673–979.

Putnam, F. W., Guroff, J. J., Silberman, E. K., Barban, L., & Post, R. M. (1986). The clinical phenomenology of multiple personality disorder: A review of 100 cases. *Journal of Clinical Psychiatry, 47,* 258–293.

Putnam, F. W., Helmers, K., Horowitz, L. A., & Trickett, P. K. (1995). Hypnotizability and dissociativity in sexually abused girls. *Child Abuse & Neglect, 19,* 645–655.

Raskind, M. A., Peskind, E. R., Hoff, D. J., Hart, K. L., Holmes, H. A., Warren, D., Shofer, J., O'Connell, J., Taylor, F., Gross, C., Rohde, K., & McFall, M. E. (2007). A parallel group placebo controlled study of prazosin for trauma nightmares and sleep disturbance in combat veterans with post-traumatic stress disorder. *Biologic Psychiatry, 61,* 928–934.

Raskind, M. A., Peskind, E. R., Kanter, E. D., Petrie, E. C., Radant, A., Thompson, C. E., Dobie, D. J., Hoff, D., Rein, R. J., Straits-Tröster, K., Thomas, R. G., & McFall, M. M. (2003). Reduction of nightmares and other PTSD symptoms in combat veterans by prazosin: A placebo-controlled study. *American Journal of Psychiatry, 160,* 371–373.

Rasmusson, A. M., Lipschitz, D. S., Wang, S., Hu, S., Vojvoda, D., Bremner, J. D., Southwick, S. M., & Charney, D. S. (2001). Increased pituitary and adrenal reactivity in premenopausal women with post-traumatic stress disorder. *Biologic Psychiatry, 50,* 965–977.

Reich, D. B., Winternitz, S., Hennen, J., Watts, T., & Stanculescu, C. (2004). A preliminary study of risperidone in the treatment of posttraumatic stress disorder related to childhood abuse in women. *Journal of Clinical Psychiatry, 65,* 1601–1606.

Resnick, H. S., Kilpatrick, D. G., Dansky, B. S., Saunders, B. E., & Best, C. L. (1993). Prevalence of civilian trauma and posttraumatic stress disorder in a representative national sample of women. *Journal of Consulting and Clinical Psychology, 61,* 984–991.

Richardson, J. T., Best, J., & Bromley, D. G. (Eds.). (1991). *The satanism scare.* New York, NY: Aldine de Gruyter.

Roelofs, K., Keijsers, G. P. J., Hoogduin, K. A. L., Näring, G. W. B., & Moene, F. C. (2002). Childhood abuse in patients with conversion disorder. *American Journal of Psychiatry, 159,* 1908–1913.

Ross, C. A. (1989). *Multiple personality disorder: Diagnosis, clinical features and treatment.* New York, NY: John Wiley & Sons.

Ross, C. A. (1995). *Satanic ritual abuse: Principles of treatment.* Toronto, Canada: University of Toronto Press.

Ross, C. A. (1997). *Dissociative identity disorder: Diagnosis, clinical features, and treatment of multiple personality.* New York, NY: John Wiley & Sons.

Ross, C. A. (2007). Borderline personality disorder and dissociation. *Journal of Trauma & Dissociation, 8*(1), 71–80.

Ross, C. A., Anderson, G., Fleisher, W. P., & Norton, G. R. (1991). The frequency of multiple personality disorder among psychiatric inpatients. *American Journal of Psychiatry, 148*, 1717–1720.

Ross, C. A., Heber, S., Norton, G. R., Anderson, D., Anderson, G., & Barchet, P. (1989). The dissociative disorders interview schedule: A structured interview. *Dissociation, 2*, 169–189.

Ross, C. A., Miller, S. D., Reagor, P., Bjornson, L., Fraser, G. A., & Anderson, G. (1990). Structured interview data on 102 cases of multiple personality disorder from four centers. *American Journal of Psychiatry, 147*, 596–601.

Ross, C. A., & Norton, G. R. (1989). Suicide and parasuicide in multiple personality disorder. *Psychiatry, 52*, 365–371.

Ross, C. A., Norton, G. R., & Fraser, G. A. (1989). Evidence against the iatrogenesis of multiple personality disorder. *Dissociation, 2*, 61–64.

Ross, S., & Health, N. (2002). A study of self-mutilation in a community sample of adolescents. *Journal of Youth and Adolescence, 31*, 67–77.

Roth, A. S., Ostroff, R. B., & Hoffman, R. E. (1996). Naltrexone as a treatment for repetitive self-injurious behaviour: An open-label trial. *Journal of Clinical Psychiatry, 57*, 233–237.

Roth, S., Newman, E., Pelcovitz, D., van der Kolk, B., & Mandel, F. S. (1997). Complex PTSD in victims exposed to sexual and physical abuse: Results from the DSM-IV field trial for posttraumatic stress disorder. *Journal of Traumatic Stress, 10*, 539–556.

Rothschild, B. (2000). *The body remembers: The psychophysiology of trauma and trauma treatment.* New York, NY: W. W. Norton.

Russ, M. J., Shearin, E. N., Clarkin, J. F., Harrison, K., & Hull, J. W. (1993). Subtypes of self-injurious patients with borderline personality disorder. *American Journal of Psychiatry, 150*, 1869–1871.

Russell, D. E. H. (1986). *The secret trauma: Incest in the lives of girls and women.* New York, NY: Basic Books.

Russell, P. L. (2006). The theory of the crunch. *Smith College Studies in Social Work, 76*(1–2), 9–21.

Rutter, M. (1987). Psychosocial resilience and protective mechanisms. *American Journal of Orthopsychiatry, 57*, 316–331.

Ruzek, J. I., Polusny, M. A., & Abueg, F. R. (1998). Assessment and treatment of concurrent posttraumatic stress disorder and substance abuse. In V. M. Follette, J. I. Ruzek, & F. R. Abueg (Eds.), *Cognitive-behavioral therapies for trauma* (pp. 226–255). New York, NY: Guilford Press.

Sakheim, D. K. (1996). Clinical aspects of sadistic ritual abuse. In L. K. Michelson & W. J. Ray (Eds.), *Handbook of dissociation: Theoretical, empirical, and clinical perspectives* (pp. 569–594). New York, NY: Plenum Press.

Sakheim, D. K., & Devine, S. E. (Eds.). (1992). *Out of darkness: Exploring satanism and ritual abuse.* New York, NY: Lexington Books.

Sakheim, D. K., Hess, E. P., & Chivas, A. (1988). General principles for short-term inpatient work with multiple personality disorder patients. *Psychotherapy, 25*, 117–124.

Salkovskis, P. M. (1989). Somatic problems. In K. Hawkin, P. M. Salkovskis, & J. W. Kirk (Eds.), *Cognitive-behavioral approaches to adult psychiatric disorders* (pp. 235–276). Oxford, England: Oxford University Press.

Sandberg, D., Lynn, S. J., & Green, J. (1994). Sexual abuse and victimization. In S. J. Lynn & J. Rhue (Eds.), *Dissociation: Clinical and theoretical perspectives* (pp. 242–267). New York, NY: Guilford Press.

Sanders, B., & Giolas, M. H. (1991). Dissociation and childhood trauma in psychologically disturbed adolescents. *American Journal of Psychiatry, 148*, 50–54.

Sansone, R. A., Pole, M., Dakroub, H., & Butler, M. (2006). Childhood trauma, borderline personality symptomatology, and psychophysiological and pain disorders in adulthood. *Psychosomatics, 47*, 158–162.

Sapolsky, R. M. (1986). Glucocorticoid toxicity in the hippocampus: Reversal by supplementation with brain fuels. *Journal of Neuroscience, 6*, 2240–2244.

Sapolsky, R. M., Krey, L. C., & McEwen, B. S. (1986). The neuroendocrinology of stress and aging: The glucocorticoid cascade hypothesis. *Endocrine Review, 7*, 284–301.

Sapolsky, R. M., Uno, H., Rebert, C. S., & Finch, C. E. (1990). Hippocampal damage associated with prolonged glucocorticoid exposure in primates. *Journal of Neuroscience, 10*, 2897–2902.

Sarchiapone, M., Jaussent, I., Roy, A., Carli, V., Guillaume, S., Jollant, F., Malafosse, A., & Courtet, P. (2009). Childhood trauma as a correlative factor of suicidal behavior—via aggression traits: Similar results in an Italian and in a French sample. *European Psychiatry, 24*, 57–62.

Sareen, J., Cox, B. J., Stein, M. B., Afifi, T. O., Fleet, C., & Asmundson, G. J. G. (2007). Physical and mental comorbidity, disability, and suicidal behavior associated with posttraumatic stress disorder in a large community sample. *Psychosomatic Medicine, 69*, 242–248.

Sareen, J., Houlahan, T., Cox, B. J., & Asmundson, G. J. G. (2005). Anxiety disorders associated with suicidal ideation and suicide attempts in the national comorbidity survey. *Journal of Nervous and Mental Disease, 193*, 450–454.

Sargant, W., & Slater, E. (1941). Amnesic syndromes in war. *Proceedings of the Royal Society of Medicine, 34*, 757–764.

Saul, L. J. (1945). Psychological factors in combat fatigue—with special reference to hostility and the nightmares. *Psychosomatic Medicine, 7*, 257–272.

Saunders, E. A., & Arnold, F. A. (1993). A critique of conceptual and treatment approaches to borderline psychopathology in light of findings about childhood abuse. *Psychiatry, 56*, 188–203.

Saxe, G. N., van der Kolk, B. A., Berkowitz, R., Chinman, G., Hall, K., Lieberg, G., & Schwartz, J. (1993). Dissociative disorders in psychiatric inpatients. *American Journal of Psychiatry, 150*, 1037–1042.

Saxe, J. G. (1851). *Poems by John Godfrey Saxe.* Boston, MA: Ticknor, Reed and Fields.

Schaaf, K. K., & McCanne, T. R. (1998). Relationship of childhood sexual, physical, and combined sexual and physical abuse to adult victimization and posttraumatic stress disorder. *Child Abuse & Neglect, 22*, 119–133.

Schacter, D. L. (1985). Priming of old and new knowledge in amnesic patients and normal subjects. *Annals of the New York Academy of Science, 444*, 44–53.

Schacter, D. L. (1987). Implicit memory: History and current status. *Journal of Experimental Psychology: Learning, Memory and Cognition, 13*, 501–518.

Schacter, D. L. (1990). Implicit memory: Multiple perspectives. *Bulletin of the Psychonomic Society, 29*, 338–340.

Schacter, D. L. (1992). Priming and multiple memory systems: Perceptual mechanisms of implicit memory. *Journal of Cognitive Neuroscience, 4*, 244–256.

Schatzhow, E., & Herman, J. L. (1989). Breaking secrecy: Adult survivors disclose to their families. *Psychiatric Clinics of North America, 12*, 337–350.

Scheflin, A. W., & Brown, D. (1996). Repressed memory or dissociative amnesia: What the science says. *Journal of Psychiatry & Law, 24*, 143–188.

Schenk, L., & Bear, D. (1981). Multiple personality and related dissociative phenomena in patients with temporal lobe epilepsy. *American Journal of Psychiatry, 138*, 1311–1315.

Schiffer, F., Teicher, M. H., & Papanicolaou, A. C. (1995). Evoked potential evidence for right brain activity during the recall of traumatic memories. *Journal of Neuropsychiatry and Clinical Neuroscience, 7*, 169–175.

Schoener, G., Milgrom, J., Gonsiorek, J., Luepker, E., & Conroe, R. (1990). *Psychotherapists' sexual involvement with clients.* Minneapolis, MN: Walk-In Counseling Center.

Schooler, J., Gerhard, E., & Loftus, E. (1986). Qualities of the unreal. *Journal of Experimental Psychology: Learning, Memory and Cognition, 12*, 171–181.

Schreiber, F. R. (1973). *Sybil.* Chicago, IL: Henry Regnery.

Schumaker, J. F. (Ed.). (1991). *Human suggestibility: Advances in theory, research, and application.* New York, NY: Routledge.

Schwartz, R. C. (1997). *Internal family systems therapy.* New York, NY: Guilford Press.

Shapiro, F. (2001). *Eye movement desensitization and reprocessing: Basic principles, protocols and procedures* (2nd ed.). New York, NY: Guilford Press.

Shapiro, S. (1987). Self-mutilation and self-blame in incest victims. *American Journal of Psychotherapy, 41,* 46–54.

Shearer, S. L. (1994). Phenomenology of self-injury among inpatient women with borderline personality disorder. *Journal of Nervous and Mental Disease, 182,* 524–526.

Shengold, L. (1979). Child abuse and deprivation: Soul murder. *Journal of the American Psychoanalytic Association, 27,* 533–599.

Shusta-Hochberg, S. (2004). Therapeutic hazards of treating child alters as real children in dissociative identity disorder. *Journal of Trauma & Dissociation, 5*(1), 13–27.

Silberg, J. L. (Ed.). (1996). *The dissociative child: Diagnosis, treatment, and management.* Lutherville, MD: Sidran Press.

Silbert, M. H., & Pines, A. M. (1981). Sexual child abuse as an antecedent to prostitution. *Child Abuse and Neglect, 5,* 407–411.

Silverman, A. B., Reinherz, H. Z., & Giaconia, R. M. (1996). The long-term sequelae of child and adolescent abuse: A longitudinal community study. *Child Abuse & Neglect, 20,* 709–723.

Simeon, D., Gross, S., Guralnik, O., Stein, D. J., Schmeidler, J., & Hollander, E. (1997). Feeling unreal: 30 cases of DSM-III-R depersonalization disorder. *American Journal of Psychiatry, 154,* 1107–1113.

Simeon, D., Knutelska, M., Nelson, D., & Guralnik, O. (2003). Feeling unreal: A depersonalization disorder update of 117 cases. *Journal of Clinical Psychiatry, 64,* 990–997.

Simon, B. (1992). "Incest—see under Oedipus Complex": The history of an error in psychoanalysis. *Journal of the American Psychoanalytic Association, 40,* 955–988.

Simon, R. I. (1999). Chronic posttraumatic stress disorder: A review and checklist of factors influencing prognosis. *Harvard Review of Psychiatry, 6,* 304–312.

Sizemore, C. C. (1989). *A mind of my own: The woman who was known as "Eve" tells the story of her triumph over multiple personality disorder.* New York, NY: William Morrow.

Sizemore, C. C., & Pittillo, E. S. (1977). *I'm Eve.* New York, NY: Doubleday.

Smith, M., & Pazder, L. (1980). *Michelle remembers.* New York, NY: Congdon & Lattes.

Solomon, S. D., Gerrity, E. T., & Muff, A. M. (1992). Efficacy of treatments for posttraumatic stress disorder. *Journal of the American Medical Association, 268,* 633–638.

Sorensen, T., & Snow, B. (1991). How children tell: The process of disclosure in child sexual abuse. *Child Welfare League of America, 70,* 3–15.

Southborough, L. (1922). *Report of the war office committee of inquiry into "shell-shock."* London, England: HMSO.

Southwick, S. M., Krystal, J. H., Bremner, J. D., Morgan, C. A., Nicolaou, A. L., Nagy, L. M., Johnson, D. R., Heninger, G. R., & Charney, D. S. (1997). Noradrenergic and serotonergic function in post-traumatic stress disorder. *Archives of General Psychiatry, 54,* 749–758.

Spanos, N. P., Weekes, J. R., & Lorne, D. B. (1985). Multiple personality: A social psychological perspective. *Journal of Abnormal Psychology, 94,* 362–367.

Spiegel, D. (1984). Multiple personality as a post-traumatic stress disorder. *Psychiatric Clinics of North America, 7,* 101–110.

Spiegel, D. (1988). Dissociation and hypnosis in post-traumatic stress disorders. *Journal of Traumatic Stress, 1,* 17–33.

Spiegel, D. (1990). Trauma, dissociation and hypnosis. In R. P. Kluft (Ed.), *Incest-related syndromes of adult psychopathology* (pp. 247–262). Washington, DC: American Psychiatric Press.

Spiegel, D., & Cardeña, E. (1991). Disintegrated experience: The dissociatve disorders revisited. *Journal of Abnormal Psychology, 100,* 366–378.

Spiegel, D., Hunt, T., & Dondershine, H. E. (1988). Dissociation and hypnotizability in posttraumatic stress disorder. *American Journal of Psychiatry, 145,* 301–305.

Spiegel, H., & Spiegel, D. (1978). *Trance and treatment: The clinical uses of hypnosis*. New York, NY: Basic Books.

Spitzer, C., Barnow, S., Gau, K., Freyberger, H. J., & Grabe, H. J. (2008). Childhood maltreatment in patients with somatization disorder. *Australian and New Zealand Journal of Psychiatry, 42*, 335–341.

Steele, K., Van der Hart, O., & Nijenhuis, E. R. S. (2001). Dependency in the treatment of complex posttraumatic stress disorder and dissociative disorders. *Journal of Trauma & Dissociation, 2*(4), 79–116.

Steele, K., Van der Hart, O., & Nijenhuis, E. R. S. (2005). Phase-oriented treatment of structural dissociation in complex traumatization: Overcoming trauma-related phobias. *Journal of Trauma & Dissociation, 6*(3), 11–54.

Stein, M. B., Kline, N. A., & Matloff, J. L. (2002). Adjunctive olanzapine for SSRI-resistant combat-related PTSD: A double-blind, placebo-controlled study. *American Journal of Psychiatry, 159*, 1777–1779.

Steinberg, M. (1994a). *Interviewer's guide to the structured clinical interview for DSM-IV dissociative disorders—revised (SCID-D-R)* (2nd ed.). Washington, DC: American Psychiatric Press.

Steinberg, M. (1994b). *Structured clinical interview for DSM-IV dissociative disorders—revised (SCID-D-R)* (2nd ed.). Washington, DC: American Psychiatric Press.

Steinberg, M. (1995). *Handbook for the assessment of dissociation: A clinical guide*. Washington, DC: American Psychiatric Press.

Steinmeyer, S. M. (1991). Some hard-learned lessons in the milieu management of multiple personality disorder. *The Psychiatric Hospital, 22*, 1–4.

Stern, D. (1997). *Unformulated experience: From dissociation to imagination in psychoanalysis*. Hilldale, NJ: Analytic Press.

Striegel-Moore, R. H., Dohm, F., Pike, K. M., Wilfley, D. E., & Fairburn, C. G. (2002). Abuse, bullying, and discrimination as risk factors for binge eating disorder. *American Journal of Psychiatry, 159*, 1902–1907.

Summit, R. (1983). The child sexual abuse accommodation syndrome. *Child Abuse & Neglect, 7*, 177–193.

Surrey, J., Michaels, A., Levin, S., & Swett, C. (1990). Reported history of physical and sexual abuse and severity of symptomatology in women psychiatric outpatients. *American Journal of Orthopsychiatry, 60*, 412–417.

Surrey, J. L. (1991). Relationship and empowerment. In J. V. Jordan, A. G. Kaplan, J. B. Miller, I. P. Stiver, & J. L. Surrey (Eds.), *Women's growth in connection* (pp. 162–180). New York, NY: Guilford Press.

Swanson, L., & Biaggo, M. K. (1985). Therapeutic perspectives on father-daughter incest. *American Journal of Psychiatry, 142*, 667–674.

Swett, C., & Halpert, M. (1994). High rates of alcohol problems and history of physical and sexual abuse among women inpatients. *American Journal of Drug and Alcohol Abuse, 20*, 263–272.

Teegen, F. (1999). Childhood sexual abuse and long-term sequelae. In A. Maercker, M. Schutzwohl, & Z. Solomon (Eds.), *Posttraumatic stress disorder: A lifespan developmental perspective* (pp. 97–112). Seattle, WA: Hogrefe & Huber.

Teicher, M. H., Ito, Y., Glod, C. A., Andersen, S. L., Dumont, N., & Ackerman, E. (1997). Preliminary evidence for abnormal cortical development in physically and sexually abused children using EEG coherence and MRI. *Annals of the New York Academy of Sciences, 821*, 160–175.

Terr, L. (1979). Children of Chowchilla: A study in psychic trauma. *Psychoanalytic Study of the Child, 34*, 547–623.

Terr, L. (1980). Medical lessons from Chowchilla. *Journal of Pediatrics, 97*, 251–252.

Terr, L. (1983). Chowchilla revisited: The effects of psychic trauma four years after a school bus kidnapping. *American Journal of Psychiatry, 140*, 1543–1550.

Terr, L. (1988). What happens to memories of early childhood trauma? *Journal of the American Academy of Child and Adolescent Psychiatry, 27*, 96–104.

Terr, L. (1990). *Too scared to cry: Psychic trauma in childhood*. New York, NY: Harper & Row.

Terr, L. (1991). Childhood traumas: An outline and overview. *American Journal of Psychiatry, 148*, 10–20.

Thigpen, C. H., & Cleckley, H. M. (1957). *The three faces of Eve*. London, England: Secker and Warbug.

Thom, D., & Fenton, N. (1920). Amnesias in war cases. *American Journal of Insanity, 76*, 437–448.

Thomas, A. (2001). Factitious and malingered dissociative identity disorder: Clinical features observed in 18 cases. *Journal of Trauma & Dissociation, 2*(4), 59–77.

Thomas, J. L., Wilk, J. E., Riviere, L. A., McGurk, D., Castro, C. A., & Hoge, C. W. (2010). Prevalence of mental health problems and functional impairment among active component and national guard soldiers 3 and 12 months following combat in Iraq. *Archives of General Psychiatry, 67*, 614–623.

Tjaden, P., & Thoennes, N. (2000). *Full report of the prevalence, incidence, and consequences of violence against women* (Research Report No. NCJ 183781). Washington, DC: U.S. Department of Justice.

Tobias, B. A., Kihlstrom, J. F., & Schacter, D. L. (1992). Emotion and implicit memory. In S.-Å. Christianson (Ed.), *The Handbook of emotion and memory* (pp. 67–92). Hillsdale, NJ: Lawrence Erlbaum.

Torrie, A. (1944). Psychosomatic casualties in the Middle East. *Lancet, 29*, 139–143.

Trujillo, K., Lewis, D. O., Yeager, C. A., & Gidlow, B. (1996). Imaginary companions of school boys and boys with dissociative identity disorder: A normal to pathological continuum. *Child and Adolescent Psychiatric Clinics of North America, 5*, 375–392.

Tucker, P., Zaninelli, R., Yehuda, R., Ruggiero, L., Dillingham, K., & Pitts, C. D. (2001). Paroxetine in the treatment of chronic posttraumatic stress disorder: Results of a placebo-controlled, flexible-dosage trial. *Journal of Clinical Psychiatry, 62*, 860–868.

Tudor, T. G., & Holmes, D. S. (1973). Differential recall of successes and failures. *Journal of Research in Personality, 7*, 208–224.

Tulving, E. (1972). Episodic and semantic memory. In E. Tulving & W. Donaldson (Eds.), *Organization of memory* (pp. 381–403). New York, NY: Academic Press.

Tulving, E. (1983). *Elements of episodic memory*. Oxford, England: Clarendon Press.

Twombly, J. H. (2005). EMDR for clients with dissociative identity disorder, DDNOS, and ego states. In F. Shapiro (Ed.), *EMDR solutions: Pathways to healing* (pp. 88–120). New York, NY: W. W. Norton.

U.S. Department of Health & Human Services, Administration for Children and Families, Administration on Children Youth and Families, & Children's Bureau. (2010). *Child maltreatment 2008*. Washington, DC: U.S. Government Printing Office.

Vaillant, G. E. (1992). The beginning of wisdom is never calling a patient borderline. *Journal of Psychotherapy Practice and Research, 1*, 117–134.

Vaiva, G., Ducrocq, F., Jezequel, K., Averland, B., Lestavel, P., Brunet, A., & Marmar, C. R. (2003). Immediate treatment with propranolol decreases posttraumatic stress disorder two months after trauma. *Biologic Psychiatry, 54*, 947–949.

Van der Hart, O., Brown, P., & van der Kolk, B. A. (1989). Pierre Janet's treatment of post-traumatic stress. *Journal of Traumatic Stress, 2*, 379–395.

van der Kolk, B., Greenberg, M., Boyd, H., & Krystal, J. (1985). Inescapable shock, neurotransmitters and addition to trauma: Towards a psychobiology of post traumatic stress. *Biologic Psychiatry, 20*, 314–325.

van der Kolk, B. A. (1983). Psychopharmacological issues in posttraumatic stress disorder. *Hospital and Community Psychiatry, 34*, 683–691.

van der Kolk, B. A. (1993). Group psychotherapy with posttraumatic stress disorders. In H. I. Kaplan & B. J. Sadock (Eds.), *Comprehensive textbook of group psychotherapy* (pp. 550–560). Baltimore, MD: Williams & Wilkins.

van der Kolk, B. A. (1994). The body keeps the score: Memory and the evolving psychobiology of posttraumatic stress. *Harvard Review of Psychiatry, 1*, 253–265.

van der Kolk, B. A. (1996). The body keeps the score: Approaches to the psychobiology of posttraumatic stress disorder. In B. A. van der Kolk, A. C. McFarlane, & L. Weisaeth (Eds.), *Traumatic stress: The effects of overwhelming experience on mind, body, and society* (pp. 214–241). New York, NY: Guilford Press.

van der Kolk, B. A. (2002). The assessment and treatment of complex PTSD. In R. Yehuda (Ed.), *Treating trauma survivors with PTSD* (pp. 127–156). Washington, DC: American Psychiatric Press.

van der Kolk, B. A., Dreyfuss, D., Michaels, M., Shera, D., Berkowitz, B., Fisler, R., & Saxe, G. (1994). Fluoxetine in posttraumatic stress disorder. *Journal of Clinical Psychiatry, 55,* 517–522.

van der Kolk, B. A., & Ducey, C. P. (1989). The psychological processing of traumatic experience: Rorschach patterns in PTSD. *Journal of Traumatic Stress, 2,* 259–274.

van der Kolk, B. A., & Greenberg, M. S. (1987). The psychobiology of the trauma response: Hyperarousal, constriction and addiction to traumatic reexposure. In B. A. van der Kolk (Ed.), *Psychological trauma* (pp. 63–87). Washington, DC: American Psychiatric Press.

van der Kolk, B. A., Greenberg, M. S., Orr, S. P., & Pitman, R. K. (1989). Endogenous opioids and stress induced analgesia in posttraumatic stress disorder. *Psychopharmacology Bulletin, 25,* 108–112.

van der Kolk, B. A., Hopper, J. W., & Osterman, J. E. (2001). Exploring the nature of traumatic memory: Combining clinical knowledge with laboratory methods. *Journal of Aggression, Maltreatment & Trauma, 4*(2), 9–31.

van der Kolk, B. A., Hostetler, A., Herron, N., & Fisler, R. E. (1994). Trauma and the development of borderline personality disorder. *Psychiatric Clinics of North America, 17,* 715–730.

van der Kolk, B. A., & Kadish, W. (1987). Amnesia, dissociation and the return of the repressed. In B. A. van der Kolk (Ed.), *Psychological trauma* (pp. 173–190). Washington, DC: American Psychiatric Press.

van der Kolk, B. A., Pelcovitz, D., Roth, S., Mandel, F. S., McFarlane, A., & Herman, J. L. (1996). Dissociation, somatization, and affect dysregulation: The complexity of adaptation to trauma. *American Journal of Psychiatry, 153*(7 Suppl.), 83–93.

van der Kolk, B. A., Perry, J. C., & Herman, J. L. (1991). Childhood origins of self-destructive behavior. *American Journal of Psychiatry, 148,* 1665–1671.

van der Kolk, B. A., Roth, S., Pelcovitz, D., Sunday, S., & Spinazzola, J. (2005). Disorders of extreme stress: The empirical foundation of a complex adaptation to trauma. *Journal of Traumatic Stress, 18,* 389–399.

van der Kolk, B. A., & Van der Hart, O. (1989). Pierre Janet and the breakdown of adaptation in psychological trauma. *American Journal of Psychiatry, 146,* 1530–1540.

van der Kolk, B. A., & Van der Hart, O. (1991). The intrusive past: The flexibility of memory and the engraving of trauma. *American Imago, 48,* 425–454.

Van IJzendoorn, M., & Schuengel, C. (1996). The measurement of dissociation in normal and clinical populations: Meta-analytic validation of the dissociative experiences scale (DES). *Clinical Psychology Review, 16,* 365–382.

Vanderlinden, J., Van Dyck, R., Vandereycken, W., Vertommen, H., & Verkes, R. J. (1993). The dissociation questionnaire (DIS-Q): Development and characteristics of a new self-report questionnaire. *Clinical Psychology and Psychotherapy, 1,* 21–27.

Vermetten, E., & Bremner, J. D. (2002a). Circuits and systems in stress: I. Preclinical studies. *Depression and Anxiety, 15,* 126–147.

Vermetten, E., & Bremner, J. D. (2002b). Circuits and systems in stress: II. Applications to neurobiology and treatment in posttraumatic stress disorder. *Depression and Anxiety, 16,* 14–38.

Vermetten, E., Dorahy, M., & Spiegel, D. (Eds.). (2007). *Traumatic dissociation.* Washington, DC: American Psychiatric Press.

Victor, J. S. (1993). *Satanic panic: The creation of a contemporary legend.* Chicago, IL: Open Court.

Vogeltanz, N. D., Wilsnack, S. C., Harris, T. R., Wilsnack, R. W., Wonderlich, S. A., & Kristjanson, A. F. (1999). Prevalence and risk factors for childhood sexual abuse in women: National survey findings. *Child Abuse & Neglect, 23,* 579–592.

Wagenaar, W., & Groenweg, J. (1960). The memory of concentration camp survivors. *Applied Cognitive Psychology, 4,* 77–87.

Waldinger, R., & Gunderson, J. G. (1987). *Effective psychotherapy with borderline patients.* Washington DC: American Psychiatric Press.

Waldinger, R. J., Schulz, M. S., Barsky, A. J., & Ahern, D. K. (2006). Mapping the road from childhood trauma to adult somatization: The role of attachment. *Psychosomatic Medicine, 68,* 129–135.

Waller, G., Hamilton, K., Elliott, P., Lewendon, J., Stopa, L., Waters, A., Kennedy, F., Lee, G., Pearson, D., Kennerley, H., Hargreaves, I., Bashford, V., & Chalkley, J. (2000). Somatoform dissociation, psychological dissociation, and specific forms of trauma. *Journal of Trauma & Dissociation, 1*(4), 81–98.

Waller, N. G., Putnam, F. W., & Carlson, E. B. (1996). Types of dissociation and dissociative types: A taxometric analysis of dissociative experiences. *Psychological Methods, 1*, 300–321.

Waller, N. G., & Ross, C. A. (1997). The prevalence and biometric structure of pathological dissociation in the general population: Taxometric and behavior genetic findings. *Journal of Abnormal Psychology, 106*, 499–510.

Wallerstein, R. S. (1986). *Forty-two lives in treatment.* New York, NY: Guilford Press.

Warner, M. D., Dorn, M. R., & Peabody, C. A. (2001). Survey on the usefulness of trazodone in patients with PTSD with insomnia or nightmares. *Pharmacopsychiatry, 34*, 128–131.

Warren, A. R., & Swartwood, J. N. (1992). Developmental issues in flashbulb memory research: Children recall the *Challenger* event. In E. Winograd & U. Neisser (Eds.), *Affect and accuracy in recall* (pp. 95–120). New York, NY: Cambridge University Press.

Watkins, J. G., & Watkins, H. H. (1997). *Ego states: Theory and therapy.* New York, NY: W. W. Norton.

Weinberg, S. K. (1955). *Incest behavior.* New York, NY: Citadel.

Welch, S. L., & Fairburn, C. G. (1996). Childhood sexual and physical abuse as risk factors for the development of bulimia nervosa: A community-based case control study. *Child Abuse & Neglect, 20*, 633–642.

Westen, D., Ludolph, P., Misle, B., Ruffins, S., & Block, M. J. (1990). Physical and sexual abuse in adolescent girls with borderline personality disorder. *American Journal of Orthopsychiatry, 60*, 55–66.

Widom, C. S. (1999). Posttraumatic stress disorder in abused and neglected children grown up. *American Journal of Psychiatry, 156*, 1223–1229.

Widom, C. S., & Hiller-Sturmhöfel, S. (2001). Alcohol abuse as a risk factor for and consequence of child abuse. *Alcohol Research & Health, 25*(1), 52–57.

Widom, C. S., & Kuhns, J. B. (1996). Childhood victimization and subsequent risk for promiscuity, prostitution, and teenage pregnancy: A prospective study. *American Journal of Public Health, 86*, 1607–1612.

Widom, C. S., & Shepard, R. L. (1996). Accuracy of adult recollections of childhood victimization: Part 2. Childhood sexual abuse. *Psychological Assessment, 9*(1), 34–46.

Widom, C. S., Weiler, B. L., & Cottler, L. B. (1999). Childhood victimization and drug abuse: A comparison of prospective and retrospective findings. *Journal of Consulting and Clinical Psychology, 67*, 867–880.

Wignall, E. L., Dickson, J. M., Vaughan, P., Farrow, T. F., Wilkinson, I. D., Hunter, M. D., & Woodruff, P. W. (2004). Smaller hippocampal volume in patients with recent-onset posttraumatic stress disorder. *Biologic Psychiatry, 56*, 832–826.

Willer, J. C., Dehen, H., & Cambier, J. (1981). Stress-induced analgesia in humans: Endogenous opioids and naloxone-reversible depression of pain reflexes. *Science, 212*, 689–691.

Williams, L. M. (1994). Recall of childhood trauma: A prospective study of women's memories of child sexual abuse. *Journal of Consulting and Clinical Psychology, 62*, 1167–1176.

Williams, L. M., & Banyard, V. L. (1997). Perspectives on adult memories of childhood sexual abuse: A research review. In L. J. Dickstein, M. B. Riba, & J. M. Oldham (Eds.), *American Psychiatric Press review of psychiatry* (Vol. 16, pp. 123–151). Washington, DC: American Psychiatric Press.

Wilsnack, S. C., Vogeltanz, N. D., Klassen, A. D., & Harris, T. R. (1997). Childhood sexual abuse and women's substance abuse: National survey findings. *Journal of Studies on Alcohol, 53*, 264–271.

Winnicott, D. W. (1965). *The maturational processes and the facilitating environment: Studies in the theory of emotional development.* Oxford, England: International Universities Press.

Wise, M. L. (1989). Adult self-injury as a survival response in victim-survivors of childhood abuse. *Journal of Chemical Dependency Treatment, 3*, 185–201.

Wonderlich, S., Donaldson, M. A., Carson, D. K., Staton, D., Gertz, L., Leach, L. R., & Johnson, M. (1996). Eating disturbance and incest. *Journal of Interpersonal Violence, 11*, 195–207.

Yehuda, R., Giller, E. L., Southwick, S. M., Lowy, M. T., & Mason, J. W. (1991). Hypothalamic-pituitary-adrenal dysfunction in posttraumatic stress disorder. *Biologic Psychiatry, 30*, 1031–1048.

Yehuda, R., Golier, J. A., Tischler, L., Harvey, P. D., Newmark, R., Yang, R. K., & Buchsbaum, M. S. (2007). Hippocampal volume in aging combat veterans with and without post-traumatic stress disorder: Relation to risk and resilience factors. *Journal of Psychiatric Research, 41,* 435–445.

Yehuda, R., Teicher, M., Trestman, R., Levengood, R., & Siever, L. (1996). Cortisol regulation in posttraumatic stress disorder and major depression. *Biologic Psychiatry, 40,* 79–88.

Young, E. A., & Breslau, N. (2004). Cortisol and catecholamines in posttraumatic stress disorder: An epidemiologic community study. *Archives of General Psychiatry, 61,* 394–401.

Ystgaard, M., Hestetun, I., Loeb, M., & Mehlum, L. (2004). Is there a specific relationship between childhood sexual and physical abuse and repeated suicidal behavior? *Child Abuse & Neglect, 28,* 863–875.

Zabriskie, E., & Brush, A. (1941). Psychoneuroses in wartime. *Psychosomatic Medicine, 3,* 295–329.

Zanarini, M. C., Gunderson, J. G., & Marino, M. F. (1987). Childhood experiences of borderline patients. *Comprehensive Psychiatry, 30,* 18–25.

Zanarini, M. C., Ruser, T., Frankenburg, F. R., & Hennen, J. (2000). The dissociative experiences of borderline patients. *Comprehensive Psychiatry, 41,* 223–227.

Zetzel, E., & Meissner, W. W. (1973). *Basic concepts of psychoanalytic psychiatry.* New York, NY: Basic Books.

Zlotnick, C., Hohlstein, L. A., Shea, M. T., Pearstein, T., Recupero, P., & Bidadi, K. (1996). Relationship between sexual abuse and eating pathology. *International Journal of Eating Disorders, 20,* 129–134.

CPSIA information can be obtained
at www.ICGtesting.com
Printed in the USA
BVOW06s1926290917

496193BV00002B/3/P

9 780470 768747